One Book Stands Alone

The Key to Believing the Bible

By Douglas D. Stauffer, Ph.D.

One Book Stands Alone

By Dr. Douglas D.Stauffer

One Book Stands Alone tackles the most pressing theological debate of our time—identifying God's preserved word in the English language. Unlike many of the controversial and sometimes caustic works in this area, this book conclusively pinpoints the present battleground and spiritual combatants of the 21st century.

As a result of his "success" in the Garden of Eden, Satan has unrelentingly posed his familiar *"Hath God said"* question to every generation. Unfortunately, his query has frequently accomplished its designed purpose, undermining one's faith in God's word and causing division between the Creator and His creation.

One Book Stands Alone identifies the counterfeit authorities guilty of giving an uncertain sound. The reader will quickly discover how to recognize Satan's multi-pronged attack aimed at:

- the deity of Jesus Christ
- scriptural purity and preservation
- salvation by grace without works
- the supremecy of preaching
- Christ's sinless perfection
- the teaching of moral absolutes
- the total elmination of certain key verses and doctrines

The main objective of this work was clearly recognized by Dr. Lee Roberson when he stated, *"One Book Stands Alone is a spiritual masterpiece. It will strengthen your faith!"* In these perilous times, most men are ever learning and never able to come to the knowledge of the truth. I trust that the Lord will use this book to strengthen your faith and help you withstand the onslaught of modern "scholarship."

About the Author:

Dr. Douglas D. Stauffer was born in Huntsville, Alabama. He was saved at the age of twenty while a member of the Air Force, stationed in Florida. Upon his honorable discharge, he was awarded the Air Force Commendation Medal for meritorious service and returned to his home in Pennsylvania.

After graduating from *The Pennsylvania State University* with a B.S. degree in Accounting, he began attending Bible college in Alabama. The Lord dealt with him about preaching during his first semester; whereupon, he dedicated himself to preaching in rescue missions, juvenile detention centers, nursing homes, jails, and prisons. In addition, he had a radio broadcast three times a week. He graduated with a B.A. in Bible and was ordained.

While attending Bible college, Dr. Stauffer passed the CPA exam. He then worked as Controller of several organizations. In 1994, he gave up his work as C.F.O. of a multi-million dollar company along with managing his own firm when God began dealing with him about dedicating his time more fully to the ministry. Since that time, he has earned his Th. M. in Theology and Ph. D. in Religion.

Dr. Stauffer currently serves as president of *Key of Knowledge Ministries*. He has thousands of hours teaching experience, ten years serving in pastoral ministries, and has authored several books. Each of these books, as taught by Dr. Stauffer, has been produced into cable television segments. One of Dr. Stauffer's most recent projects included his participation as consulting editor for *Oxford University Press*. Many of his writings have been published in Christian magazines, journals and periodicals.

Dr. Stauffer has been the featured speaker dozens of times on national and international radio broadcasts. The radio programs were heard on over 100 stations in the continental U.S., as well as, Russia, Europe, Central and South America, Asia, Australia, and India.

Doug and his wife, Judy, are traveling together with their two children, Justin and Heather, as he preaches and teaches.

Copyright © 2001
McCowen Mills Publishers
All rights reserved
Printed in the United States of America
Jacket Design by The Aslan Group · Baton Rouge, Louisiana
ISBN 0-9677016-4-3
Second Printing: October, 2005

Scripture quotations from the Authorized King James Bible (A.V. 1611) need no permission to quote, print, preach or teach. *For clarity, all scripture is in italics with reference and any emphasis in bold print. Any deviation from the King James Bible is not intentional.*

Some may object to my sometimes dogmatic assertions within the pages of this book; however, I do not apologize for them. Every Christian should believe strongly in what he deems to be truth. If I cannot persuade others of the rightness of my views and observations, my prayer is that they will be stimulated to carefully examine the evidence themselves.

For more information, contact:

McCowen Mills Publishers
Dr. Douglas D. Stauffer, President
P.O. Box 1611
Millbrook, AL 36054
(334)285-6650
Website: *www.McCowenMills.com*
Email: *dougstauffer@rightlydivided.com*

Throughout this book, the reader will notice that when the word "Bible" is used in reference to the King James Bible, it is capitalized, distinguishing it as the true, preserved word of God in the English language. The word "bible" is used when referring to any of the versions that are not the preserved word of God in the English language.

This volume is affectionately dedicated to my faithful *helpmeet*, Judy Ann, and our two children, Justin and Heather. Thank you for your support and understanding when the Lord desired another book written.

"...a woman that feareth the LORD, she shall be praised. ...Her children arise up, and call her blessed; her husband also, and he praiseth her."
(Proverbs 31:30b, 28)

Acknowledgements

The author would like to express his deepest appreciation to the following: Most preeminently, the precious Lord Jesus Christ for His saving and sustaining grace.

Those who pioneered the Bible believing efforts, thwarted the satanic advances, and provided the foundation for this work.

My devoted helpmeet Judy for her support, encouragement, and understanding through our years of marriage and ministry together. Justin and Heather for understanding when Dad took on the God-given task to complete another book.

My parents, Richard and Marianne Stauffer, who instilled in me the work ethic and the fortitude to never quit. Thank you for the character-building foundation the Lord used to convict and convince me to repent of my sins and accept the one and only Saviour.

Mr. Hugh Taylor for reading the draft during its early stages and offering many helpful suggestions. Mrs. Frances Eller for reading the early draft, providing the clever chapter titles, and assistance with the final proof reading.

Dr. Bill Grady, Dr. David Reagan, Dr. Sam Gipp, and Dr. Jerry Rockwell for technical expertise and many helpful suggestions.

Miss Michelle Goree for her many hours of proofreading and grammatical suggestions. Mr. John Hale for reading the final proof.

Mr. Tommy Ray and his wife, Lori, with the Aslan Group for their creativity reflected in another impressive cover design. Mr. Tommy Trucks for his assistance with the text design.

Finally, Pastor Steve Sanders and Victory Baptist Church of Millbrook, Alabama, for providing a learning, growing, and teaching environment for over twenty years.

Table of Contents

Foreword
A Personal Word
Introduction
Preface

Glossary of terms
Bibliography
Index
Scripture Index

Foreword

The world has never seen a greater attack on the true Word of God than the concentrated attack we witness today. The multitude of so-called Bible versions has caused many Christians, pastors, churches, colleges, and seminaries to depart from the truth. Thankfully, God has raised up some godly men in these last days to shine the light of truth upon the spiritual darkness. Dr. Doug Stauffer is one of these men *for such a time as this*.

One Book Stands Alone encourages believers to stand by the one and only inspired book of God, the King James Bible. To prove there is only one Bible is a gigantic victory for the true Bible believers. Dr. Stauffer clearly repudiates the modern versions whose main purpose seems to be to deceive and divide. This book attests to the fact that the Bible is what God has said through inspiration, and not a book or version produced by man.

The acceptance of the corrupt versions by many seminaries and colleges has had detrimental effects on Christianity. The modern versions attack all of the cardinal doctrines in God's Word. The author deals with these spurious and corrupt versions by clearly proving that Westcott and Hort greatly influenced all of them. Dr. Stauffer, in a scholarly and biblical fashion, provides an answer for those who tamper with the Word of God.

One Book Stands Alone shows how the departure from the *Massoretic Text* and the *Textus Receptus* has demoralized our nation and the world. The results have been far reaching. Many Christians have even begun to accept the degenerate lifestyles of those condemned by the scriptures. For instance, the Word of God clearly condemns homosexuality and sodomy; however, the changes made in the modern versions have obscured God's condemnation.

The chapter entitled "Bible Roots" is worth more than words can express. The author clearly reveals how we can know that our King James Bible is the pure, preserved Word of God for the English-speaking people.

Thankfully, my mother placed a King James Bible in my hands in August of 1935. I have never known anything else in my 66 years of preaching. I expect to use *One Book Stands Alone* as a textbook in Midwestern Baptist College and Midwestern Baptist Bible Seminary.

Dr. Tom Malone, Sr.
Founder and President
Midwestern Baptist College

BIOGRAPHICAL SKETCH

Dr. Tom Malone, Sr. was born in New Orleans, Louisiana and raised in Russellville, Alabama. At age 19, he was saved and immediately surrendered to preach. He left Alabama to attend Bob Jones College in Cleveland, Tennessee.

In 1942, he founded Emmanuel Baptist Church and Midwestern Baptist College nine years later. He pastored Emmanuel for over 50 years, as the church grew to over 4,000 members. He now serves as *pastor emeritus* of Emmanuel and president of Midwestern Baptist College and Seminary.

Dr. Malone holds many degrees of higher education including doctorates from Bob Jones University, Dallas Theological Seminary, the University of Detroit, and Wayne State University.

He is still in great demand and travels all over the country as an evangelist, soul winner, and revival preacher. Dr. Malone has often been called *"the preacher's preacher"* and the *"greatest pulpiteer of our generation."* He has been married for 62 years and been blessed with four children.

A Personal Word

"I have known Dr. Stauffer since 1984. He is a faithful, dependable, godly member of Victory Baptist Church and was previously a member of my staff. I highly recommend all those in search of truth to read this great book."

Pastor Steve Sanders
Victory Baptist Church
Millbrook, Alabama

"Dr. Stauffer's book is a noteworthy entry into the KJV debate. It addresses the common arguments with a fresh approach and adds some new information that must not be ignored. This book should be read by every advocate of the KJV position. Anyone serious about knowing the main arguments cannot avoid this document. Every pastor, teacher, student, Sunday school teacher, et al. should have this volume in their possession."

Dr. Jerry Rockwell
Vice President
SWORD OF THE LORD PUBLISHERS

*"**One Book Stands Alone** is well done and on point for the present struggle over God's Word. May God bless and enlighten many good brethren through this book."*

Dr. Mickey Carter
Pastor, Landmark Baptist Church
President, Landmark Baptist College
Haines City, Florida

iii

*"**One Book Stands Alone** is rich in principle, fresh in content, and extremely well-written. Dr. Stauffer is to be commended for his diligent research and meticulous preparation of the material."*

Dr. Dennis Corle, Editor
Revival Fires! Newspaper
Claysburg, Pennsylvania

"Dr. Stauffer's new book reveals the insidious effort of the enemy of souls in his fiendish attempt to stamp out the Word of God. It should convince the skeptic and will be invaluable help to the earnest seeker of truth who is perplexed about all of the so-called bibles on the market today!"

Dr. Hugh Pyle
Evangelist/Author
Panama City, Florida

"OUTSTANDING! Congratulations on a wonderful work that will be of inestimable help to many believers.

Dr. Dennis Spackman
Auckland, New Zealand

'I consider your book heaven sent because it is just the book I longed for. I am certain that it is God's will that I warn others of the deception of the modern versions. Unless the Church gets this straight, gets this right, then there is no hope for the world. I must warn others as the Lord leads me."

Mrs. Janet Teem
Franklin, North Carolina

[Note: Mrs. Janet Teem has felt burdened (and sometimes over-whelmed) in her desire to warn others of the satanic deception. She has personally distributed several cases of books to preachers as the Lord leads. Pray for her as she seeks to follow His leading.]

Introduction

Consider the average man (or woman) who enters a Christian bookstore to buy a Bible. He reminds me of the man who fell off the top of a ten-story building. At every floor on the way down you could hear him saying, "So far, so good...so far, so good...so far, so good." He simply ignored the sudden reverse of fortune awaiting him at the bottom of the first floor.

Watch the Bible-buyer as he finds the Bible section of the bookstore and flips through six or eight *hot* versions. I cannot tell you what versions this may include since every few months bookstores tout a new bible as the latest word from God. It promises to be more up-to-date, more understandable and more relevant than the 200 or so translations that preceded it over the course of the last century.

Anyway, back to our shopper. He finds a bible he likes. It has a nice look and feel. The notes seem helpful. He reads a verse or two. It sounds like modern English. The store clerk tells him that he is holding a good choice in his hands. It has been translated by the best scholars and is recommended by famous people. He lays down his $40 (or $60 or $80) and proudly carries his new possession home with him.

He has now made a financial commitment to his version and has no intention of allowing any challenges to its veracity. He rejects any hint that it might have made critical subtractions from God's word. He may sense that it does not sound the same as the Bible of his grandmother. He may be forced to admit that some verses are missing. But he chooses to keep his eyes closed. He does not notice that the present bibles have changed much more than the earlier revisions did. He does not care that future versions will make even more drastic changes. He is happily oblivious to the coming crash awaiting him at the bottom of the first floor. He might as well be saying, "So far, so good...so far, so good...so far, so good..."

This book is written for those of you who really want to know what is happening to the English Bible. If you prefer to be ignorant about the changes being made and the doctrines being diminished, perverted, or erased, then you do not need to read this book. It might upset you. It might make you notice things you have been able to ignore prior to this time. No, for your own peace of mind, just put it back on the shelf where you got it.

However, if you really want to know the truth and are not afraid of where it might lead you... if being right is more important to you than being accepted... then just keep reading. At times you will laugh and at other times you will cry. Some pages will cause your blood to boil and others will make you want to know more. As a preview, look at the New International Version and consider some of the changes being made in this popular translation.

Verses Omitted

The NIV has totally omitted seventeen verses. In it, you no longer read *Matthew 17:21; 18:11; 23:14; Mark 7:16; 9:44,46; 11:26; 15:28; Luke 17:36; 23:17; John 5:4; Acts 8:37; 15:34; 24:7; 28:29; Romans 16:24;* or *I John 5:7.* These verses deal with doctrines of great importance: the doctrine of the Trinity *(I John 5:7)*; the doctrine of hell *(Mark 9:44,46)*; the doctrine of salvation *(Matthew 18:11; Mark 15:28; Acts 8:37)*; the doctrine of prayer *(Matthew 17:21)*. Other passages remain in the NIV, but the marginal notes discredit them. These notes reveal that the NIV translators would have preferred to leave out *Mark 16:9-20* and *John 7:53-8:11.* That's an additional 24 verses. Why would someone want to remove these passages? Who would want to remove *Matthew 18:11* which states, *"For the Son of man is come to save that which was lost"*? In spite of these and even more disturbing alterations, the advocates of the new versions declare that no doctrines are changed in the new bibles.

Words Omitted

Something else is disappearing from the NIV. There are many biblically significant words that are simply no longer there. By this, I mean that these words are not mentioned even one time in the NIV. Words conspicuously absent from the NIV include all of the following words enclosed in quotation marks. There is no longer a "Godhead." There is no "Jehovah" or "blessed and only potentate." There is no "Holy Ghost" and He is not the "Comforter." God is no longer "immutable" or "omnipotent" – there goes Handel's *Messiah*!

Christ is no longer the "only begotten" or the "first begotten." We no longer need to worry about "devils" or "Lucifer" or "damnation" or "brimstone" or the "bottomless pit." Hell, which is mentioned 54 times in the KJB, is mentioned only fourteen times in the NIV and is entirely removed from the Old Testament. But why worry about hell or damnation? In the NIV, there are no "trucebreakers" or "winebibbers." No one is ever accused of being "carnal," "slothful," or "unthankful." In the NIV, there is no "backbiting," "vanity," "lasciviousness," "fornication," or "whoredom." In fact, no one is "effeminate" and there are no "sodomites." No wonder liberals so readily accept this bible.

It is a good thing that there is not much to be saved *from* in the NIV, since it is harder to get saved as well. No longer is Christ crucified on "Calvary." He is not the "testator" who brings us the New Testament or the "daysman" who stands between God and us. He has not sprinkled His blood on the "mercyseat." He was not placed in the "sepulchre" and His resurrection is no longer established by many "infallible" proofs. It only makes sense then that we are no longer "quickened" and there is no more "propitiation" or "remission" or "regeneration" in the NIV. Did you get that? No "Calvary;" no "propitiation;" no "regeneration."

All of the words in quotation marks—as well as many others that could be cited—have been totally removed from between the covers of the New International Version. Therefore, it follows that the word of

God is no longer "incorruptible." It is not the "engrafted" word of God. There is no "verity" and Christ does not say "verily, verily." There is no "science" falsely so-called and there are no "fables." Perhaps that is why the saints no longer "abide in Christ."

"Archaic" Language

Another victim of the modern versions has been the very language of the Bible that makes it sound like the Bible. English scholars recognize a category of English which they call biblical English.[1] It is the English of the King James Bible and of other English versions of that era. These same scholars point out that the modern versions of the Bible are not written in biblical English. And, despite the claim of recent translators that this is simply the language of the time, it is not. The language of the King James Bible is distinct from any spoken English of any time period of English history.

The biblical English of the King James Bible stems from two sources: the historical, "archaic" English vocabulary and grammar and the transparency of the English text that maintains the style of the Hebrew and Greek languages. Scholars most often attack the "archaic" language of the King James Bible. People may have spoken that way in 1611, they say, but we speak differently now. We need a Bible that sounds the way we talk.

Yet, the English of the King James Bible was not the way common English speech sounded in 1611. For instance, the *thee's* and *thou's* of the King James Bible were seldom used by common speakers of that time. Even when encountered in conversation, these pronouns were spoken differently from their written use in the Bible. In the Bible, *thee* and *thou* are always singular (referring to one person or group) second person pronouns, while *ye* and *you* are always plural second person pronouns. This grammatical device, by the way, retains the distinction between the singular and plural *you* as found both in Hebrew and in Greek. The modern versions lose this distinction.

We do not incorporate this distinction of singularity and plurality into modern English. We always say *you* (except when we say *you all, etc.*). But so did most of the English-speaking people of 1611. Just consider the Dedication written to King James by the translators of the KJB. (It is found in the front of many Bibles.) Throughout this document, King James is referred to as *you* and *your* even though he is obviously one person. The King James Bible and the Dedication to King James were written at the same time and by the same men. However, the documents use *you* in two totally different ways. This difference alone illustrates well that the language of the King James Bible was not the common language of 1611. It was meant to be different; it was biblical English.

Even the older verb endings (such as *–est* and *–eth*) were not commonly used in English conversation in 1611. Individuals of this era used *believe* or *believes* in talking to one another—not *believest* and *believeth*. Why then were these older forms retained in the King James Bible? Seth Lerer, in his taped course on *The History of the English Language*, states that he believes that the translators attempted "to produce a highly crafted, artificial, elevated and, at times, archaic language—a language that will stand, not just the test of time, but will contain within it the time frame of the history of English."[2] In other words, the language of the King James Bible was designed from the beginning to be distinct from all other language. It was designed, I believe, by God to stand apart from the language of any particular period. It was written in a timeless language.

Biblical English

Greek teachers of an earlier age understood that the Greek of the New Testament was not exactly like any Greek that was ever spoken. They called it Biblical Greek.[3] Because of the recent emphasis on having a contemporary language Bible, we now hear of Koine or Common Greek instead of Biblical Greek. And, concerning the Old Testament, recent research has shown that its Hebrew was distinct from the common Hebrew spoken by ancient Israelites.[4] So, we should not be surprised that the English of the King James Bible is quite different from the contemporary English of any age.

One of the main reasons for this distinction is the impact of the Hebrew and Greek languages on the English of the King James Bible. The article on "Biblical Literature" in *The New Enyclopaedia Britannica* states as follows: "The impact of Jewish sources upon the King James Version is one of its noteworthy features…The impact of the Hebrew upon the revisers was so pronounced that they seem to have made a conscious effort to imitate its rhythm and style in the Old Testament. The English of the New Testament actually turned out to be superior to its Greek original."[5] *The Oxford Companion to the English Language* states that "the vigour and simplicity of OT Hebrew and NT Greek have to a great extent been successfully conveyed in Biblical English."[6] Let me provide two examples to illustrate this point.

The Old Testament Hebrew uses the word *and* as a continual connector. Its repetitive use sets the rhythm of the text and is one of the key characteristics of the Hebrew Old Testament. This rhythm is maintained in the King James Bible. Just notice how many verses in the Old Testament begin with the word *and*. However, newer versions seem intent on updating the style and removing the repetitive *and's*.

Just consider the passage of *I Kings 17:17-24*, which deals with Elijah's raising the son of the widow of Zarapheth from the dead. The King James Bible has 22 *and's* in this short passage. This closely corresponds with the number found in the Hebrew text. However, the New International Version removes over half of them and retains only ten *and's*. This trend is seen to a greater extent in other modern versions. The Contemporary English Version includes only seven *and's*, and the *New International Reader's Version* removes all but one of them.

This may seem like a small change, but it entirely alters the way the Bible reads and sounds. It removes the biblical language of the text and creates something that is not quite Bible. Also, this is only one of several major shifts of language being made in the modern Bible versions. Let us look at one more.

The Greek New Testament is filled with long, complex sentences of seemingly never-ending clauses. These involved sentences cause the Bible student to pause and reflect so that he can carefully comprehend the complex connections being revealed by the Holy Ghost in these passages. As a rule, the King James Bible keeps these sentences intact. On the other hand, the modern versions generally split them up into smaller sentences and thereby lose many of the intended connections.

Take *Hebrews 1:1-4* as an example. This passage tells us about how God's ultimate revelation of Himself comes through His Son Jesus Christ. Any preacher worth his salt could preach a ten or twelve week series from this one passage. The complex connections between the different concepts in this passage prove the greatness of God.

In the Greek New Testament, *Hebrews 1:1-4* is made up of only one sentence. The King James Bible also has only one sentence in this passage. However, look what is being done in the modern versions. The NIV breaks the passage up into three sentences; the CEV into six sentences; and the NIRV chops this one passage up into thirteen different sentences. This last version gives you the awkward sensation of going through a series of unnecessary speed bumps.

Conclusion

The Bible has ceased to be the "last word" for most Christians. They want to know what another version says. Or, if they do not like what they read, they assume that it is a bad translation. So, instead of the word of God correcting us, we correct the word of God. In the minds of today's Christians, the Bible has ceased to be a solid substance that can be checked as an absolute authority. Rather, it has become a process that is always becoming but never quite arrives. The real authority becomes the scholar who tells us what the passage really means.

But where is this process taking us? What is God's word becoming? The book you hold in your hand records the path taken by the modern versions and shows where this path is leading. It demonstrates one by one the doctrines that are being attacked, weakened, and—in some cases—destroyed. The new versions are taking us somewhere. But, do we want to go there? From their treatment of the doctrine of salvation to the practice of fasting, this book systematically details what is happening in the new versions. Please read this book. Then, perhaps you will know better than to say, "So far, so good…so far, so good…so far, so good." Perhaps then you will be ready to get off the steadily lengthening modern version train and return to home base—to the King James Bible of 1611.

Dr. David Reagan
Pastor, Antioch Baptist Church
President, Antioch Baptist College
Knoxville, Tennessee

Introduction Endnotes

[1] *The Oxford Companion to the English Language*, 1992, s.v. "Biblical English."

[2] Lerer, Seth, *The History of the English Language*, Lecture One, *The Great Courses on Tape*, 1998.

[3] Robertson, A. T., "Language of the New Testament," in *The International Standard Bible Encyclopaedia,* 1956.

[4] Robert Alter, "Beyond King James," *Commentary*, September 1996, p. 61-62.

[5] Nahum M. Sarna, "Biblical Literature," in *The New Encyclopaedia Britannica*, 15th ed., 1979.

[6] *The Oxford Companion to the English Language*, 1992, s.v. "Bible."

Preface

The opening chapters of the book of Genesis make it clear that the forces of evil are pitted against the forces of good. In the Garden of Eden, Satan reveals his true colors as well as his ultimate objective: the destruction of the relationship between God and man. Casting doubt upon God's word has always been his most effective strategy for destroying this bond.

Immediately following the biblical account of the creation of the first man and woman, the reader is introduced to the great deceiver. In Genesis chapter 3, Satan questions God's plain statements concerning the consequences of sin. He tests Eve's willingness to believe God by casting doubt upon the very words of God. During his conversation with her, Satan directly challenges God's explicit instructions with the question: *"Yea, hath God said…" (Genesis 3:1)*.

Over the course of some six millennia, Satan's destructive methodology of undermining the authenticity and authority of God's words has remained constant. Only the means whereby he pursues his objectives have slightly changed. Today, his most effective doubt-producing tool has become the contemporary versions of the Bible. Generators of these modern versions claim simply to be updating the terminology of the King James Bible. However, as this book and the work of many others reveal, they do much more.

In fact, one cannot escape the sense that these so-called bibles, camouflaged by clever advertising and celebrity recommendations, pose the same satanic question first noted in Genesis chapter 3. Just as God permitted Satan to deceptively attack His infallible word in the Garden, He *tolerates* his attacks today. Thus, Satan has been able to effectively use the modern versions to cast doubt upon God's infallible word, creating a hostile environment against those that believe the book.

As our attention moves from the Garden to the classroom, Satan's masterful tactics do not change. The greatest damage to the authority of scripture and the faith of the young preacher generally occurs in the seminaries. Two of the most insidious men ever to influence the pulpits around the world through the seminaries were Brooke Foss Westcott and Fenton John Anthony Hort. As attested by the following words from Mr. Hort in 1867, these men knew the importance of influencing the minds of young seminary students during their formative educational years.

> *More and more I am convinced that the work of the Church must be done at the Universities – nay, at Cambridge. It is too late to shape men afterwards, even if they could be reached.* [1]

Satan's main objectives do not change when he moves from the secular colleges teaching evolution to the seminary and religious institutions teaching the "bible." He must negatively affect the truth by peddling his lies. Satan has used men like Westcott and Hort to infiltrate our seminaries because he clearly recognizes his opportunity to manipulate the future by influencing the learning process of young students. Destroying the young preacher's faith in God's perfect word is Satan's most effective device for leading that young man down a deleterious path from which many preachers never return.

Nearly 400 years of testing at the hands of generations of students has done nothing to upset or disprove the cover to cover veracity and infallibility of the King James Bible. As the ages pass, linguistics change. In response, man has produced hundreds of updated bible versions in the "modern language," proclaiming each successive translation to be "easier to read." Their stated purpose remains constant – to dethrone the one book blessed by God.

Most Christians *purchase* these new versions with *pure motives*. Their desire to better understand the word of God is admirable. The purpose of *One Book Stands Alone* is to show that the *motives* of the Bible revisers are not so pure and that millions of God-fearing, well-intentioned people are getting *more* from their new versions than they realize. They are getting distortions of doctrine and seeds of doubt as to what God has said.

An expansive rift exists between those who know the truth and those who doubt it. The author seeks to methodically present the truth in an effort to close this gap which exists within the Body of Christ.

The Bible encourages us to dwell together in unity. Disunity in a country, in a church, or in a home is extremely unpleasant. God wants us to live in unity and provides the means and method whereby to do so. *"Behold, how good and how pleasant it is for brethren to dwell together in unity!" (Psalm 133:1)*. The schisms caused by disagreement and strife quench and grieve the Holy Spirit of God *(I Thessalonians 5:19, Ephesians 4:30)*.

The only group of Christians that can enjoy true scriptural unity is one that shares a common bond and foundation. Bible believers should be the primary ones *"endeavouring to keep the unity of the Spirit in the bond of peace" (Ephesians 4:3)*. Those Christians that believe in one book are *not* the sources of the disunity in the Body of Christ. Rather, those who have no standard and no final authority create all the havoc. Dr. Mickey Carter clearly identifies the crux of the problem.

> The real purpose behind the modern versions is to cause confusion and division among God's people. It causes the unbelievers to mock and laugh asking, "Where is the REAL Bible anyway? How can I tell which one I am supposed to believe? [2]

> Every change made to God's word is one of two things: it either adds to or takes from. That is what the Bible warns about and is exactly what caused the fall of man in the Garden of Eden. Eve and Satan added to and took away from God's word (Genesis chapter 3). During the temptation recorded in Mat-

thew chapter 4, Satan quotes the word of God, changing it ever so slightly. *The Lord Jesus Christ kept responding by correcting Satan using the scripture. The battle began with the word and has continued throughout time. Satan always brings up the question, "Did God mean that literally or figuratively?" These are the areas where the spiritual battleground is set.*[3]

One of the indicators of the last days is a turning away from the truth (the word of God). *"For the time will come when they will not endure sound doctrine; but after their own lusts shall they heap to themselves teachers, having itching ears; 4 **And they shall turn away their ears from the truth,** and shall be turned **unto fables" (II Timothy 4:3).***

According to *Webster's 1828 Dictionary*, a fable is "a feigned story or tale, intended to instruct or amuse; a fictitious narration intended to enforce some useful truth or precept." In other words, the Bible predicts that people will turn from the very words of God and instead turn to a *fairy tale*. Don't be guilty of fulfilling this prophecy simply because the majority will not listen. God has already foretold that the majority will be lead astray. *"Enter ye in at the strait gate: **for wide is the gate, and broad is the way, that leadeth to destruction, and many there be which go in thereat:** 14 Because strait is the gate, and narrow is the way, which leadeth unto life, and few there be that find it" **(Matthew 7:13-14).***

Some have likened the publishing of the *English Revised Version* to the opening of a breach in a dike. Once this version appeared on the market in 1881, the floodgates immediately opened, allowing the passage of a deluge of modern versions all attempting to displace the one book that God used for centuries.

Are *all* of the changes in the modern versions blatant perversions of truth? No! Many are subtle and innocent in appearance. However, *"A little leaven leaveneth the whole lump" (Galatians 5:9).* Acceptance of certain changes as "not really a problem" or "not so very different" dulls the senses and sets a precedent for increasingly greater variance. This process escalates until, eventually, serious errors are accepted as easily as Eve accepted the first subtle, satanic perversion of God's words.

However, the principle given by God to prevent such deception is to accept **no** change, **no** error, and **no** perversion since the word of God is pure and preserved in the English language in the King James Bible. The KJB supports itself as the pure, preserved word of God while the modern versions undermine both themselves and the truth, as we shall show throughout this book.

Thousands of books have been written about the Bible. Many of them attack the King James Bible. One such book, written by James White, states that we can know God's word by diligently comparing the various translations.

> ...*English-speaking people today have access to the best translations that have ever existed, and by **diligent comparison of these translations any English-speaking person can study and know God's Word**. . . . Inconsistency in proclaiming His truth does not bring Him glory.* [4] (Emphasis mine)

> *What we have discovered is that the comparison of various translations of the Bible is often very useful in ascertaining the meaning of the passage being studied, and that the KJV is one of the many fine translations available for just that task.*[5]

The bulk of this work will do just as Mr. White has suggested. We are going to diligently compare the translations. Those familiar with White's work will quickly realize that the motive of this author is vastly different from Mr. White's. The reader will also note that the author rejects the multiple authorities accepted by Mr. White. Our goal should be to study and know God's word, thus identifying any counterfeit. The conclusions reached will be at the opposite end of the spectrum from Mr. White's, yet, we will allow the scriptures to speak for themselves. May God richly bless you in your search for truth.

Preface Endnotes

[1] Arthur Fenton Hort, *Life and Letters of Fenton John Anthony Hort,* volume I (London: Macmillan and Co., 1896), p. 292.

[2] Mickey Carter, *Things That are Different are Not the Same*, (Haines City, FL: Landmark Baptist Press, 1993), p. 174.

[3] *Ibid.,* p.160.

[4] James R. White, *The King James Only Controversy*, (Minneapolis, MN: Bethany House Publishers, 1995), p. 247-8.

[5] *Ibid.,* p. 146.

1

Purity & Preservation

---

*For this cause also thank we God without ceasing, because, **when ye received the word of God** which ye heard of us, **ye received it not as the word of men**, but as it is in truth, the word of God, which effectually worketh also in you that believe.*
(I Thessalonians 2:13)

Nearly 2,000 years ago, the Apostle Paul clearly identified Christianity's degeneration. Its effectiveness would decline in direct proportion to people's receiving the word of God as the word of men! The word of God no longer *effectually worketh* in those that believe that the Bible is the word of men. The Bible contains several promises concerning the actual words of God, but none seems any greater than the one found in Psalm chapter twelve.

God pledges the supernatural preservation of His words. The passage begins by describing the words of the Lord as pure words. According to Webster's Dictionary, for these words to indeed be *pure,* they must be free from moral defilement and without spot!

(KJB) Psalm 12:6 The words of the LORD are pure words:
as silver tried in a furnace of earth, purified seven times.

Verse six reveals the extent of the purity of God's word, likening it to that of purified silver. Nevertheless, many "scholars" refuse to accept the purity of the words of God. If people choose to disbelieve the promises of God, He will not force Himself upon them *(I Corinthians 14:38)*. Instead, He has promised to show Himself pure only to those who are pure *(Psalm 18:25-26)*.

God attaches His solemn promise to these pure words. He promises to providentially keep **and preserve** His *pure* words in *every* generation.

> *(KJB) Psalm 12:7 Thou shalt keep **them*** (the pure words of the preceding verse), *O LORD, thou shalt preserve **them*** (the pure words of the preceding verse) *from this generation for ever.*

God promises to *keep* and *preserve* His very w-o-r-d-s in every generation. This promise includes the generations of the 20th and 21st centuries. As the centuries have elapsed, God has *not* somehow become impotent to preserve His word just because man has turned his back on God and become a god unto himself.

One book stands alone, proclaiming God's promise to preserve His words.

These important truths concerning God's word and His *promise to preserve* His words are removed from almost every modern translation. This study focuses primarily on one of the most widely used versions on the market today, the New International Version (NIV). As a means of introduction, compare what the King James Bible (KJB) says concerning God's promise of providential preservation to the corresponding words found in the New International Version.

> *(NIV) Psalm 12:6 And the words of the LORD are flawless, like silver refined in a furnace of clay, purified seven times.*

According to the NIV, the words of the Lord are no longer pure. What does the Bible say about this? *"Unto the pure all things are pure:* ***but unto them that are defiled and unbelieving is nothing pure; but*** *even their mind and conscience is defiled" **(Titus 1:15)**.* Instead, the

NIV says the words of God are simply flawless. Furthermore, the NIV makes no mention of God's solemn promise to *preserve* His words in every generation. Note also that the NIV changes the entire context of the passage in the next verse.

(NIV) Psalm 12:7 O LORD, you will keep us safe and protect us from such people *forever.*

Although the change in context is easily identified, read the verses together to be sure you do not miss this extraordinary alteration.

(NIV) Psalm 12:6 And the words of the LORD are flawless, like silver refined in a furnace of clay, purified seven times. 7 O LORD, you will keep us safe and protect us from such people forever.

The NIV changes the very context of this passage from the *words of the LORD* in verse six to *people* in verse seven. The revisers' objective is easy to recognize. The Christian cannot be allowed to know God's promise to preserve His word for every generation. Otherwise, the entire premise of man's supposed need for their "newer and better" revisions would lack any justification.

If these contemporary translations were to reveal God's promise to preserve His words for each generation, would these truths impact the lucrative bible market? If Christians could know from reading a modern version that God promised to preserve His word for every generation, they could recognize their individual responsibility to find the pure, preserved word of God.

Recent inquiries concerning the changes in the New American Standard Version (NASV) have prompted the author to address the NASV in this opening chapter and again in chapter 13. These two discussions of the NASV are alone sufficient to establish the translation as just another corrupt bible. Most of the corrupted NIV passages used for comparison throughout this book are also corrupted in the NASV. In fact, in many cases, the NASV perverts the truth even further.

(NASV) **Psalm 12:6** *The words of the LORD are pure words; As silver tried in a furnace on the earth, refined seven times. 7 You, O LORD, will* **keep them***; You will* **preserve him** *from this generation.*

Read that again! You will keep *them*? You will preserve *him*? The NASV makes even less sense than the NIV! Take note that the 1995 updated NASV changes the pronouns in verse seven from "You" to "Thou."

Not only did God promise to provide every generation with His word; He also instructed man to live by *every* word of God. Man cannot live by every word "if" the Lord has failed to preserve every one of His words for us.

(KJB) **Luke 4:4** *And Jesus answered him, saying, It is written, That* **man shall** *not* **live** *by bread alone, but* **by every word of God.**

One promise and one command: God promises to preserve His word for every generation and commands that man live by *every* word of God. Once again, the modern version revisers seem unwilling to allow the child of God to know or believe this truth. Otherwise, the whole purpose for the existence of these versions would be invalid.

(NIV) **Luke 4:4** *Jesus answered, "It is written: 'Man does not live on bread alone.'"*

According to the NIV, the Lord Jesus Christ did not say that man is to *live by every word of God*! Does God require this or doesn't He? Did the Lord say this or didn't He? One can imagine that Satan hated to hear these words leveled against him in the first century. Even at that time, he probably began plotting how he would one day rip the words right out of the Lord's mouth. The Bible records that Satan's scribes were busy soon after the epistles were penned *(II Corinthians 2:17)* and even before the completion of the New Testament. Now, the Bible revisers of the 20th century have simply picked up where these corrupters of old left off. What about the NASV?

(NASV) Luke 4:4 And Jesus answered him, "It is written, 'MAN SHALL NOT LIVE ON BREAD ALONE.'"

The updated NASV, previously mentioned, includes the phrase about *living by every word of God*, after having omitted it for the previous 35 years (1960-1995). Consistency is certainly not one of the hallmarks of these modern versions.

Since God promised to preserve His word, where is it today? One book truly stands alone, and all the other versions find it necessary to compare themselves with that one book – the King James Bible. Why do they all seem to be in collusion against this one book? Has someone convinced them that they must try to dethrone the King before they have any chance to succeed with their respective revisions?

Every modern version originates from, or is significantly influenced by, a set of manuscripts different from the one from which the King James Bible originated. For example, the New Testament of the KJB comes from the *Textus Receptus* (Received Text), whereas the modern versions emanate from the corrupt Westcott and Hort Greek Text and the equally corrupt Nestle's Greek Text.

When the root is corrupt, so is the fruit. Pure fruit can come only from a pure tree *(Matthew 7:15-20)*. That is the way God made His word, and that is the way He preserved it. However, Satan has always had his "garden variety" fruit tree *(Genesis 3:4-5)*. The Bible gives clear warning concerning the necessity of determining the type of tree from which a fruit originates *(Matthew 7:20)*.

In the following chapters, this book compares the fruit produced by the *Textus Receptus*-derived King James Bible with the fruits of the modern versions. Each of these modern versions is significantly influenced by the Westcott and Hort/Nestle's/United Bible Society texts. The purpose of this book is not to provide manuscript evidence.

Although one chapter delves into this area, many fine works exist which provide sufficient evidence for the accuracy of our King James Bible. (See Bibliography for a list of such works.) Surely, a reasonable person will agree that there is something sinister about any book claiming to be a bible that attacks the virgin birth, the blood atonement, salvation by grace, and the deity of the Lord Jesus Christ. All of the modern versions do just these things and many more. Thankfully, as we shall see, the King James Bible preserves, protects, and presents these sacred truths, as well as all other truths God intended for us.

God describes His word with such penetrating terminology. For example, the following passage states that a person is born again by the *incorruptible* word of God. Therefore, the true word of God is not corruptible!

> *(KJB) I Peter 1:23 Being **born again**, not of corruptible seed, but of **incorruptible, by the word of God**, which liveth and abideth for ever.*

No matter the opinion of all the so-called Bible scholars, God does *not* lie. His word is *not* corruptible. The modern translations cannot allow anyone to know this truth. Their basis for "updating" God's word would be destroyed if they claimed it to be truly incorruptible. The true word of God is incorruptible. Nevertheless, beginning in the first century, mankind has made repeated attempts to alter it.

The Apostle Paul makes this point in the following verse. *"For we are not as many, which corrupt the word of God..."* **(II Corinthians 2:17)**. The word of God is incorruptible; therefore, once corruption enters the text it is no longer God's word. This corruption took place during the first century. Even counterfeit letters began circulating **(II Thessalonians 2:2)**. So much for the claim of the **oldest manuscripts** being the best simply based upon their *age*! Even in the first century, scribes were intentionally influencing others by inserting their own beliefs into copies of the manuscripts. Someone does not want you to know that God says His true word is **incorruptible**.

> *(NIV) I Peter 1:23 For you have been born again, not of perishable seed, but of **imperishable**, through the living and enduring word of God.*

Here, the NIV presents its changes. No longer is one taught the truth concerning God's promise to *preserve* His *incorruptible* word. The NIV merely says it is imperishable, as does its predecessor the NASV.

*(NASV) I Peter 1:23 for you have been born again not of seed which is perishable but **imperishable**, that is, through the living and enduring word of God.*

The self-proclaimed scholars of today seem to have no problem with these alterations. James White is a prime example of a Bible "scholar" who believes that the oldest manuscripts are the best simply because of their antiquity. He states: *"Most scholars today (in opposition to the KJV Only advocates) would see the Alexandrian text-type as representing an earlier, and hence more accurate, form of text than the Byzantine text-type."* [1] Of course, he has swallowed Satan's plan completely.

All of the modern versions elevate the "older, more reliable" manuscripts from Alexandria, Egypt over those that were used to produce the King James Bible. How important is the word of God? What are the promises of God concerning His word? Six truths from the King James Bible concerning God's word are as follows:

1. God promises that His word will stand forever.

*Isaiah 40:8 The grass withereth, the flower fadeth: but **the word of our God shall stand for ever.***

2. God promises that His word can make you clean.

*John 15:3 Now ye are **clean through the word** which I have spoken unto you.*

3. God promises blessings to those that hear and keep His word.

*Luke 11:28 But he said, Yea rather, **blessed** are they that **hear** the word of God, **and keep** it.*

4. God promises the blessings only to those that accept His word as authoritative.

> *I Samuel 15:23 For rebellion is as the sin of witchcraft, and stubbornness is as iniquity and idolatry. **Because thou hast rejected the word of the LORD, he hath also rejected thee** from being king.*

This application is not limited to an Old Testament king. It applies to the New Testament Christian as well. If a Christian rejects God's word, might not the Lord justifiably deny that person a reign with Him *(II Timothy 2:12)*?

5. God promises that if we continue in His word, we will know the truth and the truth will make us free.

> *(KJB) John 8:31 Then said Jesus to those Jews which believed on him, **If ye continue in my word**, then are ye my disciples indeed; 32 And **ye shall know the truth, and the truth shall make you free.***

Failing to compare this change would be tantamount to negligence. First of all, the NIV changes "word" to "teachings," detracting from the authority of the entire word of God. This changes the emphasis from the *Author of the word* to the *teacher of the teaching*.

> *(NIV) John 8:31 To the Jews who had believed him, Jesus said, "If you hold to my **teaching**, you are really my disciples. 32 Then you will know the truth, and the truth will **set you free.**"*

The NIV further changes "make you free" to "set you free." *Make* is more active than the passive *set*. God's word doesn't just release us to freedom, it empowers us to experience it totally. It *makes* us free. When a person gives up his KJB, he gives up some of his freedom to be all God wants him and enables him to be.

6. God promises that He will judge us with the same word we are to live by.

*John 12:48 He that rejecteth me, and receiveth not **my words,** hath one that judgeth him: the word that I have spoken, **the same shall judge him** in the last day.*

If you don't receive God's words, you have rejected Him. What basis will God use to judge man and hold him accountable for his actions? The only justifiable basis is His holy, written word provided for man to follow. God magnifies His word above all else. An attack against the word of God is an attack against the very person of God. Proverbs clearly reveals this truth through the personification of the word of God.

*Proverbs 30:5 Every word of God is pure: **he** is a shield unto them that put their trust in him.*

God personifies His word, relating it to His Son, the Lord Jesus Christ *(John 1:1, 1:14)*. God provides man with His pure word and He expects man to live by it today. We are to live by every word of God; therefore, God has provided man with *every* word of God.

*Matthew 4:4 But he answered and said, It is written, **Man shall** not **live by** bread alone, but by **every word that proceedeth out of the mouth of God.**

The Bible does not say we are to live by every word that "proceeded" (past tense) out of the mouth of God. It uses the word "proceedeth." The use of the present verb tense reveals that the word is *alive (I Peter 1:23)*. It is not that we are adding to it, but that *it* is adding to us. The word of God is not something that stopped after the "originals" were penned. Second Timothy conveys the same thought: *"All scripture **is given** by inspiration of God..." (II Timothy 3:16)*.

God's word is the most powerful thing known to man. God says it is quick, powerful, sharp, piercing, and able to discern a person's thoughts and intentions. Oh, how powerful it is!

*Hebrews 4:12 For **the word of God is** quick, and powerful, and sharper than any twoedged sword, piercing even to the dividing asunder of soul and spirit, and of the joints and marrow, and is a discerner of the thoughts and intents of the heart.*

Most "scholars" agree that God gave man His perfect word. With the importance God places on His word, the conclusion that some have drawn makes no sense. Their actions imply that God has allowed His word to be lost through the centuries. If His word has in fact disappeared, one must conclude that God has permitted His piercing, dividing, and discerning sword to be replaced with a sword that has no power to pierce or destroy the enemy. However, the Lord has magnified His word *above* even the name of God. This would include the precious name of Jesus. *Name* here signifies His reputation and character.

*Psalm 138:2 I will worship toward thy holy temple, and praise thy name for thy lovingkindness and for thy truth: **for thou hast magnified thy word above all thy name.***

He has magnified His word above all of His name. Why would He do this? Think about it. A man's name is only as good as His word. If a man's word is no good, His name is certainly tarnished. This holds true concerning the Creator, too. God's name is only as good as His word. Actually, His word *is* His name! *"In the beginning was the Word, and the Word was with God, and the Word was God" (**John 1:1**)*. Only a good name can display integrity and honor.

God is powerful. His word is powerful. It is therefore logical that Satan would dedicate his resources in an attempt to destroy a Christian's faith in the word of God. He is very busy working to accomplish this end! Satan knows that if he can destroy a person's faith in the word of God, he can make that word unprofitable in his life. Read for yourself:

*Hebrews 4:2 For unto us was the gospel preached, as well as unto them: **but the word preached did not profit them, not being mixed with faith in them that heard it.***

Has your faith been destroyed? If so, think back to when and how this destruction occurred. Unfortunately, many preachers lose their faith in the seminaries. In turn, many others lose their faith sitting under the preaching of these seminary graduates. How did you lose yours? Regardless of the pathway taken, Satan has gained victory over you in this area if he has destroyed your faith.

God rebuked the Jews for their lack of faith *(Deuteronomy 32:20)*. We are told that the Old Testament examples are given to us to help us avoid repeating Israel's sins. They are given to us for *examples* and *ensamples (I Corinthians 10:6, 11)*. Many Christians are ignorant of God's word and its applications. This is especially true of those that have been busy perverting God's word – the modern version producers.

The 23rd chapter of Jeremiah shows God's disgust with those responsible for perversion of His word. When the prophets prophesied falsely, attributing their lies to the Almighty, the reader can sense the Lord's anger. Finally, we see Him rebuking the prophets for stealing *His words* from their neighbors.

> *(KJB) Jeremiah 23:30 Therefore, behold, I am against the prophets, saith the LORD, that **steal my words** every one from his neighbour.*

How does someone steal the words from another person? The context of the passage shows that they were passing off their own words as the very words of God. The modern version editors are guilty of the same thing. Consider the NIV reading that once again casts doubts upon whether the words were God's or *supposedly* His!

> *(NIV) Jeremiah 23:30 "Therefore," declares the LORD, "I am against the prophets who steal from one **another words supposedly from me.***

It seems reasonable for God to rebuke the prophets for stealing His words from their neighbors. However, the NIV says that God was upset because the prophets were stealing words that were SUPPOSEDLY from Him. Does it seem logical that the Lord would be rebuking these prophets for stealing words that were not really His at all? Again, the

NIV casts doubt upon the word of God and makes His word seem pointless. There is little hope of recovery for those that see no problem with these changes.

This book is written for all those interested in re-establishing or further strengthening their faith in God's word. Simple verse-to-verse comparisons allow you to easily see the pattern of corruption in the modern versions. Topical chapters in this book highlight the modern versions' clear attack on specific truths and doctrines of God. May your faith be strengthened, restored, or established in God's holy word. Pray that you will magnify His word and give it the prominence God expects.

Chapter 1 Endnotes

---

[1] White, *The King James Only Controversy, op. cit.*, p.43.

2

Deity Denied

*For if the true New Testament text came from God, whence came
the erroneous variant readings ultimately save from the evil one;
and how could the true text have been preserved save through
the providence of God working through His Church?* [1]
David Otis Fuller

The Lord addresses the problem at the root of all of the modern
versions. Modern version proponents try to convince us of their
desire to elevate the *incarnate* word while attacking the *written*
word. According to the Lord Jesus Christ, you can't have one without
the other. He equates His spoken words to those written by Moses.

> *John 5:46 For had ye believed Moses, ye would have believed
> me: for he wrote of me. 47 **But if ye believe not his writings,
> how shall ye believe my words?***

For decades now, modern versions have been hitting the market at
the rate of several per year. As a result, we now have hundreds of different versions on the market. How did it all begin? To answer this
question, we must revisit the early formative years of the modern debate concerning updating the word of God. The first modern version to
appear on the market was the English Revised Version (ERV) of 1881.
It was supposed to be a revision of the KJB but became a new translation. The American Standard Version (ASV) was first published in 1901
in America as a revision of the 1881 English Revised Version.

The ERV and the ASV are the great *granddaddies* of all the modern translations. They initiated the changes that are so common today. These versions also included study footnotes for the reader. Examining the footnotes found in these early versions, one can quickly ascertain the thoughts and intentions of the earliest revisers. Although its copyright page claims the ASV to be a revision of the King James Bible, it is not.

The claimed purpose of this older translation, as well as the stated purpose of today's translations, is simply to modernize the language and render these versions easier to read and understand. If the intention of the revisers was merely to modernize the language of the King James Bible, why then do these modern versions all attack the deity of our Lord Jesus Christ?

Jesus – Accepts Worship

The American Standard Version died out long ago. It is no longer an acceptable version, having been replaced by the more than 200 more modern choices. For this reason, only a single verse from the ASV, along with its corresponding footnote, will be considered in the present study.

> *(KJB) John 9:38 And he said, Lord, I believe. And he worshipped him.*

Amazingly, we have agreement between the two texts. The ASV says the exact same thing as the King James Bible.

> *(ASV) John 9:38 And he said, Lord, I believe. And he worshipped him.*

In this case, the problem does not involve a change in the text itself. Instead, the attack manifests itself in the footnotes of the ASV. Both versions reveal that **the Lord Jesus Christ received worship**. However, the footnote corresponding to this verse in the ASV blasphemes God. Here, in the great granddaddy of all the modern versions, the deity of the Lord Jesus Christ is vehemently and overtly attacked. By examining this footnote, one can quickly see that the revisers did not believe Jesus to be God.

The footnote: *"The Greek word denotes an act of reverence, **whether paid to a creature (as here), or to the Creator."** [2]* Translators of the American Standard Version and the English Revised Version believed our Lord and Saviour Jesus Christ to be *a created being.* Since Jesus was the One being worshipped in this passage, the translators reveal their *unbelief* that He is the Creator of the universe. Many other passages could be considered. However, such a flagrant attack on the deity of Christ should suffice to illustrate the point.

Another major revision to hit the market was the Revised Standard Version (RSV) published in 1952. It was a revision of the American Standard Version. The copyright page of the RSV says that it is a revision of the English Revised Version of 1881-1885 and the American Standard Version of 1901.

From the above information taken from the copyright page, one can see that the RSV is a child or a grandchild of the American Standard Version. As we have seen, the translators of the American Standard Version had a problem with the Lord Jesus Christ's receiving worship. After publishing the ASV, it appears that these revisers realized they could still communicate their message while better disguising their intent by tampering only with the verses rather than expressing their true beliefs in their footnotes.

> *(KJB) Luke 24:51 And it came to pass, while he blessed them, he was parted from them, and carried up into heaven. 52 **And they worshipped him**, and returned to Jerusalem with great joy:*

Instead of bringing doubt upon the Lord's deity through a footnote, the RSV simply deletes the fact that the Lord Jesus Christ received worship. The scripture teaches that only God is to receive worship *(Matthew 4:10)* and we have already read the revisers' footnote revealing how they felt concerning this matter.

> *(RSV) Luke 24:51 While he blessed them, he parted from them. 52 And they returned to Jerusalem with great joy.*

Of course, the 1960 NASV follows its predecessor by omitting worship. Interestingly, the updated 1995 NASV places worship back into the text after having omitted it from the text for 35 years.

Jesus – the Son of God

Not only do the revisions attack the Lordship of Jesus Christ, but they also attack every other major attribute concerning His deity, including His virgin birth. Most Bible students recognize the prophecy contained in Isaiah chapter seven to be critical to a true understanding of the redemptive work of the Lord Jesus Christ. The KJB states that *a virgin* shall conceive, establishing that a supernatural act would take place and result in the conception of the Son of God in human form.

> *(KJB) Isaiah 7:14 Therefore the Lord himself shall give you a sign; Behold, **a virgin** shall conceive, and bear a son, and shall call his name Immanuel.*

The removal of *virgin* from Isaiah chapter seven in the RSV directly attacks the deity of the Lord Jesus Christ. The fact that Mary was a virgin made the conception and birth of Christ a supernatural act, also eliminating the sinful blood of Adam's race from His veins.

> *(RSV) Isaiah 7:14 Therefore the Lord himself will give you a sign. Behold, **a young woman** shall conceive and bear a son and shall call his name Immanuel.*

Satan knows that if the doctrine of the virgin birth is eliminated, likewise the efficacy of the blood shed on Calvary's cross is destroyed. The Bible says that God shed His own blood *(Acts 20:28)*, not the blood of a mere sinful man of Adam's race. Sometimes a new translation goes too far in its attack of the truth. This passage from the RSV is just such a case. Immediately upon discovery of this attack in the early 1950's, an uproar against the RSV commenced. The blatant infidelity of the RSV eventually brought about its own demise.

Although the attack from Isaiah chapter seven was well-publicized, another less obvious attack by the RSV on the virgin birth went unnoticed.

(KJB) Luke 1:34 Then said Mary unto the angel, How shall this be, seeing I know not a man?

When a woman says, *I know not a man;* she is a virgin. But what about a person with no husband – does this mean by default that she is always a virgin?

(RSV) Luke 1:34 And Mary said to the angel, "How shall this be, since I have no husband?"

Obviously, these two verses do not say the same thing. One proves the virgin birth (KJB) and the other leaves room for doubt (RSV). A woman that states that she does not have a husband proves nothing concerning her virginity. There are many more examples from the RSV that attack the virgin birth, but these two should suffice. Therefore, we will look at the most popular modern version – the New International Version (NIV).

Because the Lord Jesus Christ is the virgin born Son of God, the Bible carefully points out that Joseph is *not* His father. Only the King James Bible remains true to God's defined plan. It clearly distinguishes between *Joseph* and the *mother* of the Lord, preserving a distinction of paternity. Mary is called His mother, but Joseph is *not* called His father.

*(KJB) Luke 2:43 And when they had fulfilled the days, as they returned, the child Jesus tarried behind in Jerusalem; and **Joseph and his mother** knew not of it.*

The peculiar wording of *Joseph and his mother* is sure to stand out as rather odd-sounding to the reader. God wants His word to be especially unique – uniquely God-like! The NIV removes this distinction and changes its impact by replacing the distinctive wording with the vague "his parents."

*(NIV) Luke 2:43 After the Feast was over, while **his parents** were returning home, the boy Jesus stayed behind in Jerusalem, but they were unaware of it.*

It is not necessarily incorrect to say that Joseph and Mary were the parents of the Lord *(Luke 2:41)*. However, it is wrong when God desires to point out that Joseph's relationship to the Lord *differs* from Mary's relationship to Him.

> *(KJB) Luke 2:33 And **Joseph** and his mother marvelled at those things which were spoken of him.*

Satan is never satisfied with an *indirect* attack on truth. He must go for the kill. However, when he does so, it is much easier to identify his handiwork. No matter how one feels about the preceding verse from the NIV, the attack grows even stronger and more direct as we continue the comparison. The next verse directly attacks the Lord's deity by destroying the doctrine of the virgin birth. See for yourself:

> *(NIV) Luke 2:33 **The child's father** and mother marveled at what was said about him.*

Joseph was not the father of the virgin born Son of God! However, he was the father of all of Mary's other children *(Matthew 13:55)*. The King James Bible only refers to Joseph as the father of the Lord one time. This happens as Mary rebukes her son for staying behind in the temple conversing with the religious leaders. Mary says, *"Son, why hast thou thus dealt with us? behold, **thy father** and I have sought thee sorrowing."* How does her Son (THE Son of God) respond?

The Lord Jesus Christ corrects her. Her words were misguided and the Lord corrects her as follows: *"How is it that ye sought me? wist ye not that I must be about **my Father's business?"** (Luke 2:48-49)*.

God the Son corrected His earthly mother when she inaccurately stated that Joseph was His father. God never leaves truths like these open to mere chance. He settles the matter and holds each person responsible for how he handles these precious truths. Any bible that addresses Joseph as the father of the Lord Jesus Christ (uncontested) is a deceptive counterfeit *(II Corinthians 2:17)*. The Lord thought the distinction important enough to correct His own mother. One can imagine what will happen to these bible revisers when they stand before Him in the day of judgment.

Jesus – the Creator

The Jehovah's Witnesses do not believe that Jesus is God. Therefore, their own version of the bible, called the New World Translation (NWT) serves their purposes. It is usually a green book and claims to be rendered from the original languages by the New World Bible Translation Committee with a revision date of "1961 C.E."

Even the use of C.E. in the copyright date is a blatant attack on the deity of the Lord Jesus Christ. Use of the C.E. implies a failure to recognize A.D. – *Ano Domini* (translated "in the year of our Lord"). "C.E." stands for *Common Era*, representing nothing, but certainly denying the Lord.

An important point to consider is that the Christ-rejecting NWT originated from the same set of manuscripts as the other modern translations on the market. Granted, the NWT goes *farther* than any of the others, but the association still exists.

(KJB) John 1:1 In the beginning was the Word, and the Word was with God, and the Word was God.

The NWT (and the Jehovah's Witness doctrine) directly attacks our Lord and Saviour by claiming that He was only *a god.*

(NWT) John 1:1 In the beginning the Word was, and the Word was with God, and the Word was a god.

The New World Translation need not be concerned with how it portrays the Lord Jesus Christ since it has a captive audience *(II Timothy 2:26).* This audience is the cult known as the Jehovah's Witnesses. Nevertheless, we can learn much by considering that they chose to use the same corrupt manuscripts as the other "versions." The Jehovah's Witnesses teach that Jesus was a created god, rather than having eternally existed with the Father and Holy Spirit. However, God's word states that the Lord Jesus Christ was not created, but was instead the Creator of all things. Colossians chapter one states this truth superbly.

(KJB) Colossians 1:16 For by him [by the Son – mentioned in verse 13] *were all things created, that are in heaven, and that are in earth, visible and invisible, whether they be thrones, or dominions, or principalities, or powers: all things were created by him, and for him: 17 And he is before all things, and by him all things consist.*

Since the Jehovah's Witness doctrine demeans the Lord Jesus Christ, one should not be surprised by this next change. Notice how the NWT repetitively adds **one word** and changes the whole meaning of the passage. In doing so, the NWT directly attacks the person and character of our Lord and Creator.

*(NWT) Colossians 1:16 because by means of him all **other** things were created in the heavens and upon the earth, the things visible and the things invisible, no matter whether they are thrones or lordships or governments or authorities. All **other** things have been created through him and for him. 17 Also, he is before all **other** things and by means of him all **other** things were made to exist,*

This passage states that the Lord created all *other* things. What are the implications? This change implies that Jesus created everything, *except Himself.* It means He was created by God, but God used Him to create everything else. Sheer blasphemy!

The foreword to the NWT (copyright 1961) states, *"The translators who have a fear and love of the divine Author of the Holy Scriptures feel especially a responsibility toward **Him to transmit his thoughts and declarations** as accurately as possible."* **The translators of the word of God** are to transmit *His words,* not simply his *thoughts.* However, this same translation philosophy underlies all of the modern versions (such as the NIV) which purport to follow the dynamic equivalency theory.

The foreword continues. *"They also feel a responsibility toward the searching readers of the **modern translation who depend upon the inspired Word of the Most High God for their everlasting salvation.** It* *was with such a sense of solemn responsibility that the committee of dedicated men have produced the New World Translation of the Holy Scriptures . . ."*

The writers of the NWT realize that people will trust in the NWT for their everlasting salvation! This salvation is based on a structure built on sinking sand *(Matthew 7:26)*. Can you imagine knowing that others would stake their salvation on something you produced, which missed the mark so badly? People are trusting in it for their salvation, just as people are trusting in the other modern versions for theirs. They miss the mark too!

Can a person get saved by reading *Romans 10:13* in the NWT? It reads: For "everyone who calls on **the name of Jehovah** will be saved." This reading attempts to point a person away from our Lord and Saviour Jesus Christ by not mentioning that one must call upon the name of the *Lord* (Jesus Christ) to be saved.

Is any further proof required for one to declare this translation a corrupt piece of trash? The NWT openly attacks Jesus in these and many other verses. The most recently developed versions do too, but much more subtly *(Genesis 3:1)*, making the newer versions even more dangerous. Hundreds of additional verses from the NWT could be used to further illustrate this heresy, but why waste the space and time? *"Wherefore by their fruits ye shall know them" (Matthew 7:20).*

Keep in mind that the majority of the verses compared with the NIV in this book could also be compared with the NWT. The results would be profound. Usually when the modern versions (such as the NIV, NASV, Living Bible, etc.) differ from the KJB, they align themselves more closely with the Christ-rejecting bible of the Jehovah's Witnesses. Get a copy of the NWT, and compare the changes yourself. The NIV and NWT align in concert *against* the KJB *(Amos 3:3)*.

The following example reveals the NIV's association with the NWT. The NIV attacks Jesus as the Creator, too. The Bible says the Father did not create anything by Himself. The Father created *all* things by the Son. Yet, in Genesis chapter one, the Bible says *"And God said."*

Consequently, Jesus must be the person of the Godhead that spoke everything into existence in the beginning. Ephesians provides another great proof text for the deity of the Lord Jesus Christ.

> *(KJB) Ephesians 3:9 And to make all men see what is the fellowship of the mystery, which from the beginning of the world hath been hid in God, **who created all things by Jesus Christ**:*

Once again, the modern versions alter a passage in the KJB so that it no longer proves the Lord Jesus Christ to be the Creator. This attack is reminiscent of the assault found in the great granddaddy version, the ASV (like father, like son). The Bible foretells the result of the blind leading the blind – they both fall *(Matthew 15:14)*.

> *(NIV) Ephesians 3:9 and to make plain to everyone the administration of this mystery, which for ages past was kept hidden in **God, who created all things**.*

According to the NIV, the Lord Jesus Christ is not the Creator. Something that destroys such an important doctrine and aligns itself with the most perverted version ever written needs further examination.

Jesus – Manifest in the Flesh

One book stands alone in claiming "without controversy" that GOD was manifest in the flesh. When something is *without controversy* it is not controversial and it is indisputable . . . at least when you read it in the King James Bible. God became a man; therefore, He was manifest in the flesh. Jesus claimed to be that man and the Bible says that He is. That makes Jesus God. This is the end of controversy when one reads the clear testimony of the King James Bible.

> *(KJB) I Timothy 3:16 And **without controversy** great is the mystery of godliness: **God was manifest in the flesh**, justified in the Spirit, seen of angels, preached unto the Gentiles, believed on in the world, received up into glory.*

Believing the King James Bible, there can be no doubt Who was manifest in the flesh. It was God. However, the New International Version attacks the deity of the Lord Jesus Christ in very subtle ways. The *indisputable* truth proclaimed by the KJB cannot be found in the same passage of the New International Version. The Bible plainly states it was **God** that was manifest. The NIV no longer makes this truth evident, but replaces "God" with "He."

(NIV) I Timothy 3:16 Beyond all question, the mystery of godliness is great: He appeared in a body, was vindicated by the Spirit, was seen by angels, was preached among the nations, was believed on in the world, was taken up in glory.

The NIV says absolutely nothing. To say that "**He** appeared in a body…" means nothing. Everyone has appeared in a body. When the KJB states that "God was manifest in the flesh…" a critical statement is made and a crucial truth is conveyed. The NIV is not even grammatically correct. *He* is a pronoun that refers to a noun or antecedent. There is no antecedent in the context. Therefore, this verse cannot be used as a proof text for the deity of the Lord Jesus Christ and does not even conform to common grammatical rules. As the ancient landmarks are removed *(Proverbs 22:28)*, is it any wonder the world stands confused?

Jesus – from Everlasting

Now we come to a particularly overt attack on the Lord's deity. The Old Testament book of Micah prophesies of the coming Messiah from Bethlehem *(Matthew 2:1)*. The verse plainly says that the ruler in Israel one day is to be the Lord who is "from everlasting."

(KJB) Micah 5:2 But thou, Bethlehem Ephratah, though thou be little among the thousands of Judah, yet out of thee shall he come forth unto me that is to be ruler in Israel; whose goings forth have been from of old, from everlasting.

Undeniably, the one *from everlasting* has no beginning, otherwise He could not be from everlasting. The Lord Jesus Christ is from everlasting, and therefore no beginning can be attributed to Him. The blasphemous NIV instead asserts that Jesus had an *origin*. Thus, the NIV creates doubt about the Lord's eternal pre-existence (before taking upon Himself human flesh). That is blasphemous! The Jesus I serve is God and has *no* beginning; He has *no* origin.

> *(NIV) Micah 5:2 "But you, Bethlehem Ephrathah, though you are small among the clans of Judah, out of you will come for me one who will be ruler over Israel, whose **origins** are from of old, from ancient times."*

The NIV claims that the Lord Jesus Christ had a starting point. If He has an **origin** (or a beginning), He is not God! One should not fail to grasp this truth. God has no beginning. If Jesus has origins then He is *a god*, just as the Jehovah's Witnesses claim! God the Son was present in *Genesis 1:1, "In the beginning..."* This same heresy was also very evident in the Revised Standard Version of 1952 which includes the same falsehood in the book of Hebrews: *"For he who sanctifies and those who are sanctified have all **one origin**. That is why he is not ashamed to call them brethren." (Hebrews 2:11).* The Lord has no origin, regardless of how many of the modern perversions agree together against the testimony of God's one book.

If the motive of the new versions is simply to update the language, then why do they pervert the truth and in fact destroy it? The Lord Jesus Christ has no beginning and will have no end! Otherwise, He would not be God and the Saviour of the world.

The Bible refers to the Lord Jesus Christ as the **only** begotten Son *(John 1:18, 3:16, 3:18)* thus emphasizing the distinction between Him, *the begotten Son*, and believers who are *adopted sons (Ephesians 1:5)*. The New American Standard Version, following the lead of the corrupt Vaticanus and Sinaiticus Greek manuscripts, have God the Father creating (begetting) another lesser god in *John 1:18*. However, Acts chapter 13 in the King James Bible clearly refers to the begotten **Son**.

> *(KJB) Acts 13:33 God hath fulfilled the same unto us their children, in that he hath raised up Jesus again; as it is also*

*written in the second psalm, Thou art my Son, **this day have I begotten thee**.*

When the Father said this to the Son, it was not at His birth. It was at His resurrection. He became the *"...first **begotten** of the dead..." (Revelation 1:5).* God did not become the Lord's Father when He was born of Mary or at His resurrection. He is from everlasting, with no beginning. The Son always was... but not so in the NIV.

*(NIV) Acts 13:33 he has fulfilled for us, their children, by raising up Jesus. As it is written in the second Psalm: "`You are my Son; **today I have become your Father**.'*

The Lord Jesus Christ did not become *the Son* of God at any time during His earthly life or ministry *(Psalm 2:12).* The Lord Jesus Christ (God the Son) can be found throughout the Old Testament. Numerous appearances are revealed prior to His being born of Mary. A great passage in proof of this truth is located in the book of Daniel when Shadrach, Meshach, and Abednego are thrown into the fiery furnace. Notice who else shows up – the *eternal* Son of God.

*(KJB) Daniel 3:25 He answered and said, Lo, I see four men loose, walking in the midst of the fire, and they have no hurt; and the form of the fourth is like **the Son of God**.*

They recognized the fourth figure in the furnace for who He was and who He is. For the Son of God to show up in the fiery furnace, He must have existed prior to His becoming a man in Matthew chapter one. Can this be proven using an NIV?

*(NIV) Daniel 3:25 He said, "Look! I see four men walking around in the fire, unbound and unharmed, and the fourth looks like **a son of the gods**."*

The NIV fails to reveal who the fourth person in the furnace is. He is the Son of God. The NIV aligns itself with the Christ-rejecting Jehovah's Witness bible by refusing to identify the Lord Jesus Christ. Considering that the sons of God can have a negative connotation as reflected in **Genesis 6:2** and **Job 1:6**, further compounds the error. The Apostle Paul tells us of the second Adam, showing that He is "the Lord" from heaven (present tense).

> *(KJB) I Corinthians 15:47 The first man is of the earth, earthy: the second man is **the Lord** from heaven.*

The second man refers to the Lord Jesus Christ. He had no beginnings, no origin. He is "the Lord" from heaven. This is another proof of His deity (at least in a King James Bible).

> *(NIV) I Corinthians 15:47 The first man was of the dust of the earth, the second man from heaven.*

No longer is He **the Lord** from heaven. No longer can one use these very clear testimonies of the Lord's deity in the perverted New International Version. They don't say the same thing.

Jesus – Without Sin

The NIV stoops so low as to attack the sinlessness of our Lord and Saviour Jesus Christ. Most Bible students are aware that the Lord became angry when he saw the hypocrisy of His fellow Jewish brethren. The Lord's anger is illustrated in the following passage where the hypocritical Pharisees are watching to see if He will heal on the Sabbath day.

> *(KJB) Mark 3:5 And when he had looked round about on them **with anger**, being grieved for the hardness of their hearts, he saith unto the man, Stretch forth thine hand. And he stretched it out: and his hand was restored whole as the other.*

In this case the New International Version agrees with the King James Bible. Both verify that the Lord got angry.

> *(NIV) Mark 3:5 He looked around at them **in anger** and, deeply distressed at their stubborn hearts, said to the man, "Stretch out your hand." He stretched it out, and his hand was completely restored.*

Although a man's anger is frequently sinful, it would be blasphemous to claim that the Lord sinned when he became angry. The King James Bible protects the sinlessness of our Lord by explaining that one can be angry with His brethren without sinning as long as there is a cause (or reason) for this anger. Anger, however, cannot be justified *without a cause* or reason.

> *(KJB) Matthew 5:22 But I say unto you, That whosoever is angry with his brother **without a cause** shall be in danger of the judgment: and whosoever shall say to his brother, Raca, shall be in danger of the council: but whosoever shall say, Thou fool, shall be in danger of hell fire.*

No true child of God would ever claim that the anger of the Lord was unjustified. He certainly had cause. However, the NIV removes that important phrase ("without a cause") and makes a blanket condemnation of anyone who becomes angry for *any* reason. According to the NIV, anyone that becomes angry with his brother is a sinner, including our Lord.

> *(NIV) Matthew 5:22 But I tell you that **anyone who is angry** with his brother will be subject to judgment. Again, anyone who says to his brother, 'Raca,' is answerable to the Sanhedrin. But anyone who says, 'You fool!' will be in danger of the fire of hell.*

This verse in the NIV makes the Lord Jesus Christ a sinner. It says "anyone who is angry!" The Lord Himself got angry! Verses such as these infuriate true Bible believers. Was there not a cause *(I Samuel 17:29)*? David knew there was a cause when Goliath was reproaching Israel and His God. Bible believers know there is a cause when man attacks God's word and work. *Be ye angry, and sin not: let not the sun go down upon your wrath: (Ephesians 4:26).*

God – Laid Down His Life

First John contains another passage that undeniably proves the deity of the Lord Jesus Christ. In this text, the pronoun "he" refers to the antecedent "God."

*(KJB) I John 3:16 Hereby perceive we the love of **God**, because **he** laid down his life for us: and we ought to lay down our lives for the brethren.*

Since the KJB indisputably proves the deity of the Lord Jesus Christ, one can well imagine Satan's opposition. Read the NIV and sense the hostility against the truth. Unlike the KJB, this verse in the modern versions cannot be used to prove the deity of the Lord Jesus Christ.

*(NIV) I John 3:16 This is how we know what love is: **Jesus Christ** laid down his life for us. And we ought to lay down our lives for our brothers.*

Yes, Jesus Christ laid down His life, but the purpose of the passage is lost in the modern versions. We are to see that it was God that died for our sins in the form of human flesh.

Jesus – The Morning Star

Now that the modern versions' attack on the deity of the Lord Jesus Christ has been clearly identified, we turn our attention toward the source of this attack. Satan is identified as **Lucifer** only *one time* in the word of God. Before we look at the passage in the book of Isaiah, which identifies Lucifer, reveals his past, and foretells his future, we must first establish who Lucifer is *not*. For this reason, we must take note of the identity of the *morning star.*

*(KJB) Revelation 22:16 I **Jesus** have sent mine angel to testify unto you these things in the churches. I am the root and the offspring of David, and **the bright and morning star.***

The Bible and the modern versions both state that Jesus is *the bright and morning star*. Now, having established the identity of the morning star, our attention is directed to Isaiah chapter fourteen – the only place in the Bible that mentions *Lucifer* by name. He is the *son of the morning* that was created perfect until pride destroyed him. Notice the five times that he uses the personal pronoun "I."

(KJB) Isaiah 14:12 How art thou fallen from heaven, O Lucifer, son of the morning! how art thou cut down to the ground, which didst weaken the nations! 13 For thou hast said in thine heart, I will ascend into heaven, I will exalt my throne above the stars of God: I will sit also upon the mount of the congregation, in the sides of the north: 14 I will ascend above the heights of the clouds; I will be like the most High. 15 Yet thou shalt be brought down to hell, to the sides of the pit.

Satan, Lucifer, the Devil, that crooked serpent – all the same. Praise God, one day Lucifer will be brought down to hell. The KJB proclaims this truth in this singular biography and identification of Lucifer. However, this is not the case in the blasphemous NIV. Instead of being brought low, the NIV allows Lucifer to become the imposter he desires so much to be *(II Thessalonians 2:4)*.

Instead of revealing Satan to be the archenemy of God and man, the finger is pointed in the Saviour's direction as though He is the imposter. Remember who the book of the Revelation identified as the *morning star*...now, look at the One to whom the NIV blasphemously points its finger – Jesus Christ!

*(NIV) Isaiah 14:12 How you have fallen from heaven, O **morning star**, son of the dawn! You have been cast down to the earth, you who once laid low the nations! 13 You said in your heart, "I will ascend to heaven; I will raise my throne above the stars of God; I will sit enthroned on the mount of assembly, on the utmost heights of the sacred mountain. 14 I will ascend above the tops of the clouds; I will make myself like the Most High." 15 But you are brought down to the grave, to the depths of the pit.*

The NIV fails to reveal Lucifer, but instead attributes the history and future of Lucifer to *the morning star*. According to **Revelation 22:16,** the morning star is the Lord Jesus Christ – not Lucifer! Thus, the NIV indicates that the Lord, rather than Satan, was actually the One that fell. This passage in the KJB is the only place Lucifer shows up by name. He remains hidden in the NIV.

Displacing the Lord has always been the goal of Satan. All of this has been done in preparation for the day when the antichrist will outwardly claim that he is God. The Bible foretells this future event: *"so that he as God sitteth in the temple of God, shewing himself that he is God" (II Thessalonians 2:4)*. The NIV makes that deception all the more possible. The antichrist will claim that the Lord Jesus Christ was the false Messiah and that he is the true one. Can you imagine how much easier the deception will be when he picks up one of these modern versions to "prove" his point?

In his book which attacks the King James Bible, the author James White answers these legitimate concerns with the following response. *"The person under discussion in Isaiah 14 is obviously not the Lord Jesus Christ, and how anyone could confuse the person who is obviously under the wrath of God in that passage (note verse 15) with the Lord Jesus is hard to imagine."* [3] My concerns for misunderstanding are not self-motivated. I know to whom the passage refers because my King James Bible tells me it is *Lucifer*.

However, the lost person of the future may *only* have exposure to the modern versions. The Bible says Satan will come "with all deceivableness of unrighteousness..." *(II Thessalonians 2:10)*. This passage may be one of the key tools used by him to deceive many people *(Mark 13:5-6)*. The Bible says many will come in the name of Christ (imposters) *(Luke 21:8),* claiming that He never came in the flesh *(II John 7)*. We can expect that they will point to the Lord Jesus Christ (the Morning Star) as the *true* deceiver *(Matthew 27:63)*. The Bible foretells that deception will increase dramatically in the last days *(II Timothy 3:13)*. For someone, such as Mr. White, to defend these changes while understanding their implications is complete biblical infidelity!

For instance, consider the implications during the Tribulation of the NIV's saying that Christians are marked. (See *Ephesians 1:13* discussion in chapter four.) The NIV Christians are marked. The future consequences of such an error are more bleak than can be conveyed within the pages of this book *(Revelation 13:16)*. After the rapture, when the modern versions finally displace the King James Bible, will those left behind be convinced by these modern perversions that "God's people" truly do take the mark...then why should they resist it? The battle for the Bible pits the Bible believer against the "father of lies" *(John 8:44)*. Whose side do you find yourself on?

Jesus – in the Old Testament

Many of the changes revealed so far have shown a direct attack on the deity of the Lord Jesus Christ. One book stands alone in painting clear pictures of Christ's deity in the Old Testament. One of the author's favorite Old Testament pictures of our Saviour occurs in the story of Abraham and Isaac. When Isaac asks about the lamb sacrifice, Abraham reveals the future sacrifice of the Lamb of God. The Bible does not simply say God will provide *a* lamb. It implies that He will provide Himself !

> *(KJB) Genesis 22:8 And Abraham said, My son, God will provide himself a lamb for a burnt offering: so they went both of them together.*

The Bible says that God will provide *himself* a lamb. Recall that a ram was caught in the thicket *(Genesis 22:13)*. God provided a *ram* at that time. This seemingly insignificant detail actually adds further significance to Abraham's comment concerning the future coming of a *Lamb (John 1:29)*. This poignant picture, along with many others, is destroyed by the modern versions.

> *(NIV) Genesis 22:8 Abraham answered, "God himself will provide the lamb for the burnt offering, my son." And the two of them went on together.*

Yes, God will provide a lamb, but the greater truth is revealed when one realizes that Abraham was prophesying of the day when the Lord would provide **Himself** as the sacrifice for our sins! What picture does your version convey?

Jesus – the Judge

The Lord Jesus Christ is not *only* the Creator of the universe, but will also be the Judge of the same. However, only God can judge on the last day. Thus, the following passage further proves the deity of the Lord Jesus Christ. Christians will stand at His judgment seat.

> *(KJB) Romans 14:10 But why dost thou judge thy brother? or why dost thou set at nought thy brother? for we shall all stand before **the judgment seat of Christ**.*

All Christians will stand before the judgment seat of Christ. Each of us will have his work judged to determine whether or not he will receive an eternal reward. Clearly, the One who died for us – the Lord Jesus Christ – will be our Judge. Not so clear in the NIV, which fails to refer to this as the judgment seat of Christ.

> *(NIV) Romans 14:10 You, then, why do you judge your brother? Or why do you look down on your brother? For we will all stand before **God's judgment seat**.*

Not only is the deity diminished, but the NIV contradicts the truth. God the Father has assigned all judgment to the Son. The NIV passage contradicts this truth as presented in the NIV and the KJB in *John 5:22*. *"For the Father judgeth no man, but **hath committed all judgment unto the Son**."*

Jesus – Omnipresent

When the Lord Jesus Christ was talking to Nicodemus, He gave proof of His deity and oneness with the Father. According to this verse, while the Lord was physically on earth, He was in heaven as well. We may not fully understand these truths because of our finite abilities of comprehension, but the truth remains. Jesus was in heaven while He was walking on the earth.

> *(KJB) John 3:13 And no man hath ascended up to heaven, but he that came down from heaven, even the Son of man **which is in heaven**.*

The evidence continues to mount. Verse after verse shows the attack on the deity of the Lord Jesus Christ. The truth is easy to see when one compares the modern versions to the standard *(Jeremiah 50:2)*. Unfortunately, there is no opportunity for comparison when a person uses only one of these modern versions. The problems can only be recognized when a comparison is made. Only a person that has read and memorized the King James Bible can recognize the existence or magnitude of these changes .

(NIV) John 3:13 No one has ever gone into heaven except the one who came from heaven-the Son of Man.

In the NIV, this verse no longer reveals that the Lord was in more than one place at a time. He is one with the Father. The Lord Jesus Christ was walking on this earth at the same time that He was in heaven. His hearers must have thought Him crazy or heretical…I think Him to be God. The Jews understood the meaning. Look at their reaction when the Lord Jesus Christ proclaimed: *I and my Father are one. 31 Then the Jews took up stones again to stone him. (John 10:30-31).*

Jesus – the Resurrection

Next, we consider the attack on the resurrection of the Lord. The Lord told His hearers that, shortly, they would no longer see Him because He was going to the Father. Upon their death, the souls of all Old Testament saints were sent to the heart of the earth in paradise. But the eternal, sinless Son of God was resurrected FROM the dead *(Mark 9:9-10)* and went to the Father.

*(KJB) John 16:16 A little while, and ye shall not see me: and again, a little while, and ye shall see me, **because I go to the Father**.*

Satan hates the resurrection with a passion. When he finds an opportune time to destroy it, he opens his penknife *(Jeremiah 36:23)*. No mention of the resurrection is made in the following verse from the NIV. The NIV sounds more like a magician's disappearing act.

*(NIV) **John 16:16** "In a little while you will see me no more, and then after a little while you will see me."*

The resurrection has been attacked and has disappeared from the verse! Jesus foretold His death many times *(John 12:33)*. The KJB points out that He would be going to the Father (who is in heaven). This statement foretells of His resurrection and the fact that His body would not remain in the grave, nor would His soul remain in the heart of the earth.

Jesus – Equal with God

As we have seen, the King James Bible clearly declares the deity of the Lord Jesus Christ time and again. If Christ was not in fact God manifest in the flesh as He claimed to be, He was the great deceiver. If His claims to be equal with God were false, everything He said could be questioned. However, He was and is God and did not think it robbery of God's glory to claim it for Himself.

*(KJB) **Philippians 2:6** Who, being in the form of God, thought it not robbery to be **equal with God:***

The NIV again subtly denies the deity of our Lord and Saviour by stating that equality with God was not something to be grasped. Grasped by whom? By man or Jesus Himself?

*(NIV) **Philippians 2:6** Who, being in very nature God, **did not consider equality with God something to be grasped,***

All of these truths about the Lord Jesus Christ must eventually disappear in order for Satan to complete his deception *(II Thessalonians 2:4)*. Some would have us believe we should simply accept these verses and fallacies, since the truth can be found elsewhere in most of the modern versions. Not so! We must recognize these warning signs as satanic attacks on something that is holy and pure.

The modern versions apparently have a motive other than simply revising the language of the Bible. From the preceding examples, it is clear that they instead shape and support an agenda to dethrone Jesus Christ as *"My Lord and my God!" (John 20:28)*.

The modern versions come and go, but the King James Bible cannot be dethroned. A typical justification for the existence of the modern versions is their supposed readability. The underlying premise is that our understanding of the modern languages evolved into something superior to that in 1611 and we have older and better manuscripts now. These false presumptions are dealt with in later chapters, but why do we have so many different versions? The preface to the New American Standard (a version that has fallen upon hard times too) gives great insight as to why so many have been produced. None of them can stand the test of time.

The ASV was heralded as a replacement for the KJB when it was published in 1901. Twenty-three years later it went broke and sold its copyright to the National Council of Churches. According to the preface of the New American Standard, the Lockman Foundation realized that the ASV had fallen into disuse. Quoting from the preface of the NASV:

The producers of this translation were imbued with the conviction that interest in the American Standard Version should be renewed and increased. Perhaps the most weighty impetus for this undertaking can be attributed to a disturbing awareness that the ASV of 1901 was fast disappearing from the scene. [4]

A modern version bible publisher had a conviction ($) that interest in their copyrighted text ($) should be renewed and increased. They were disturbed that their version was disappearing from the scene (i.e. the lucrative bible market $). Of course, their motive had nothing to do with money *(I Timothy 6:10)*.

Here is the typical position of the modern day Bible critic as expressed in a book published in 1999. The first paragraph refers to a quote from a century earlier before the Bible version debate had heated up. The next two paragraphs update their position and reveal the infidelity involved in preaching from a book one does not believe.

Do not needlessly amend our Authorized Version. It is faulty in many places, but still it is a grand work taking it for all in all, and it is unwise to be making every old lady distrust the only Bible she can get at, or what is more likely mistrust you for falling out with her cherished treasure. Correct where correction must be for truth's sake, but never for the vainglorious display of your critical ability. [5]

...not one word of God's Word has been lost to us. And in the cases where we may not be sure which variant most accurately repeats the original wording, not one doctrine is affected. Not one truth is compromised. [6]

But the fact is, most of us trying to preach Christ are doing so out of the King James Version. We love and honor it... [7]

What is the point? Twofold: even some great preachers from a century earlier did not understand the issue, and it is easy to justify preaching from a book that you do not believe if your audience does not know what you truly believe. The modern critic teaches that there is no significant difference between the underlying Greek texts, no significant differences between the resultant bible versions, and I suppose no issue to discuss. The fact that they are *using* a Bible that they do not believe matters not to them.

Addendum to Second Printing

After preaching a message on the deity of Jesus Christ, someone asked me if I knew of the changes to *Revelation 1:6* affecting my subject. This change not only detracts from the deity of Jesus Christ, but also attacks the doctrine of the Godhead existing in three persons *(Colossians 2:9)*. The Bible says that Christ made us *"kings and priests"* when He *"...washed us from our sins in his own blood (verse 5)."*

*(KJB) Revelation 1:6 And hath made us kings and priests **unto God and his Father;** to him be glory and dominion for ever and ever. Amen.*

Because Christ made us all priests, this has become known as *the priesthood of the believer*, negating the need for a separate class of priests like that which existed under the Old Testament economy. Christ as our High Priest offered the final *blood* sacrifice—now we are to present ourselves as living sacrifices to Him *(Romans 12:1-2)*. The modern version change is very simple. They move the personal pronoun "his" making a plurality of Gods or eliminating the Son as God altogether. Now it becomes "his" God.

*(NIV) Revelation 1:6 And has made us to be a kingdom and priests to serve **his God and Father**—to him be glory and power for ever and ever! Amen.*

Christ now has a God—referred to as *his* God. If Christ had a God then what was He? You would either have to take the position of the Jehovah's Witnesses or the unbeliever. The unbelievers do not believe that God has ever existed in three persons and the Jehovah's Witnesses teach that Christ was a lesser god and a created being.

Some would point to Christ's question on the cross as contradictory to this point. Although Jesus cried out on the cross, *"My, My God, my God, why hast thou forsaken me?"* He was not saying that there was more than one God. It was more of a figure of speech used by many today to take the Lord's name in vain (ie. "Oh, *my God*"). He certainly was not proclaiming a plurality of Gods by referring to the Father as "My God.'

Another very interesting point came from reading a book by Dr. Sam Gipp entitled, *For His Pleasure* which points out why we exist on this earth. The King James Bible is very clear when it says that we are and were created for the pleasure of the Creator—Jesus Christ.

*(KJB) Revelation 4:11 Thou art worthy, O Lord, to receive glory and honour and power: for thou hast created all things, and **for thy pleasure they are and were created.***

Imagine how simple (how wonderful) life would be if every single person would realize that they owed their very existence to a supernatural Creator (now named *Intelligent Design*). Imagine if everyone determined to live in such a way as to bring pleasure to the Creator. Sam Gipp wrote that *"We are here to put a smile on God's face."* [8] Every thought, every action, every deed should bring pleasure to the Lord Jesus Christ. What does the NIV do to this simple truth?

> ***(NIV) Revelation 4:11*** *"You are worthy, our Lord and God, to receive glory and honor and power, for you created all things, and **by your will they were created and have their being.**"*

The NIV completely distorts the point altogether. Every effort by those responsible for the modern versions seems to be made to avert one's attention away from Jesus Christ. The attack is most vehement when the verse speaks of Christ as Creator, Judge, and equal with the Father. Since we were created for His pleasure, Satan must attack and hide this truth through his cronies who are willing to do his bidding for the glory of man (or money). We were created for the pleasure of Him that created us. How should this influence our behavior?

The next chapter addresses one of the most insidious books written on this subject. It unapologetically attacks the KJB, though the author claims to be unbiased in his presentation. He concludes that the modern versions are superior to the KJB specifically relating to the subject at hand – the deity of our Lord Jesus Christ.

Chapter 2 Endnotes

[1] David Otis Fuller, *Which Bible?*, (Grand Rapids, MI: Grand Rapids International Publications, 1975), p. 97.

[2] *American Standard Version*, (NY: Thomas Nelson and Sons, American Bible Society, 1901, 1929), p. 114.

[3] White, *The King James Only Controversy, op. cit.*, p. 139.

[4] *New American Standard Version,* (Glendale: Gospel Light Publications, 1971), p. iv, v.

[5] James B. Williams, ed., *From the Mind of God to the Mind of Man*, (Greenville, SC: Ambassador-Emerald International, 1999), p. 93.

[6] *Ibid.*, p. 96.

[7] *Ibid.,* p. 98.

[8] Samuel C. Gipp, For His Pleasure, (Miamitown, OH: DayStar, 2005).

3

What's Right? vs. James White

*He that is **our** God is **the** God of salvation; and unto God the Lord belong the issues from death. 21 But God shall wound the head of his enemies, and the hairy scalp of such an one as goeth on still in his trespasses.*
(Psalm 68:20-21)

The previous chapter reveals the magnitude of the changes in the modern versions concerning the deity of our Lord Jesus Christ. Even the most precious of Bible doctrines fall prey to Satan's penknife. Despite the immense variations, many of the modern version gurus fail to admit the problems associated with these differences. Some of the least honest Bible critics go so far as to claim that the modern versions are *superior* in this area!

The next passage is a favorite of those proclaiming the superiority of the modern versions. Of course, all attempts to elevate the modern versions must first try to prove the inferiority and mistranslation of the King James Bible! For this reason, extra attention is devoted to completely refuting this errant position.

One man that has written an entire book attacking the KJB is James White. Mr. White mentions the next passage on *eleven* different pages in his book and devotes four full pages in an attempt to prove that the modern versions are superior to the King James Bible in their treatment of the *deity* of the Lord Jesus Christ. On the surface, it may appear that he uses credible evidence for this verse, but not if one fully considers the implications of these differences.

> *(KJB)* **Titus 2:13** *Looking for that blessed hope, and the glorious appearing of* **the** *great God and* **our** *Saviour Jesus Christ;*

> *(NIV)* **Titus 2:13** *while we wait for the blessed hope-the glorious appearing of* **our** *great God and Savior, Jesus Christ,*

The main differences between the two versions are clearly seen: *"...the great God and our Saviour Jesus Christ"* in the KJB versus *"...our great God and Savior, Jesus Christ"* in the NIV. James White provides a chart listing 12 verses (including the subject verse) and concludes that *"...we can see that the NIV provides the clearest translations of the key passages that teach the deity of Christ, the NASB just a bit less so, and the KJB the least of the three."* He also claims that the NIV and NASV are clear; whereas the King James Bible is ambiguous.[1] If necessary, go back to the previous chapter and see if you arrive at the same conclusion concerning the NIV's supposed superiority in its treatment of the deity of Jesus Christ. A few pages later, Mr. White's attack on God's word concerning this passage continues.

> *The insertion of the second 'our' in* **the AV translation makes it possible to separate 'God' from 'Savior,'** *as indeed those who deny the deity of Christ would assert.* **But this is an error,** *as is demonstrated elsewhere. The fact is that* **the KJV provides an inferior translation in these passages,** *one that unintentionally detracts from the presentation of the full deity of Jesus Christ.* **The willingness of the KJV defenders to overlook this fact is most disturbing.** [2] [Emphasis mine]

This "KJV defender" (the author) does not feel compelled to *overlook* this passage. In spite of devoting almost 300 pages to the attack of the King James Bible, Mr. White's book contains an introduction which emphasizes that, *"This book is not against the King James Version."* [3] Such a statement would be similar to my claiming that this book is *not* against the New International Version. I would be a hypocritical, deluded liar if I made such a ridiculous claim and expected anyone to believe me.

In addition to those pages already mentioned, Mr. White spends four entire pages (pages 267 to 270) discussing *Titus 2:13* in an attempt to prove the inferiority of the King James Bible. Here is another of his comments, *"The KJV translators, through no fault of their own, obscured these passages through less than perfect translation. Modern versions correct their error."* He then runs to the Greek and *Granville Sharp's Rule* attempting to prove his point. What exactly is his point? (See additional material at the end of the chapter concerning Granville Sharp's Rule.)

He claims that when the KJB says *"...the great God and our Saviour Jesus Christ,"* the use of "our" between God and Saviour makes it possible to separate "God" from "Saviour." This is TRUE and exactly what the Holy Spirit intended to convey. **However, the separation of God and Saviour does *not* make the KJB inferior.** In fact, the reading from the KJB should bolster one's faith in the inspiration and preservation of God's perfect word as found in the pages of one book – the King James Bible. Let me explain.

"The" is used in reference to "**the** great God" because there is only *one* great God. This fact holds true whether a person accepts the Lord Jesus Christ as his personal Saviour or not. The reason that "our" is used before Saviour is because He may be **the** great God, but *not* one's *personal* Saviour. Therefore, Paul proclaims that we are looking toward the day when **the** great God and **our** Saviour returns (because he addressed a saved man in the book of Titus). Jesus is **the** great God, but a personal, conscious decision must be made to make Him one's personal Saviour (the **our** in the verse). When the NIV and all of the other modern versions change the passage to read: *our great God and Savior, Jesus Christ*, it can imply that there is more than one great God – our great God and their great God.

This reading allows those that claim false gods to have an "out." With the wording of the NIV, one could construe that there is *our* great God (the Christian God) and *their* great God of choice. One does not have this problem when allowing the King James Bible to remain the standard. According to the Bible, when the Lord returns, He will be THE great God and OUR Saviour to those that have trusted in Him.

However, He will not be everyone's Saviour. *For therefore we both labour and suffer reproach, because we trust in the living God, who is the Saviour of all men, specially of those that believe (I Timothy 4:10).*

Furthermore, the construction in each of the three chapters of Titus in the King James Bible testifies to the design planned by God. The parallel composition of each chapter does *not* indicate that there are two Saviours, but instead that the Lord Jesus Christ and God the Father are one and the same. The modern versions retain the construction in chapters one and three, but arbitrarily eliminate it in chapter two. Take note of the unique construction of the KJB:

> *"...God our Saviour" (Titus 1:3)*
> *"...Lord Jesus Christ our Saviour." (Titus 1:4)*
>
> *"...the doctrine of God our Saviour ..." (Titus 2:10)*
> *"...our Saviour Jesus Christ" (Titus 2:13)*
>
> *"...love of God our Saviour..." (Titus 3:4)*
> *"...through Jesus Christ our Saviour" (Titus 3:6)*

In each case, **God** is pointed out as the Saviour, then **Jesus Christ** is pointed out as the Saviour. The modern versions eliminate the construction of the second chapter, but retain it in the first and third chapters. Moving the "our" in *Titus 2:13* in front of "great God" as the new versions do, destroys the parallelism and weakens the truth.

One cannot devote the time or the space necessary to refute all the errors and inconsistent treatment against the KJB by those claiming the superiority of the modern versions. However, when we consider how the critics emphasize and then distort the truth concerning *Titus 2:13*, their position in other areas becomes equally suspect. Mr. White and others use the same tactic concerning a similar passage in the book of Jude.

Another favorite "proof text" used by the modern Bible critic to attack the King James Bible is *Jude 4*. Again, KJB critics claim that the modern versions are actually stronger concerning the deity of the

Lord Jesus Christ. Once again, Mr. White states that *"Few KJV Only works address this passage, though it would seem like consistency would demand at least some explanation of the difference between the KJV and the modern texts."* I do not find it necessary to dodge any of the passages that Mr. White claims Bible believers must avoid. Once again he misinterprets the passage by reading the corrupt translation of the modern version and concludes, *"The last passage we will examine wherein the deity of the Lord Jesus is more plainly revealed in modern translations than in the KJV is Jude 4."* [4]

He goes on to say that the TR (*Textus Receptus*) adds one word here, "God," which he says disrupts the flow and introduces a second person into the text. He implies that the "the Lord God" should not be differentiated from the Lord Jesus Christ. He concludes by saying that most would feel that "Lord God" refers to the Father.

(KJB) Jude 4 For there are certain men crept in unawares, who were before of old ordained to this condemnation, ungodly men, turning the grace of our God into lasciviousness, and denying the only Lord God, and our Lord Jesus Christ.

He says that *"the modern texts contain a very clear testimony to the deity of Christ."* Once again, his virulent attack against the word of God is without basis. The confusion caused by the mistranslation of the text **in the NIV** has caused the readers to miss God's purpose for the distinctions given by the King James Bible. Once again, the NIV inexcusably fails to make any distinction between THE only Lord God and OUR Lord Jesus Christ.

(NIV) Jude 4 For certain men whose condemnation was written about long ago have secretly slipped in among you. They are godless men, who change the grace of our God into a license for immorality and deny Jesus Christ our only Sovereign and Lord.

Mr. White's argument sounds quite plausible on the surface; however, like so many of his other statements, this one has no basis in truth. The King James Bible differentiates between the only Lord God and our Lord Jesus Christ. God is "THE only Lord God"! However, He is only "OUR Lord Jesus Christ" to those that have trusted in Him as Lord and Saviour.

Clearly showing his true colors, Mr. White attacks the foundation for the King James Bible in his concluding comments concerning this passage. He says that *"the KJV's rendering obscures this by following **inferior manuscripts**, resulting in a reading that allows one to distinguish between the 'Lord God' and the Lord Jesus Christ."* [5] The "inferior manuscripts" to which he refers are those used by the churches for centuries and known as the Received Text *(Textus Receptus)*. In their place, he elevates two Roman Catholic texts.

Mr. White believes that the Westcott and Hort Greek text (with the *Codex Sinaiticus* and *Vaticanus* as their basis) are the most reliable manuscripts. He calls the Sinaiticus a **great** codex that was found in a wastebasket by Tischendorf in a monastery of St. Catherine. [6] So much for supernatural preservation.

Mr. White states that he is fully aware that these two *(corrupt)* manuscripts were used by *(corrupt)* men to eventually produce the glut of *(corrupt)* bibles on the market. He states: *"Wescott and Hort used* (Sinaiticus) *and* (Vaticanus) *to produce their New Testament, a work that displaced the text used by the KJV, later known as the Textus Receptus, **in scholarly studies**."* [7] This is the main reason that the modern versions differ from the King James Bible.

The differences are not due to the "scholars'" desire to simply update the Bible into today's modern language. All of the modern versions have a significantly different foundation. Mr. White points out that these (corrupt) Greek texts replaced the true text *in scholarly studies.* That means that the seminaries moved away from the *Textus Receptus/* Received Text King James Bible first. No wonder our seminaries are creating scholarly infidels.

Hopefully, the comparisons between the KJB and the NIV have sufficiently convinced the reader of the infidelity of the Bible critic. However, the scriptural evidence is not limited to simply comparing the truth with the counterfeit. It was common practice in the word of God for the writer to refer to *our Lord Jesus Christ*. In fact, one will find the phrase 56 different times in the New Testament and in each and every one of Paul's epistles save one.

Finally, take note of the clear distinction between **the** LORD and **our** Lord given in Psalm chapter 135. *For I know that **the LORD is great**, and that **our Lord** is above all gods (Psalm 135:5).*

David distinguishes between **the** LORD that is great and **our** Lord that is above all gods. The Bible will never lose its capacity to silence the critic. However, for those that still need a little more evidence – examining the reason that the Bible distinguishes between Lord and LORD reveals much. The Hebrew word *Jehovah* is translated as "LORD" (all capitals) in the King James Bible to distinguish it from the Hebrew word *Adonai*, which is translated as "Lord" (only the L capitalized). Could the variation be significant? Read the next passage, keeping this distinction in mind.

> *Psalm 110:1 **The LORD** said unto **my Lord**, Sit thou at my right hand, until I make thine enemies thy footstool.*

The Lord Jesus Christ quotes David's remarks unmistakably revealing their meaning. One can see that the second Lord is Christ Himself.

> *Matthew 22:41 While the Pharisees were gathered together, Jesus asked them, 42 Saying, **What think ye of Christ? whose son is he?** They say unto him, The Son of David. 43 He saith unto them, **How then doth David in spirit call him Lord**, saying, 44 **The LORD said unto my Lord**, Sit thou on my right hand, till I make thine enemies thy footstool? 45 If David then call him Lord, how is he his son? 46 And no man was able to answer him a word, neither durst any man from that day forth ask him any more questions.*

David understood the significance between THE great God and OUR Lord. The passages say *"The **LORD** (the Father) said unto my Lord (the Son)..."* Too bad history does not repeat itself today in the bible-rejecting seminaries around the world. Obviously, from the reaction of the Pharisees (in verse 46), they were much more convicted and quickly silenced than the critics of today. One day, the enemies of our Lord and Saviour will be made His footstool and silenced forever *(Hebrews 10:12-13).*

At the great supper of the Lamb everyone will finally realize that OUR Lord is THE great God too. No more excuses for those that have rejected Him. *"And I saw an angel standing in the sun; and he cried with a loud voice, saying to all the fowls that fly in the midst of heaven, Come and gather yourselves together unto the supper of the great God"* *(Revelation 19:17).*

Just as the King James Bible says, one day He will be revealed as THE great God! The gods of these false religions will not be able to protect the lost. Either they accept Him as their personal Saviour or suffer the consequences. God requires a personal relationship!

(KJB) Titus 2:13 Looking for that blessed hope, and the glorious appearing of the great God and our Saviour Jesus Christ;

I hope the reader realizes that He is not to be just THE great God, but every person must make a personal, conscious decision whether to include himself in the statement when we say, "He is OUR Saviour Jesus Christ." Is He YOUR Saviour?

James White – Further Comments

The introduction to a book is used to introduce the basic premise of the book to the reader. Here is one statement from the introduction of Mr. White's book.

This book is not against the King James Version. [8]

James White makes the previous statement in the introduction to his book. However, the facts seem to indicate otherwise. Here is just a **sampling** of comments gleaned from just two chapters of his book to prove the absurdity of his stated position on the King James Bible. Can one really trust a man that seems to have such a hatred and disdain for the King James Bible, all the while claiming that he is not against it?

Therefore we see that, in reality, the KJV rendering is inferior to all the modern translations, which more faithfully bring out what Paul is referring to. [9]

Here the KJV rendering is better than it was in the previous example, though it is still found to be inferior to the modern versions. [10]

*...we discover that the modern translations are **much** more accurate than the rather free, and misleading, translation of the KJV at this point.* [11]

The KJV is the favorite version of a number of groups that promote works-salvation. [12]

Yet, this is a case in which the modern translations are more literal, and more correct, than the KJV. [13]

...cultic groups such as Jehovah's Witnesses have made great use of the KJV's ambiguous rendering of words that have to do with the afterlife...this is one place in which many modern translations far surpass the KJV in accuracy. [14]

While the KJV's translation of these terms is certainly unfortunate... [15] [Emphasis mine]

Any honest person must admit that the modern translations provide a much needed element of clarity and precision that is lacking in the AV. [16]

*Again we find the modern translations quite **honestly** surpassing the KJV in clarity and exactitude.* [17]

The modern translations recognize the context in which this word is found and translate it accordingly, bringing out the meaning that is, quite simply, obscured in the KJV. [18]

The great scholars who labored upon the AV would have been the first to admit that their work was liable to correction and revision as the study of biblical languages and the textual history of the Bible advanced. (Better known as the evolution of mankind – see **II Timothy 3:1-2, 7.**) *Surely they would have welcomed the study undertaken by Granville Sharp late in the 1790s. Sharp's work resulted in a rule of koine Greek that bears his name,* **a rule that was not fully understood by the KJV translators.** *Because of his work, we are able to better understand how plain is the testimony to the deity of Christ that is found in such places as Titus 2:13 and 2 Peter 1:1.* **The KJV translators, through no fault of their own, obscured these passages through less than perfect translation. Modern translations correct their error.** [19] [Emphasis mine]

He goes on to justify the changes already discussed in the body of this chapter, but the humorous statement comes on the next page. After he spends a full page justifying why the Granville Sharp rule would have changed the outcome of the wording of the King James Bible in *II Peter 1:1*, he makes the following statement.

The little book of 2 Peter contains a total of five 'Granville Sharp' constructions. They are 1:1; 1:11; 2:20; 3:2; and 3:18. **No one would argue that the other four instances are exceptions to the rule.** [20]

Let me try to rephrase Mr. White's "insightful" comments. This rule that did *not* exist when the King James translators did their work is being used to justify changes that are unnecessary and unscriptural. Furthermore, his arguments for the changes in the modern versions are bolstered by a rule that he says applies five times in one book, but four of them are clearly EXCEPTIONS to the rule???!!! Here is a better rule: *Any rule that contradicts the plain teaching of scripture is satanically inspired and has no basis in truth.* (See **Psalm 12:6-7, Matthew 24:35, Hebrews 4:12.**)

The purpose of this book is to keep our discussions simple; however, answering the critic sometimes necessitates a more technical rebuttal. Please pardon the technical nature of this short answer to Mr. White's scriptural infidelity. Mr. White fails to recognize that the statement "God and **our** Saviour" is a Hebraism called Hendiady (en dia dis). This means "one by means of two." Other such constructions can be found in many scriptures such as *I Timothy 1:1, II Timothy 1:2,* and *Titus 1:4.*

Other examples of the Hebraism are found throughout the Old Testament. Here are three.

Zechariah 9:9 ...riding upon an ass, and upon a colt the foal of an ass

Isaiah 49:7 ...the Redeemer of Israel, and his Holy One

Isaiah 45:21 ...a just God and a Saviour

Each of these examples reveals a clear Hendiady. They are all one by means of two. In addition to the fact that the construction of *II Peter 1:1* is correct, the style is plainly the Apostle Peter's style of writing.

The Apostle Peter's inspired style of writing is *"our Lord Jesus Christ," Jesus our Lord,"* and *"our Lord and Saviour Jesus Christ."* (See *II Peter 1:1, 1:2, 1:8, 1:11, 1:14, 1:16,* etc.).

Now consider the passage in Second Peter under attack by Mr. White. Once again, OUR Bible (like OUR Saviour) differentiates between God and our Saviour. Over and over again, the true word places an emphasis upon a personal relationship with Jesus Christ.

(KJB) II Peter 1:1 Simon Peter, a servant and an apostle of Jesus Christ, to them that have obtained like precious faith with us through the righteousness of God and our Saviour Jesus Christ:

The importance of a personal relationship with our Saviour Jesus Christ cannot be overemphasized. The KJB correctly makes this distinction; the modern versions fail to do so. In the NIV, the personal relationship is confused because the "our" is moved out of place. Instead of salvation being emphasized, it seems as though more than one God could be recognized – *our* God and *their* God.

> *(NIV) II Peter 1:1 Simon Peter, a servant and apostle of Jesus Christ, To those who through the righteousness of **our God and Savior Jesus Christ** have received a faith as precious as ours:*

Anyone can create a rule that supposedly corrects an error, but first you must prove that the error exists and then prove the veracity of the rule in its application to the particular passage. In this case, once again, the critic fails on both counts. He cannot prove the error and fails to establish that this rule applies or even exists. Furthermore, he cannot even justify that the rule is valid.

Men like Mr. White and his cohorts should read the next passages very carefully. Pay particular attention to the fact that there is a distinction concerning our God (versus their God), and that OUR God is THE God of salvation. The verse thus distinguishes between OUR God and the God of the heathen. Their God does not save and our God will not save anyone that does not know Him personally.

> *Psalm 68:20 He that is **our** God is **the** God of salvation; and unto God the Lord belong the issues from death.*

Mr. White's book and many others like his attack the greatest book ever given to man. As we have seen, some of their arguments are very easy to disprove. God foreknew that books like his would be written, and I believe that is why He included verse 20 to stop the mouth of the gainsayer. God's warning follows in the very next verse (21). Be warned!

> *Psalm 68:21 But God shall wound the head of his enemies, and the hairy scalp of such an one as goeth on still in his trespasses.*

God is not mocked; one day, He will judge the infidelity of those that attack His precious word. Why would anyone want to continue in error when the truth is so plain and the judgment is so certain?

Chapter 3 Endnotes

[1] White, *The King James Only Controversy, op. cit.*, p.197.
[2] *Ibid.*, p. 201-202.
[3] *Ibid.*, p. vi.
[4] *Ibid.*, p. 206.
[5] *Ibid.*, p. 206.
[6] *Ibid.*, p. 32.
[7] *Ibid.*, p. 33.
[8] *Ibid.*, p. vi.
[9] *Ibid.*, p. 114.
[10] *Ibid.*, p.115.
[11] *Ibid.*, p. 132.
[12] *Ibid.*, p. 133.
[13] *Ibid.*, p. 133.
[14] *Ibid.*, p. 137.
[15] *Ibid.*, p. 138.
[16] *Ibid.*, p. 141.
[17] *Ibid.*, p. 142.
[18] *Ibid.*, p. 145.
[19] *Ibid.*, p. 267.
[20] *Ibid.*, p. 268.

4

Salvation Sure & Simple

*He that is our God is the God of salvation; and unto God the
Lord belong the issues from death.*
(Psalm 68:20)

S ome of the changes in the modern versions seem quite innocent.
However, in some instances, the "modernization" of the words of
God constitutes heresy. Much of this heresy surrounds the most
important truth for a person to understand – that is, the means of salvation.

For instance, the word of God plainly teaches that salvation occurs at
a *point in time* in a man's life after he realizes his lost condition and
acknowledges his need for a Saviour. The *moment* he accepts the Saviour, he is saved! The modern versions distort God's *instantaneous*
salvation into some sort of *progressive* salvation that occurs over time.

The Apostle Paul teaches the church that salvation involves *no works*
(Ephesians 2:9, II Timothy 1:9, Titus 3:5); however, the modern versions alter this truth as well. Rather than teaching salvation by grace,
many of their verses pervert the gospel by including *works*. Though the
problems with these versions neither begin nor end with these two critical distortions, these two highly significant issues will be the primary
emphasis of this chapter.

As the King James Bible (KJB) is compared to the New International
Version (NIV), keep in mind that the changes discussed are *not* limited

solely to the NIV. Because the modern versions rely upon the same corrupt foundation, the other contemporary versions also manifest these same erroneous alterations.

The Greek and Hebrew texts accepted as authentic by the churches for 1,500 years, and used to translate the KJB, have been rejected by the modern version authors. Instead, these individuals consistently chose to base their changes on the corrupt interpretations provided by the Westcott and Hort Greek Text. Such a basis amounts to a foundation of sinking sand. James White gives the position of the modern version critic quite succinctly.

> *The simple fact of the matter is that no textual variants in either the Old or New Testaments in any way, shape, or form materially disrupt or destroy any essential doctrine of the Christian faith.* [1]

Doug Kutilek, another modern day critic, agrees with Mr. White's assessment, adding "credibility" to his position by finding someone that agreed with him during the early 1900's. He quotes Sir Frederic G. Kenyon. In discussing the differences between the traditional text (King James Bible text) and the Alexandrian text-types (the modern versions), Kenyon writes:

> *We may indeed believe that He would not allow His Word to be seriously corrupted, or any part of it essential to man's salvation to be lost or obscured; but the differences between the rival types of text is not one of doctrine. No fundamental point of doctrine rests upon a disputed reading: and the truths of Christianity are as certainly expressed in the text of Westcott and Hort* (all modern versions) *as in that of Stephanus* (King James Bible). *Even advocates and defenders of the supremacy of the Byzantine over the Alexandrian text agree in this assessment.* [2]

Of course, I do *not* agree with the assessments of White, Kutilek, or Kenyon. All of the modern versions follow or have been infected by the Westcott and Hort, Alexandrian text types. You be the judge whether these changes are significant. The souls of men rest upon the truths of

God's word! Who would want to change these precious truths and pervert them so?

Christ Came to Save the Lost . . . or Did He?

As the result of sin, every person born into the world *deserves* to be eternally separated from God. In fact, Adam's sin created this division six thousand years ago, passing it upon all future generations. *"Wherefore, as by one man sin entered into the world, and death by sin; and so death passed upon all men, for that all have sinned:"* *(Romans 5:12)*. However, God's eternal plan provided for the redemption of man from the very beginning. Man was not to be left without hope.

The Lord Jesus Christ would provide the ultimate sacrifice as payment for our sins – His blood shed on the cross of Calvary. The Bible plainly teaches that He descended from heaven's glory *to save sinners.* Since we have all sinned *(Romans 3:23)*, He came to save each and every one of us from the penalty that we all deserve – eternal separation from a holy, perfect, and just God.

(KJB) Luke 9:55 But he turned, and rebuked them, and said, Ye know not what manner of spirit ye are of. 56 For the Son of man is not come to destroy men's lives, but to save them. And they went to another village.

The Bible emphasizes that Jesus came to save and not to destroy men's lives! History clearly reveals that religion has done just the opposite – destroyed much and saved none. Christ came to save from the penalty of sin: *"For the wages of sin is death; but the gift of God is eternal life through Jesus Christ our Lord" (Romans 6:23)*. By removing 70 percent of this passage from Luke, the NIV fails to state Christ's mission for becoming a man.

(NIV) Luke 9:55 But Jesus turned and rebuked them, 56 and they went to another village.

The Bible frequently provides multiple witnesses in order to emphasize important truths. Consequently, another very clear passage concerning the purpose for God's becoming a man is found in the book of Matthew. In this instance, the verse tells exactly who He came to save – *the lost*. Praise God for His infinite mercy, and provision for the salvation of man.

(KJB) Matthew 18:11 For the Son of man is come to save that which was lost.

One should always be mindful of this great truth and never tire of hearing it repeated. The Lord Jesus Christ came to save the lost! Praise God for this simple truth so vehemently attacked in every modern version on the market. Now read the same verse in the NIV (if you can find it). The verses before and after verse eleven are given for context.

(NIV) Matthew 18:10-12
10 "See that you do not look down on one of these little ones. For I tell you that their angels in heaven always see the face of my Father in heaven.

12"What do you think? If a man owns a hundred sheep, and one of them wanders away, will he not leave the ninety-nine on the hills and go to look for the one that wandered off?

Did you notice that verse eleven is completely omitted in the NIV? Who would not want man to know the purpose of God's Son coming to earth? Satan, of course. There are many other verses missing in these modern versions, too. For instance, try to locate the following references in modern counterfeit bibles:

Matthew 17:21	*Mark 11:26*	*Acts 15:34*
Matthew 23:14	*Mark 15:28*	*Acts 24:7*
Mark 7:16	*Luke 17:36*	*Acts 28:29*
Mark 9:44	*Luke 23:17*	*Romans 16:24*
Mark 9:46	*John 5:4*	*I John 5:7*

The list goes on. Later in this study, we will look at one more missing verse from Acts chapter eight to further demonstrate the pattern of corruption. It should be obvious who is behind these inexcusable omissions.

The first two passages discussed, from Luke and Matthew respectively, showed that Jesus came "to save" sinners and "to save that which was lost." It should be obvious that Satan and the NIV have blatantly attacked these two truths.

Jesus Christ – the Object of our Belief

As other verses are compared, a pattern will appear. For instance, the Bible teaches that salvation comes from simple belief on the Lord Jesus Christ.

(KJB) John 6:47 Verily, verily, I say unto you, He that believeth on me hath everlasting life.

The modern versions distract the reader and detract from the necessary object/Person of our belief – the Lord Jesus Christ. Satan has always desired worship, to the point of beckoning the Lord to bow down to him *(Matthew 4:9)*. Is it any wonder then that the Devil has eroded the very foundations of this truth? Elimination of these truths remains his ultimate goal. The modern versions have taken many steps in that direction. Upon whom are you to believe according to the NIV?

*(NIV) John 6:47 I tell you the truth, **he who believes** has everlasting life.*

He who believes on *what* or *whom*? Jesus said to believe "on me." The Devil wants to decide *what* you are supposed to believe in and in *whom* you are to believe. If we leave this crucial choice to Satan, he will eliminate God's truth so that many more people remain confused, bewildered, *and lost*. Consider all the religions of the world offering *substitute* saviors that cannot save.

Salvation – Simple or Difficult?

When all of a person's physical needs are almost effortlessly satisfied, his spiritual needs can easily be overlooked and ignored. Such is the warning conveyed in the following verse concerning priorities. When someone elevates money above all else, a misplaced trust results. He finds it hard to trust in anything but his riches; therefore, he does not realize his need for Christ.

*(KJB) Mark 10:24 And the disciples were astonished at his words. But Jesus answereth again, and saith unto them, Children, how hard is it for them **that trust in riches** to enter into the kingdom of God!*

The KJB does *not* say that salvation is difficult to attain. In fact, it affirms the simplicity that is in Christ *(II Corinthians 11:3)*. Throughout time, Satan has gradually eroded the truth in an effort to achieve his ultimate goal: to completely change the truth of God into a lie *(Romans 1:25)*. The next passage achieves this goal in the NIV by stating that salvation is a hard thing to attain.

*(NIV) Mark 10:24 The disciples were amazed at his words. But Jesus said again, "Children, **how hard it is to enter the kingdom of God!**"*

The NIV changes the whole point of the passage. It eliminates the dire warning to those who trust in riches and makes salvation sound difficult to everyone. Do the KJB and the NIV say the same thing? Do they teach the same truths? Obviously not! Salvation is not hard. Manmade religion makes salvation hard. What must you do to be saved?

- Realize you are a sinner *(Romans 3:23)*.
- Believe that the Lord Jesus Christ died for your sins *(Romans 5:8)*.
- Repent of trusting in anything else to save you *(Romans 2:4-5)*.
- Accept the free gift of salvation *(Romans 6:23)*.
- Believe in the Saviour to forgive your sins *(Romans 10:9-13)*.

One cannot trust in his church membership, his baptism, or his good works to save him. One must simply trust in the Lord Jesus Christ alone by *believing* on Him. You can't say, "I am trusting in Jesus" *and* believe that your good works will merit a place for you in heaven. Anyone so doing has failed to believe solely on the Lord Jesus Christ and is sadly trusting in his own good works to merit that which cannot be earned – heaven's glory. The Lord Jesus Christ and He alone must be the object of our trust.

*(KJB) Ephesians 1:13 In whom ye also **trusted**, after that ye heard the word of truth, the gospel of your salvation: in whom also after that ye believed, ye were sealed with that holy Spirit of promise,*

When a person hears the truth, he must decide whether he will accept this truth over everything else. Once a person repents of *trusting* in anything other than Christ, a simple heart belief in the payment Christ has made is sufficient to save any lost sinner. The Bible tells us that once we have "believed," the Holy Spirit of God seals us "unto the day of redemption" *(Ephesians 4:30)*.

These are precious truths no matter how frivolously the modern versions handle them. How does the NIV present these same truths? The NIV states that a person becomes *included* in Christ by simply hearing the word of truth!

*(NIV) Ephesians 1:13 And you also were **included** in Christ **when you heard the word of truth**, the gospel of your salvation. Having believed, **you were marked in him with a seal**, the promised Holy Spirit,*

What a mess! How confusing! No one is *included* in Christ by simply hearing the truth. Even the parable of the sower clearly contradicts this teaching. *"And these are they by the way side, where the word is sown; **but when they have heard, Satan cometh immediately, and taketh away the word that was sown in their hearts."** (Mark 4:15).* The NIV seems to indicate that church attendance, faithful viewing of televangelists, or listening to the Bible on tape saves.

One must first act upon the truth he hears. A person must TRUST in Him **by believing** that He died for his sins. No one is included in Christ simply by *hearing* the truth; such a statement is equivalent to claiming to have been born a Christian. No one is physically born a Christian. Rather, being born a Christian is a matter of the spiritual rebirth *(I Peter 1:23)*.

Notice that the NIV also mentions being marked toward the end of the verse – *"you were marked in him with a seal."* Christians are not marked, nor do they have to be concerned about the future mark of the Beast *(Revelation 13:16-17, Revelation 19:20)*. However, since these modern versions seem to be the end-times bibles of choice, this verse could be used by the antichrist to convince people in the Tribulation that taking the Mark of the Beast is an important element in the life of a "child of God." How confusing! The Bible says, *"...God is not the author of confusion..." (I Corinthians 14:33)*.

Salvation – Before or After Baptism?

The Devil desires to confuse anyone seriously searching for the truth. Many times those searching are at a crossroad in their lives. As a result, these individuals are exceptionally vulnerable to satanic attack. Such was the case with the Philippian jailer. After attempting to take his own life, he exclaimed, *"Sirs, what must I do to be saved?"* The jailer certainly posed his question to the right two men. Paul and Silas responded in unison, *"...Believe on the Lord Jesus Christ, and thou shalt be saved, and thy house" (Acts 16:31)*. Don't let the Devil convince you that you will be *included* by any other means. Many pew sitters have realized that they must act upon what they have heard in order to be saved.

Salvation does not come by simply hearing the truth, nor does it come as a result of works or baptism. It comes as a result of believing that Christ died in your place and that you have no hope apart from Him. Acts chapter eight provides one of the clearest examples of the inefficacy of baptism for salvation. Baptism has no power to save. This passage also convincingly demonstrates that baptism *follows* salvation and is *not* a part of the gospel.

*(KJB) Acts 8:36 And as they went on their way, they came unto a certain water: and the eunuch said, See, here is water; what doth hinder me to be baptized? 37 **And Philip said, If thou believest with all thine heart, thou mayest. And he answered and said, I believe that Jesus Christ is the Son of God.** 38 And he commanded the chariot to stand still: and they went down both into the water, both Philip and the eunuch; and he baptized him.*

According to this passage, what hinders a person from being baptized? More precisely, what momentarily delayed the eunuch's baptism? Of course, the eunuch's lost spiritual condition initially disqualified him as a candidate for baptism. We all need to realize, preach, and teach this truth. Once Peter came to an understanding concerning the Gospel of the Grace of God, he said, *"...we believe that through the **grace** of the Lord Jesus Christ we shall be saved, even as they" (**Acts 15:11**)*. He did *not* include baptism as a requirement for salvation, but preached that salvation was all of grace. The Apostle Paul separates baptism from the Gospel of the Grace of God in his epistle to the Corinthians *(**I Corinthians 1:17**)*.

This passage in Acts also proves that babies *cannot* and should not be baptized since they do not have the knowledge, capabilities, or will to believe on the Lord Jesus Christ to be saved. The *Church of Christ* incorrectly teaches a regenerating power of baptism. They do not like Philip's answer and wish him to remain silent. Conveniently, because of the modern version deletions, they do not have to face their false teachings. Satan has already silenced Philip for them in the modern perversions.

(NIV) Acts 8:36 As they traveled along the road, they came to some water and the eunuch said, "Look, here is water. Why shouldn't I be baptized?" 38 And he gave orders to stop the chariot. Then both Philip and the eunuch went down into the water and Philip baptized him.

The eunuch's question is never answered in the NIV. See if you can find it. For that matter, see if you can find verse 37 at all. One submits to baptism because he is saved, not in order to attain salvation. Any teaching contrary to this truth is heretical. Notice that the NIV's verse enumeration in this passage reflects that found in the King James Bible; however, verse number 37 is completely skipped. Anyone teaching baptismal regeneration loves this deletion *(**Deuteronomy 4:2**)*.

The Gospel & the Blood of Jesus Christ

Many of the changes to the word of God are so subtle *(**Genesis 3:1**)* that one may not immediately notice them or recognize their full impact.

The next passage is one such example. The change is subtle, but the ramifications are far reaching. The Apostle Paul declares the gospel in this passage.

> **(KJB) I Corinthians 15:1** *Moreover, brethren,* **I declare unto you the gospel** *which I preached unto you, which also ye have received, and wherein ye stand; 2 By which also ye are saved, if ye keep in memory what I preached unto you, unless ye have believed in vain. 3 For I delivered unto you first of all that which I also received,* **how that** *Christ died for our sins according to the scriptures; 4 And* **that** *he was buried, and* **that** *he rose again the third day according to the scriptures:*

In the instance of this passage, the very meaning of the gospel is changed by the omission of a single word in the modern versions. Notice the seemingly insignificant word *how* in bold print in the third verse. The inclusion of this one word eliminates the notion that the Gospel of the Grace of God includes **only** the *death, burial,* and *resurrection* without considering the "how" of Jesus' death. Because preachers fail to account for this one word, some of them erroneously teach that the *how* of Jesus' death is not important. For instance, some discount the necessity of the shedding of blood for the remission of sins.

One of the most recognizable teachers of this serious error is John MacArthur, pastor of Grace Community Church in Sun Valley, California. He has stated that the Lord's *death* is important, *not His blood.* This error is a direct result of not believing in the divine preservation of the King James Bible. Here are segments of a letter he published in 1976 entitled "Not His Bleeding But His Dying."

> *It was His death that was efficacious, not His blood. ...The gospel in I Corinthians 15:4 hits the issue "Christ died". ...The shedding of blood has nothing to do with bleeding, it simply means death, violent sacrificial death. ...***Nothing in His human blood saves.*** ...I may add a note on Revelation 1:5, a passage which is* **confusing in the King James Version.** *The word "washed" is not correct. The Greek word is "delivered". ...It is not His bleeding that saved me, but His dying.* [1] [Emphasis mine]

What makes a man who has been preaching for many years arrive at these conclusions? The answer is very simple. When a preacher places himself as judge and ultimate authority over God's perfect word, the light of spiritual illumination dims. Many passages of the Bible prove that it was not *human* blood that was shed on the cross of Calvary. For instance, the book of Acts says: *"...feed the church of **God, which he hath purchased with his own blood"** (Acts 20:28).* It was clearly the blood of God shed on Calvary's cross for you and me!

Seven years after he published the previous letter written to one of his church members, Moody Bible Institute published Mr. MacArthur's commentary on the book of Hebrews. After many people publicly questioned his views and stand, his commentary shows that his views did not change.

> It was **not Jesus' physical blood** that saves us, but **His dying on our behalf,** which is **symbolized** by the shedding of His physical blood. [2] [Emphasis mine]

The King James Bible proves Mr. MacArthur completely wrong when it gives the gospel in First Corinthians chapter fifteen. In verse one, Paul says he declared the gospel. He proceeds to tell us what the gospel is in verses three and four. The "**how** that Christ died for our sins" is part of that gospel! However, the modern versions drastically change the gospel by eliminating one little word – that word is "how." *How* that Jesus died is a part of the gospel that we preach (unless one uses one of the modern versions).

> *(NIV) I Corinthians 15:1 Now, brothers, I want to remind you of the gospel I preached to you, which you received and on which you have taken your stand. 2 By this gospel you are saved, if you hold firmly to the word I preached to you. Otherwise, you have believed in vain. 3 For what I received I passed on to you as of first importance: **that** Christ died for our sins according to the Scriptures, 4 **that** he was buried, **that** he was raised on the third day according to the Scriptures,*

The modern versions remove this very important aspect of the gospel – the *how* of His death. *How* that Christ died is part of the Gospel of the Grace of God. In order for a person to receive the gospel, he must understand what it is. That one little word shifts the emphasis from the simple fact that Christ died, placing the emphasis on the "how" of His death.

How did He die? **He died on the cross; He shed His blood; He became sin for us.** Each of these particulars is an aspect of the gospel because of that one little word *"how."* Remove this single word, and the whole gospel changes. We are told that *"Every word of God is pure..." (Proverbs 30:5).* We are also warned, *"Ye shall not add unto the word which I command you, neither shall ye diminish ought from it..." (Deuteronomy 4:2).* When we ignore the clear teachings and commands from scripture, we open ourselves up to every kind of error and heresy.

Since we are to spread *the gospel,* our preaching is to include the "power of the cross" . . . the **how** of Jesus' death. It is also to include the blood . . . the **how** of Jesus' death. We must inform people concerning what the Bible says about *why* His death can save anyone from eternal separation from God. All of these are different facets of the gospel. He suffered for us; He died for us; He shed His blood for us; He went to hell for us *(Acts 2:31).* Redemption and the forgiveness of sins come through the blood (shed by God on Calvary's cross).

*(KJB) Colossians 1:14 In whom we have redemption **through his blood,** even the forgiveness of sins:*

The **how** of Jesus' death is a part of the gospel. When preachers allege that Jesus could have *drowned* in the sea for our sins, one should not be surprised since the revisers' changes have distorted and perverted the truth. Once the Gospel of the Grace of God has been changed, the blood is the next to go. The Bible says a little leaven leaveneth the whole lump *(Galatians 5:9).* See if you can find the blood in this same verse in the NIV:

(NIV) Colossians 1:14 in whom we have redemption, the forgiveness of sins.

The Christian has redemption *through His blood* regardless of what the modern versions delete and no matter what the popular preachers profess. Forgiveness of sins is a direct result of our Lord and Saviour's *shedding of His blood*. The Bible clearly states that *"...without shedding of blood is no remission" (Hebrews 9:22)*. Anyone that claims otherwise is a heretic.

This false teaching of the "human" blood of Jesus did not begin with people like John MacArthur. During the early church, liberal teachings were making a distinction between the *human Jesus* and the *divine Christ*. The Apostle Paul warned of such corruption *(II Corinthians 2:17)* during the first century.

The humanistic philosophy was known as *Doceticism*. Proponents of this cult taught that Jesus WAS the son of Joseph *(Luke 2:33* NIV), but He became deity (Christ) the moment He was baptized by John the Baptist. They taught that He remained deity until the moment He was nailed to the cross. According to this teaching, He lost His deity and became "just Jesus" again. [3]

The King James Bible says that the blood of Jesus *Christ* cleanses us from all sin.

(KJB) I John 1:7 But if we walk in the light, as he is in the light, we have fellowship one with another, and the blood of Jesus Christ his Son cleanseth us from all sin.

Satan wants to destroy the association of the divine title "Christ" with its human counterpart "Jesus." Notice the change in the next verse with the removal of one word – Christ.

(NIV) I John 1:7 But if we walk in the light, as he is in the light, we have fellowship with one another, and the blood of Jesus, his Son, purifies us from all sin.

The elimination of the word "Christ" from this verse may not appear significant on the surface until one considers its full implications. The change deliberately attacks the deity of the Lord Jesus Christ. In this case, the change attacks the ultimate sacrifice of God – the shedding of His own sinless blood. Thus, the Bible student is missing another convincing proof that the blood of Calvary is more than merely human blood, but rather the cleansing blood of Christ – the anointed one.

Salvation – a Fact Proven or a Fickle Process

Since the Bible revisers take free reign to attack the word of God, they do not hesitate to attack the mode that God has chosen to propagate His truth – through preaching. God uses *preaching* to convince the world of sin, judgment, and condemnation, thus making men conscious of their need to be saved.

> *(KJB) I Corinthians 1:18 For the **preaching** of the cross is to them that perish foolishness; but unto us which **are saved** it is the power of God.*

Satan will do anything within his power to stop the preaching of the word. Therefore, the new versions place the emphasis on the *message*, rather than the *preaching*. You can see the results in today's churches. The power of God is gone because their bibles no longer emphasize the supreme importance of preaching. Preaching has been replaced by every imaginable program and gimmick. Churches have diminished the importance of preaching because modern versions, like the NIV, have de-emphasized it and in many cases eliminated it.

> *(NIV) I Corinthians 1:18 For the **message** of the cross is foolishness to those who are perishing, but to us who are **being saved** it is the power of God.*

In this passage, the NIV not only eliminates preaching, but also communicates *salvation as a process*. Rather than stating that Christians *are* saved, the NIV changes the verse to read that Christians are *being* saved. Are you saved, or are you being saved? Every true Bible believing child of God knows that no legitimate Bible teaches progressive salvation. The NIV ridicules the message preached three verses later (verse 21) by referring to the *foolishness of what is preached*. What part of the preaching do you suppose this verse in the NIV could be referring to as foolish: the blood, the cross, the Saviour, etc.?

As we have seen, God's righteousness is not something deserved, nor is it the result of any human effort. His righteousness comes without man's works to bring it to pass. At the moment of salvation, an individual becomes a new creature in Christ Jesus *(II Corinthians 5:17)* by being *made* the righteousness of God. God makes the lost sinner righteous *(John 1:3)*.

*(KJB) II Corinthians 5:21 For he hath made him to be sin for us, who knew no sin; that we might be **made** the righteousness of God in him.*

God's righteousness is applied to a person instantaneously and completely, apart from any work done by that person. The Christian is not "becoming" righteous by exerting some personal effort. He is *made* righteous by an outside source (God) and cannot *become* righteous by any other way. God does *all* of the work. A person plays no part in the *work* of salvation. One must only believe on the Lord Jesus Christ in order to be saved. All of the work was finished on the cross of Calvary... not so according to the NIV.

*(NIV) II Corinthians 5:21 God made him who had no sin to be sin for us, so that in him we **might become** the righteousness of God.*

The NIV once again makes salvation a process. It would be interesting but sad to know how many people have remained lost because of the false teachings promulgated by these modern versions.

Another example of the progressive salvation propagated by these modern versions occurs in the book of Acts. During the early Acts period, the Apostles were concerned about the Gentiles and the many conflicting instructions they were receiving from the converted Jews. Therefore, the Apostles came to the following conclusion concerning the **saved** Gentiles that had *turned to God*.

*(KJB) Acts 15:19 Wherefore my sentence is, that we trouble not them, which from among the Gentiles are **turned to God**: 20 But that we write unto them, that they abstain from pollutions of*

idols, and from fornication, and from things strangled, and from blood.

These saved Gentiles had too many chiefs instructing them in what they should do *after salvation*. Remember that these people did not have the luxury of simply picking up the Bible and thereby knowing how to carry out the will of God. Instead, the Apostles instructed them in writing regarding how to maintain a good testimony for the sake of the Jews in their city. They were to abstain from certain things particularly offensive to the Jews in order to be an effective witness to them. The main point to realize is that these instructions *for Christian service* were directed toward *saved* people... not so with the NIV.

*(NIV) Acts 15:19 "It is my judgment, therefore, that we should not make it difficult for the Gentiles **who are turning to God**. 20 Instead we should write to them, telling them to abstain from food polluted by idols, from sexual immorality, from the meat of strangled animals and from blood.*

Instructions on how to live godly are never given to someone "turning to God." This would cloud the issue of salvation. In the NIV, the letter written by the Apostles is no longer addressed to those who *have turned to God* (past tense), but instead, to the Gentiles *who are turning to God* (present tense). As a result, the letter is transformed from one which instructs regarding Christian testimony, to one which recommends works to be done by the lost – presumably for their salvation!

Hopefully, one more nail in the coffin will suffice to bury these modern versions and their false teachings. Another verse teaching progressive salvation is found in Paul's second letter to the Corinthians. The true Bible believer knows that he is either saved or lost. God leaves no middle ground, and salvation does not occur over a process of time.

*(KJB) II Corinthians 2:15 For we are unto God a sweet savour of Christ, in them that **are saved**, and in them that perish:*

The NIV?

*(NIV) II Corinthians 2:15 For **we** are to God the aroma of Christ among those **who are being saved** and those who are perishing.*

According to the NIV, the man that wrote more books of the Bible than anyone else was not even sure he was saved. The NIV says "we...who are being saved." This verse identifies the author of Second Corinthians (Paul) as one of those that is *being saved*. Is it any wonder so many Christians struggle with the assurance of their salvation when reading verses from these modern versions?

Pulpits have lost their effectiveness because of perversion of truth. The preacher may preach and teach salvation by grace and eternal security of the believer, but the modern versions confuse the reader by not conveying this same truth. And we know that *"...God is not the author of confusion..." (I Corinthians 14:33)*. God is not the author of these modern versions either! Many other verses in the modern versions teach this same heresy.

Will Christ Disown His Children?

Some would point to the following verse in the King James Bible as "proof" that the King James Bible teaches that one can lose his salvation too. However, the context of any verse always determines its meaning. The context of this passage deals with a Christian's future reign with Christ as a reward for his suffering for Christ while on this earth.

*(KJB) II Timothy 2:12 If we **suffer**, we shall also **reign** with him: **if we deny him, he also will deny us:***

Just as God promises a future reign to those who suffer, He denies a reign to all those who refuse to live godly and thereby avoid the suffering. "If we deny him" (by not suffering), he also will deny us (a reign). The verse does not mean, nor does it say, that the Lord will somehow deny the child of God a place in heaven. **Remember context always determines the meaning of a passage.** Does the NIV transmit this same truth?

*(NIV) II Timothy 2:12 if we **endure**, we will also **reign** with him. If we **disown him, he will also disown us;***

Notice that the NIV changes *suffer* to *endure*, thus eliminating the possibility of our most basic Bible study tool – the cross-reference word search. Further, by choosing the word *endure*, this passage in Timothy aligns itself with passages such as **Matthew 24:13 and Mark 13:13**, which are applicable to individuals living during the Tribulation.

Although the change to the first part of this verse is awful, the second part of the passage gets even worse. The NIV states that a Christian who *disowns* the Lord will be *disowned* by Him. The Lord will never *disown* one of His own! If you are saved, you are a child of God; He cannot disown you. The comedy of errors gets even more pathetic when reading the very next verse in the NIV.

*13 if we are faithless, he will remain faithful, for **he cannot disown himself.***

Verse twelve says He will disown the Christian and the very next verse states that He cannot disown him because He would be disowning Himself! Do you get it? At least verse thirteen speaks the truth, but it surely contradicts the preceding verse in the NIV. The Lord cannot disown a Christian because to do so would mean that a member of the Body of Christ would be lost *(I Corinthians 12:27, Ephesians 5:30)*. However, this true statement in verse thirteen contradicts the previous false statement concerning disownment found in verse twelve, and thus the satanic goal of creating confusion is accomplished. The saying comes to mind, "he who sets out to deceive will be deceived." (See Jacob in the Old Testament.)

Must We Confess or Simply Acknowledge?

Satan always tries to cloud the waters. He does not want people to confess Jesus Christ as Lord and Saviour. *"That if thou shalt **confess** with thy mouth the Lord Jesus, and shalt believe in thine heart that God hath raised him from the dead, thou shalt be saved" (**Romans 10:9**)*. With this truth in mind, read the next passage concerning the spirits.

*(KJB) I John 4:2 Hereby know ye the Spirit of God: Every spirit that **confesseth** that Jesus Christ is come in the flesh is of God: 3 And every spirit that **confesseth not** that Jesus Christ is come in the flesh is not of God: and this is that spirit of antichrist, whereof ye have heard that it should come; and even now already is it in the world.*

We are commanded to try the spirits *(I John 4:1)* to see if they are of God. If the spirit does not *confess* that Jesus is come in the flesh, he is not of God. Look at this satanic change! *Confess* is changed to simply *acknowledge.*

*(NIV) I John 4:2 This is how you can recognize the Spirit of God: Every spirit that **acknowledges** that Jesus Christ has come in the flesh is from God, 3 but every spirit that does **not acknowledge** Jesus is not from God. This is the spirit of the antichrist, which you have heard is coming and even now is already in the world.*

The wicked spirits that we read about in Jesus' day had no problem acknowledging that the Son of God had come in the flesh. For instance, the two possessed men that came out of the tombs *"...cried out, saying, What have we to do with thee, Jesus, thou Son of God? art thou come hither to torment us before the time?" (Matthew 8:29).* They **acknowledged** Him, but did not **confess** Him. The difference can be more clearly seen when considering the difference between *acknowledging* and *confessing* a crime. There is much more personal involvement in and identification with *confessing* to a crime versus *acknowledging* that a crime took place.

A person may acknowledge Jesus as having existed, and yet he may simultaneously fail to confess Him as Lord and Saviour. The difference between *confessing* and *acknowledging* is the difference between believing on Him and simply admitting that He existed. The evil spirits have no reservations about acknowledging that Jesus Christ has come in the flesh. They certainly acknowledged Him by recognizing Him as the Son of God. However, they will be tormented (in hell – Luke 16) one day because they refuse to believe upon and accept Him and therefore do not *confess* Him.

Final Thoughts – The *New* King James Version

The focal point of this study is the New International Version; however, the other versions are just as harmful. We will look at a few passages in the New King James Version to prove this point, although many others could be included too.

*(KJB) Matthew 7:13 Enter ye in at the strait gate: for wide is the gate, and broad is the way, that leadeth to destruction, and many there be which go in thereat: 14 Because strait is the gate, and **narrow** is the way, which leadeth unto life, and few there be that find it.*

The KJB says *narrow is the way, which leadeth unto life*. The NKJV blatantly changes *narrow* to *difficult*, thus making salvation seem a hard thing to attain. This contradicts the plain teaching of scripture and contributes to the strong biases many have against the simplicity of salvation. Religion remains Satan's most effective tool to control the masses. His most effective method is to create a difficult system for salvation supported by the changes in the modern versions.

*(NKJV) Matthew 7:13 "Enter by the narrow gate; for wide is the gate and broad is the way that leads to destruction, and there are many who go in by it. 14 Because narrow is the gate and **difficult** is the way which leads to life, and there are few who find it."*

The New King James Version is just as confusing about these matters as the other modern versions are. However, it is more subtle because it does not make the number of changes that its modern counterparts do and seems more acceptable to some Christians. The Bible says that the resurrection is part of the gospel. Without it we would not have a living Saviour, seated at the right hand of God.

*(KJB) Romans 4:25 Who was delivered for our offences, and was **raised again for our justification**.*

The Lord Jesus Christ was resurrected so that we may be justified. It was for our justification. Praise God! Notice how confusing the NKJV makes this simple truth.

(NKJV) **Romans 4:25** *who was delivered up because of our offenses, and* **was raised because of our justification.**

Dr. Mickey Carter analyzes the changes: *"When the NKJV says that the Lord was raised* **because of our justification** *it sounds like we paid for our own sin and guilt which caused Christ to be raised again."* [4]

Hopefully, this short study has assisted the student of God's word in realizing that the modern versions have contributed to the heresies of man. Many of these revisions attack the very fabric of everything Christians hold sacred. For instance, the NIV completely removes Calvary from the text of the Bible *(Luke 23:33)*.

It does not matter whether you choose the NIV, NASV, Living Bible, or any other modern version. The foundation of each of these is corrupt. All of the modern versions are built upon the same corrupt sinking-sand foundation. The Bible says, *"Blessed is he that readeth..."* *(Revelation 1:3)*. One can be blessed by simply reading the Bible, but it does matter which bible one chooses. The blessings do not come from picking up one's favorite version. They come from reading God's book and God only wrote one book!

Chapter 4 Endnotes

[1] John MacArthur Jr., *"Not His Bleeding But His Dying,"* Letter to a member, 1976.

[2] John MacArthur, *Hebrews (The MacArthur New Testament Commentary)*, Moody Bible Institute, 1983, p. 237.

[3] Al Lacy, *Can I Trust my Bible?* (Littleton, CO: Al Lacy Publications, 1991) p. 279.

[4] Carter, *Things That are Different are Not the Same, op. cit.*, p.193.

5

Godly Language vs. the Modern Lingo

The words of the LORD are pure words: as silver tried in a furnace of earth, purified seven times.
(Psalm 12:6)

The modern versions communicate impurely. Rather than immediately looking at many of the ways they do so, one example should show the magnitude of the problem associated with producing these modern versions.

The book of Zechariah gives a very clear prophecy of the crucifixion. It reveals that the Lord would be wounded in the house of His friends (the Jews). The wounds in His hands clearly signified His manner of death. *"Then saith he to Thomas, reach hither thy finger, and behold my hands; and reach hither thy hand, and thrust it into my side: and be not faithless, but believing" (John 20:27).* The Bible never records that Thomas took the Lord up on His offer, but he could plainly see the wounds in His hands and side.

However, Satan has been attacking the crucifixion for thousands of years. Consider this prophecy and realize its fulfillment by the Lord Jesus Christ, our Saviour.

*(KJB) Zechariah 13:6 And one shall say unto him, **What are these wounds in thine hands?** Then he shall answer, Those with which I was wounded in the house of my friends.*

Every modern translation must have enough changes to warrant a copyright. By law, new bible versions cannot be copyrighted if they are derivative works. Words must be changed to legally qualify for copyright protection. Did the prophecy say *hands* . . . or *body*?

(NIV) Zechariah 13:6 If someone asks him, 'What are these wounds on your body?' he will answer, 'The wounds I was given at the house of my friends.'

. . . or *back*?

(RSV) Zechariah 13:6 And if one asks him, 'What are these wounds on your back?' he will say, 'The wounds I received in the house of my friends.' "

. . . or *between your arms*?

(NKJV) Zechariah 13:6 "And one will say to him, 'What are these wounds between your arms?' Then he will answer, 'Those with which I was wounded in the house of my friends.'

. . . or *your chest and your back*?

(LB) Zechariah 13:6 "And if someone asks, `Then what are these scars on your chest and your back?' he will say, `I got into a brawl at the home of a friend!'

A brawl? – this is outright blasphemy! The reason that Bible believers get such a bad rap is because they have seen this foolishness for too long – it is angering *(Ephesians 4:26)*. Two other things to take note of concerning the blasphemous Living Bible above – the Lord Jesus Christ had no scars and He did not get into **a brawl.** He willingly laid down His life. *"He was oppressed, and he was afflicted, yet **he opened not his mouth**: he is brought as a lamb to the slaughter, and as a sheep before her shearers is dumb, so he openeth not his mouth" (Isaiah 53:7).*

If the words of the Lord are pure (and the KJB is), and if the word of God commands us to put off filthy communication (as the KJB does), why then is the language of the modern versions so impure? The following is a sampling of the improper language used in the modern versions.

The Living Bible – the Unholy Word

Kenneth Taylor claimed to have written the Living Bible so that children could understand the Bible. He addressed the page following the contents page of his 1972 *Children's Living Bible* to his *Dear Young Friends*. He told them he had written the Living Bible (LB*) "in easy words, so you can understand all of it if you read it carefully."* Mr. Taylor went on to instruct his young readers: *"These books of the Bible are God's letters to you, Pray and ask him to speak to you as you read."* [1] As the following passages are discussed, consider how an adult could truly justify providing children with more explicit language and, in some instances, blatant gutter language in order to help them better "understand the Bible."

Adam knew Eve

The King James Bible uses very tactful language to discuss the marital relationship of two of the most well known Bible characters – Adam and Eve. Adults reading these passages from the KJB can readily grasp the understanding of the delicate subjects they address, without a child so much as raising an eyebrow at their content. No modest man or woman would be embarrassed to read the same verse, either in public or in private.

(KJB) Genesis 4:1 And Adam knew Eve his wife; and she conceived, and bare Cain, and said, I have gotten a man from the LORD.

A child reading the King James Bible does not even think to inquire concerning the meaning of the statement that "Adam *knew* Eve." This is God's way. Notice that Eve said that she *received* (or had gotten) a man from the LORD. Since she was not God, she did not claim to have *created* Cain. Now, compare this passage from the KJB with the following verse from the Living Bible.

*(LB) Genesis 4:1 Then **Adam had sexual intercourse with Eve his wife**, and she conceived and gave birth to a son, Cain (meaning "I have created"). For, as she said, "With God's help, **I have created a man!**"*

Sexual intercourse? Most children reading this verse from the Living Bible would have their curiosity piqued sufficiently to ask the meaning of sexual intercourse. Why would any parent want *plainer* language such as this for his children?! However, explicit language is only half of the problem associated with this one verse.

In addition to the more explicit language, Eve claims in the Living Bible to be the creator of Cain. To create means *to produce; to bring into being from nothing; to cause to exist.* Cain was produced from an egg and sperm – not from nothing. Eve did not cause Cain to exist. God did.

Lest one think that the explicitness of the Living Bible is confined to a single verse and a single couple, a further examination of this translation will reveal that Adam and Eve are only the beginning of the problems. You be the judge: are the motives of these modern versions pure? Regardless, the words and the thoughts they convey to our youth certainly are not.

(KJB) Leviticus 18:19 Also thou shalt not approach unto a woman to uncover her nakedness, as long as she is put apart for her uncleanness.

*(LB) Leviticus 18:19 "There must be no **sexual relationship** with a woman who is **menstruating**;*

Does your eight year-old know what "menstruating" means? Should she be reading this in her bible and bringing these matters to mind before her parents think it best to explain them to her?

The next passage from the Living Bible not only uses both terms dealt with so far, but also aligns itself with the Roman Catholic Church's practice of excommunicating its parishioners.

(KJB) Leviticus 20:18 And if a man shall **lie with a woman having her sickness,** and shall uncover her nakedness; he hath discovered her fountain, and she hath uncovered the fountain of her blood: and both of them shall be cut off from among their people.

(LB) Leviticus 20:18 If a man has **sexual intercourse** with a woman during her **period of menstruation,** both shall be **excommunicated,** for he has uncovered the source of her flow, and she has permitted it.

Does God excommunicate people? Excommunicate *means "to expel from communion; to eject from the communion of the church, by an ecclesiastical sentence, and deprive of spiritual advantages."* Was Leviticus written to the church? Did they partake in communion? The Living Bible raises more unnecessary questions than it answers.

(KJB) Isaiah 8:3 And **I went unto the prophetess;** and she conceived, and bare a son. Then said the LORD to me, Call his name Maher-shalal-hash-baz.

(LB) Isaiah 8:3 Then **I had sexual intercourse with my wife** and she conceived and bore me a son. And the Lord said, "Call him Maher-shalal-hash-baz.

Would you like your eight-year old child to ask you if you have sexual intercourse with your wife? We should strive to keep our children's minds pure rather than expose them to the explicit language originating from a supposed bible. The next verse explains the three reasons that we are commanded to *"Love not the world, neither the things that are in the world..." (I John 2:15).*

(KJB) I John 2:16 For all that is in the world, **the lust of the flesh,** and the lust of the eyes, and the pride of life, is not of the Father, but is of the world.

We are *not* to love the world because the world is made up of the lust of the flesh, the lust of the eyes, and the pride of life. These are not of the Father. The Living Bible changes the whole meaning of the passage and limits its application considerably. It changes the "lust of the flesh" and limits it to the "craze for sex"!

*(LB) I John 2:16 for all these worldly things, **these evil desires-the craze for sex**, the ambition to buy everything that appeals to you, and the pride that comes from wealth and importance-these are not from God. They are from this evil world itself.*

The *lust of the flesh* is not limited to "sex" as the Living Bible claims. One example should sufficiently prove this truth. The temptation of Eve included the lust of the flesh, the lust of the eyes, and the pride of life; however, her temptation and fall did not involve sex. *"And when the woman saw that the tree was **good for food (the lust of the flesh)**, and that it was **pleasant to the eyes (the lust of the eyes)**, and **a tree to be desired to make one wise (the pride of life)**, she took of the fruit thereof, and did eat, and gave also unto her husband with her; and he did eat" (Genesis 3:6).*

The Living Bible seems to have been written with a fixation upon things sexual. The initial text copyright for the Living Bible was issued in 1971. Therefore, this fixation upon sex in a so-called Bible preceded the world's almost total obsession with things of a sexual nature by over one decade. For proof of the veracity of this statement, simply watch the first few minutes of any sitcom produced within the last 15 years!

Elijah and the Prophets

In the book of First Kings, Elijah challenges the prophets of Baal to a contest to determine which group was serving the true God. Each side was to dress a bullock and place it on the altar, and then call upon the name of its respective God or gods. The one that answered by fire would be the true God. The prophets of Baal called upon their god from morning until noon to no avail. We pick up the story when these prophets of Baal, out of exasperation, finally leap upon the altar.

(KJB) I Kings 18:27 And it came to pass at noon, that Elijah mocked them, and said, Cry aloud: for he is a god; either he is

*talking, **or he is pursuing**, or he is in a journey, or peradventure he sleepeth, and must be awaked.*

I guess this is one of those cases where "the oldest and best manuscripts" said something different from the "old, archaic" King James Bible. Can you imagine the prophet Elijah speaking in the manner attributed to him by Mr. Taylor? The Living Bible brings the word of God down to a level that is a disgrace to any spiritually minded child of God. With "spiritual" examples such as the following, is it any wonder that parents must constantly fight against the influence of corrupt language on children today?

*(LB) I Kings 18:27 And about noontime, Elijah began mocking them. "You'll have to shout louder than that," he scoffed, "to catch the attention of your god! Perhaps he is talking to someone, **or is sitting on the toilet**, or maybe he is away on a trip, or is asleep and needs to be wakened!"*

Is this Mr. Taylor's idea of *helping the children* relate to Elijah? We need to help our children rise up out of the mediocrity of the day, not promote it by providing them with these types of examples. By condoning and actually encouraging this kind of nonsense, parents may be part of the problem rather than part of the solution. We must assist our children so they can be an example to other Christians *"...**in word**, in conversation, in charity, in spirit, in faith, in **purity**" (I Timothy 4:12).*

Saul's anger

The first example dealt with the Living Bible's fixation upon sex. The second dealt with Elijah's supposed comments to the prophets of Baal. Now, we shall examine the comments of a father to his son.

*(KJB) I Samuel 20:30 Then Saul's anger was kindled against Jonathan, and he said unto him, **Thou son of the perverse rebellious woman**, do not I know that thou hast chosen the son of Jesse to thine own confusion, and unto the confusion of thy mother's nakedness?*

This example is provided almost without comment due to its absurdity. However, the point must be made that the words recorded below are supposed to be the words of a father to his son.

> *(LB) I Samuel 20:30 Saul boiled with rage. "You s__ of a b____!" he yelled at him. "Do you think I don't know that you want this son of a nobody to be king in your place, shaming yourself and your mother?"* [Note: the actual words were included in the text of the Living Bible.]

Warning: After many people raised quite a fuss about this needless profanity, the editors of the Living Bible removed SOB from their text. Its very removal further demonstrates the total lack of respect for the word of God among promoters of the modern versions. They can change the Bible at will because they have very little regard for what God has promised concerning His infallible holy word.

The language of our children, and of society in general, has suffered rapid degradation. Certainly, the Bible should not contribute to this decline in quality of speech.

The word of God is sacred. Every new version claims to "make the Bible easier to understand." However, the word of God is spiritually discerned *(I Corinthians 2:14)*. It is not intended to be read like some cheap paperback novel. This is God's book!

The primary purpose for updating the modern translations almost annually seems to be money *(I Timothy 6:10)*. The common excuse of trying to make the Bible easier to understand is indeed pretty lame, especially when one considers that some things are best left unsaid or written in such a way that a child does not completely understand their meaning.

In the mid-90's, the Living Bible was still selling about one-half million copies per year! In fact, for many church-goers, the Living Bible remains the *only* version of the Bible they read or carry to church. A few of the worst problems and most pathetic examples contained in the Living Bible have been discussed. However, the doctrinal errors it contains are far more serious. Entire books could be devoted to the doctrinal error and attack on the truth that steep the pages of the Living Bible.

We must never be sold the Devil's bill of goods, especially where our youth are concerned. Youth can be as spiritual as any adult Christian can. However, the adults must do their part. Let us encourage our children to live above the fray, rather than bring God's word down to the lowest common denominator.

Much more space could be devoted to exposing the Living Bible's indiscriminate handling of delicate subjects. The New International Version exhibits the same inability to address these matters in a fashion pleasing to God. Once again, by comparing the NIV with the King James Bible, we can see that God intended these subjects to be handled discretely. Praise God!

The Custom of Women

(KJB) Genesis 31:35 And she said to her father, Let it not displease my lord that I cannot rise up before thee; for the custom of women is upon me. And he searched, but found not the images.

Many years ago, this subject would never have been discussed in public, let alone on television commercials or as the butt of jokes. Commercial television began frankly discussing this subject in the 1990's. However, the NIV preceded this degrading practice by two decades. Thus, the indiscriminate handling of this particular subject did not begin outside the church! Anytime this passage was read publicly, *corrupt communication* was promoted by the church *(Ephesians 4:29)*.

(NIV) Genesis 31:35 Rachel said to her father, "Don't be angry, my lord, that I cannot stand up in your presence; I'm having my period." So he searched but could not find the household gods.

Contemporary society has come to discuss certain subjects in mixed company that our parents and grandparents would never have considered appropriate. Much of this discussion would have been deemed indecent, even if it were carried out only amongst women. We don't need our Bible modernized; we need our minds cleansed and our mouths washed out with soap.

Filthy Communication

The Apostle Paul instructs us to put off *"filthy communication out of your mouth" (Colossians 3:8)*. The next verse from the King James Bible may not be one commonly used for memory work, yet it does not convey the same sense of disgust that is communicated by the modern versions.

(KJB) Ezekiel 23:20 For she doted upon their paramours, whose flesh is as the flesh of asses, and whose issue is like the issue of horses.

The NIV continues the onslaught upon common decency in the next passage. Someone needs to explain how a person can obey God by keeping his mind pure while "feasting" upon trash like the NIV. No other version on the market reads as indecently as the NIV.

*(NIV) Ezekiel 23:20 There she lusted after her lovers, whose **genitals** were like those of donkeys and whose emission was like that of horses.*

When I first began teaching these comparisons of Bible versions in churches, I used overhead transparencies. Because I had the preceding verse from the NIV printed on the overhead, I would cover the bottom part of the transparency, explaining that I could not show this particular verse from the NIV in mixed company, let alone in a church service.

However, the first time I taught it using the overheads, someone using an NIV was sitting in the second row of pews. She and her husband turned to the passages as I covered each one. You can imagine their reaction when they read this verse from the NIV. You could hear the woman gasp from the back of the church.

The Old Paths

Most of the comparisons addressed in this chapter concern the degradation of language. Although this next verse does not impact the Bible in the same manner, I find it just as deplorable. Even a seemingly pure motive of modernizing the language of the Bible can have a profound effect on modern-day worship. The new versions even affect our favorite old hymns of the faith! *"Thus saith the Lord, Stand ye in the ways, and see, and **ask for the old paths**, where is the good way, and walk therein, and ye shall find rest for your souls. But they said, We will not walk therein" (**Jeremiah 6:16**).*

A common misconception today is the notion that churches must change their style of music in order to keep pace with the changing whims of the people. With the modern style of music has come a modern form of worship which eliminates the use of the old hymns. In the modern versions, one can find little or no basis for singing songs like *At Calvary*. Read the words to this great song and see the great heritage of which many have become ignorant.

At Calvary

Years I spent in vanity and pride,
Caring not my Lord was crucified,
Knowing not it was for me He died
On Calvary.

Chorus
Mercy there was great, and grace was free,
Pardon there was multiplied to me,
There my burdened soul found liberty
At Calvary.

By God's Word at last my sin I learned –
Then I trembled at the law I'd spurned,
Till my guilty soul imploring turned
To Calvary.

Now I've given to Jesus everything,
Now I gladly own Him as my King,
Now my raptured soul can only sing
Of Calvary

O the love that drew salvation's plan!
O the grace that brought it down to man!
O the mighty gulf that God did span
At Calvary!

The only reason we know about Calvary is because of the King James Bible. The book of Luke mentions Calvary only one time. Furthermore, Luke is the only book of the Bible to mention Calvary at all.

(KJB) Luke 23:33 And when they were come to the place, which is called Calvary, there they crucified him, and the malefactors, one on the right hand, and the other on the left.

Satan wants to destroy the old paths by creating a generation that has very little or no knowledge of its rich heritage. When the Antichrist shows up, he will point to the cross as an example of a man getting His just rewards. Constantly, the liberals are rewriting history in order to distort the truth and the past. Are the liberals the only ones? In the NIV, none of the Gospel books mentions Calvary because Calvary has been removed from the one book that mentions it in the word of God.

(NIV) Luke 23:33 When they came to the place called the Skull, there they crucified him, along with the criminals-one on his right

What reason would there be to sing a song like *At Calvary*, if no one even knows what it symbolizes? One might respond – well, of course everyone knows what Calvary means. Only because of the King James Bible!!! A future generation with all of their modern versions will have no knowledge of this place that churches have sung about for centuries. Satan knows that man must become ignorant of his past before he can effectively be deceived. Satan must displace the Lord Jesus Christ. Music is only one of the very powerful media he will use to accomplish this end.

I travel quite extensively these days. On one of my trips with the *Baptist Historical Preservation Society*, we went to Cox's Creek Baptist Church (now a Southern Baptist Church) in Cox's Creek, Kentucky. We sang *At Calvary* using their hymnal produced by the Southern Baptists. As I sang from the hymnal, I noticed that all of the songs included a verse of scripture in the header. This one included the verse that references Calvary *(Luke 23:33)* only they quoted it from the NIV: *"When they came to the place called the Skull, there they crucified him, along with the criminals-one on his right, the other on his left."* How can the significance be missed? **Calvary** is a Bible term like many of the others found within the pages of the real Bible.

Christians need to learn the terminology of the Bible. It is a lame excuse to claim that these words should be deleted since man does not know them. When did the common man ever understand justification, sanctification, atonement, regeneration, and repentance? When did the unbeliever ever understand this terminology? The answer is: Never! These terms are peculiar and special and our business as preachers is to show that our gospel message is peculiar and not talking about ordinary matters. Consider this: When did the natural man ever understand the true meaning of *John 3:16*? Read the next story and see if the natural man can really comprehend the depths of God's love.

John 3:16

In the city of Chicago, one cold, dark night, a blizzard was setting in. A little boy was selling newspapers on the corner; the people were in and out of the cold. The little boy was so cold that he wasn't trying to sell many papers.

He walked up to a policeman and said, *"Mister, you wouldn't happen to know where a poor boy could find a warm place to sleep tonight would you? You see, I sleep in a box up around the corner there and down the alley and it's awful cold in there for tonight. Sure would be nice to have a warm place to stay."*

The policeman looked down at the little boy and said, *"You go down the street to that big white house and you knock on the door. When they come out the door you just say John 3:16, and they will let you in.* " So he did. He walked up the steps and knocked on the door, and a lady answered.

He looked up and said, *"John 3:16.* " The lady said, *"Come on in, Son.* "

She took him in and she sat him down in a split bottom rocker in front of a great big old fireplace, and she went off. The boy sat there for a while and thought to himself: **John 3:16...I don't understand it, but it sure makes a cold boy warm.**

Later she came back and asked him *"Are you hungry?* " He said, *"Well, just a little. I haven't eaten in a couple of days, and I guess I could stand a little bit of food.* " The lady took him in the kitchen and sat him down to a table full of wonderful food. He ate and ate until he couldn't eat any more. Then he thought to himself: **John 3:16...Boy, I sure don't understand it but it sure makes a hungry boy full.**

She took him upstairs to a bathroom to a huge bathtub filled with warm water, and he sat there and soaked for a while. As he soaked, he thought to himself: **John 3:16... I sure don't understand it, but it sure makes a dirty boy clean.** You know, I've not had a bath, a real bath, in my whole life. The only bath I ever had was when I stood in front of that big old fire hydrant as they flushed it out.

The lady came in and got him. She took him to a room, tucked him into a big old feather bed, pulled the covers up around his neck, kissed him goodnight and turned out the lights. As he lay in the darkness and looked out the window at the snow coming down on that cold night, he thought to himself: **John 3:16...I don't understand it, but it sure makes a tired boy rested.**

The next morning the lady came back up and took him down again to that same big table full of food. After he ate, she took him back to that same big old split bottom rocker in front of the fireplace and picked up a big old Bible. She sat down in front of him and looked into his young face.

"Do you understand John 3:16?" she asked gently. He replied, *"No, Ma'am, I don't. The first time I ever heard it was last night when the policeman told me to use it."* She opened the Bible to John 3:16 and began to explain to him about Jesus. Right there, in front of that big old fireplace, he gave his heart and life to Jesus. He sat there and thought: **John 3:16...I don't understand it, but it sure makes a lost boy feel safe.**

You know, I have to confess I don't understand it either, how God was willing to send His Son to die for me, and how Jesus would agree to do such a thing. I don't understand the agony of the Father and every angel in heaven as they watched Jesus suffer and die. I don't understand the intense love for ME that kept Jesus on the cross till the end. I don't understand it, but it sure does make life worth living. *– Author Unknown*

*For God so loved the world, that he gave his only begotten Son, that whosoever believeth in him should not perish, but have everlasting life (**John 3:16**).*

Chapter 5 Endnotes

[1] Kenneth Taylor, *The Children's Living Bible*, (Wheaton, IL: Tyndale House   Publishers, 1972).

6

Godly Living vs. Good Intentions

---

*And they that be wise shall shine as the brightness of the firmament; and **they that turn many to righteousness** as the stars for ever and ever.*
(Daniel 12:3)

If the modern translations are making the Bible easier to understand, why do they make it so difficult for Christians to know how to live right? The modern versions do not teach the Christian the living standards God expects, nor do they stress the importance of living a godly life to the same extent as the King James Bible.

Satan's schemes are not difficult to recognize. He knows that without an absolute authority, pastors and Christians alike have no definite criteria by which to judge what is right and what is wrong. Without a true standard of judgment, one cannot take the kind of firm stand for righteousness that God expects. As the following passages are presented, consider whether the modern versions or the King James Bible glorifies God the most by presenting a holy standard of living.

Your Reasonable Service

God wants the Christian completely devoted for His service. The Devil wants the Christian satisfied with mediocrity. Comparing the King James Bible with the NIV should demonstrate God's will versus the hand of Satan. The contrast between complete devotion and simple mediocrity should become clear.

*(KJB) Romans 12:1 I beseech you therefore, brethren, by the mercies of God, that ye present your bodies a living sacrifice, holy, acceptable unto God, which is **your reasonable service**.*

God commands that Christians present their bodies as living sacrifices to God. If people obey this command by sacrificing everything for the Lord Jesus Christ, God does not consider this to be a noteworthy feat. Instead, He considers it only *reasonable* that we do this in light of what the Lord has sacrificed on our behalf. The NIV changes something deemed "reasonable service" by God into a "spiritual act of worship."

*(NIV) Romans 12:1 Therefore, I urge you, brothers, in view of God's mercy, to offer your bodies as living sacrifices, holy and pleasing to God-this is **your spiritual act of worship**.*

The NIV sounds as though the sacrificing of our lives is something super spiritual, when God says it is simply *reasonable* service. The NIV definitely changes the context of this act so that it seems highly commendable in the eyes of God, an accomplishment of which one should be proud.

If we do not present our bodies as living sacrifices, we will allow the flesh to rule us. Christians must realize, contrary to Satan's plan, that their "old man" is corrupt with absolutely no redeeming qualities *(Mark 10:18, Romans 3:10)*.

*(KJB) Ephesians 4:22 That ye put off concerning the former conversation the old man, **which is corrupt** according to the deceitful lusts;*

Every Christian should realize that until God delivers us from *"...the body of this death..." (Romans 7:24)* and changes our *"...vile body, that it may be fashioned like unto his glorious body..." (Philippians 3:21)*, we are stuck with our corrupt old man. Of course, the NIV even changes this vivid terminology from *vile* body to *"lowly"* body in the book of Philippians. There is a big difference between these two descriptions, just as there is a big difference between the NIV and the KJB in the following passage from Ephesians. The KJB clearly states that our old man *is* corrupt. However, the NIV states that it is *being corrupted* (a process that occurs over time).

*(NIV) Ephesians 4:22 You were taught, with regard to your former way of life, to put off your old self, **which is being corrupted** by its deceitful desires;*

There is a considerable difference between something that *is* corrupt and something that is *being* corrupted. Something that is in the process of corruption can have redeeming qualities. However, our old man *is* corrupt and we must *"...walk in the Spirit..."*, *(Galatians 5:16)* in order to **put off** the old man and his deeds.

These changes are bad enough. Amazingly, they can and *do* get worse. Literally, hundreds of verses in the modern versions could be provided to illustrate their corruption and reveal the satanic attack against godly living. Here is another case in point. The Lord wants us to understand that the only way for old age, and the signs of old age, to be a blessing is for an individual to live a righteous life. Thus, Solomon includes the word "if" to indicate the conditional promise attached to the man or woman that is living for God as they age.

*(KJB) Proverbs 16:31 The hoary head is a crown of glory, **if** it be found in the way of righteousness.*

The only way for old age, signified by the hoary head *(Leviticus 19:32, Isaiah 46:4)*, to be a crown of glory is IF it is found in the way of righteousness. There is no such conditional promise attached to old age in the NIV. The NIV states that all gray-headed men and women have lived a righteous life. This is ludicrous!

*(NIV) Proverbs 16:31 **Gray hair is** a crown of splendor; it is **attained by a righteous life.***

The NIV states that gray hair is attained by a righteous life. This means that every person with the signs of age (and those prematurely grayed) have attained this *crown of splendor* through righteous living. As much as we would like this to be true, it is another of Satan's lies contrived to produce mediocrity and a false sense of accomplishment.

Suffering for Christ's Sake

The only way to take a firm stand for righteousness is to know that you base your spiritual position on something that is absolutely infallible in its guidance. No modern version on the market provides a person with the assurance needed to take the appropriate godly moral stand. For example, the King James Bible makes a definite statement concerning the results of living godly.

> *(KJB) II Timothy 3:12 Yea, and all that will live godly in Christ Jesus shall suffer persecution.*

The King James Bible says that a godly person will suffer persecution. It is imperative for Christians to understand God's expectations. God *expects* Christians to live godly and will reward them one day for doing so. If a child of God suffers persecution because he lives a godly life for Jesus, God will reward him in the future. (We will see this truth even more clearly in the next comparison.)

The NIV, in a very subtle way, encourages the Christian to feel satisfied with himself as long as he *desires* to live godly. Unlike the statement from the KJB, the NIV no longer *requires* the child of God to put into action what he desires. It says that one need only "want" to live godly, and he will suffer persecution. This is simply not a true statement, but Satan would like every Christian to be satisfied with his standard of mediocrity!

> *(NIV) II Timothy 3:12 In fact, everyone who wants to live a godly life in Christ Jesus will be persecuted,*

We can identify the far-reaching ramifications of this change by considering some practical applications of the verse. According to the NIV, if a person decides that he *wants* to begin witnessing, he will be persecuted for that *desire* alone. Or if a person decides that he *wants* to take a stand against profanity at the workplace, he will be persecuted for that *desire* alone. One who "wants to live a godly life" (the NIV) and one who "will live godly" (the KJB) are two different people, exhibiting two entirely different types of behavior.

The King James Bible's standard requires one's desires to be put into action – merely possessing the right intentions is not sufficient to elicit suffering. These changes are critical when one considers the promises of future reward (found in the next comparison) as they relate to the suffering a Christian experiences in this life.

When comparing scripture with scripture from the KJB, one can ascertain the full revelation concerning living godly and obtaining future rewards. God has attached some important promises to suffering. The next passage from the KJB says that if we suffer, we will reign with the Lord Jesus Christ (as joint-heirs *Romans 8:17*).

(KJB) II Timothy 2:12 If we suffer, we shall also reign with him: if we deny him, he also will deny us:

Combining the truths taught in *II Timothy 2:12* with *3:12* from the KJB gives a clear picture of God's expectations and His promised rewards. The KJB shows that reigning with the Lord Jesus Christ is directly associated with suffering for Him in this life. If a person lives godly, he will suffer persecution; if he suffers persecution, he will reign with the Lord. If he denies the suffering by failing to live godly, God will deny him the future opportunity to reign with Him.

Only by comparing scripture with scripture *(I Corinthians 2:13)* can one arrive at this vital truth. Needless to say, the *wording* must remain intact to enable one to cross-reference these scripture verses. A concordance word search for "suffer" will yield two different results, depending upon the version searched. The NIV destroys this important truth and eliminates any opportunity for cross-referencing by changing *suffer* to "endure."

*(NIV) II Timothy 2:12 if we **endure**, we will also reign with him. If we **disown** him, he will also disown us;*

One should recognize that the NIV not only changes the truth, but completely perverts a Church Age doctrine by relating a person's faithfulness to a Tribulation word – "endure" *(Matthew 24:13)*.

Although dealt with in chapter four, this point bears repeating. When the NIV changes *deny* to *disown*, it changes the truth of God into a lie *(Romans 1:25)*. To *disown* someone is a much more severe action than *to deny* him something. If we deny God our service and suffering, He will deny us the reward of reigning with Him. However, we will still be His and will remain with Him for eternity because He cannot deny Himself. God is faithful to His word even if we are not *(I Corinthians 1:9)*.

When *disown* is used in the NIV, God appears to contradict Himself by *disowning* us (severing His relationship with us). He has assured us repeatedly elsewhere that He will not do that. Consequently, the NIV makes God a liar! What kind of standard for godly living is that? The contradictions and errors do not stop at these two glaring blunders.

The next passage *(II Timothy 2:13)* in the NIV continues to compound the comedy of errors. It says, *"If we are faithless, he will remain faithful, for **he cannot disown himself.**"* Try to make sense of it all. Verse 12 **in the NIV** says that God will disown the Christian, and then verse 13 **in the NIV** says that God *cannot* disown the Christian because He cannot disown himself. How ridiculous!

One loses the opportunity for effective Bible study by using these modern versions. The Bible issue debate is not simply a fight against modernizing the reading to update the language. Comparing scripture with scripture is one of THE keys to effective Bible study. When the words are changed, one no longer has the basic tools necessary for Bible study. I have never met a *Bible Believing* new version advocate. When asked, they will timidly admit that they do not accept any English Bible as God's perfect word. Ask them if you can get an honest response.

No matter how some men try to belittle those who are truly searching for the truth, one must carefully consider the evidence for himself. Look at the comparisons and see which one elevates our Lord and Saviour. James White is a good example of an individual who attacks those that examine the evidence from a Bible believing perspective. In his book *The King James Only Controversy*, his introduction disparages the true student of God's word: *"Most biblical scholars and theologians, even of the most conservative stripe, do not feel the issue worthy of any real investment of time."*

He goes on to say, *"Our relationship with Jesus Christ is not based upon a particular Bible translation."* [1] However, it should be evident that the scholars and theologians should be investing their time to find out the truth, and our relationship with the Lord Jesus Christ *is* dependent upon the truth revealed in His word. Thus, our relationship with Jesus Christ IS based upon a particular Bible translation! Each chapter in this book proves that the modern versions leave the Christian less accountable and provide a lower standard of living, directly affecting one's relationship with Jesus Christ.

The issue of bible translations is how to qualify for a new copyright. In order to qualify for a new copyright, the revisers know that they must change a significant amount of the text. Consequently, they must deceive the public by using slick Hollywood advertising to convince people that they need *"the most up-to-date, modern, smooth-talking version produced for the common man... written in easy to understand English."* However, when the words are changed, the opportunity for proper study is lost *(II Timothy 2:15)* and the truth becomes error.

Bear Your Own Cross

Luke depicts a beautiful picture of a Christian's responsibility to bear his own cross. *"And whosoever doth not bear his cross, and come after me, cannot be my disciple" (Luke 14:27)*. Too many people are failing to recognize their responsibility to suffer for His sake.

*(KJB) Luke 23:26 And as they led him away, they laid hold upon one Simon, a Cyrenian, coming out of the country, and on him they laid the cross, **that he might bear it after Jesus.***

Simon had to literally bear the cross of Jesus Christ giving us a beautiful picture of our responsibility to spiritually bear His cross. The KJB retains this poignant illustration. However, no picture is seen here in the NIV.

(NIV) Luke 23:26 As they led him away, they seized Simon from Cyrene, who was on his way in from the country, and put the cross on him and made him carry it behind Jesus.

The extraordinary wording of the King James Bible did not happen by accident. God providentially planned for His message to be conveyed literally and figuratively. We cannot completely comprehend the depth of the riches found within God's word. Satan wants to ensure that our opportunities to appreciate His goodness are reduced and frequently totally eliminated.

Higher Standards

As we have seen, God promises to reward all those who suffer persecution for living a godly life. As is evident from studying God's expectations, not everyone will be rewarded for simply being a Christian. God gives Christians some high standards following salvation. Here is another of those high expectations. The child of God not only has a responsibility to abstain from evil, but also must abstain from anything that *appears* to be evil.

(KJB) I Thessalonians 5:22 Abstain from all appearance of evil.

Even if the act or action is not evil in and of itself, one must abstain from the act or action if it even *appears to be* wrong. What a tremendous truth to know. Many Christians are falling into sin because they are not reading from the right book. The modern bibles no longer warn Christians about potentially destructive situations and God's prescribed method for staying out of trouble.

(NIV) I Thessalonians 5:22 Avoid every kind of evil.

The NIV lowers God's standards. It seems obvious that one should avoid every kind of evil. But what about something that has the capacity to destroy your testimony, but is not evil of itself? God commands us to abstain from these things, too. The KJB embodies a higher standard than that expressed in the modern translations. God says to abstain from that which even *appears* evil. Many things look evil or have a potential for evil, but are not evil in and of themselves.

Being a Talebearer – Blessing or Curse?

The King James Bible rebukes the talebearer (one that slanders or gossips about another). This is a serious offense and one that causes much harm to the cause of Christ. The damage done to the lost person and weak brothers and sisters in Christ is incalculable. The Judgment seat of Christ will expose the damage done to the ministry of the local church by such gossip.

*(KJB) Proverbs 26:22 The words of a talebearer are as **wounds**, and they go down into the innermost parts of the belly.*

A talebearer harms his victim. The Bible says that the tongue is an *"unruly evil, full of deadly poison" (James 3:8)*. With the same mouth, we bless God and curse men. Proverbs says these words are as *wounds*. They are injurious. Does the NIV convey this same sense of harm and destruction?

(NIV) Proverbs 26:22 The words of a gossip are like choice morsels; they go down to a man's inmost part.

The NIV seems to encourage the despicable act of gossiping. The NIV says that a gossip's words are like *choice morsels*. Choice morsels are the best part of something. They are to be desired. The NIV may not warn its readers, but both parties are guilty – the one who gossips and the one who listens. No wonder the world sees little difference between the one that attends church regularly and the one that finds other "more important" things to do on Sunday.

Faith to Believe God's Promise

If the motive of the new translations is to update the language of the King James Bible, then why do they differ so greatly on the subject of faith? Although this verse was addressed in an earlier chapter, it will again be discussed with a slightly different application.

(KJB) Psalm 12:6 The words of the Lord are pure words: as silver tried in a furnace of earth, purified seven times. 7 Thou shalt keep them, O Lord, thou shalt preserve them from this generation for ever.

God has promised to preserve His word for every generation. Every Christian should ask himself: "Where is the preserved word of God today?" Since God has promised to preserve His word, where can it be found? The King James Bible is the only version that has preachers proclaiming to the world that it is perfect and without error.

I believe God's promises. Therefore, I believe we have His word without error. However, I cannot convince the faithless. There are difficult passages in the word of God that *seem* to be contradictory and thus *appear* to contain error. How does one handle these potential bombshells? Only by faith can some of these be studied, understood, and believed! **Faith** is a requirement for the word of God to do an effectual work in a person's life.

The word of God says that *"...whatsoever is not of faith is sin" (Romans 14:23)*. This truth applies to a failure to have faith in the actual words of God, too. It is sin!

The word of God goes on to say that faith is a necessary element in order to please God. *"But without faith it is impossible to please him..." (Hebrews 11:6)*. This truth applies also to a failure to have faith in the actual words of God. It is impossible to please God without faith!

A lack of belief causes the work of God to suffer today, just as it did during the Lord's earthly ministry. His opportunity to do a great work was limited by the lack of faith. *"And he did not many mighty works there because of their unbelief" (Matthew 13:58)*. Because people do not accept the word of God as it is in truth – the word of God – the mighty works that God wishes to accomplish in their lives are limited.

A constant state of confusion best describes the world today. Part of this crisis is attributable to the ineffectiveness of the preaching from pulpits. But what has caused the ineptitude of the pulpits? Although preachers bear their share of the blame, the influence of the modern translations on the *faith* of the believers has had a far greater impact than is readily apparent. Satan has accomplished his objective of destroying the works of God by undermining the believer's faith. *"...but the word preached did not profit them, not being mixed with faith in them that heard it"* (**Hebrews 4:2**).

The word of God *must* be mixed with faith for it to be profitable. Moreover, it must be accepted as God's word for it to work effectively in an individual's life. *"For this cause also thank we God without ceasing, because, when ye received the word of God which ye heard of us, ye received it not as the word of men, but as it is in truth, the word of God, which effectually worketh also in you that believe"* (***I Thessalonians 2:13***).

If the Christian lacks faith in the word of God or considers it to be the word of men, the word of God will be unprofitable and ineffectual in him. When the next passage (verses six and seven from Psalm chapter 12) is considered from the NIV, the resultant widespread destruction of faith can be clearly foreseen as the Devil's handiwork.

(NIV) Psalm 12:6 And the words of the LORD are flawless, like silver refined in a furnace of clay, purified seven times.

The NIV promises no preservation and then changes the entire context of the verse, from a preservation of the word of God to a protection of man.

(NIV) Psalm 12:7 O LORD, you will keep us safe and protect us from such people forever.

We are not to trust in man's wisdom. However, this warning has generally gone unheeded by the revisionists. Every modern version claims to be the product of the very best scholars, and masquerades as newer and better than all its predecessors. God explicitly warns man concerning the outcome of trusting in this so-called scholarship: *"...preach the gospel: not with wisdom of words, lest the cross of Christ should be made of none effect"* (***I Corinthians 1:17***). Because the Church has trusted more in *scholarship* than in God, the pulpits have lost much of their effectiveness. (See *Ecclesiastes 12:11* in the NKJV for a case in point.)

The next passage reveals that faith comes from hearing the word of God. Faith does not come from simply hearing a message someone preaches…it comes from hearing the very words of God. Since these modern translations are not really the word of God, the lack of faith can be easily attributed to these so-called bibles.

(KJB) Romans 10:17 So then faith cometh by hearing, and hearing by the word of God.

The first thing one should notice when reading the modern translations is the move away from the word of God and the emphasis on *the message* instead. There are more ways of *hearing* than by a *message*. The *scriptures themselves* speak – at least according to the KJB *(Romans 9:17, Galatians 3:8)*. If the appropriate scripture is not speaking to a person, how can he hear and thereby receive the faith he needs *(I Corinthians 14:8)*? A message that does not contain the words of God creates a very superficial Christian. Faith comes from the very words of God, which are so vehemently attacked and undermined today.

(NIV) Romans 10:17 Consequently, faith comes from hearing the message, and the message is heard through the word of Christ.

There are a number of Christian teaching "personalities" today, whose influence in Christendom stems more from their charismatic teaching style than from the word of God. These individuals can (and do) pick and choose from the various modern versions in order to construct and support their man-pleasing, ear-tickling *message*. If they refer to the King James Bible, it is usually apologetically, asking the audience to excuse the use of the "archaic" King James for the sake of its poetic "renderings." People are being taught that a man's personality and his *message* are more authoritative than the very words of God.

For instance, James White, in his book on the King James Bible, states: *"We strongly encourage Christians to purchase and use multiple translations of the Bible so that comparison can be made between translations. It is best not to be limited to just one translation when studying Scripture. Cross-reference between such fine translations as the New King James Version, the New American Standard Bible, and the New International Version will allow the student of the Bible to get a firm grasp upon the meaning of any particular passage."* [2]

The next thing that should be evident from the passage in Romans is the focus being redirected from the word of God in general to the "word of Christ" in particular. I asked a group of young people what "the word of Christ" was, and they informed me it was contained only in the four Gospel books. One of them even said, *"It is the red letters in the Bible."* Many of the publishers place the words of Christ in red. The NIV rendering of *Romans 10:17* indicates that the way for a person to receive faith is by simply reading the four Gospel books of Matthew, Mark, Luke, and John – the words spoken by Christ while on earth.

(NIV) Romans 10:17 Consequently, faith comes from hearing the message, and the message is heard through **the word of Christ.**

Through diligent study, one can easily determine that our Apostle is Paul and the thirteen epistles bearing his name as their first word give us our primary doctrine. Satan wants our focus directed away from the Apostle Paul *(I Corinthians 11:1, II Timothy 2:7).* The NIV actually elevates the earthly words of Christ above the rest of **His word.** This is unscriptural and weakens one's faith..

Necessity of Bible Study

Those that understand how to **study** the Bible realize that proper, effective study requires a person to *rightly divide* the Bible *(II Timothy 2:15)* and *consider* what the Apostle Paul tells the Church first *(II Timothy 2:7).* The NIV and Satan have joined forces to keep the Christian from understanding these truths.

Based on the number of Bible study books sold, it seems that everyone wants an easy to understand, step-by-step guide to studying the

Bible. Studying God's word is important. However, only *one* verse in the Bible commands a person to study God's word and then explains how to go about doing so. This command is found in *II Timothy 2:15*.

*(KJB) II Timothy 2:15 Study to shew thyself approved unto God, a workman that needeth not to be ashamed, **rightly dividing the word of truth.***

If a person fails to study God's word, he will not be approved unto God. The same point holds true concerning the person that fails to study using God's prescribed method of Bible study. He will not be approved and will be ashamed. This shame may manifest itself both in the present life and at the Judgment Seat of Christ. (Reference the author's book on this subject – *One Book Rightly Divided*.)

As the King James Bible is compared with the NIV, Satan's handiwork becomes much clearer. The two key points of this verse are gone. No longer is the Christian commanded to study, and no longer does this verse reveal *how to study*.

*(NIV) II Timothy 2:15 **Do your best** to present yourself to God as one approved, a workman who does not need to be ashamed and who **correctly handles** the word of truth.*

While God does want us to do our best, He wants us to know *how* to do our best – by studying. Then He wants us to know *how* to study His way. The modern versions leave it up to everyone to do what is right in his own eyes. Meanwhile, the King James Bible tells us both *what* to do and *how* to do it God's way!

God does not want you simply to do *your* best! He commands you to study even when you don't have the time or the inclination to do so. Moreover, He does not want the preacher, teacher, and student simply to *correctly handle* the word of God. He wants them to know *how* to study His book. Christians that know their Bibles pose the greatest threat to Satan's control.

The King James Bible contains the word *study* only three times; however, only one verse contains *the command* to study with instructions on how to do so. Christians reading the modern translations will not be convicted about their lack of Bible study. God requires us to study. Without the required study, a baby Christian never matures to adulthood, and Satan wins!

It is ludicrous to think that a Christian at the Judgment Seat of Christ will have the opportunity to answer God with the excuse, *"I did my best."* Yet, we have bible translations that change the most important verse concerning Bible study into a vague "do your best" mentality. The baby Christian could conclude that he will be able to answer God with the excuse of "having tried," and so be acquitted of ignoring clearly presented truth.

The Tare and the Wheat

A tare in the field looks exactly like the wheat as it grows and matures. However, wheat produces fruit and tares do not. The Lord said to let them grow together until the time of the harvest. He would have to separate the tares and the wheat because *"...the Lord knoweth them that are his" (II Timothy 2:19).*

(KJB) Matthew 13:27 So the servants of the householder came and said unto him, Sir, didst not thou sow good seed in thy field? from whence then hath it tares?

The modern versions distort the doctrine of the fake Christian. The reason the Lord used tares in the parable is because one cannot distinguish between the wheat and the tares, just as one cannot always distinguish between the true Christian and the lost person within the local church.

(NIV) Matthew 13:27 "The owner's servants came to him and said, `Sir, didn't you sow good seed in your field? Where then did the weeds come from?'

Due to their visual similarities, God chose *wheat* and *tares* to describe his harvest. One fails to comprehend this truth when the modern versions change *tares* to *weeds*. One can easily distinguish between these two—wheat and weeds—and the whole point is lost.

Of course, the modern versions not only destroy the doctrine, but also encourage a person to be an imitator of God. The NIV says: *"Be imitators of God, therefore, as dearly loved children" (NIV – Ephesians 5:1)*. However, the Bible commands that we be *followers* of God, not *imitators* of the real thing. We don't need any more imitation Christians.

Chapter 6 Endnotes

[1] White, *The King James Only Controversy, op.cit.,* p. III, V.

[2] *Ibid.,* p. 7

7

Muddy Morality

What one generation fights with inconsistency, the next generation tolerates. Finally, the third generation endorses and embraces and the fourth generation propagates and promotes.[1]
Dr. Dennis Corle

If the new versions really just want the Bible to be easier to read, then why do they so obviously lend a "helping hand" to the homosexual agenda and an increasingly sexually permissive society? Absolute standards are a necessity in the area of sexuality.

Many Christians incorrectly limit the definition of fornication as sexual relations between two people who are not married to each other. However, the biblical definition of fornication is unchanging. The Bible defines fornication as *any* sexual union outside the bounds of marriage (including sodomy, bestiality, etc.).

Flee Fornication

With this definition in mind, there can be no doubt concerning the intent of the warning contained in the next verse. The Christian is warned to flee (run away) if he finds himself tempted to become sexually involved outside the bounds of marriage.

(KJB) I Corinthians 6:18 Flee fornication. Every sin that a man doeth is without the body; but he that committeth fornication sinneth against his own body.

God need not make the message of this verse any clearer for those who truly desire to stay true to Him. His feelings about intimate relationships outside of marriage are clearly communicated. One is to run away from such dangerous and ungodly relationships. The "updating" in the modern Bible versions certainly does not serve to make this truth plainer. What warning do these versions give?

(NIV) I Corinthians 6:18 Flee from sexual immorality. All other sins a man commits are outside his body, but he who sins sexually sins against his own body.

The new versions tell the reader to flee from *sexual immorality*, rather than using the more precise wording of the KJB – warning us to flee *fornication*. Immorality carries with it no precise definition of what is right or wrong. Thus, each person defines the ambiguous *sexual immorality* terminology for himself, and so acts as his own god.

Morality changes as cultural views waiver. Our sexually permissive society has redefined the meaning of immorality. The list of acts deemed moral or immoral by society will continue to fluctuate. However, the definition of *fornication* is not open to debate. It is fixed. One does not debate whether an act involves fornication if it is done outside of the marriage boundaries.

As our sexually permissive society continues to degrade, "sexual immorality" will continue to be redefined. Society has turned away from God and liberalized its definitions to include only the most shocking actions within the realms of sexual immorality. With such a liberal mindset, many would claim that a sexual relationship between two *consenting* adults is not sexually immoral. A person holding this liberal point of view and looking to the NIV for guidance might then justify these actions and be convinced that they do not fall within the realm of God's condemnation.

Other individuals might limit their definition of sexual immorality to "same sex" sexual encounters. However, we are warned about this type of perversion elsewhere. Still others might limit the bounds of sexual immorality to include only actions which involve children. However liberal the definition of sexual immorality, God ensures that fornication carries no such limitation.

In the preceding verse, the NIV uses vague terminology which necessitates the search for a more precise (and progressively more permissive) definition. In contrast, the KJB's use of the word *fornication* in this same verse provides man with an absolute moral standard by which to judge sexual conduct.

Today, situational ethics and the claim that all truth is relative run rampant. Sinful man wants no absolutes. God's word, however, provides us absolute standards by which to judge our actions and determine if they are right or wrong. American courts have judged that even pornography is a protected constitutional right, handed down by the forefathers of our nation! When there is no absolute standard by which to discern the morality of actions, the situation of man is precisely that of Israel when it had no leadership. *"In those days there was no king in Israel, but every man did that which was right in his own eyes" (Judges 17:6).*

This country has had Presidential executive orders forbidding the homosexual from being discharged from the military. We have even had a President who claimed to be innocent of the legal definition of sexual relations with a young woman other than his wife. Man does not need to be his own judge as to what is right and wrong. *"...Let God be true, but every man a liar..." (Romans 3:4).*

The Body is not for Fornication

God warns us in the King James Bible to flee from potentially damaging situations involving our bodies. Our bodies are not to be used for any relationship outside of marriage.

*(KJB) I Corinthians 6:13 Meats for the belly, and the belly for meats: but God shall destroy both it and them. **Now the body is not for fornication**, but for the Lord; and the Lord for the body.*

God's word is very clear. God's warnings are not to be limited only to those acts which people may consider offensive or sexually immoral. The body is not for fornication. Fornication involves physical intimacy outside of marriage. The warning from the King James Bible (from God) encompasses not only those acts which people find repugnant or perverted. This warning in the KJB, instead, includes *all* sex outside of marriage. Not so in the NIV.

(NIV) 1 Corinthians 6:13 "Food for the stomach and the stomach for food"-but God will destroy them both. **The body is not meant for sexual immorality,** *but for the Lord, and the Lord for the body.*

Once again, the modern version has diluted and changed God's clear warning. Decent people might limit their definition of sexual immorality to include only the acts of sodomites and pedophiles, while justifying their own behavior or the behavior of their children. Many carnal Christians are looking for the slightest opportunity to avoid responsibility for their sinful actions. Satan is always willing to assist them.

Fornication Eliminated

Consider the following verse from the King James Bible which contains a clear warning concerning the sin of fornication.

(KJB) Romans 1:29 Being filled with all unrighteousness, ***fornication,*** *wickedness, covetousness, maliciousness; full of envy, murder, debate, deceit, malignity; whisperers,*

Satan "aids" the sinner by allowing him to commit his sin with little or no guilt. He accomplishes this by providing a bible that does not directly mention the sin. Look at what the modern versions do with this same verse from Romans chapter one. In this verse in the NIV, the word *fornication* is removed completely and is not replaced with any other word. The condemnation of *fornication* must be eliminated in order to create a progressively desensitized and depraved culture. This is Satan's ultimate goal. Great and powerful societies have historically crumbled from within through such vices.

(NIV) Romans 1:29 They have become filled with every kind of wickedness, evil, greed and depravity. They are full of envy, murder, strife, deceit and malice. They are gossips,

As we have seen, fornication is ripped out of Romans chapter one and is changed elsewhere in the modern versions. No wonder Christians frequently have no greater conviction than the lost concerning the things they watch *for entertainment.* Numerous television programs continually celebrate and glorify even the most perverse and explicit types of behavior. What we need to do is open our Bible and follow the example of Joseph and *flee fornication.*

Society has already redefined homosexuality as a sexual *orientation,* rather than as previously defined – a sexual *preference.* Popular culture now claims that the sodomite was "born that way." Thus, he had no choice. Schools are even teaching that a certain percentage of the population is born with a *"sexual orientation toward the same gender."* The military provides and sometimes requires *Homosexuality Sensitivity Training Courses!* The "don't ask, don't tell" military policy is a direct result of a society gone crazy. Even the medical profession has not been able to stand against the homosexual agenda. The American Psychological Association has yielded to external pressure and claimed that the sodomite (KJB word) cannot help himself. A *Montgomery Advertiser* article from the early 1990's clearly reveals the current trend.

> The American Psychological Association called on mental health professionals to *"take the lead in removing the stigma of mental illness that has long been associated with homosexual orientation."* Kim Mills, a representative of the Human Rights Campaign, a lesbian and gay political group, said the resolution *"reaffirms the fact that since there is nothing wrong with homosexuality, there is no reason that gay, lesbian or bisexual people should try to change."* [2]

The Roman Catholic Church claims to have over one billion (1,000,000,000) followers. Its decrees, although ignored by many of the less faithful Catholics, still carry substantial weight. One finds the softening of the position on homosexuality within the Catholic pronouncements. The *Catholic Worker* paper of May 2001 reveals the stance of the Roman Catholic Church: *"Another issue that complicates discussion of homophobia, is that the victims of this oppression are seen to have 'chosen' their fate. Though some doubts do linger in the minds of many as to the origins of homosexuality, the Catechism of the Catholic Church states that homosexuality is innate, not chosen."* [3]

Homosexuality has been redefined in order to remove any suggestion of choice. No longer is it a matter of what one prefers ("sexual preference"). Now, society claims that these poor "sick" souls cannot help themselves because homosexuality is determined genetically ("sexual orientation"). In 1993, a geneticist from the National Cancer Institute claimed to have found a "gay gene" residing on a region of the maternally inherited X chromosome. His research was based on a finding that 33 of 40 pairs of "gay" brothers shared certain genetic markers not common between heterosexual brothers. To date, no one has been able to duplicate the results of this study. [4] However, it is frequently cited as justification for a more lenient policy.

This entire issue boils down to yet another instance of man's blaming his sinful actions upon his Creator. The Bible disagrees with this supposition that homosexuality is not a matter of choice... unless you are using one of the modern versions which homosexuals helped produce.

Virginia Mollenkott, a literary consultant for the NIV, worked on the translation the entire time it was being translated and reviewed. Although many examples can be given, one should suffice. This information is well reported and documented in books and on the internet for all to read. In 1978, Virginia Mollenkott co-authored (with Letha Scanzoni) a book entitled *Is the Homosexual My Neighbor?* in which she called for nondiscrimination toward homosexuality. The book argues that the Sodom account in Genesis teaches not the evil of homosexuality, but the evils of violent gang rape and inhospitality to strangers.

The book also claims that "the idea of a life long homosexual orientation or 'condition' is never mentioned in the Bible" (p. 71), and that

Romans chapter one does not "fit the case of a sincere homosexual Christian" (p. 62). This is the exact position taken by one of the actual translators of the NIV, Dr. Marten H. Woudstra, in a report he assisted in producing for the Christian Reformed Church in 1973.

It is also well reported that Dr. Marten H. Woudstra, a bachelor all his life, believed that lifelong 'loving monogamous relationships' between homosexual men or women were acceptable to God. He believed that there was nothing in the Old Testament (his special area of technical expertise) that addressed the 'homosexual orientation.' He believed that the 'sodomy' of the OT simply involved temple rites and gang rape.

Considering the influence on the modern versions exerted by individuals sympathetic to the perverted homosexual lifestyle, it should come as no surprise that the NIV completely removes *sodomy* from its text. Of course, in doing so, the NIV becomes much more politically correct.

Political climate and educational climate go hand-in-hand. Educators are attempting to convince our children at very early ages that the homosexual lifestyle is normal rather than aberrant. Two books, *Daddy's Roommate* and *Heather Has Two Mommies,* are prime examples of tools being used to lead youth down the path of degeneracy, and society toward total moral decay. These books are intended for first and second graders! The former presents a young boy being raised by two homosexual men. The latter portrays a young girl being raised by two lesbians. Both groups are presented as happy, healthy, normal family environments.

The homosexual agenda goes far beyond demanding tolerance. Instead, it seeks endorsement that its aberration is normal.

No More Whores and Sodomites

The Lord condemns the whore and the sodomite in the same scripture. He does this to show that there are two distinct groups involved in His rebuke. They are not one and the same.

*(KJB) Deuteronomy 23:17 There shall be no **whore** of the daughters of Israel, nor a **sodomite** of the sons of Israel.*

Instead of highlighting the sin of homosexuality, the NIV limits the context of this condemnation to those involved in the immorality of the pagan religions. Whores and sodomites have "proclaimed their sexuality" while marching in the streets of many major cities. Read the modern versions which lack the convicting properties of the word of God.

(NIV) Deuteronomy 23:17 No Israelite man or woman is to become a shrine prostitute.

When was the last time you saw a "shrine prostitute"? By including the word shrine in a translation that allegedly makes the bible easier to understand, it further dilutes any convicting properties.

The NIV replaces *sodomite* with *prostitute* in order to redefine the sin addressed by this verse. With this change, only one that *prostitutes* (sells) his or her body is condemned; those that are "lovingly devoted to one partner" are not condemned – even if that partner is of the same gender. Given the changes in this and other passages of the NIV, sex for payment is an abomination, while uncompensated whoredom and homosexuality are not issues of moral concern. To readers of the NIV, the emphasis of the text concerns the crass commercial exploitations of these practices, rather than the practices themselves. The sexual perversion itself is no longer the point of moral contention.

Consider the number of years by which the NIV preceded today's politically correct environment, including "hate crime legislation" and the legal recognition and protection of sodomites. Remember that the NIV preceded today's wicked moral climate by decades. Who do you suppose knew the direction in which he was steering the world *(II Corinthians 4:4)*? How has Satan been able to pull off these changes with hardly a whimper from many churches?

Sodomites Gone Again

Today, if one lifts his voice against the sodomite, he is labeled as politically incorrect, bigoted, and "homophobic." However, one that proclaims the truth is the servant of God and should remain unconcerned about the voices contributing to society's moral decay through their abominable acts. The word of God points to the sodomite as being cast out of the land when Israel conquered it. The sodomites were those involved in the sin of sodomy – modern day homosexuals. God does not sound very "understanding" or "open-minded," but definitely condemnatory.

> *(KJB) I Kings 14:24 And there were also **sodomites** in the land: and they did according to all the abominations of the nations which the LORD cast out before the children of Israel.*

Satan's ultimate plan, to produce a sexually promiscuous climate, began long before its results became evident. Satan has been leading the world down a gloomy path that looks deceptively bright to those unfamiliar with the truth.

> *(NIV) I Kings 14:24 There were even **male shrine prostitutes** in the land; the people engaged in all the detestable practices of the nations the LORD had driven out before the Israelites.*

One day it will be considered a "hate crime" simply to voice God's warnings concerning the sodomite. Preachers will be jailed for preaching the truth conveyed in the King James Bible. Any person who maintains a biblical belief today concerning sodomites is called homophobic and bigoted. Schools are being told not to treat homosexuality as sinful or unhealthy. They are attributing higher suicide rates among homosexuals to the "prejudice" and discrimination against them, rather than to remorse for their sinful lifestyles. Yet, even apart from suicides, the life expectancy for homosexuals remains much lower than for heterosexuals.

Today, hate crime legislation exists to protect a person's sexual "orientation." The news media portrays sodomites as victims of violence and rarely as the perpetrators. When a homosexual is involved in a sex crime, homosexual activists do not want a parallel to be drawn between the crime and the perversion of the perpetrator.

The sodomite knows that society's perception is very important. Homosexuals cannot reproduce. They must recruit in order to perpetuate their practice. To do this most effectively, they must downplay the negative aspects of their deviant lifestyle and promote it as something perfectly natural and normal. Unlike the modern versions, the King James Bible clearly and authoritatively condemns homosexuality.

Where are we Headed?

Without the absolute authority of God's word in society and culture, man tends to revert to his "natural state" – that of abominable wickedness. Here are a few examples:

In 1994, Governor William Weld of Massachusetts created the first-ever "Governor's Commission on Gay and Lesbian Youth." This state became the first state to pass into law a "Gay Rights" law for schools. The law required that, *"...all certified teachers and educators receive training in issues relevant to the needs and problems faced by gay and lesbian youth. Such training should be a requirement for teacher certification and school accreditation."* [5]

In 1996, the NEA (National Education Association) adopted as part of its bylaws Resolution B-7. This resolution deals with "racism, sexism, and sexual orientation discrimination." It calls for policies to eliminate all discrimination against "gays" and specific curricula to "educate" all age groups in public schools in the acceptance of homosexuals. [6]

In 1998, the NEA, in conjunction with Washington State University, invited every high school and junior high school student in the state of Washington to participate in a three-day conference on homosexuality. This conference was described as a *"...kind of Camp Queer experience."* [7]

In March 2000, the Vermont House approved legislation allowing sodomites to form "civil unions" that would entitle them to be recognized as married couples. Among other benefits, this provision would then allow homosexual couples to file a joint state income tax return. [8]

In June 2001, delegates to the Presbyterians' national assembly voted to abolish the church's ban on actively *"homosexual clergy and lay officers."* This vote followed an open letter signed by a majority of

Bible professors at Presbyterian Seminaries – 33 out of 58 – urging the delegates to lift the ban.

One professor fighting the ban said, *"Our context* (in the twentieth century) *is so significantly different that I don't think the words* (of the Bible) *are any longer living, but dead words if we try to read them without contextually understanding them."* This is a good point, but in no way excuses their complete scriptural infidelity.

The professors summed up their arguments for lifting the ban in their letter. They stated that Bible passages about homosexuality should be understood for *"their meaning in their own time."* On careful reading, the words of scripture *"seem to be advocating values such as hospitality to strangers, **ritual** purity or the sinfulness of all human beings before God."*

"The concept of homosexuality as now understood is probably not something the ancient biblical writers could have known." [See *II Timothy 3:7*. Man is obviously, *"Ever learning, and never able to come to the knowledge of the truth."*] The article goes on to say, the church should honor *"the rule of love"* rather than *"pronouncing judgment upon **a specific behavior of a whole category of persons.**"* They claim that *"the Bible's overarching principles are inclusivity and justice."* ⁹

I wonder if this same "rule of love" philosophy applies to pedophiles (child molesters), who make up **a whole category of persons with a specific behavior**? It is really hypocritical to selectively apply these guidelines only to those that have convinced the politicians and medical community that their deviant, chosen lifestyle should be morally accepted and legally protected.

Final Thoughts

Now, read the remaining verse comparisons to discern from whence this wicked humanistic, rationalistic philosophy stems.

God's word:

(KJB) *I Kings 15:12 And he took away the* **sodomites** *out of the land, and removed all the idols that his fathers had made.*

Satan's tool:

(NIV) *I Kings 15:12 He expelled the* **male shrine prostitutes** *from the land and got rid of all the idols his fathers had made.*

God's word:

(KJB) *I Kings 22:46 And the remnant of the* **sodomites,** *which remained in the days of his father Asa, he took out of the land.*

Satan's device:

(NIV) *I Kings 22:46 He rid the land of the rest of the* **male shrine prostitutes** *who remained there even after the reign of his father Asa.*

God's word:

(KJB) *II Kings 23:7 And he brake down the houses of the* **sodomites,** *that were by the house of the LORD, where the women wove hangings for the grove.*

Satan's design:

(NIV) *II Kings 23:7 He also tore down the quarters of the* **male shrine prostitutes,** *which were in the temple of the LORD and where women did weaving for Asherah.*

Satan knows that *"Righteousness exalteth a nation: but sin is a reproach to any people"* **(Proverbs 14:34)**. He knows that a powerful nation must crumble from within, because no outside force is sufficiently powerful to destroy it. When people change the truth of God into a lie and hold the truth in unrighteousness, God judges. *"For the wrath of*

*God is revealed from heaven against all ungodliness and unrighteousness of men, **who hold the truth in unrighteousness" (Romans 1:18).*** America holds the truth in unrighteousness; the judgment is here and coming.

Even science can prove that homosexuality is dangerous. God requires a monogamous heterosexual marital relationship. This is the greatest protection against the spread of sexually transmitted diseases. It has been shown that homosexual activities shorten a person's life span by as much as 30 years. [10] *"Be not over much wicked, neither be thou foolish: why shouldest thou die before thy time?" (Ecclesiastes 7:17).* The judgment of God abides upon the homosexual.

__Romans 1:27__ And likewise also the __men, leaving the natural use of the woman,__ burned in their lust one toward another; men with men working that which is unseemly, and __receiving in themselves__ (AIDS or GRIDS) that recompence of their error which was meet. [28] And even as they did not like to retain God in their knowledge, __God gave them over to a reprobate mind,__ to do those things which are not convenient;

The AIDS epidemic did not begin with that name. This disease began with the acronym of GRIDS – *Gay Related Immune Deficiency Syndrome.* It has become the only politically protected disease, allowing it to reach pandemic and soon to be epidemic proportions. Can you see the Devil's handiwork? However, we cannot blame the world completely for these sweeping problems. The root cause *(I Timothy 6:10)* for the lack of resolve to fight against this wickedness lies at the feet of the Church, who has too willingly accepted the latest marketed version of the bible. Due to the modern version changes and resultant lack of understanding and conviction concerning this issue, Christians no longer have the resolve to fight against the homosexual agenda.

Conclusion

The Bible warns that God will give people up to uncleanness if they change His truth into a lie. The context of this passage illustrates that America stands guilty. We have become wise, changing the glory of the incorruptible God into an image made like to corruptible man, and to birds, and four-footed beasts, and creeping things.

(KJB) Romans 1:25 Who changed the truth of God into a lie, *and worshipped and served the creature more than the Creator, who is blessed for ever. Amen.*

This country appears to care more about a beached whale or a spotted owl (the creature) than about the God who created them. These United States have certainly devolved because of their rejection of God's truth. God's condemnation is carried out against those that have the truth (the United States) and then change this truth into a lie.

The revisers have changed the truth into the opposite of the truth – that is, into a lie. To have the truth, and then to change it, is a much more serious offense to God than simply *exchanging* the truth for a lie. The person that *exchanges* the truth for a lie may do so ignorantly; the person that *changes* the truth into a lie is the mastermind underlying the error.

(NIV) Romans 1:25 They exchanged the truth of God for a *lie, and worshiped and served created things rather than the* *Creator-who is forever praised. Amen.*

There is a vast difference between the KJB and the NIV. The first condemns the perpetrator, while the second condemns the victim. No longer are God's condemnatory remarks against those *changing* the truth of God into a lie present in the modern versions. Those that are busy changing this truth do not want to put out a version of the Bible that condemns their very actions. The modern versions attack the virgin birth, the deity of Jesus Christ, the blood atonement, the sinlessness of Christ, and all other important doctrines. Those that exchange their King James Bible for one of these modern versions are condemned, while the real culprit – the one actually changing the scripture – stands condemned by the KJB.

Consider the difference between "change" and "exchange." Historically, Bible changes have been made via small incremental alterations which build over time. These changes have occurred very gradually. Like the frog in the kettle boiling to death as the heat is slowly turned up, most Christians have been completely unaware of this steady, stealthy process of Bible changes. On the other hand, to *exchange* is to turn the Bible in for something absolutely false. Such wide scale corruption would shock most people into refusing it. For that reason, the Devil "changes" the truth of God into a lie to make the gradual changes more palatable to the unsuspecting reader.

The modern versions change the truth of God into a lie. Plain and simple! If you have the truth (the King James Bible) and a modern version says something contrary to the KJB, what does that make the modern version? If it contradicts or changes the truth, it is a lie.

For purely lucrative reasons (specifically, the generation of over $400 million annually), English bible versions are produced. The love of money is the root of all evil. If these groups were truly interested in disseminating the truth, they would instead expend their energies to translate the Bible into languages that are currently without the word of God. There are thousands of languages worldwide in which there is no Bible, simply because monetary means are lacking in these areas. These publishers are concerned not with spreading truth, but with making money and gaining glory from mankind for their scholarly contributions to the supposed enlightenment of the masses.

The only way to make money is to qualify for a copyright. The only way to qualify for a new copyright is to make a sufficient number of changes to an existing text. Since the same bible publishers generally own copyrights on multiple versions, sales must come from the one book nobody owns. That is why all the modern versions compare themselves with the King James Bible. It is the standard. However, publishers cannot copyright the KJB. Instead, they are forced to make comparisons with it and attack it, with the ultimate goal of replacing it. Only by replacing the KJB can these publishers make their sales and win a substantial portion of the lucrative American Bible market.

According to a June 2001 article in the *USA Today* entitled "Protestants Face Annual Sexual Divide," the following are the leading questions that must be addressed: *"Should gay clergy be ordained? Are same-sex unions blessed before God the same as the marriage of a man and woman? May a woman lead a church?"* The article goes on to say, *American Protestantism can be a free-for-all when supposedly like-minded believers get together. ...these touchy topics may dominate – or derail – their agendas."* [11]

The one thing man learns from history is that he has failed to learn from history. God gave the Old Testament for our learning and admonition. However, we are just like Israel of old with a "whore's forehead" because we refuse to be ashamed.

*Jeremiah 3:3 Therefore the showers have been withholden, and there hath been no latter rain; and **thou hadst a whore's forehead, thou refusedst to be ashamed.***

Because we have accepted more and more wickedness, we can no longer blush.

*Jeremiah 8:12 Were they ashamed when they had committed abomination? nay, they were not at all ashamed, **neither could they blush:** therefore shall they fall among them that fall: in the time of their visitation they shall be cast down, saith the LORD.*

Should these issues really be controversial? In today's sexual climate, they are. The modern versions have played a big role in creating controversy by muddying the waters. No longer are the absolutes taught because the underlying foundations have been destroyed. Society has become increasingly more permissive because the modern versions have eroded God's explicit guidelines. The division is caused by those that accept any version, not those that believe God's principles are unchanging and absolute. It will only get worse unless we return to the one book that kept America great and strong!

Lenin knew more truth than many of the supposedly religious men of today. He said, *"Destroy the family and the society will collapse."* Destroy the family and you can destroy the church. Destroy the church and everything else follows. Mission accomplished through the modern versions' contribution to the degradation of society. This may seem a logical point with which to end this discussion, but there is more.

As we have seen, Lucifer's identity has been hidden. (See *Isaiah 14:12* comparison.) The identity and character of the Antichrist has also been changed. The book of Daniel reveals that he will be of Jewish descent (the God of his fathers) and indicates that he may be homosexual.

*(KJB) Daniel 11:37 Neither shall he regard **the God of his fathers**, nor **the desire of women**, nor regard any god: for he shall magnify himself above all.*

He will not regard (or want) the desire of women. Many Bible students believe this to mean that he will desire the attention of men only. Does the NIV adequately identify Lucifer? No! Does the NIV adequately identify the Antichrist? No!

*(NIV) Daniel 11:37 He will show no regard for **the gods of his fathers** or for the **one desired by women**, nor will he regard any god, but will exalt himself above them all.*

The KJB says he will have no regard for:
  1 – God (will be Jewish)
  2 – the desire of women (will be homosexual)
  3 – any god (will exalt himself as supreme)

The NIV says he will have no regard for:
  1 – the gods of his fathers (undefined)
  2 – the one desired of women (unclear)
  3 – any god (okay)

The Antichrist's identity is hidden along with his "sexual preference" for men. Or should I say, his "sexual orientation" remains a mystery? Who would most likely be the mastermind of such deception? These changes are not man-made but Satan inspired. *"For we wrestle not against flesh and blood, but against principalities, against powers, against the rulers of the darkness of this world, against spiritual wickedness in high places" (Ephesians 6:12).*

Chapter 7 Endnotes

[1] Dennis Corle, *Elements of a Godly Character,* (Claysburg, PA: Revival Fires Publishers, 1996) p. 61, 73.

[2] The Montgomery Advertiser, *"Homosexuality Not a Disorder, Experts Say,"* Chicago press release (file copy – date unknown).

[3] *Catholic Worker* Vol LXVIII, No. 3, May 2001, 36 East First Street, New York, NY.

[4] The Montgomery Advertiser, *"Study Offers Challenge to 'Gay Gene'"* Washington press release (file copy – date unknown)

[5] Mark A. Underwood, *King James Bible Newsletter,* October 1998, Volume II, Issue 10, page 3.

[6] *Ibid,* p. 2.

[7] *Ibid,* p. 3.

[8] The Montgomery Advertiser, *Vermont House Approves Landmark Gay Rights Bill,* March 17, 2000, p. 4A.

[9] News and Record, *Church Debates Homosexuality,* Richard Osling, July 28, 2001, P. B7, B8.

[10] Family Research Institute, *"Study Indicates Homosexual Acts Shorten Lifespan,"* Colorado Springs, CO.

[11] USA Today, *Protestants Face Annual Sexual Divide,* June 6, 2001, p. 19-20.

8

The Monetary Motive

---

*For there are many unruly and vain talkers and deceivers, spe-
cially they of the circumcision: Whose mouths must be stopped,
who subvert whole houses, **teaching things which they ought
not, for filthy lucre's sake.***
(Titus 1:10-11)

The publisher of each new, "best" bible translation that emerges
on the market hopes to capture a substantial portion of the $400
million dollars Americans annually devote to the purchase of
"Bibles." If the Bible revisers' motives are simply to assist their customers in better understanding the word of God, then why does it appear
that they publish these books for monetary gain? A consideration of the
changes made by the revisers to biblical passages containing God's warnings concerning money causes one to wonder whether these alterations
are intentional acts of deception. Regardless of the intention behind such
changes, the fact remains that the revisers are guilty of making them!

It is often said that how a person handles *money* reveals a great deal
about his character. This fact holds true with regard to the modern versions as well. The character of these versions can be discerned from
careful study of their treatment of monetary wealth.

The Deceitfulness of Riches

As the Lord began to teach, great multitudes of people gathered
around to hear His words. One of the teachings He shared with the

multitudes included the parable of the sower. When the Lord was alone with His twelve disciples, they asked Him the meaning of the parable. Jesus explained that the seeds sown *among the thorns* represent individuals who hear the word but are distracted by the cares of this world, and specifically by the *deceitfulness* of riches.

(KJB) Mark 4:19 And the cares of this world, and the deceitfulness of riches, and the lusts of other things entering in, choke the word, and it becometh unfruitful.

Mark chapter four reveals that riches can be deceitful. Furthermore, the warning of this passage is for one not to *trust* in riches because of their deceitful nature. Notice how the **Revised Standard Version** changes God's negative statement concerning money into something vague and confusing.

(RSV) Mark 4:19 but the cares of the world, and the delight in riches, and the desire for other things enter in and choke the word, and it proves unfruitful.

Take note that one can be deceived by riches *without* finding any delight in that wealth. In fact, the list of people is endless who have accumulated vast sums of money, but find no real *delight* in the money itself. The accumulation of the wealth, rather than the enjoyment of that which has been accumulated, becomes top priority. The problem with many people who are caught up in the act of accumulating wealth is that they do not realize how *deceived* they are by the very thing they so greatly desire.

Amschel Rothchild is a primary example of a man who was *deceived by riches*, but who evidently found *little delight* in them. He hanged himself in a luxury hotel in Paris at the age of 41! He was the man anticipated to assume control of the British merchant bank N.M. Rothchild and Sons. Instead, his lifeless body was discovered by a cleaning lady at the Hotel Bristol. He could certainly testify about the deceitfulness of riches now!

The Root of All Evil

Our first comparison dealt with the little-used 1952 Revised Standard Version. The remainder of these comparisons concerning money will illustrate that the NIV clearly follows the lead of its 1952 predecessor.

God and His word have no problem giving absolutes. This principle remains true concerning the issue of money as well. The most explicit biblical warning concerning money is found in the book of First Timothy. Satan does not want man to be warned about the dire consequences associated with the *love of* money.

*(KJB) I Timothy 6:10 For the love of money is **the root** of all evil: which while some coveted after, they have erred from the faith, and pierced themselves through with many sorrows.*

At first glance, it is obvious that God has no problem using absolute terminology. In fact, He says that *the love of money is **the** root of all evil.* How can God be so dogmatic? How can God make such a bold claim *(Romans 9:20)*?

The modern versions (and their authors) seem to have difficulty admitting some truths about money. If the real purpose of the modern bibles is simply to update God's words using current language, then these newer versions should still agree with the Bible version our Founding Fathers used to create the American system of government *(Isaiah 33:22)*. However, the King James Bible and the modern versions do not agree. Clearly, both cannot be correct!

*(NIV) I Timothy 6:10 For the love of money is **a root** of all **kinds of** evil. Some people, eager for money, have wandered from the faith and pierced themselves with many griefs.*

If God says that the love of money is **the** root of **all** evil, it is not **a** root of all **kinds** of evil, as the modern versions would have us believe. You cannot straddle the fence. God wants you to choose *(Joshua 24:15)*.

He cannot tolerate Christians who "sit on the fence" with a lukewarm attitude toward everything *(Revelation 3:16)*.

The apparent driving force behind the production of these modern versions is money and the overwhelming desire (love) for its accumulation. Therefore, the result of every sin caused by these modern versions, as well as their failure to dispense the truth, can be attributed to "the love of money." The reason we have hundreds of versions to choose from is that the publishers and backers of the modern versions are all trying to gain a share of this lucrative market. There are 400 million reasons ($) why this is true. The following is one illustration of how the love of money is **the** root of **all** evil.

Chapter six discussed the differences in God's expectations versus the modern versions' lowered moral standards. The King James Bible says to *"Abstain from all appearance of evil"* *(I Thessalonians 5:22)*. The New International Version changes this truth to *"Avoid every kind of evil."* The meaning of these two passages differs considerably. They are not even close in meaning. The King James Bible conveys a much higher moral standard and loftier spiritual expectation.

For example, given this first command from the KJB concerning appearances, every man or woman should realize that he or she should *not* be alone with a member of the opposite sex to whom he or she is not married. The reason to *abstain* from this situation is not because it is evil, but because it has the *appearance of evil*.

For a man and woman, not married to each other, to be alone in a room is *not* necessarily evil. However, the preacher without the KJB misses the clear warning from scripture to abstain from these things because of their appearance. If he uses one of the modern versions, such as the NIV, he is not warned to *abstain from all appearance of evil*. He is only told to *avoid every kind of evil*. He knows it is *not* necessarily evil to be alone with a woman, so he might never consider God's warnings. Frequently, in these matters, he may not realize how his problems might have been avoided until things have progressed beyond repair.

There have been many pastors (and employers, in general) that have run off with their secretaries (and employees) because they have not been scripturally warned. How does one attribute God's statement concerning *the love of money as the root* of this pastor's *evil?* The logic is very simple to follow. The modern perversions have been hitting the market at lightening speed with an underlying money-making motive. This pastor, who reads only the NIV, does *not abstain from the appearance of evil* and ends up with a much more serious problem when he becomes involved emotionally and then physically with his secretary.

The modern versions do not warn anyone to abstain from the appearance of evil. Their money-making motive for producing another bible causes men and women to miss this clear warning from God, which the standard (the KJB) has been giving for hundreds of years. Therefore, the revisers' love of money is the *root* of this evil and of **everything** that results from this one act (and all similar acts). *The love of money is the root of all evil.*

Copyrighting the bibles

If these Bible revisers' motives are pure, why do they place a financial copyright upon "the word of God"? The reason they copyright their respective versions is to gain the royalties associated with them. They, not God, wrote the words of these translations; why should they not want to profit from them? In contrast, the Apostle Paul tells us to pray *"...that the word of the Lord may have free course" (II Thessalonians 3:1) "... that we might know the things that are freely given to us of God (I Corinthians 2:12).*

The copyright makes it illegal to copy a modern "scripture" version without obtaining permission from its publisher. Reference the definition of "copyright" found in the *New Standard Encyclopedia*, vol. 3, page 565: *"The legal protection given to authors and artists to prevent reproduction of their work without their consent. The owner of a copyright has the exclusive right to print, publish, copy and sell the material covered by the copyright."* The mass copyrighting of these versions by Bible Societies and corporations indicates that these are the words of men and not the words of God *(II Thessalonians 2:13).*

The following incident further illustrates this point considering the lucrative Bible market. When Bible study computer programs first became popular, I found one program that I particularly liked. I called the designer of this program in Ontario, Canada and asked him about adding another version to it. I wanted to be able to easily compare the NIV with the KJB so that I could show others the contradictions. He said he could not afford to pay the royalties for adding the NIV to his program. How much did they want in royalties for him to include the NIV in his program? $5,000. Writing and printing these modern versions is a money-making business and has caused much evil. *"The love of money is the root of all evil."*

The modern version texts are copyrighted, allowing only a prescribed number of verses to be "quoted and/or reprinted" without *express written permission of the publisher.* The copyright page of the 1973 and 1978 NIV limited the number of verses to **100**! The 1984 version printed by the International Bible Society changed the number to **500**. *"The NIV text may be quoted in any form (written, visual, electronic, or audio), up to and inclusive of five hundred (500) verses without express written permission of the publisher..."* However, Zondervan also printed a 1984 version allowing **1,000** verses to be used without permission! Obviously, the financial incentives to control the usage of this translation were much greater during its early life.

One book stands alone without a financial copyright. The King James Bible may be freely copied, printed, or published without permission. The notes and formatting within the printed pages of King James study Bibles are copyrighted; the text has no copyright. However, the privilege of printing Bibles in England has belonged to the royal printer since the mid-1500's.

Upon publication of the Authorized Version, King James I of England assigned to that work a *Cum Privlegio* (meaning *with privilege*) in the name of the Crown. The Cambridge and Oxford Bibles (printed only in England) contain *Cum Privlegio* on their title pages. This measure has protected the integrity of the text from those producing King James Bibles containing altered text. No such protection exists in the United States, where KJB imposters such as the *New Scofield* Versions have arisen. In England, the responsibility of printing the Bible has always been considered to be too important to entrust to anyone other than the King and those appointed by him to do the printing.

Today, all Bibles printed in England are printed by the university presses of Cambridge and Oxford. Considering the spelling changes made within the King James text (whether inadvertently or intentionally) by Nelson and Zondervan publishers, it is a shame that the same standards have not been incorporated in countries outside of England in order to protect the text from the unscrupulous. The Cambridge and Oxford Bibles are some of the best quality (material) and most trusted (typographically). One need not be concerned about their altering the text (yet).

Peddling the Word

The revisers justify their changes by saying the "oldest and best manuscripts" say something different from the King James Bible. Paul negated this argument long before any of these bible perverters ever invented this scheme. During the first century, Paul made note of the "many" which were corrupting the word of God. Even as Paul penned the scripture, these scribes were doing their dirty work.

*(KJB) II Corinthians 2:17 For we are not as many, which **corrupt** the word of God: but as of sincerity, but as of God, in the sight of God speak we in Christ.*

It seems that the NIV editors do not want Christians to be aware of the far-reaching effect of Satan's hand. They do not want the believer to know that the corruption began as soon as the word of God was penned. Considering the Garden of Eden, one can show that Satan's plan of corruption was placed into action soon after the creation of man *(Genesis 3:1)*. While corrupting the word of God and selling it for a profit, these bible editors have the audacity to change the word *corrupt* to *peddle* in the modern versions!

*(NIV) II Corinthians 2:17 Unlike so many, we do not **peddle** the word of God for profit. On the contrary, in Christ we speak before God with sincerity, like men sent from God.*

Those who are peddling the word of God hide their involvement in its corruption. By doing so, they make themselves guilty of both the sin of corruption, and of the sin of hypocrisy by peddling it. Hitler once said, *"If you tell a lie enough times, people will believe it as truth."* The NIV editors not only corrupt the truth, but also change *"...the truth of God into a lie..." (Romans 1:25).* This perversion of truth did not begin after the printing press was invented.

Jeremiah told the religious leaders of his day, *"...for ye have perverted the words of the living God ..." (Jeremiah 23:36).* Solomon said, *"The thing that hath been, it is that which shall be; and that which is done is that which shall be done: and **there is no new thing under the sun" (Ecclesiastes 1:9).*** These modern publishers only duplicate the act of Satan in the Garden...this is nothing new.

By changing the scripture from *corrupt* to *peddle,* the modern versions are also attacking every bookstore that sells Bibles (KJB) and bibles for a profit. Obviously, a bookstore could not stay in business long without making a profit. Nevertheless, the NIV condemns this practice.

Supposing that Gain is Godliness

The New York Bible Society (now known as the International Bible Society) received a copyright on the text of the NIV in 1973. As evident from the copyright, this group is in fact peddling "the word of God" for profit! They may point to all the copies they sell as proof of "God's blessings." However, the Bible clearly warns us to withdraw from those that believe that profitability proves the spiritual state of someone or of some group.

> *(KJB) I Timothy 6:4 He is proud, knowing nothing, but doting about questions and strifes of words, whereof cometh envy, strife, railings, evil surmisings, 5 Perverse disputings of men of corrupt minds, and destitute of the truth, **supposing that gain is godliness: from such withdraw thyself.***

Christians are warned to withdraw from those teaching that "gain is godliness." In other words, withdraw yourself from any ministry that points to the things it possesses (in the form of money, buildings, or numbers) as proof that it is a godly ministry. One cannot look at the outward appearance and judge what is inside. The NIV does *not* warn anyone to withdraw from others because unity at all costs pervades today's "politically correct" atmosphere. In fact, the NIV actually *reverses* God's explicit warning!

> *(NIV) I Timothy 6:4* he is conceited and understands nothing. He has an unhealthy interest in controversies and quarrels about words that result in envy, strife, malicious talk, evil suspicions 5 and constant friction between men of corrupt mind, who have been robbed of the truth and **who think that godliness is a means to financial gain.**

Contrary to the NIV, living a godly life *should be* the only means to financial gain. Any claim to the contrary would be ludicrous. That is what the NIV does. If everyone believed that the only way to true financial success was through a godly lifestyle, the whole economic and financial landscape would transform. The NIV rebukes this type of thinking. If the motives of the modern revisers are not as wrong as they appear, the results of their handiwork certainly are!

Motives are Important

The King James Bible attacks the motives of those teaching false doctrine. Church leaders must *not* be **motivated** by the financial benefits of the ministry, although it is *not* a sin to take wages for one's ministry. Serving the Lord Jesus Christ, rather than earning money, is to be one's motive for ministry.

> *(KJB) Titus 1:10* For there are many unruly and vain talkers and deceivers, specially they of the circumcision: *11* Whose mouths must be stopped, who subvert whole houses, **teaching** things which they ought not, **for filthy lucre's sake.**

In this scenario, the KJB refers to the money as *filthy lucre* (money) because of the motives with which it is associated. The individuals referred to in this passage are teaching false doctrine for the sake of money.

The emphasis in the NIV changes from a rebuke against teaching for financial gain, to a rebuke for being dishonest about doing so.

(NIV) **Titus 1:10** *For there are many rebellious people, mere talkers and deceivers, especially those of the circumcision group. 11 They must be silenced, because they are ruining whole households by* **teaching** *things they ought not to teach-and that* **for the sake of dishonest gain.**

The NIV's rebuke is against *dishonest* gain, rather than a general rebuke against those teaching falsely for the sake of money. If a person teaches false doctrine and does so in a sincere ("honest") fashion, he might experience no conviction from reading the NIV – even if his motive is based on money (contrary to the true word of God). In other words, such an individual might consider his motives to be sincere, though they are not scripturally based, simply because he does not have God's absolute standard of truth convicting him.

Many of these modern version publishers may claim otherwise, but their motives remind me of a letter once written by a college student with his motives somewhat camouflaged. See if you can read between the lines.

Dear Dad,

$chool i$ really great. I am making lot$ of friend$ and $tudying very hard. With all my $tuff, I $imply can't think of anything I need, $o if you would like, you can ju$t $end me a card, a$ I would love to hear from you.

Love,
Your $on.

Concerning the purchasing of these modern bibles, we should take a hint from the father's letter back to his son concerning the veiled requests for money.

Dear Son,

I kNOw that astroNOmy, ecoNOmics, and oceaNOgraphy are eNOugh to keep even an hoNOr student busy. Do NOt forget that the pursuit of kNOwledge is a NOble task, and you can never study eNOugh.

Love,

Dad

The endless parade of modern versions will not end until the Lord returns. The financial incentives are too great for sinful man to resist. Dr. William P. Grady, in his book *Final Authority,* quotes from Jack Lewis who aptly, and probably inadvertently, pointed out the insanity behind the modern version mania.

If one should ask if there are too many translations, the reply must be that the question is really irrelevant. The translations are here; they are not going away; and they must be dealt with. To hide one's head in the sand will not make the translations disappear; it will not bring back the so-called "good old days" when everyone read one translation. As long as there is financial gain in it, publishers will push translations, old or new. [1]

Of course, the word of God reveals the true motive, too: *"For* ***the love of money*** *is the root of all evil: which while some coveted after, they have erred from the faith, and pierced themselves through with many sorrows" (**I Timothy 6:10**).*

Chapter 8 Endnotes

---

[1] Grady, *Final Authority, op. cit.,* p. 298.

9

How Shall They Preach?

What is the chief end of preaching? I like to think ...it is to give men and women a sense of God and His presence. ...I can forgive the preacher almost anything if he gives me a sense of God, if he gives me something for my soul, if he gives me the sense that, though he is inadequate himself, he is handling something which is very great and very glorious...[1]

Martyn Lloyd-Jones

If the motive underlying the translation of new bible versions is to make the word of God easier to understand, why then do these translations reduce the importance of preaching the word of God? Keep in mind two points concerning this topic as it is addressed. First: God elevates preaching. Second: Satan despises it! The Lord commends those that preach the gospel; Satan mounts his fiercest attack against these same men.

God Commends Preaching

God did not choose man's wisdom to convey His truth to the world. He chose *"the foolishness of preaching to save them that believe."* (*I Corinthians 1:21*). He chose a foolish method to confound the wise. The Lord even uses one of the most uncomely parts of the body, the feet, to commend preaching. He describes as beautiful the feet of a man who preaches the gospel.

(KJB) Romans 10:15 And how shall they preach, except they be sent? as it is written, How beautiful are the feet of them that **preach the gospel** *of peace, and bring glad tidings of good things!*

Because of the ongoing battle between the forces of good and evil, pastors must be ever conscious of Satan's attempts to destroy that which God highly exalts. Satan has many tools at his disposal. God elevates preaching; thus, any version that does not exalt this God-ordained medium for proclaiming truth is one of Satan's tools. Does the NIV promote preaching of the gospel as the KJB does?

(NIV) Romans 10:15 And how can they preach unless they are sent? As it is written, "How beautiful are the feet of those **who bring good news!***"*

This statement in the NIV does not even come close to matching the truth conveyed by the corresponding passage in the King James Bible. The simple bringing of good news does not necessarily convey, connote, or suggest the preaching of the gospel. God bestows this description of beauty only to a person who obediently follows Him by preaching the gospel. Delivering good news can cover a wide variety of activities, including the preaching of the gospel. However, preaching is not necessarily the first activity in this category to come to mind.

Martyn Lloyd-Jones understood and expressed man's highest calling: *"...the work of preaching is the highest and the greatest and the most glorious calling to which anyone can ever be called."* [2] Over thirty years ago, Mr. Jones hit the nail on the head concerning preaching's decline from its once prominent position. *"I would not hesitate to put in the first position: the loss of belief in the authority of the Scriptures, and the diminution in the belief of the Truth. I put this first because I am sure it is the main factor."* He goes on to clearly identify the ever-increasing problem. *"While men believed in the Scriptures as the authoritative Word of God and spoke on the basis of that authority you had great preaching."* [3] We do not have the great preaching or preachers of times past because of the overt attack upon God's word and the attempt by some to "preach" from these modern perversions.

Preaching Establishes the Believer

Many churches are replacing the preaching of God's word (and His gospel) with every conceivable program. Absolutely nothing should supplant the preeminence of preaching. It is the only means by which a Christian becomes established in the faith. If the Devil can blind a person to this truth, he has won. The Christian never realizes God's true purpose and plan for him apart from the preaching of God's word.

*(KJB) Romans 16:25 Now to him that is of power to **stablish** you according to my gospel, and the **preaching** of Jesus Christ, according to the revelation of the mystery, which was kept secret since the world began,*

When a man preaches Jesus Christ according to the revelation of the mystery revealed to the Apostle Paul, the Christian can be established in the faith. The NIV assists the Devil in concealing this truth. As seen in the NIV, the preeminence of preaching is diminished. Who hates preaching more than all others?

*(NIV) Romans 16:25 Now to him who is able to establish you by my gospel and the **proclamation** of Jesus Christ, according to the revelation of the mystery hidden for long ages past,*

The world loves these modern versions because the Holy Ghost conviction that comes from reading them is reduced and sometimes entirely eliminated. The Bible commands us to preach the word. Furthermore, it commands that we not be guilty of *"forsaking the assembling of ourselves together, as the manner of some is; but exhorting one another* (primarily through preaching)*: and so much the more, as ye see the day approaching" (**Hebrews 10:25**).* In our busy society, it has become too easy to skip church. The Bible says when we do so, we are forsaking the assembling of ourselves together!

As a result of the influence of these modern versions, people want to go to church and hear someone "share," rather than to listen and respond to preaching that convicts the soul. Churches need good, old fashioned, soul stirring, Holy Ghost preaching. What churches do not need is to become social clubs, devoid of spiritually vital preaching. Many prime examples of such "ecclesiastical social clubs" exist throughout the United States. The following is a case in point.

Temple Baptist Church (located just outside Detroit, Michigan) is a church with a rich history. It was founded by J. Frank Norris and later pastored by G. Beauchamp Vick. Dr. Norris actually traveled between Texas and Michigan and pastored two churches simultaneously. A flyer sent out by Temple Baptist (now called NorthRidge Church), belittled preaching by proclaiming the 101 reasons people skip church. Number 54 was because of the "Sermonator," an offshoot from Arnold Schwarzenegger's *Terminator* image!

The advertisement for this modern, up-to-date church further proclaimed: *"If your idea of a pastor is the Bible-thumping, finger-pointing, hellfire-preaching variety, then think again. At NorthRidge Church, you'll discover there's something for everyone."* The first on the list of six items is "relevant talks!" According to the flyer, the NorthRidge Senior Pastor Brad Powell *"is sharing talks through November called: 'Free to Choose.'"* How could a church move so quickly away from its rich heritage? The answer is very simple. Once men displace the King James Bible with modern versions, and replace preaching with every conceivable program – the ultimate objective of the church becomes nothing more than increasing its numbers. Of course, the same flyer also made mention of "energized music." I wonder if they think there is such a thing as "Christian Rock." They certainly have the wrong bible.

Their statement of beliefs can be found on their website at *www.NorthRidgeChurch.com.* Under the heading "What We Believe" you will find another heading entitled "Bible Beliefs." As I pressed the button, I expected to find their position on the Bible. Instead, three paragraphs appeared. The first sentence in each paragraph reads as follows:

1. *"Essential Beliefs – We believe there should be **unity**."* They quote portions of Ephesians 4:4-6 from the NIV. (Note: Unity must never become a goal to be achieved at the expense of the truth.)

2. *"Nonessential Beliefs* – *We believe there should be **liberty**."* They quote Romans 14:1, 4, 12, and 22 from the NIV. Conveniently, they leave verse 22 off of the list of verses included in their quote and they only quote one-half of the verse. What part of verse 22 did they omit? *"Blessed is the man who does not condemn himself by what he approves" (Romans 14:22b – NIV).* When the Devil tried to tempt the Lord Jesus Christ, he quoted scripture out of context, too.

Compare *Matthew 4:6* with *Psalm 91:11-13*. Matthew records the fact that the Devil quotes verses 11 and 12 from Psalm 91, but omits verse 13 which reads: *"Thou shalt tread upon the lion and adder: the young lion and the dragon shalt thou trample under feet."* The part Satan omitted foretells his demise! Go back and read the part of the verse omitted in the statement by NorthRidge church. They chose the NIV, reduced preaching to relevant talks, and now emphasize unity, liberty, and love. Unity, liberty, and love are important, but not at the expense of the truth.

3. *"In All Our Beliefs* – *We believe that we must maintain **love** toward each other."* They quote I Corinthians 13:2 from the NIV. (Note: The King James Bible uses the word "charity" referring to something far greater than love. We have limited charity to the giving of our possessions to those in need. However, the charity spoken of in the word of God is far greater than love. Shamefully, most of us lack the capacity to understand the true concept of charity in this sin-sick, hardened world.)

As we turn our thoughts back to the type of preaching that occurred in days gone by, Martyn Lloyd Jones again gives us a fresh perspective on preaching:

Is it not clear, as you take a bird's-eye view of Church history, that the decadent periods and eras in the history of the Church have always been those periods when preaching had declined? What is it that always heralds the dawn of a Reformation or of a Revival? It is renewed preaching. So my answer so far, my justification of my statement that preaching is the primary task of the Church, is based in that way on the evidence of the Scriptures, and the supporting and confirming evidence of the history of the Church. [4]

*Any true definition of preaching must say that that man is there to deliver the message of God, a message from God to those people. ...he is 'an ambassador for Christ'. ...he is standing there as the mouthpiece of God and of Christ to address these people. In other words he is not there merely to **talk** to them, he is not there to entertain them. ...Preaching should make such a difference to a man who is listening that he is never the same again.* [5]

Amen! Does your view of preaching line up with the modern contemporary "relevant talk" or Bible-based sermons by Spirit filled men of God?

The Astonishing Word

A church giving preeminence to any activity other than the preaching of the word of God lessens the importance of the main purpose for assembling together. Too many churches are frequently allowing the song service to replace the time formerly allotted to preaching. If done on a consistent basis, carnality rises in that church because people need the preaching of God's word. God says His word has power!

*(KJB) Luke 4:32 And they were astonished at his doctrine: for his **word** was with power.*

As we have seen, the modern versions replace **preaching** with the message. They also change the **word**, giving misplaced emphasis to the message. Satan knows he cannot completely destroy the truth; therefore, he does the next best thing – he supplants it! He convinces the multitudes that there is no difference among the various bibles.

Even James White's book, which shrewdly attacks the King James Bible, admits that the modern versions used a different set of manuscripts. He wrote, *"The textual differences between the KJV and the modern versions derive from the Hebrew and Greek texts from which they were translated."* [6] These self-proclaimed scholars have convinced themselves and others that we no longer have God's word; therefore, the *message* becomes more important than the literal words of God. See the change:

> *(NIV) Luke 4:32 They were amazed at his teaching, because his message had authority.*

These changes are far more significant than one might realize. The *message* has no authority without the *word*. To give the message preeminence, one has to debase the authority of the word. If we elevate the message over the word, we likewise unscripturally elevate the messenger.

Preach Doctrine

All scripture is profitable. God says the first thing that scripture is profitable for is *doctrine!* Doctrine is dogmatic! One must never waiver on the doctrines of God.

> *(KJB) II Timothy 3:16 All scripture is given by inspiration of God, and is profitable for **doctrine**, for reproof, for correction, for instruction in righteousness:*

A man can *teach* anything, but the doctrines of God are unique. The doctrines of God come from the scriptures . . . they are the very words of God. The NIV diminishes the importance of God's doctrines, by instead elevating teaching. If we elevate the teaching over doctrine, we likewise unscripturally elevate the teacher.

> *(NIV) II Timothy 3:16 All Scripture is God-breathed and is useful for **teaching**, rebuking, correcting and training in righteousness,*

When the NIV says that the scripture is useful for *teaching,* it states nothing more than the obvious. However, when the Bible mentions *doc-*

trine, this means something much more concrete than teaching alone. Doctrine is something that is accepted as authoritatively true and indisputable. Doctrine is dogmatic truth. Christianity is dogmatic concerning the fact that there is *"...none other name under heaven given among men, whereby we must be saved" (Acts 4:12).* This is the doctrine of salvation. A man's teachings do not carry the same weight of authority as God's doctrines. Satan hates God's doctrines and tries to diminish their importance.

Pray that the Word has Free Course

It is the *word* that gives authority to the message. Paul's prayer request for the Thessalonians elevates the word. His desire was that God's *word* would have free course and be glorified.

*(KJB) II Thessalonians 3:1 Finally, brethren, pray for us, that the **word** of the Lord may have **free course**, and be glorified, even as it is with you:*

The emphasis in the NIV is misplaced. Once again, the *word* is changed to the *message*. The carnal church of today is more concerned with numbers. Thus the emphasis is placed on the speed of getting out *a message*, rather than on the word's being unhindered and having free course *(I Thessalonians 2:18).*

*(NIV) II Thessalonians 3:1 Finally, brothers, pray for us that the **message** of the Lord may **spread rapidly** and be honored, just as it was with you.*

The NIV sounds more like a disease (like GRIDS/AIDS) – it is spreading rapidly. The mushroom growth of the contemporary unscriptural churches shows how the message of the NIV has spread rapidly. In its wake arise churches like Northridge Church.

The Word Saves

The priests and the Sadducees were grieved that Peter and some of the other Apostles taught the people and preached the resurrection **from** the dead. Therefore, they arrested them and put them in prison. However, many of them which heard the word, believed and were saved.

*(KJB) Acts 4:4 Howbeit many of them which heard the **word** believed; and the number of the men was about five thousand.*

Again, the emphasis in the King James Bible is upon the word of God. People are saved by the word, not some three-point outline devised by a man. The *message* must always originate from the word, elevate the word, and preach the word. Can you find the *word* in this same passage from the NIV?

*(NIV) Acts 4:4 But many who heard the **message** believed, and the number of men grew to about five thousand.*

Satan wants man to be elevated, while he desires that God and His word be cheapened. What is important? **If the message is supreme, the messenger is most important. If the word is supreme, its Author is most important!!!** *"...Let God be true, but every man a liar..." (Romans 3:4).* As a vessel, man needs to take God's word and pray that God gives it free course and that Satan does not reign victorious. When the word is elevated, the messenger becomes less significant. John aptly said, *"He must increase, but I must decrease."(John 3:30).* We need to be vessels, submitted and empty, *"meet for the Master's use" (II Timothy 2:21).*

Calvin Linton, an NIV editor, said the Bible is *"God's message and not his words."* He calls Christians *"amusingly uninformed"* who *"presume the Holy Spirit dictated the actual words of the text of the original writers."* [7] With this type of demeaning attitude, no wonder our seminaries have become breeding grounds for every type of heresy. I wonder what Mr. Linton will think when he stands before the "Dictator" of the word?

Matthew 5:18 For verily I say unto you, Till heaven and earth pass, one jot or one tittle shall in no wise pass from the law, till all be fulfilled.

According to Webster's 1828 Dictionary, the definitions of jot and tittle are very simple.

JOT, n. [Heb. yod.] An iota; a point; a tittle; the least quantity assignable.

TIT'TLE, n. [from tit, small.] A small particle; a minute part; a jot; an iota.

God promises that not one iota, point, or minute part of the word will fall by the wayside. God does not care what man thinks; His thoughts are far above our thoughts. Where man sees only the impossibilities, God sees victory.

> *Isaiah 55:7 Let the wicked forsake his way, and the unrighteous man his thoughts: and let him return unto the Lord, and he will have mercy upon him; and to our God, for he will abundantly pardon. 8 **For my thoughts are not your thoughts, neither are your ways my ways, saith the Lord.** 9 For as the heavens are higher than the earth, so are my ways higher than your ways, and my thoughts than your thoughts.*

We are responsible for aligning our thoughts as close as possible with those of the Lord. We need to be more spiritually minded, and the only way to achieve this lofty goal is to saturate our thoughts with His true word.

Some concluding thoughts concerning preaching: *"Preaching is that which deals with the total person, the hearer becomes involved and knows that he has been dealt with and addressed by God through this preacher."* [8] Oh, to experience more of that type of preaching today! How can one expect to attain this lofty goal if he does not even have God's word *(Jeremiah 23:28)*? It is unachievable without God's word to guide and direct the preacher and hearer. Satan knows this!

> *One reason many preachers are shying away from preaching is because true preaching has power. "...if there is no power it is not preaching. True preaching, after all, is God acting. It is not*

just a man uttering words; it is God using him....Since God is on the outside of many of these churches knocking on the door, it would be a misnomer to call the activity from the stage, preaching. [9]

The world needed preaching one hundred years ago. It needs preaching today. The world needed churches that were busy preaching God's word. The world needs churches like this today. These modern versions have corrupted the truth and have caused many people to err. Shamefully, Christians have not been very quick to listen to the problems associated with these modern versions. The Bible believer cannot take this rejection in a personal way. What if a man rejects God's warnings concerning His infallible word? God reveals His thoughts concerning this man, too. *"But if any man be ignorant, let him be ignorant"* (*I Corinthians 14:38*).

Chapter 9 Endnotes

[1] D. Martyn Lloyd-Jones, *Preaching and Preachers*, (Zondervan, Grand Rapids, MI, 1972), p. 97, 98.
[2] *Ibid.*, p.9.
[3] *Ibid.*, p.13.
[4] *Ibid.*, p. 24, 25.
[5] *Ibid.*, p. 53.
[6] White, *The King James Only Controversy, op. cit.*, p.28.
[7] Kenneth L. Barker, *The NIV: The Making of a Contemporary Translation*, (Grand Rapids, Michigan: Zondervan Publishing House, 1986), p. 17-19.
[8] Jones, *Preaching and Preachers, op. cit.*, p. 56.
[9] Jones, *Preaching and Preachers, op. cit.*, p. 95.

10

NKJV: Those Pesky Little Pronouns

---

*The first time the devil shows up in the Bible he is sitting under
the tree of knowledge and he hasn't moved since.*
Martin Luther

T he New King James Version (NKJV) should be classified as one
of the subtlest versions on the market *(Genesis 3:1)*. The success
of the NKJV, albeit limited, is attributable to two factors: the
retention of *King James* in its title and the recommendation of this version
by some of the more conservative Christian television and radio
personalities.

Because this version is promoted as an authentic King James Bible,
many people who would not even consider picking up one of the other
modern versions have been misled into buying the NKJV. Although the
changes found in the NKJV are less pervasive than those found in the
other modern versions, the New King James Version corrupts truth just
the same.

The New King James Version is the modern translation most similar
to the King James Bible. Nevertheless, the NKJV makes an estimated
100,000 translation changes to the KJB. This figure averages to over 80
changes per page, and approximately three changes per verse. While
claiming to follow the Majority Text of the King James Bible, the NKJV
frequently accepts the corrupt readings of the Alexandrian manuscripts.[1]

The changes found in the NKJV are too numerous to list completely. Some significant *removals* in the NKJV are as follows:

22 omissions of *hell*
23 omissions of *blood*
44 omissions of *repent*
48 omissions of *heaven*
51 omissions of *God*
66 omissions of *Lord*

In addition to the above deletions, the words *devils, damnation, JEHOVAH,* and *New Testament* are omitted completely from the text of the NKJV! In the New Testament alone, the NKJV removes 2,289 words from the KJB! The Old Testament is replete with changes as well. The changes begin in Genesis and continue through the book of the Revelation. The student of God's word should realize that *things that are different are not the same.*

To begin the comparison on the NKJV, consider the various influences brought to bear on this modern version. God promised the first man a help meet. Do both of the following verses convey the same thought and meaning?

(KJB) Genesis 2:18 And the LORD God said, It is not good that the man should be alone; I will make him an help meet for him.

The Bible says that God made a *help meet* for Adam. Notice the New King James Version's slant toward the women's liberation philosophy in this verse.

(NKJV) Genesis 2:18 And the LORD God said, "It is not good that man should be alone; I will make him a helper comparable to him."

"A helper comparable to him" sounds too much like the 50-50 concept promoted by many modern marriage counselors. The love, respect, and loyalty should be equal; the marriage itself should not be. The husband is the head of the home *(Ephesians 5:23)* and the wife is to be

subject to him *(Ephesians 5:24)*. The environment in most homes (Christian homes included) does not align itself with the scriptures in this respect, and chaos abounds.

The Bible does not say that the man is better, but that the woman was made for the man. The husband should consider that God gives him only one key instruction, but has to repeat it three times. Husbands are to love their wives *(Ephesians 5:25, 28, 33)*.

Although Thomas Nelson Publishers decided to begin their version with a slant toward the women's liberation movement, the main focus of this chapter is the NKJV's deletion of many of the pronouns found in the KJB. These pronouns help convey the true meaning of many passages.

The Pronouns: *Thee, Thy, Thine,* and *Ye*

The New King James Version claims its pronoun changes to be a positive feature of the version. The NKJV changes *thee, thy, thine,* and *ye* to the appropriate conjugations of the generic pronoun *you*. This alteration appears to be very simple, but is it really a positive feature? The Introduction to the New King James Version reads as follows:

> *Readers of the Authorized Version* (their primary advertising focus and the majority of their customer base) *will immediately be struck by the absence of several pronouns: thee, thou, and ye are replaced by the simple you, while your and yours are substituted for thy and thine as applicable. ...These pronouns are no longer a part of our language. ...Throughout their investigations,* **the publishers** *have observed that the real character of the Authorized Version does not reside in its archaic pronouns...*[2] [Emphasis mine]

What authority do the *publishers* (Thomas Nelson Publishers, Inc.) have to determine whether something in the Bible is necessary? Are the pronouns really archaic, or are they simply the language of the Bible? Furthermore, what saith the scripture? *"Ye shall not add unto the word which I command you, neither shall ye diminish ought from it..." (Deuteronomy 4:2).* Scriptural justification exists for leaving these words alone. Likewise, as will be demonstrated shortly, these pronouns are grammatically necessary for a clearer understanding of the text.

Purpose of the various pronouns: *thee, thy, thine,* **and** *ye.* Does God have a reason for using these particular pronouns, or can they simply be eliminated? Are these particular pronouns important, or can the generic "you" replace them and convey precisely the same message?

Background: The Greek and Hebrew languages utilize different words for the second person *singular* and second person *plural* pronouns. Since the King James Bible is a word-for-word translation, rather than an eclectic translation of the Hebrew and Greek texts, the usage of these separate pronouns (singular *thee* and plural *ye*) is retained in the KJB. The generic *"you"* would not meet the criteria used by the King James Bible translators. Though the English language has changed considerably over the centuries, using the imprecise word *you* for both singular and plural second person pronouns in the word of God is not justifiable.

God has provided a simple tool for determining the singular or plural nature of a particular pronoun. If the pronoun begins with "t" (thou, thy, thine), it is *singular.* If the pronoun begins with "y" (ye, you), it is *plural.* Simple as that! "T" is singular. "Y" is plural. O.T. Oswald Allis investigated the matter rather thoroughly and stated his conclusions quite succinctly. Allis informs us that the pronouns used in the KJB are not simply a reflection of the contemporary words used by the translators and their contemporaries in 1611.

It is incorrect to claim that the "thou" represents the usage of the 1611 period when the AV was prepared and that that usage is out of date and should be rejected for that very reason. Such a claim misrepresents the facts. The AV usage is not Jacobean or 17th century English. It is biblical English. The Greek of the New Testament distinguishes between the singular and the plural forms of the second person. The AV makes this distinction simply because NT Greek does so, and because that is the only way to translate the Bible correctly. [3]

Do not miss the point: When the generic "you" of the New King James Version replaces the singular and plural pronouns of the King

James Bible, text clarity and understanding are sacrificed. What may seem to be a simple change actually has far reaching implications. This truth bears out in the Old Testament Hebrew to English translation, as well as the New Testament Greek to English translation!

Examples: Thousands of passages could be given. However, only five illustrations are provided which demonstrate the singular and plural nature of the pronouns of the KJB, and communicate the importance of retaining the use of these separate pronoun groups. Each example shows both the singular and plural usage of the pronouns.

Acts chapter five records the story of Ananias and Sapphira and their disobedience. Peter discusses with Sapphira her own sin and that of her husband. He says: "...*ye* have agreed together..." – they were in collusion. Next, Peter turns his attention to Sapphira and tells her that the men have carried out "*thy* husband" and will "carry *thee* out" next. The passage illustrates the plural and then the singular usage of the second person pronouns.

*(KJB) Acts 5:9 Then Peter said unto her, How is it that ye have agreed together to tempt the Spirit of the Lord? behold, the feet of them which have buried **thy** husband are at the door, and shall carry **thee** out.*

Although one can sometimes determine the singular or plural nature of a pronoun by its context, this is not always the case. The NKJV uses the generic "*you*" in place of the more precise *ye, thy,* and *thee* of the King James Bible.

*(NKJV) Acts 5:9 Then Peter said to her, "How is it that **you** have agreed together to test the Spirit of the Lord? Look, the feet of those who have buried **your** husband are at the door, and they will carry **you** out."*

This example from Acts chapter five shows the differences in pronoun usage between the NKJV and the KJB. In this case, the singular or plural meaning of the word *you* is easily discernable simply from the context of the passage. However, this determination is often much more difficult to make.

The Bible's explicit instructions frequently refer to a general audience and then become more specific, dealing on an individual basis. In Revelation chapter two, we read that many believers will be persecuted for ten days. The passage further states that if the *individual* is faithful unto death, he will receive a reward.

*(KJB) Revelation 2:10 Fear none of those things which **thou** shalt suffer: behold, the devil shall cast some of **you** into prison, that **ye** may be tried; and **ye** shall have tribulation ten days: be **thou** faithful unto death, and I will give **thee** a crown of life.*

In other words, only those saints who withstand the ten days of persecution will be rewarded with a crown of life. Not all of the "ye" spoken of in this passage will *endure to the end (Matthew 24:13)*. It would be incorrect to say "be *ye* faithful unto death, and I will give *you* a crown of life." The rewards are **individually** based, not collectively earned as a group. No such distinction is made in the parallel passage from the NKJV or any of the other modern versions.

*(NKJV) Revelation 2:10 Do not fear any of those things which **you** are about to suffer. Indeed, the devil is about to throw some of **you** into prison, that **you** may be tested, and **you** will have tribulation ten days. Be faithful until death, and I will give **you** the crown of life.*

In the next comparison, the NKJV passage will be provided first. Read the following verse from the New King James Version and then answer the questions found after the passage. Each of the answers should be either the *Apostles collectively* or *Peter alone*.

*(NKJV) Luke 22:31 And the Lord said, "Simon, Simon! Indeed, Satan has asked for **you**, that he may sift **you** as wheat. 32 But I have prayed for **you**, that **your** faith should not fail; and when **you** have returned to Me, strengthen **your** brethren."*

Who did Satan desire to sift as wheat? Who did the Lord pray for? Who was to strengthen the brethren? This passage illustrates another clear example of the loss of truth resulting from this simple change of pronouns. *"Every word of God is pure..." (Proverbs 30:5)*. Now read the corresponding passage from the true King James Bible and notice the singular and plural natures of the pronouns used.

*(KJB) Luke 22:31 And the Lord said, Simon, Simon, behold, Satan hath desired to have **you**, that he may sift **you** as wheat: 32 But I have prayed for **thee**, that **thy** faith fail not: and when **thou** art converted, strengthen **thy** brethren.*

The King James Bible is much clearer as a result of using numerically specific second person pronouns. The Lord is speaking to Simon Peter and telling him that Satan desired to have the apostles (you – plural). But the Lord says to Simon Peter that He prayed for him (thee – singular) that his faith (thy – singular) would not fail. He was told to strengthen (thy – singular) brethren when he (thou – singular) was converted. There is much to be lost by tampering with the word of God. The Lord did not pray for Judas Iscariot to strengthen the brethren. Judas is not included in the *thee* of the KJB.

Here is another example to further drive home the point. Notice that the Lord is speaking to Moses and says, "Thus *thou* shalt say...*Ye* (Israel) have seen... (I think you get the idea).

*(KJB) Exodus 20:22 And the LORD said unto Moses, Thus **thou** shalt say unto the children of Israel, **Ye** have seen that I have talked with **you** from heaven. 23 **Ye** shall not make with me gods of silver, neither shall **ye** make unto **you** gods of gold. 24 An altar of earth **thou** shalt make unto me, and shalt sacrifice thereon **thy** burnt offerings, and **thy** peace offerings, **thy** sheep, and **thine** oxen: in all places where I record my name I will come unto **thee**, and I will bless **thee**.*

God instructs Moses on what he is to say to the nation of Israel. God commands Moses to remind Israel that God has spoken directly to **them** and that they are not to make their own gods. However, when Moses addresses Israel regarding the appropriate sacrifices, he is instructed by God to bring the issue down to an individual level. One can only grasp this truth through the usage of the singular pronouns *thy, thine,* and *thee.*

(NKJV) Exodus 20:22 Then the LORD said to Moses, "Thus you shall say to the children of Israel: 'You have seen that I have talked with you from heaven. 23 You shall not make anything to be with Me—gods of silver or gods of gold you shall not make for yourselves. 24 An altar of earth you shall make for Me, and you shall sacrifice on it your burnt offerings and your peace offerings, your sheep and your oxen. In every place where I record My name I will come to you, and I will bless you.

In another example, Nicodemus comes to the Lord secretly. In this passage, a *single* person is addressed, concerning a *multitude* of people (the nation of Israel).

*(KJB) John 3:7 Marvel not that I said unto **thee**, Ye must be born again.*

Jesus speaks to Nicodemus (thee) about the nation of Israel (Ye). He tells Nicodemus that the nation must be born again. Jesus then continues and explains to Nicodemus several truths concerning the Spirit.

*(KJB) John 3:8 The wind bloweth where it listeth, and **thou** hearest the sound thereof, but canst not tell whence it cometh, and whither it goeth: so is every one that is born of the Spirit. 9 Nicodemus answered and said unto him, How can these things be? 10 Jesus answered and said unto him, Art thou a master of Israel, and knowest not these things? 11 Verily, verily, I say unto **thee**, We speak that we do know, and testify that we have seen; and **ye** receive not our witness. 12 If I have told **you** earthly things, and **ye** believe not, how shall **ye** believe, if I tell **you** of heavenly things?*

The Lord emphasized to Nicodemus that the nation of Israel had not received His witness. He told them about things He knew and had seen, but they remained in unbelief. Jesus is not simply referring to Nicodemus in the discussion. This truth is evident from the usage of plural pronouns in the passage. The NKJV does not provide a clear presentation of the truth.

*(NKJV) **John 3:7** Do not marvel that I said to **you**, 'You must be born again.' 8 "The wind blows where it wishes, and you hear the sound of it, but cannot tell where it comes from and where it goes. So is everyone who is born of the Spirit." 9 Nicodemus answered and said to Him, "How can these things be?" 10 Jesus answered and said to him, "Are **you** the teacher of Israel, and do not know these things? 11 Most assuredly, I say to **you**, We speak what We know and testify what We have seen, and **you** do not receive Our witness. 12 If I have told you earthly things and **you** do not believe, how will **you** believe if I tell you heavenly things?*

All pronouns in these verses from the NKJV are changed to the generic *you*. God has a purpose for even the pronouns He uses. These pronoun changes in the NKJV cause the passage to sound as if the Lord is simply rebuking Nicodemus when, in reality, He is rebuking the entire nation of Israel.

There are literally thousands of examples of this nature which could be cited. Why give up these pronouns when they are excellent tools for further understanding the word of God? God gives us light and He expects us to turn toward it. When we reject this light, for whatever reason, God is not obligated to provide any further light.

Along with illuminating the scripture, these pronouns also have a rich heritage in our hymns. Unfortunately, these hymns themselves, along with the Bible from which they originate, are likewise undergoing revisions at the hands of modern critics. If revisionists are to be consistent in making these changes, each of the following hymns would need to be updated or eliminated. Note that these titles do not hold the same meaning without the pronouns **from a King James Bible**. Remember, the excuse for deleting them from the modern translations is to make things easier to understand. Read the updated song titles; see how they sound; and think about what you lose as a consequence of this indiscriminate change.

"Come **Thou** Almighty King" – "Come **You** Almighty King"
"How Great **Thou** Art" – "How Great **You** Are"

"Come **Thou** Fount" – "Come **You** Fount"
"Be **Thou** My Vision" – "Be **You** My Vision"
"My Country, 'Tis of **Thee**" – "My Country, 'Tis of **You**"

If the hymns above should be updated, then what do you do with the songs below?

"Great is **Thy** Faithfulness"
"He is Able to Deliver **Thee**"
"I am **Thine**, O Lord"
"I Need **Thee** Every Hour"
"More Love to **Thee**"
"My Jesus, I Love **Thee**"

It is estimated that the King James Bible's use of *thee* and *ye*, versus the generic *you*, gives greater accuracy to the translation and the interpretation of the Bible in some 2,000 different passages.[4]

The problems of the NKJV are far more widespread than the simple changing of second person pronouns. As the next chapter will demonstrate, many doctrines are also attacked in this version because its translators allowed the Alexandrian manuscripts (which underlie all other modern versions) to supersede the authority of the *Textus Receptus*. The next discussion reveals the embarrassment that comes to those allowing their names to be associated with the modern versions.

Billy Graham's NKJV New Testament.

The preface to *The New King James New Testament – Billy Graham Counselor's Edition* has many different sections. In the section entitled *Grasping God's Word*, a picture illustrates a hand gripping the Bible, with a word written on each of the fingers.

Each finger represents a practice which can be employed in order to help a person gain an understanding of the word of God - hence enabling them to *"grasp the word of God."* The five topics are "hear, read, **study**, memorize, and meditate." The advice is good; however, the pre-

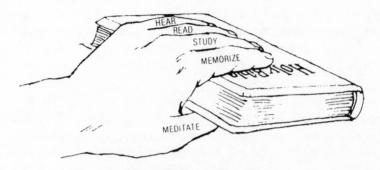

"Grasping God's Word"
© 1979 The New King James New Testament,
Thomas Nelson Publishers, Nashville, TN, p. 8.

sentation is comical. A person would better know how to understand God's word by doing the five things mentioned.

We will examine only one of these suggested practices: studying. Each of the sections cites numerous quotes from the **New** King James Version as support. The middle finger says STUDY, and the first three paragraphs found in that section are as follows.

From the Billy Graham Counselor's Edition of the New King James New Testament:

STUDY: Study is working at what we read with the intention of understanding, retaining, and utilizing the information. We retain about fifty percent of what we study.

*Paul wrote in II Timothy 2:15, **Be diligent** to present yourself approved to God, a worker who does not need to be ashamed, rightly dividing the word of truth. (p. 331).*

*What does study mean? It means getting a pencil and paper and recording the truths that God shows you as you study. It means asking questions and answering them. It means comparing verse with verse, looking up a topic and studying all you can about it. It means always asking the question, **"What does the Bible say about this subject?"*** [5] [Emphasis mine]

What does *II Timothy 2:15* in the **New** King James Version have to do with studying the Bible? This version has changed *study* to "be diligent." This particular translation gives a nice aid to help people spiritually, but it has no spiritual basis for doing so, since the NKJV deletes any reference to studying in the passage quoted to emphasize its point!

To add insult to injury, note the final question in bold. The revisers present the question: *what does the Bible say about this subject* – referring to any topic studied. However, answering the question concerning the topic at hand is more fun. The NKJV, along with every other modern perversion, removes the command to study; therefore, the answer to their question is as follows. The NKJV says **absolutely nothing about the subject of studying God's word!** The revisers quote the **right verse, but the wrong version.** Read the same verse in the **real** King James Bible, and you will see where the editors of this version got the idea to use this verse from Second Timothy to emphasize the importance of Bible study.

(KJB) II Timothy 2:15 Study to shew thyself approved unto God, a workman that needeth not to be ashamed, rightly dividing the word of truth.

One might classify this as the ultimate *faux pas*. However, it is neither the funniest nor the dumbest thing these revisers come up with. Here is another one. The Thomas Nelson advertising campaign sounds as evolutionary as Darwin's theories. We are continually evolving according to this advertisement.

*Every word of the New King James Version has been checked against the original **in light of the increasing knowledge about the Greek and Hebrew languages**. Nothing has been changed except to make the original meaning clear.* [6] [Emphasis mine]

In light of their claim to have increasing knowledge in the languages of Greek and Hebrew, has anyone told these publishers about the annual decline in ACT scores and the dumbing down of school standards? Or, better yet, has anyone informed them as to what the real Bible says concerning the last days? It is a matter of choice. Who are you going to believe . . . the counterfeiters or God? *"This know also, that in the last days perilous times shall come.* 2 *For men shall be lovers of their own selves ...7 ever learning, and never able to come to the knowledge of the truth." (II Timothy 3:1, 2, 7).*

Why no revival? Satan uses the domino effect. The standard advice given to the seminary student who then infects his congregation is as follows: *"The student's . . . goal must be to determine what God actually said and apply it to his life. To accomplish this he can rely on trustworthy translations and seek the aid of those who are acquainted with biblical languages."* [7] (That is: the ultimate authority rests with the Greek and Hebrew professors and the student's loyalty must always be to his alma mater.)

These Bible revisers claim to be making the Bible easier to understand. How is this goal accomplished when they remove the Bible's sole command to study and then make reference to a verse that has been corrupted in their version *(II Corinthians 2:17)* in order to teach people the importance of studying the Bible? The NKJV verse cited no longer remotely resembles a command to study. How did Thomas Nelson venture out in this "new" direction? Here is the answer, in their own words.[8]

In the early 1970's, there appeared to be a growing concern over the fact that the revisions of 1881, 1901, and 1952 had used a Greek text that largely ignored the great majority of biblical manuscripts. Some were concerned that the words of men had begun to change the Word of God, even if only in subtle ways.

The comments of the Thomas Nelson Publishers attack the English Revised Version (1881), the American Standard Version (1901), and the Revised Standard Version (1952) – stating that they did in fact use a different Greek text, ignoring the Majority Text of the King James Bible! Furthermore, take note that the last sentence recognizes the *subtlety* of the changes as designed by the instigator of all of this modernization *(Genesis 3:1).*

In 1975 Thomas Nelson Publishers, successor to the British firm that had first published the English Revised Version

(1885), the American Standard Version (1901), and the Revised Standard Version (1952), determined to assess the depth of this concern.

How convenient to attack these other versions that had already lost their market share! Notice that this excerpt makes no mention of any of the modern versions still heavily marketed by Thomas Nelson. It appears that these bible producers were instead assessing the depth of the pockets of their potential customers. Take note who is left out of the following list.

Because any revision of the Scriptures must meet the needs of the public worship, Christian education, personal reading and study, leading clergymen and lay Christians were invited to meetings in Chicago, Illinois, and Nashville, Tennessee, in 1975, and in London, England, in 1976, to discuss the need for a new revision. Almost one hundred church leaders from a broad spectrum of Christian churches attended those meetings.

*The expression of concern which **Nelson Bible editors** had been hearing for several years was confirmed by those in attendance. And there was a strong sentiment that the King James Bible should once more be sensitively revised in a way that would retain everything that could be retained of the text and language of that historic translation.*

*Each of the selected scholars signed a statement of faith, declaring his belief that **the Scriptures in their entirety are the uniquely inspired Word of God, free from error in the original autographs.*** (Emphasis mine)

Thomas Nelson Publishers worded the statement very carefully. They knew what they were doing. They eliminated the possibility that any Bible believer could attend this meeting. How? Everyone had to agree with the following statement: "the Scriptures in their entirety are the **uniquely** inspired Word of God, free from error in the **original autographs.**" No true Bible believer believes that the original autographs are *uniquely* free from error. He believes that God has preserved His word and not *uniquely* limited His perfection to the "originals." Anyone who signed this statement of exclusivity could not claim the King James Bible to be free from error because of the word *unique*. Thus, the scholars were freed from those pesky King James Bible believers.

What Saith the Scriptures?

Dr. Bill Grady, in his book *Final Authority*, gives a great illustration from the scripture as to why the true Bible believer will reject the NKJV as corrupt.

In II Samuel 23:9-10 and I Chronicles 11:12-14, we have the brief account of Eleazar's engagement with the Philistines. While Chronicles details the *spoil* of Eleazar's victory – *"a parcel of ground full of barley,"* Samuel divulges the *secret* of his success – *"and his hand clave unto the sword."*

From 1611 to 1881, God's foot soldiers wielded KJV swords while defending spiritual barley fields against Jesuits armed with the Douay-Rheims Version. Their grip grew tighter from 1881-1974 as one Alexandrian imposter after another was driven from the field.

Suddenly, a profit-oriented corporation (the same crowd who manufactured the *enemies'* swords) would prevail upon the church to believe that the Holy Spirit had abruptly ordered the *weapon change – in the very heat of battle!* Their corrupt rendering of Romans 1:25 says it best. Instead of the KJV's "changed" we read, "who exchanged the truth of God for a lie." A true Bible believer will never exchange his KJV for a NKJV.[9]

Dr. Grady continues to point out that, although the NKJV claims to be translated from the *Textus Receptus*, its departure to the corrupt Westcott and Hort readings is easily identifiable.

With the main English Scripture **supposedly** translated from the traditional *Textus Receptus*, 774 instances appear where two alternative Greek texts are presented for consideration. These are the Old Westcott and Hort readings, perpetrated by the Nestles/United Bible Societies text, designated as "NU" and the Hodges-Farstad-Nelson Majority Greek text, denoted by "M" in the footnotes.[10]

Dr. Grady, quoting Dr. D.A. Waite, states: *"Conservative estimates of the total translation changes in the NKJV are generally put at over 100,000! (This is an average of 82 changes for each of the 1219 pages in the NKJV.)"* [11]

That is a tremendous amount of change. However, when they slap *King James* on the title, they fool many Christians into believing that it is simply an updated KJB with some minor variations. The evidence proves otherwise. Here is another case in point – another "updated" King James Bible. This time they call it the *King James Version 2000*. What was the impetus behind another bible version? According to the *Citrus Chronicle* news article:

> *When Bob Curic was growing up and memorizing scrip-ture in the Southern Baptist Church, he stumbled over the "thees" and "thous," the "haths" and "wots" of the King James Version (KJV) of the Bible that was used in his Sunday School classes. As a teenager just as the Bible was beginning to be translated into modern language, he often wondered why some-one didn't just take the KJV and update it. After all, most people had already memorized many of the verses. Besides newer trans-lations lacked much of the poetry of the KJV.* [12]

Isn't that what the New King James Version translators claimed to be doing? The insanity will not stop until people realize that they have no business messing with God's word. Many of the changes in these *newer* "KJV's" align themselves with the most corrupt versions on the market – the New World Translation, the New Century Version, and the Contemporary English Version. We do not have time, nor space to deal with them all. However, the two following chapters address fur-ther textual corruption in the NKJV. Though not an exhaustive presentation on this subject, enough material is provided to enable any Bible student to make an informed decision.

Chapter 10 Endnotes

[1] D.A. Waite, *Defects in the NKJV*, (Collingswood, N.J.: Dean Burgon Society, 1988), p. 7.

[2] The Holy Bible, New King James Version (Nashville, Tenn.: Thomas Nelson, 1982), Introduction, page vi.

[3] Oswald T. Allis, *The New English Bible, The New Testament of 1961, A Comparative Study* (n.p., 1963), p. 69.

[4] Carter, *Things That are Different are Not the Same, op. cit.* p. 150.

[5] The New King James New Testament, Billy Graham Counselor's Edition. (Nashville, Tenn.: Thomas Nelson, 1979), p. 9.

[6] "Advertisement," *Moody Monthly*, June 1982, back cover.

[7] James B. Williams, ed, *From the Mind of God to the Mind of Man*, (Greenville, SC: Ambassador-Emerald International, 1999), p. 28.

[8] The Holy Bible, New King James Version (Nashville, Tenn.: Thomas Nelson, 1982), p. 1233-1234.

[9] William P. Grady, Ph.D., *Final Authority*, (Schererville, Ind.: Grady Publications, 1993), p. 303.

[10] *Ibid*, p. 304.

[11] *Ibid*, p. 305.

[12] The Citrus Chronicle, *King James Version 2000 Makes Language Plain*, February 10, 2001.

11

They Call This New?

No Bible believer should be deceived by the parading of great names in the field of Biblical "scholarship," when these very men are but the parrots of the rationalists of another century. The case they present is not their own but a modern presentation of an ancient heresy. By lowering the Bible from the heaven of its divinity to depraved earth they declare it to be but an ordinary book of mere human production. [1]
Ian Paisley

Thomas Nelson Publishers placed an advertisement on the back cover of the June 1982 *Moody Monthly Magazine* stating that "nothing has been changed except to make the original meaning clearer." [2] Thus began the "career" of one of the most insidious bibles ever to hit the market – the New King James Version.

Rather than making the Bible more understandable, the New King James Version often obscures or changes the meaning of biblical passages. The modern versions, including the NKJV, generally align themselves with one another. They incorporate parallel renderings of the scriptures which contradict corresponding passages found in the King James Bible. These modern versions also align themselves closely with the Christ-rejecting Jehovah's Witness version of the Bible, the New World Translation. To establish the pattern of corruption found in the modern translations, the following verse comparisons will include some or all of the following versions.

Versions compared, with respective first year of copyright:
King James Bible (KJB) – no financial copyright
New World Translation (NWT) – 1970
New International Version (NIV) – 1973
New King James Version (NKJV) – 1979
New Century Version (NCV) – 1987
Contemporary English Version (CEV) – 1995

Uncovering the changes to the NKJV is the main emphasis of the next two chapters. Take note that the changes incorporated into the text of the NKJV align it with not only the NIV, but also the corrupt NWT of the Jehovah's Witnesses.

Too Superstitious or Very Religious?

The book of Acts records Paul's missionary journeys. When the apostle arrives in Athens, he finds the people worshipping their false gods in the midst of Mars' hill.

(KJB) Acts 17:22 Then Paul stood in the midst of Mars' hill, and said, Ye men of Athens, I perceive that in all things ye are too superstitious.

Paul rebukes these people for having created a multitude of gods to govern every facet of life, and for even going so far as to create a "catch-all" idol inscribed TO THE UNKNOWN GOD. Paul declares this unknown God to them by preaching Jesus. He adamantly scolds them for being too superstitious – asserting that their beliefs were absurd. The New International Version changes the tone of this verse from one of *condemnation* to seeming *commendation* for dedicated religious service.

(NIV) Acts 17:22 Paul then stood up in the meeting of the Areopagus and said: "Men of Athens! I see that in every way you are very religious.

In some cases, being very religious can be commendable. For instance, it is a good thing to be very religious about going to church or praying consistently. Consider the example found four chapters earlier.

Those that were *religious* were persuading Paul and Barnabas to continue in the grace of God! *"...many of the Jews and religious proselytes followed Paul and Barnabas: who, speaking to them, persuaded them to continue in the grace of God" (Acts 13:43)*. Were they superstitious or religious?

With this first comparison, note that the NKJV retains much of the wording of its beloved predecessor, but aligns itself in meaning with the modern versions.

(NKJV) Acts 17:22 Then Paul stood in the midst of the Areopagus and said, "Men of Athens, I perceive that in all things you are very religious;

Two newer versions, the New Century Version (NCV) and the Contemporary English Version (CEV), also line up with the corrupt readings of the NIV and the NKJV. As we will see time and again, the King James Bible stands alone. Both the New Century Version and the Contemporary English Version follow the lead of their corrupt predecessors.

(NCV) Acts 17:22 Then Paul stood before the meeting of the Areopagus and said, "People of Athens, I can see you are very religious in all things.

(CEV) Acts 17:22 So Paul stood up in front of the council and said: People of Athens, I see that you are very religious.

These modern versions consistently agree in meaning with one another because they were produced or influenced by the same underlying manuscripts. The Greek and Hebrew used to produce the modern versions is not the Greek and Hebrew of the King James Bible.

Will Christ Sit on David's Throne?

(KJB) Acts 2:30 Therefore being a prophet, and knowing that God had sworn with an oath to him, that of the fruit of his loins, according to the flesh, he would raise up Christ to sit on his throne;

The KJB refers to the person of Christ sitting on the throne of David one day. This verse also highlights the resurrection of Christ, in reference to the future millennial reign of the Lord Jesus Christ. The NWT of the Jehovah's Witnesses completely obliterates these truths. This corrupt translation fails to reveal Who will sit on the throne of David and ignores the resurrection.

*(NWT) Acts 2:30 Therefore, because he was a prophet and knew that God had sworn to him with an oath that he would **seat one from the fruitage of his loins** upon his throne.*

The Christ-rejecting NWT of the Jehovah's Witnesses not only perverts the truth, but sounds absurd as well. The NIV, although not sounding so absurd, states that "one of his descendants" will sit on the throne. Christ is removed entirely from the verse (and from His rightful throne) in both of these modern versions.

*(NIV) Acts 2:30 But he was a prophet and knew that God had promised him on oath that he would place **one of his descendants** on his throne.*

Take note of the subtle change in the New King James Version.

*(NKJV) Acts 2:30 Therefore, being a prophet, and knowing that God had sworn with an oath to him that of the fruit of his body, according to the flesh, He would **raise up the Christ** to sit on his throne,*

Satan has instigated these changes to mislead. No matter how pure the motives of some of the revisers, Satan's goal is accomplished with the changes. The New King James Version says "the" Christ will sit on his throne. This particular wording denotes a position, rather than a Person – Jesus Christ. The end result cleverly removes Christ from His throne. Can you find Christ in the next two versions?

*(NCV) Acts 2:30 He was a prophet and knew God had promised him that he would make **a person from David's family** a king just as he was.*

Remember the modern versions must make enough changes in order to qualify for their respective copyrights. Can all of these variations have arisen from the Greek manuscript from which these versions claim to be derived? It is a money making scheme to dupe unsuspecting Christians and keep them and the lost in the dark concerning the truth.

*(CEV) Acts 2:30 But David was a prophet, and he knew that God had made a promise he would not break. He had told David that **someone from his family** would someday be king.*

What did God *really* say about the one who would sit upon the throne of David? Who will it be?

a) One from the fruitage of his loins
b) One of his descendants
c) The Christ
d) A person from David's family
e) Someone from his family
f) None of the above

During a test, no matter how close the answer (for instance, "c"), *none of the above* is still the correct answer. The Bible says that God promised to raise up **Christ** to sit on His throne. This is not *the* Christ or simply some person from David's family. No matter how many of the modern versions are compared, no two read exactly the same. Changes are necessary in order to justify a new copyright. No copyright means no control. No control means no money. No money, no profit, no stock sales!

Hell, Hades, or Simply the Grave?

Since *Acts 2:27* and *2:31* are very similar verses, they will be compared together. The previous verse attacks Christ's rightful place on the throne and ignores His resurrection. However, as any Bible believer knows, Christ was indeed resurrected. But, from where was the Son raised? According to the King James Bible, God raised His Son up from paradise, after He crossed over the great gulf from hell. The Bible student understands that the Lord tasted death for every man...even the eternal death of the lost in hell. *"But we see Jesus, who was made a little lower than the angels for **the suffering of death**, crowned with glory and honour; that he by the grace of God should **taste death for every man" (Hebrews 2:9).***

For this reason, when the Son of God died on the cross of Calvary, His soul went to hell and *tasted* the death of the lost. However, Jesus did not die for His own sins; therefore, hell could not hold Him. Furthermore, His body saw no corruption.

*(KJB) Acts 2:27 Because thou wilt not leave **my soul** in **hell**, neither wilt thou suffer thine Holy One to see **corruption**.*

*(KJB) Acts 2:31 He seeing this before spake of the resurrection of Christ, that **his soul** was not left in **hell**, neither **his flesh** did see **corruption**.*

One must recognize that two different entities are dealt with in these passages – the *soul* and the *flesh* of the Lord Jesus Christ. Christ's flesh did not corrupt in the sepulcher, neither was His soul left in hell. The Bible says that His soul was made an offering for sin. *"Yet it pleased the LORD to bruise him; he hath put him to grief: when **thou shalt make his soul an offering for sin...**" (Isaiah 53:10).* However, His soul was not left in hell, but the Father brought Him up. Some say Jesus only went into the paradise **part** of the heart of the earth. Were this the case, the plain teachings of scripture, which show that he went into the lower **parts** (plural) of the earth, would be violated. *"Now that he ascended, what is it but that he also descended first into the lower **parts** of the earth?" (Ephesians 4:9).* Let us return to the comparison.

The New World Translation's changing of hell to Hades is understandable since the Jehovah's Witnesses do not believe in the Lord Jesus Christ or in a literal hell.

*(NWT) Acts 2:27 because you will not leave **my soul** in **Hades**, neither will you allow your loyal one to see corruption.*

(NWT) Acts 2:31 he saw beforehand and spoke concerning the resurrection of the Christ, that neither was he forsaken in Hades nor did his flesh see corruption.

The Jehovah's Witnesses teach that a man's existence ends at the grave. Thus, followers of Jehovah's Witness doctrine are particularly difficult to reach with the gospel. Take note how the Jehovah's Witnesses reject the Lord in the second passage by referring to "the Christ." Now read the NIV and see what conclusions can be reached concerning these verses. No wonder the saved and lost alike are questioning the very existence of hell when hell is changed to the grave in so many versions. The NIV has no reference to **His soul** in **hell**, but changes the application to "me" and the "grave."

(NIV) Acts 2:27 because you will not abandon me to the grave, nor will you let your Holy One see decay.

(NIV) Acts 2:31 Seeing what was ahead, he spoke of the resurrection of the Christ, that he was not abandoned to the grave, nor did his body see decay.

Eventually, hell will be removed from the modern versions altogether. Hell has already been removed 40 times in the NIV, with the NIV addressing hell in only fourteen instances, compared with the KJB's 53. The 40 removals equate to 75% of the time! Satan does not want man to comprehend his fate, nor does he want man to consider the repercussions of rejecting Christ as Saviour.

In its introduction, the NKJV claims to make the King James Bible much clearer by *updating obsolete words. Hell* must be one of those obsolete words. The NKJV replaces the word *hell* 23 times with the words *Hades* and *Sheol.*

Webster's New Collegiate Dictionary defines *Hades* as the *"underground abode of the dead in Greek mythology."* Therefore, according to the dictionary, *hades* is not always a place of torment! For instance, the Assyrian *Hades* is an abode of blessedness with silver skies called

Happy Fields. Furthermore, the New Age Movement describes *hades* as an intermediate state of purification! Now read the NKJV.

*(NKJV) Acts 2:27 For You will not leave my soul in **Hades**, Nor will You allow Your Holy One to see **corruption**.*

*(NKJV) Acts 2:31 he, foreseeing this, spoke concerning the resurrection of **the Christ**, that His soul was not left in **Hades**, nor did His flesh see **corruption**.*

Hell is removed from the NKJV. What purpose, other than copyright justification, is served by changing *hell* to *Hades*? Is the Bible made clearer? Is the saint edified? Certainly not!

It is obvious from newer translations such as the NCV and the CEV that the modern versions are grasping for newer words. Like the NIV, the NCV uses the word *grave*, but replaces *decay* with the word *rot*.

*(NCV) Acts 2:27 because you will not leave **me** in the **grave**. You will not let your Holy One **rot**.*

*(NCV) Acts 2:31 Knowing this before it happened, David talked about **the Christ** rising from the dead. He said: 'He was not left in the **grave** his body did not **rot**.'*

Rot! Obviously, this is a new word used by a rotten translation vying for a new copyright. Can you imagine David referring to the Son, and saying that the Father would not let Him *rot*? The CEV, in this case, aligns itself with the words chosen by the NIV. On occasion, revisers can do this and still qualify for a new copyright – so long as other verses pick up the slack!

*(CEV) Acts 2:27 The Lord won't leave **me** in the **grave**. I am his holy one and he won't let my body **decay**.*

*(CEV) Acts 2:31 David knew this would happen, and so he told us that Christ would be raised to life. He said that God would not leave **him** in the **grave** or let his body **decay**.*

The versions have gone full circle. The modern versions have gone from *Hades* (NWT) to the *grave* (NIV), back to *Hades* (NKJV), and finally back to the *grave* (NCV & NEV). Of course, each translation claims to be clearer than the one before it. Clear as mud!

When someone mentions the most recognized passage in the Bible concerning hell, Luke chapter 16 usually comes to mind. Of course, this is the case only if you have not already traded in your King James Bible for the *"New" (Ecclessiastes 1:9) King James Version* or some other modern perversion. Read about the rich man:

> *(KJB) Luke 16:23 And in **hell** he lift up his eyes, being in **torments**, and seeth Abraham afar off, and Lazarus in his bosom.*

Consistent with its otherwise corrupt teachings, the NWT changes *hell* to *Hades*.

> *(NWT) Luke 16:23 And in **Hades** he lifted up his eyes, he existing in **torments**, and he saw Abraham afar off and Lazarus in the bosom (position) with him.*

How can one justify the NKJV's alignment with the doctrine of the Christ-rejecting Jehovah's Witnesses? The NKJV was supposed to have been produced by "fundamentalists" for fundamentalists. The bible publishers could not steal many of the faithful until they found a better disguise for their corrupt readings – then, along came the NKJV.

> *(NKJV) Luke 16:23 And being in **torments** in **Hades**, he lifted up his eyes and saw Abraham afar off, and Lazarus in his bosom.*

I cannot imagine any preacher worth his weight in salt standing in the pulpit and preaching about the rich man in *Hades*! Maybe it goes something like this: "Our message today is on...*Hades!!!* Turn in your *New* King James Versions to Luke chapter 16 and we will begin reading." Next comes a big yawn from the audience. Even the lost will be falling asleep on that one. No wonder Satan has finally achieved his ultimate objective – to create such confusion and discord that everyone will point his fingers at someone else.

Let us next examine the versions produced in the 1980's and 90's. No longer do the versions discuss *hell* or even *Hades*. Instead, in these newest versions, hell has become *the place of the dead!*

> *(NCV) Luke 16:23 In the place of the dead, he was in much pain. The rich man saw Abraham far away with Lazarus at his side.*

How can anyone justify this further perversion of truth? God warned us thousands of years ago not to change His word. What happens when we accept a small change? *"A little leaven leaveneth the whole lump" (Galatians 5:9).* When one allows for a little change, the floodgates soon open. Satan is never satisfied with a small perversion of the truth. His ultimate goal is the condemnation of man. These versions are the very tools capable of making his ultimate goal all the more attainable.

Notice that *torments* is changed to *pain* also. There is a significant difference between these two. Pain can be something as simple as a mild headache. *Torment* connotes a much greater degree of suffering. Likewise, implicit with the use of the word *torment* is an understanding that such suffering is actively inflicted upon the recipient.

Since Luke chapter 16 is the most-preached passage concerning *hell* in the King James Bible, consider another portion of this chapter. The most descriptive terminology in the Bible describing hell is also provided here. The KJB's depiction of hell as a place of torment is powerful, convincing, and revealing in this passage. The rich man in hell (or *Hades, the grave,* or *the place of the dead*) is in torment and wants to warn his five brothers. He does not want them to also go to hell (or *Hades, the grave,* or *the place of the dead*).

> *(KJB) Luke 16:28 For I have five brethren; that he may testify unto them, lest they also come into this place of torment.*

For this verse, we will compare only the most extreme versions. When reading the two most modern versions, if this subject were not so serious, it would be funny. Instead of *hell* being referred to as a *place of torment*, the NCV describes *the place of the dead* as a *place of pain*. How ridiculous! The word of God conveys the only truth we know about God, salvation, eternal life, and damnation.

(NCV) Luke 16:28 I have five brothers, and Lazarus could warn them so that they will not come to this place of pain.'

No matter how ridiculous the changes, there seems to be no limit to them. Once again, the modern translators have run out of words. Now, *hell – the place of torment – is just a horrible place*. The slums in some inner cities could fit the same description, but they are not hell. Some third world countries contain horrible places, but these locations are not hell. No one could label any of these places "this place of torment."

(CEV) Luke 16:28 Let him warn my five brothers, so they won't come to this horrible place."

No wonder preaching has lost its power. Preachers have no hope for power from God in their preaching when they use one of these modern versions (even for comparative purposes). There is no conviction and no light. There is no comparison, no Bible study. However, the confusion continues to run rampant.

First Corinthians refers to death and its aftermath. The body is placed in the grave. The King James Bible correctly uses the word *grave*, while the NKJV changes grave to *Hades* in this passage. We have already seen that the NKJV changed *hell* to Hades, and now it changes *grave* to Hades. Is one to draw some type of parallel? Is the grave really hell, as the Jehovah's Witnesses proclaim and as the NKJV purports?

First, consider the background: When the Apostle Paul begins to reflect on the day when the mortal bodies **of the saved** will be changed into their glorified bodies, he has reason to shout. One of the greatest accounts given is found in the book of First Corinthians. Paul says to the Christian, *"...We shall not all sleep, but we shall all be changed, 52 In a moment, in the twinkling of an eye, at the last trump: for the trumpet shall sound, and the dead shall be raised incorruptible, and we shall* *be changed. 53 For this corruptible must put on incorruption, and this mortal must put on immortality"* **(I Corinthians 15:51-53).**

He continues: *"So when this corruptible shall have put on incorruption, and this mortal shall have put on immortality, then shall be brought to pass the saying that is written, Death is swallowed up in victory"* **(I Corinthians 15:54).** When the Lord returns for those that are His, death and the grave will lose their strength because Christians will go to heaven without dying.

(KJB) I Corinthians 15:55 *O death, where is thy sting? O* **grave,** *where is thy victory?*

Christians living at the time of the rapture will never experience *death*; therefore, *death* and the *grave* will lose their power over the child of God, just as *hell* loses its power over the Christian at the moment of salvation.

Once again, the NKJV must incorporate enough changes to justify the issuance of a new copyright. The authors decided to change the *grave* to *Hades*! These changes are made at the expense of truth and Bible doctrine. This change is heretical when it is combined with the rich man in *Hades* in Luke chapter 16.

(NKJV) I Corinthians 15:55 *"O Death, where is your sting? O* **Hades,** *where is your victory?"*

The consequences of these combined changes are incomprehensible. Confusion results when the lost rich man of Luke chapter 16 is found in the very place (Hades) that the saved Christian feared until the point of the rapture (Hades)! This is doctrinally unsound. Long before the rapture, the Christian does not have to be concerned about hell (or *Hades,* or *the place of the dead!*). To indicate otherwise is to place doubt upon the doctrine of eternal security, the efficacy of the cross, and the blood atonement.

For the sake of conciseness, a simple list of similar NKJV changes should suffice. The NKJV removes *hell* in all of the following passages:

II Samuel 22:6, Job 11:8, Job 26:6, Psalm 16:10, Psalm 18:5, Psalm 86:13, Psalm 116:3, Isaiah 5:14, Isaiah 14:15, Isaiah 28:15, Isaiah 28:18, Isaiah 57:9, Jonah 2:2, Matthew 11:23, Matthew 16:18, Luke 10:15, Luke 16:23, Acts 2:27, Acts 2:31, Revelation 1:18, Revelation 6:8, Revelation 20:13, and Revelation 20:14.

Many of these other verses could be studied in more depth, but the core problem has been already thoroughly identified. It has been said that anyone trying to *air condition* hell is probably getting ready to move in there. What conclusion may be drawn concerning a person attempting to get rid of it altogether? Not only are they going there, but they are causing others to join them.

Jesus Accepts Worship

Satan knows the scripture better than we do. The Lord rebuked him for seeking worship. *"And Jesus answered and said unto him, Get thee behind me, Satan: for it is written, **Thou shalt worship the Lord thy God,** and him only shalt thou serve" (Luke 4:10).* Satan hated these words because he desires more than anything to be worshipped. He hates the Lord and does not want man to worship Him at all. The Devil also knows that the Lord's acceptance of worship is a proof of His deity. The alternatives are sobering. If He accepted worship and was not God, He was an imposter.

*(KJB) Matthew 20:20 Then came to him the mother of Zebedee's children with her sons, **worshipping him,** and de-siring a certain thing of him.*

In typical fashion, the Jehovah's Witness version sets a precedent by making drastic changes. It changes worship to obeisance!

*(NWT) Matthew 20:20 Then the mother of the sons of Zebedee approached him with her sons, doing **obeisance** and asking for something from him.*

The NIV follows the trend of the Jehovah's Witnesses and steals worship away from the Saviour, too.

(NIV) Matthew 20:20 Then the mother of Zebedee's sons came to Jesus with her sons and, **kneeling down**, asked a favor of him.

The NWT, NIV, and NKJV are three peas in a pod! The NKJV follows the suit of the two previous corruptions. One person's kneeling down before another does not necessarily indicate that the first person is worshipping the second.

(NKJV) Matthew 20:20 Then the mother of Zebedee's sons came to Him with her sons, **kneeling down** and asking something from Him.

Remember the copyright! Further translations cannot simply say "kneeling down"…two of the other versions have already used those words. Instead, in the newest versions, Zebedee's wife just *bows* down.

(NCV) Matthew 20:20 Then the wife of Zebedee came to Jesus with her sons. She **bowed before him** and asked him to do something for her.

Remember the copyright requirements. This time, the past tense of the NIV and the NKJV will suffice – she *knelt* down.

(CEV) Matthew 20:20 The mother of James and John came to Jesus with her two sons. She **knelt down** and started **begging** him to do something for her.

We have moved from obeisance (NWT), to kneeling down (NIV, NKJV), to bowing before him (NCV), and now to kneeling down…and begging (CEV). Another copyright granted – more money should be flowing in soon! Satan knows that begging for something does not bring to mind the act of worship. Had the earliest modern versions never paved the way, the current changes could not have become so radical.

God Laid down His Life

The book of First John provides another of the great verses proving the deity of the Lord Jesus Christ.

(KJB) I John 3:16 *Hereby perceive we the love of **God**, because* ***he*** *laid down his life for us: and we ought to lay down our lives for the brethren.*

He (God) laid down His life for us. Thank God for this clear-cut proof of the deity of the Lord Jesus Christ. After reading this verse, one cannot question the fact that Jesus is God. Unless, of course, one uses the NWT, NIV, NKJV, NCV, CEV, or any of a host of other modern versions.

(NWT) I John 3:16 *By this we have come to know love, because **that one** surrendered his soul for us; and we are under obligation to surrender our souls for our brothers.*

God is gone! The Christ-rejecting NWT gives no indication of who laid down His life. One can understand the justification underlying this change. The Jehovah's Witnesses do not hide their hatred for the Lord Jesus Christ when they refer to Him as *a god* in *John 1:1*. But one would think that the NIV and all of the other "Christian-produced" versions would be more protective of the verses that substantiate the Lord's deity.

(NIV) I John 3:16 *This is how we know what love is: **Jesus Christ** laid down his life for us. And we ought to lay down our lives for our brothers.*

The NIV follows suit by naming Jesus Christ, thus eliminating clear documentation of the Lord's deity. The NIV no longer enables the reader to use this verse to prove that Jesus Christ is God. What about the NKJV that is supposed to be a "modernized" King James Bible? Par for the course! This time, *God* is missing altogether.

(NKJV) I John 3:16 *By this we know love, because **He** laid down His life for us. And we also ought to lay down our lives for the brethren.*

Did God lay down His life on the cross of Calvary? All of the modern versions attack this clear proof of the Lord's deity by watering down the text. The NCV and the CEV bring Jesus back (as does their sister NIV), but neither provides any proof of Christ's deity in this passage.

(NCV) I John 3:16 This is how we know what real love is: Jesus gave his life for us. So we should give our lives for our brothers and sisters.

(CEV) I John 3:16 We know what love is because Jesus gave his live for us. That's why we must give our lives for each other.

The modern versions claim to *contain* the major doctrines; and, in some cases, this is true. However, Bible corruption is a process. Initially, not every instance of a particular doctrine is removed from a given version. Satan knows that patience is the key to deception. The perversion of truth occurs one step at a time *(Proverbs 22:28)*. The Devil could not have produced and sold the NCV or the CEV twenty years ago. The world was not yet ready to accept them, without first experiencing the influence of earlier, pioneering bible revisions (perversions). The changes found in the NCV and CEV would have been considered far too pervasive when the earliest versions appeared on the market decades ago.

Too many people in decades gone by would have stood up and condemned these versions. They would have noticed the verse changes, and yelled: "The blood's gone; the gospel's gone; preaching's gone; the deity is gone; the virgin birth is gone. Throw this piece of junk in the trash can." But these versions sell well today to those who have been gradually weaned off the truth by subtle and gradual changes incorporated into the earlier modern versions.

A person who reads the NIV will likely pick up the NCV and not recognize the serious problems. However, a person that reads and studies the KJB will see many problems with the NCV and will not likely be deceived by the Hollywood hype surrounding such versions. The Holy Spirit can still reveal glaring errors in the modern versions when they are compared with the KJB.

Individuals who use these modern versions have no idea of the magnitude of difference between what their bibles say and what they *should* say. However, a person who jumps from using the KJB to reading the NCV or CEV will liken the difference to moving from day to night. The glaring degree of apostasy in the modern versions is evident to such an individual.

When God's Wrath is Revealed

We are commanded to study the word *(II Timothy 2:15)*. The King James Bible says that God's wrath is *not* revealed all of the time. It is *not* revealed against *all* unrighteousness. With a little study of the next passage, one can easily understand when God's wrath *is* revealed against man.

(KJB) Romans 1:18 For the wrath of God is revealed from heaven against all ungodliness and unrighteousness of men, who hold the truth in unrighteousness;

God's wrath is revealed against all the ungodliness and unrighteousness of people *who hold* (possess) *the truth* and nevertheless live unrighteously. These possessors of the truth evidently ignore the light of the truth and continue to participate in unrighteous acts, and God judges them for it.

Citizens of the United States should heed this warning. More so than any other nation in the world, people of the United States should recognize God's warning as directly applicable to them. We Americans have held the word of God for centuries. Today, more than ever, we are holding it *in unrighteousness* and God's wrath is being revealed against us more and more. Look at the corruption in our three branches of government. Look at our less desirable weather patterns, rampant crime rates, the break up of the family, and the acceptance of perversion as the norm. We are a guilty nation; we hold the truth in unrighteousness. The judgment of God awaits around the corner.

Does the Christ-rejecting NWT convey this same truth? Does it warn those that are holding the truth in unrighteousness? No, it changes the meaning of this verse entirely.

(NWT) Romans 1:18 For God's wrath is being revealed from heaven against all ungodliness and unrighteousness of men who are suppressing the truth in an unrighteous way,

The Jehovah's Witnesses change the truth into a lie. Their version no longer asserts that the wrath of God comes upon all those who simply *hold* the truth in unrighteousness. Instead, their translation changes this warning to be applicable only to those who *suppress* the truth. This change really becomes somewhat humorous because the rebuke is additionally limited to those that suppress the truth "in an unrighteous way." I guess if they were more righteous in their suppression of the truth, this would be acceptable!? Either way, the authors of this change fall under the preceding warning because, as they change the truth, they suppress it too. However, no matter what these Christ-rejecting infidels say, God's wrath is not limited to those who suppress His truth. Who do the NIV and NKJV align themselves with . . . the truth or the Jehovah's Witnesses?

(NIV) Romans 1:18 The wrath of God is being revealed from heaven against all the godlessness and wickedness of men who suppress the truth by their wickedness,

(NKJV) Romans 1:18 For the wrath of God is revealed from heaven against all ungodliness and unrighteousness of men, who suppress the truth in unrighteousness,

The NIV and the NKJV follow the example of the Jehovah's Witnesses, an unholy alliance which alone should raise red flags! However, most modern versions go even further in their destruction of truth. The NCV says that God's anger is shown against all of the bad things people do. Each of us should be thankful that this is not really the word of God and that God's anger is not always manifested as they claim.

(NCV) Romans 1:18 God's anger is shown from heaven against all the evil and wrong things people do.

The NCV completely eliminates God's mercy, grace, and longsuffering. The CEV reverts to the suppression of the truth taught by the corrupt NWT, NIV, and NKJV. However, it embraces new terminology.

(CEV) Romans 1:18 From heaven God shows how angry he is with all the wicked and evil things that sinful people do to crush the truth.

Ignore this lie! **God's judgment comes against all those that have the truth and yet remain unrighteous.** Although the modern versions limit this application, God does not. Crime, wickedness, divorce, and abortion rates have steadily increased since 1963 when the United States Supreme Court began making new laws by ignoring legal precedent. Their goal seemed to be to rid the public of the influence of Christianity. The United States has not been the power it once was since that time. As a nation, America is guilty of holding the truth in unrighteousness. As a country, we have experienced and are experiencing a taste of God's judgment for that very reason.

Changing the Truth of God into a Lie

The Bible warns that God will give up to uncleanness any people that change the truth of God into a lie.

(KJB) Romans 1:25 Who changed the truth of God into a lie, and worshipped and served the creature more than the Creator, who is blessed for ever. Amen.

America is guilty once again. For instance, almost every state in the nation once had laws recognizing sodomy and pornography as illegal. Today, *hate crime laws* have been enacted to give legal protection to sodomites, while lawyers claim the First Amendment to protect the "rights" of those who distribute illicit trash. We have legitimized that which God condemns in His book. **We have changed the truth of God into a lie** by claiming that sodomy is merely an alternative lifestyle and that the rights of pornographers are equal to the rights of legitimate authors. No wonder our schools graduate the illiterate and have become killing grounds for teens and preteens alike.

God admonishes those who possess the truth and then *change* the truth into a lie. Instead, the NWT gives a completely different connotation in this passage.

*(NWT) Romans 1:25 even those who **exchanged** the truth of God for the lie and venerated and rendered sacred service to the creation rather than the One who created, who is blessed forever. Amen.*

Instead of warning those busy *changing* the truth, the NWT directs its rebuke against those who pick up the lies of these modern versions and use them. *Changing the truth* is a much more serious offense than *exchanging the truth* for the lie created by someone else. Of course, the NIV follows the course charted by the NWT. **In contrast, the KJB warns the perpetrator and condemns his actions.** The modern versions condemn those who may innocently exchange the truth (KJB) for a lie (NWT, NIV, NKJV, NCV, CEV, etc.).

*(NIV) Romans 1:25 They **exchanged** the truth of God for a lie, and worshiped and served created things rather than the Creator-who is forever praised. Amen.*

The NKJV follows suit.

*(NKJV) Romans 1:25 who **exchanged** the truth of God for the lie, and worshiped and served the creature rather than the Creator, who is blessed forever. Amen.*

The NCV uses new words, but basically follows the same path taken by the corruptions that preceded it.

*(NCV) Romans 1:25 They **traded** the truth for a lie. They worshipped and served what had been created instead of the God who created those things, who should be praised forever. Amen.*

The CEV decided to dig into the depths of the "original Greek!" What did they find? They gave up the truth. Again, the CEV attacks the innocent victim rather than the perpetrator. These bible producers must wear out the thesaurus trying to find the synonyms.

*(CEV) Romans 1:25 They **gave up** the truth about God for a lie, and they worshipped God's creation instead of God, who will be praised forever. Amen.*

God warns those that change the truth of God into a lie. The modern translations change this truth into something God did not say and rebuke all those that exchange or trade the truth (KJB) for the lie perpetrated by the modern versions. The difference between *changing* and *exchanging* would be equivalent to condemning the innocent recipient of a counterfeit bill, rather than the one creating the counterfeit. Which book stands alone?

KJB = changed
NWT = exchanged
NIV= exchanged
NKJV = exchanged
NCV = traded
CEV = gave up

What do you prefer? Take your pick. All of the versions stand together in solidarity against the King James Bible. Has the version that God has blessed above all others, the KJB, been lying all of this time and only now do we have its true meaning or meanings? Or has the Devil finally been able to convince enough greedy people to change the truth into a lie? No wonder we do not have the great and wonderful revivals of past generations – the lies of Satan are designed to destroy revival!

Chapter 11 Endnotes

[1] Ian Paisley, *My Plea for the Old Sword*, (Belfast Northern Ireland, 1997), p. 13, 14.
[2] Advertisement, *Moody Magazine*, (820 N. LaSalle Boulevard, Chicago, IL 60610, June 1982).

12

No New Thing under the Sun

Truth is not only violated by falsehood. It may be equally out-raged by silence.

Henri Frederic Armiel

Anyone who attacks the cross does so because he thinks the cross is a foolish thing. God says that such a person finds it silly because he is still spiritually lost. True preaching always magnifies the significance of the cross. In this chapter, like the previous chapter, we will be making comparisons directly to the Jehovah's Witnesses' New World Translation (NWT) – the most insidious of all the modern versions. Once this cultic bible version is compared to the standard, the other modern versions will be compared to it.

*(KJB) I Corinthians 1:18 For the **preaching** of the **cross** is to them that perish foolishness; but unto us which **are saved** it is the power of God.*

Do you want a bible that aligns itself with something that replaces the cross with a *torture stake*? Hopefully not!

*(NWT) I Corinthians 1:18 For the **speech** about the **torture stake** is foolishness to those who are perishing, but to us who are **being saved** it is God's power.*

How can anyone justify producing a bible that aligns itself with the Christ-rejecting New World Translation? The importance of preaching is diminished (and simply called speech); the cross is eliminated (and changed to the torture stake); and salvation is taught as a process (one is *being* saved). Some reader enamored of the modern versions might assert that at least they don't go as far as the NWT. But how far is far enough?

(NIV) I Corinthians 1:18 For the message of the cross is foolishness to those who are perishing, but to us who are being saved it is the power of God.

The NIV agrees with two out of the three changes in the New World Translation. Preaching is deleted in the NIV. But, instead of using the word *speech* as the NWT does, the NIV uses the word *message*. Both the NWT and NIV agree that a person is *being saved* (a process). However, the authors of the NIV would not have been so foolish as to follow the NWT's example and insert the terminology of the *torture stake*. The "Christian bibles" must leave the cross in the text although they delete *Calvary (Luke 23:33)*. Thus, the damage is still done. The supremacy of preaching is lessened and the verse now teaches salvation as a process. Ditto for the New King James Version.

(NKJV) I Corinthians 1:18 For the message of the cross is foolishness to those who are perishing, but to us who are being saved it is the power of God.

Answer this question: Do you know that you have eternal life? If you answered "yes," then you are not *being saved*. This verse alone may be sufficient to convince a baby Christian that he must work to stay "saved." The cults know how to use these so-called bibles more effectively to gain converts to their false teachings than lazy Christians who have the truth and know the truth, but fail to stand up for it. The New Century Version (NCV) had to produce further changes in order to secure its copyright.

(NCV) I Corinthians 1:18 The teaching about the cross is foolishness to those who are being lost, but to us who are being saved it is the power of God.

Evidently, the Contemporary English Version (CEV) had enough differences to qualify for that copyright and could use the same changes as the NIV and NKJV. Of course, "the cross doesn't make any sense to lost people" was enough of a change to qualify. Do you see what they are doing?

> *(CEV) I Corinthians 1:18 The message about the cross doesn't make any sense to lost people. But for those of us who are being saved, it is God's power at work.*

The only thing lost is the truth! Every preacher should be Christ-like. He should elevate preaching and preach that salvation is a point in time when a person accepts the Saviour and becomes *a new creature (II Corinthians 5:17)*. He does not become a new *creation* (NIV, NKJV, etc.) over a process of time.

Blasphemous Trash

The all-*wise* God (*Jude 25*, but not if you read an NIV), proclaims that preaching is foolish. To have one man stand up and rant and rave out of the same book week after week seems foolish to an unregenerate world. However, God chose this *foolish* method to save man.

> *(KJB) I Corinthians 1:21 For after that in the wisdom of God the world by wisdom knew not God, it pleased God by the foolishness of preaching to save them that believe.*

The NWT changes the object of the foolishness from *the act of preaching* to *that which is preached*. This is downright blasphemy!

> *(NWT) I Corinthians 1:21 For since, in the wisdom of God, the world through its wisdom did not get to know God. God saw good through the foolishness of what is preached to save those believing.*

Of course, we know that the editors of the NWT must find preaching about the cross foolish because they change it to the torture stake. One must consider the implications of the NIV's agreeing with the Jehovah's Witness bible concerning that which is preached.

*(NIV) I Corinthians 1:21 For since in the wisdom of God the world through its wisdom did not know him, God was pleased through the **foolishness of what was preached** to save those who believe.*

Unless you consider what is being said very carefully, you may miss the point. What is a preacher preaching? The blood...the cross...the Saviour...the virgin birth...godly living, etc. It is blasphemy to call these things foolish! Yet, Christians are not aware that their bibles show such a disregard for preaching. The NKJV joins ranks with the NWT and the NIV to blaspheme our Saviour and His work, as well.

*(NKJV) I Corinthians 1:21 For since, in the wisdom of God, the world through wisdom did not know God, it pleased God through the **foolishness of the message preached** to save those who believe.*

The NCV needed its copyright; note the resultant changes.

*(NCV) I Corinthians 1:21 In the wisdom of God the world did not know God through its own wisdom. So God chose to use the **message that sounds foolish** to save those who believe.*

The CEV uses similar measures.

*(CEV) I Corinthians 1:21 God was wise and decided not to let the people of this world use their wisdom to learn about him. Instead, God chose to save only those who believe **the foolish message** we preach.*

The message is not foolish! The method chosen of God is! One should not view a man or woman who believes in the authority and supremacy of one book as a weirdo or a fanatic. Rather, such a person should be thanked for keeping the battle going *(I Timothy 6:12)* and not being weary in well doing *(II Thessalonians 3:13)*. However, the Bible believer should *not* berate someone unfamiliar with the differences either. *"Brethren, if a man be overtaken in a fault, ye which are*

spiritual, restore such an one in the spirit of meekness; consider-
ing thyself, lest thou also be tempted" *(Galatians 6:1).*

Doctrine Changed to Teaching

Paul preached doctrine. Bible doctrines refer to sound teaching based
on the word of God. The Bible calls this doctrine the doctrine of the
Lord. In other words, Paul preached the Lord's doctrine, not his own.

*(KJB) Acts 13:12 Then the **deputy**, when he saw what was
done, believed, being astonished at **the doctrine of the Lord.***

All of the modern versions claim to make the Bible easier to understand. It is hard to identify where the modern versions make the Bible
easier to comprehend, considering the changes they have introduced.
How is clarity achieved by changing *deputy* to *proconsul?* Certainly one
would not claim that the New World Translation makes the word of God
any clearer or easier to understand.

*(NWT) Acts 13:12 Then the **proconsul**, upon seeing what had
happened, became a believer, and he was astounded at **the
teaching of Jehovah.***

If the NWT is *not* easier to understand, then neither is the NIV. The
NIV follows the example set by its predecessor, the NWT. Why do both
versions use the same word? Could it be that they arise from the same
source? At least the NIV does not change Lord to Jehovah. But it does
remove *the doctrine of the Lord* by changing it into *the teaching about
the Lord.* Doctrine is a Bible word with spiritual connotations!

*(NIV) Acts 13:12 When the **proconsul** saw what had happened,
he believed, for he was amazed at **the teaching about the Lord.***

Ditto concerning the NKJV. Instead of using the word *about*, the
NKJV changes this verse to read "*of* the Lord." Just another effort to
attain a copyright! A few words altered here and there produces two
different bibles, two separate copyrights, and twice the publication profits.

*(NKJV) Acts 13:12 Then the **proconsul** believed, when he saw what had been done, being astonished at **the teaching of the Lord.***

The NKJV changes the wording to *the teaching of the Lord*. When reading this verse, one wonders: "Who is teaching?" Was the Lord giving one of His famous sermons, or was the Apostle Paul preaching? No wonder people are confused about the Bible.

Now we move forward to the versions produced in the 1980's and 90's. These newest versions shift from using either *deputy* or *proconsul* to deciding on *governor*. It is difficult to discern exactly what this man's title really was. Read a few other versions not addressed herein and see what other words these bible editions have used.

*(NCV) Acts 13:12 When the **governor** saw this, he believed because he was amazed at the **teaching** of the Lord.*

*(CEV) Acts 13:12 When the **governor** saw what had happened, he was amazed at this **teaching** about the Lord. So he put his faith in the Lord.*

A person should be dogmatic about the doctrines of the Lord. Paul was. He did not waiver on these doctrines. The whole emphasis in the modern versions has changed from a dogmatic faith to a superficial type of belief. We need to be dogmatic about Bible doctrines – such as the infallibility of scripture, God's mercy and grace, eternal security of the believer, and man's responsibility to live holy. These are Bible truths (from the old black Book) that have convicted the sinner, converted the soul, and kept the Christian's walk with God on an even keel for millennia.

All Modern Versions Peddle the Word

During the first century, the supposed "oldest and best" manuscripts were being corrupted. Therefore, the age of the manuscript does not automatically impart to it credibility, as proponents of the modern versions would have one believe. See footnotes attached to the passages they claim to clarify. As a matter of fact, the older the manuscript, the longer it has lasted. In all likelihood, such a manuscript may owe its longevity to its rejection by the church. Manuscripts regularly used by the church were worn out, recopied, and burned. "Oldest and *best*" is more aptly dubbed "oldest and *worst*."

> **(KJB) II Corinthians 2:17** *For we are not as many, which* **corrupt** *the word of God: but as of sincerity, but as of God, in the sight of God speak we in Christ.*

Thank God for His promises concerning His word. The true word of God is *incorruptible* **(I Peter 1:23 KJB).** However, during the first century, some scribes were already busy trying to confuse the brethren and destroy the faith. None of the modern versions own up to this truth, but again make themselves doubly guilty. They not only corrupt the true word of God, but also transgress their own new standard by *peddling* their particular version of the bible. Notice how the birds of a feather flock together.

> **(NWT) II Corinthians 2:17** *We are; for we are* **not peddlers** *of the word of God as many men are, but as out of sincerity, yes, as sent from God, under God's view, in company with Christ, we are speaking.*

> **(NIV) II Corinthians 2:17** *Unlike so many, we do not* **peddle** *the word of God for profit. On the contrary, in Christ we speak before God with sincerity, like men sent from God.*

> **(NKJV) II Corinthians 2:17** *For we are not, as so many,* **peddling** *the word of God; but as of sincerity, but as from God, we speak in the sight of God in Christ.*

> **(NCV) II Corinthians 2:17** *We do not sell the word of God* **for a profit** *as many other people do. But in Christ we speak the truth before God, as messengers of God.*

Are we to believe that they do not sell the New Century Version for a profit?!! I guess these bible publishers want to convince us that publication of the NCV was simply a labor of love. Now, read the 1995 version:

*(CEV) II Corinthians 2:17 A lot of people try to get **rich from preaching** God's message. But we are God's sincere messengers, and by the power of Christ we speak our message with God as our witness.*

It almost seems a waste of time and energy to comment further on these modern perversions. They are all peddling and they are all using corrupt manuscripts. They certainly do *not* all say the same thing. The CEV may have a valid point, but it seems quite hypocritical to emphasize the preacher's sin, while ignoring its own shortcomings.

God Cares about Appearances

Satan does not want dedicated Christians living up to the standards God sets forth in His word. Although addressed earlier, here is one such case in point.

*(KJB) I Thessalonians 5:22 Abstain from all **appearance of evil**.*

It is clear that God demands a high standard of living once a person has accepted Christ. Not only does He expect a person to live above the wickedness of this world, but he also expects us to be conscious of our testimony at all times. For this reason, we are to abstain from everything that even looks suspicious of sin. In the KJB, God commands us to abstain from even the appearance of evil. Compare this command with what is found in the modern versions. This time, four additional comparisons are provided to emphasize the insanity of the modern translations.

*(NWT) I Thessalonians 5:22 Abstain from every **form** of wickedness.*

*(NIV) I Thessalonians 5:22 Avoid every **kind** of evil.*

*(NKJV) I Thessalonians 5:22 Abstain from every **form** of evil.*

*(NCV) I Thessalonians 5:22 and stay away from **everything** that is evil.*

(CEV) I Thessalonians 5:22 and don't have anything to do with evil.

Each version must have unique qualities to qualify for a copyright. Take notice that every one of these modern versions fails to proclaim God's true expectations. Their proclamations limit the warning only to those things that are evil or wicked in themselves, rather than including the things that have a simple appearance of evil. Sin abounds because the modern versions fail to adequately warn against the wiles of the Devil.

For instance, a young teenage boy inviting a girl to his home without any parental supervision is not evil in and of itself. Yet, it certainly has the potential to destroy the reputation of each of them. It also can lead to some very serious problems created by an enticing environment. On the contrary, if we teach our children to live by the higher standard of the word of God (KJB), they will not find themselves in the precarious situations that cause many unwanted pregnancies, spread sexually transmitted diseases, and destroy many an innocent reputation and life.

The Love of Money

As we have already seen, the modern versions have a real problem revealing God's explicit warnings concerning money, getting gain, and an inordinate affection for the same.

*(KJB) I Timothy 6:5 Perverse disputings of men of corrupt minds, and destitute of the truth, **supposing that gain is godliness**: from such withdraw thyself.*

We are to withdraw ourselves from anyone that thinks that gain (the accumulation of wealth) *proves* the godliness of an individual or group. If the amount owned is an indication of godliness, then everyone should join the Roman Catholic Church. According to figures compiled in June 1965, the Roman Catholic Church had accumulated a minimum of $80 billion in real estate in the United States. [1]

Better yet, if wealth is the draw, join fellowship with the Jehovah's Witnesses or the Mormon Church. These entities also have amassed great wealth, though not to the extent of the Catholic Church.

The NWT does not warn you to separate from anyone. This is standard operating procedure for the shallow type of un-biblical modern Christianity condoned and promoted today. Unity at all costs!

*(NWT) I Timothy 6:5 violent disputes about trifles on the part of men corrupted in mind and despoiled of the truth, thinking that **godly devotion is a means of gain.***

The KJB warns us to withdraw from any individual who thinks a person's wealth signifies his spiritual station. The NWT makes no such pronouncement and gives no warning. Instead, the NWT makes a contradictory statement. It warns against those that think "godly devotion is not a means of gain." Is it not? Living for God should be encouraged as the only means of gain. Notice how the NIV aligns itself with the NWT.

*(NIV) I Timothy 6:5 and constant friction between men of corrupt mind, who have been robbed of the truth and who think that **godliness is a means to financial gain.***

Likewise, the NKJV aligns itself with both the NWT and the NIV.

*(NKJV) I Timothy 6:5 useless wranglings of men of corrupt minds and destitute of the truth, who suppose that **godliness is a means of gain.** From such withdraw yourself.*

These versions rebuke someone that thinks that godliness is a means to gain. When in actuality, godliness should be the only means of gain. The alternative is to ascribe ungodliness as the only means of gain. This is not true in all cases – there are some men and women that have gained wealth by living a spiritual life. Praise God! This time, the next two corrupt versions are closer to conveying some truth than the NIV, NKJV, and NWT combined.

(NCV) I Timothy 6:5 and constant quarrels from those who have evil minds and have lost the truth. They think that serving God is a way to get rich.

(CEV) I Timothy 6:5 and nasty quarrels. They have wicked minds and have missed out on the truth. These people think religion is supposed to make you rich.

The King James Bible says one thing, and all of the other versions another. The KJB says *"...supposing that gain is godliness: from such withdraw thyself."* By lining up the modern versions together, the consistent pattern of corruption becomes plainer.

"...thinking that godly devotion is a means of gain." (NWT)
"...who think that godliness is a means to financial gain." (NIV)
"...who suppose that godliness is a means of gain. From such withdraw yourself." (NKJV)
"...They think that serving God is a way to get rich." (NCV)
"...These people think religion is supposed to make you rich." (CEV)

The New King James Version comes closest to matching the KJB. The NKJV begins with a reading similar to the KJB and deliberately inserts the corrupt Alexandrian text readings, thus conveying a false premise. Think about what it actually says! Instead of warning against those that look at the possessions and bank accounts to determine one's spirituality, they rebuke anyone that thinks the only way to become prosperous is through spirituality.

Here is another example concerning money in which the NKJV follows the corruption of its predecessor. The love of money is the root of all evil.

*(KJB) I Timothy 6:10 For the love of money is **the root of all evil**: which while some coveted after, they have erred from the faith, and pierced themselves through with many sorrows.*

The version the Jehovah's Witnesses have crafted changes this truth dramatically. No longer is the rigid warning concerning an inordinate affection for money given.

*(NWT) I Timothy 6:10 For the love of money is **a root of all sorts of injurious things**, and by reaching out for this love some have been led astray from the faith and have stabbed themselves all over with many pains.*

The New World Translation says "a root of all sorts of injurious things." The NIV and the NKJV follow suit with the Christ-rejecting Jehovah's Witnesses. What justification do the Christian revisers use for aligning themselves with this blasphemous group? The same excuse used by the authors of the NWT – "the oldest and best manuscripts."

*(NIV) I Timothy 6:10 For the love of money is **a root of all kinds of evil**. Some people, eager for money, have wandered from the faith and pierced themselves with many griefs.*

*(NKJV) I Timothy 6:10 For the love of money is **a root of all kinds of evil**, for which some have strayed from the faith in their greediness, and pierced themselves through with many sorrows.*

Of course, the NCV and the CEV always pervert the truth to a greater degree than their predecessors. *Root* is completely missing in the newest versions. We have moved from the love of money being *the* root (KJV), to *a* root (NIV, NKJV), to *no* root at all (NCV, CEV). The root nourishes the plant, just as the love of money feeds all evil. This is not to say that sin does not exist apart from the love of money. It does, but when one considers all manner of evil in the world, he can usually very easily trace any form of it back to the love of money.

*(NCV) I Timothy 6:10 The love of money **causes all kinds of evil**. Some people have left the faith, because they wanted to get more money, but they have caused themselves much sorrow.*

The CEV not only removes the *root*, but also the *evil*. Comparisons like this should dispel the claim that all the bibles read alike. The modernization of the Bible sheds no light on the truth, and instead places a person in darkness.

(CEV) I Timothy 6:10 The love of money causes all kinds of trouble. Some people want money so much that they have given up their faith and caused themselves a lot of pain.

In Closing...

Why, you may wonder, have these truths and their associated falsehoods not been well publicized? They have been, but who is listening? The seminaries rejected these truths long ago and only now are some of them having to face the error of their ways. This phenomenon is occurring only as a result of the grass roots efforts of many who have not given up on the fight... men and women that fear God more than man.

Why not join in this fight for the faith? If you don't let your voice be heard, how will others know where you stand? Maybe there are others just waiting for that one voice *(Acts 24:21)*, that one man or woman to speak up and speak out. There are indeed many people who can see these truths just as plainly as you. There is a time for silence, and there is a definite time to let your voice be heard *(Romans 13:11)*.

Chapter 12 Endnotes

---

[1] Avro Manhattan, *The Vatican Billions* (Chino, Calif.: Chick Publications, 1983), 188.

13

The Road to Rome

The printing of the English Bible has proved to be by far the mightiest barrier ever reared to repel the advance of Popery, and to damage all the resources of the Papacy. Originally intended for five or six millions who dwelt within the narrow limits of the British Islands, it at once formed and fixed their language, till then unsettled; and has since gone with that language to the isles and shores of every sea. [1]
Alexander McClure

We must now explore the corrupting influence of those sympathetic to the dogmas of the Roman Catholic Church. By "up dating" the bible, the modern versions have included the false teachings of Catholicism within their pages. Although only thirteen of the errors are covered, these false teachings include: the confession of sins to a priest, Mariolatry, Mary's perpetual virginity, and celibacy of the priest. No longer are the clear warnings given against idol worship, the elevation of tradition, the selling of "masses," and repetitious prayers like *the rosary*. Here are thirteen of the false teachings that align the NIV with the false teachings of the Roman Catholic Church:

I. Both Teach Confession of Sins to a Man

Our relationship to other believers is of utmost importance. However, sometimes these relationships become strained and need to be repaired. For that reason, the book of James instructs confession of one's *faults* to each other. When one confesses *his faults*, he confesses to the individual he has wronged, rather than to some priest who can change nothing.

> *(KJB) James 5:16 Confess your faults one to another, and pray one for another, that ye may be healed. The **effectual fervent** prayer of a righteous man availeth much.*

Asking for forgiveness and prayer go hand in hand with the confession of one's faults to another person. The Bible promises that the *effectual fervent prayer* of a righteous man does much good. Nowhere in God's word are we told to confess **our sins** to any person! The NIV changes the truth and supports the heretical teachings of the Roman Catholic Church. The Catholic Church effectively uses this teaching to control its followers through the confessional.

> *(NIV) James 5:16 Therefore confess your **sins** to each other and pray for each other so that you may be healed. The prayer of a righteous man is powerful and effective.*

Christians do not need to divulge their sins to any mere mortal. No man (or woman) is sufficiently able to listen to someone else's sinful thoughts and actions and remain unaffected. To force someone to divulge these sins under the threat of condemnation is tantamount to blackmail. The person hearing one's innermost thoughts and sinful actions potentially gains control over the life of the confessor. When *absolution* from the penalty of sin is "granted" by the priest, the individual feels absolved from his actions no matter how heinous the crime. (The Nazi Holocaust and the actions of the Italian Mafia are great examples of what can happen when men feel completely absolved after confessing their sins to a priest. After a time, their conscience becomes hardened to the point that they can sin without feeling remorse or a need to confess to a priest.)

The Jesuit English Roman Catholic Bible agrees with the NIV. In its explanatory note for the preceding verse, this version states: *"Ver. 16. Confess your sins one to another. **That is, to the priests of the church**, whom (ver. 14) he had ordered to be called for, and brought in to the* *sick; moreover,* **to confess to persons who had no power to forgive sins, would be useless.** *Hence the precept here means, that we must confess to men whom God hath appointed, and who, by their ordination and jurisdiction,* **have received the power of remitting sins in his name.** *"* (Douay-Rheims, 1610, pages 262-263) [Emphasis mine]

These modern versions continually align themselves with the teachings of the Roman Catholic Church because of the corrupt Greek manuscripts from which they both emanate. The Roman Catholic Church need not print its own version of the Bible when men like Westcott and Hort have influenced every modern version on the market with the same heresies taught by the Roman Catholic Church. (See chapter fourteen – *"The Men Behind the Madness."*)

Also, take further note that the King James Bible, unlike the NIV, qualifies *the type* of prayer that is effective. It says that only **effectual, fervent** prayer is powerful, and not just any prayer thrown up to heaven without the heart. Once again, the NIV obscures the truth; this time, by eliminating the type of prayer pleasing to God.

II. Both Elevate Mary

There are two general types of errors – errors of commission and errors of omission. In the following passage, the NIV commits the error of omission by leaving out the word "among" when referring to Mary's status.

(KJB) Luke 1:28 And the angel came in unto her, and said, Hail, thou that art highly favoured, the Lord is with thee: blessed art thou among women.

When the reader of the King James Bible realizes that Mary is blessed *among* women, he understands that she is *not* blessed *above* them.[2] As long as the KJB reigns supreme, the Catholic searching for the truth can be shown that Mary has not been given a place of superiority over other women. Certainly, she was blessed; but she is not to be artificially elevated above other women. Once Christians displace the King James Bible – convinced that they cannot understand it – the unscriptural elevation of

206 ONE BOOK STANDS ALONE

Mary can be perpetrated upon those unfamiliar with the truth contained in His true word.

> *(NIV) Luke 1:28 The angel went to her and said, "Greetings, you who are highly favored! The Lord is with you."*

The NIV does not reveal God's simple truth about Mary. Mary's humanity is too plainly communicated in the KJB for anyone desiring to elevate her to a god-like status. When a person recognizes that Mary is blessed *among* women, no longer can she be lifted up above other women. Mary is not to be elevated, worshipped, or prayed to! She is not all knowing; she cannot hear the prayers of a billion Catholics (or of even one) because she is *not* God.

The Bible teaches that only Mary needed purification, not Mary and Joseph or Mary and Jesus.

> *(KJB) Luke 2:22 And when the days of **her** purification according to the law of Moses were accomplished, they brought him to Jerusalem, to present him to the Lord;*

Mary was a sinner that needed to bring a sacrifice. She was obediently following the requirements of the Law found in *Leviticus 12:2-8.* The Law of God called for a burnt-offering and a SIN-OFFERING. The priest was to make atonement for HER! The Law did not address the mother's husband, but the NIV does.

> *(NIV) Luke 2:22 When the time of **their** purification according to the Law of Moses had been completed, Joseph and Mary took him to Jerusalem to present him to the Lord*

The NIV is a lie. Read Leviticus yourself. The NIV downplays the fact that Mary was a sinner in need of a sin-offering.

III. Both Elevate Mary to a Co-Redemptress Level

It is Jesus alone that has power to save. He purged our sins by himself. Mary had no part in it. *"Who being the brightness of his glory,* *and the express image of his person, and upholding all things by the word of his power, when he had **by himself** purged our sins, sat down on the right hand of the Majesty on high;" **(Hebrews 1:3)**.* Mary was not involved in the work of the cross. Mary cannot hear anyone's prayers and has nothing to do with the purging of our sins.

(KJB) I John 5:7 *For there are three that bear record in heaven, the Father, the Word, and the Holy Ghost: and these three are one.*

The Bible proclaims that there are only **three** that bear record in heaven – the Father, the Word, and the Holy Ghost. No mention of Mary. The NIV masks this truth by eliminating the majority of this verse!

(NIV) I John 5:7 *For there are three that testify:*

The NIV makes way for Mary by removing this important truth from the scripture. Is it any wonder why Christians do not know how sufficiently to minister to the Catholics? The truth is blurred, eliminated, or distorted.

IV. Both Attempt to Teach that Mary had no Other Children

The Roman Catholic Church began elevating Mary centuries ago. However, they could not elevate her to a god-like status until they could "prove" she was no ordinary human being at birth or throughout her entire life. Therefore, they began teaching, among other things, that Mary was supernaturally born **without** sin, that she never committed sin, and that she never had normal intimate relations with her husband Joseph. The first teaching is called the *immaculate conception*; the last is referred to as her *perpetual virginity*. Of course, this would mean that she caused her husband, Joseph, to be a perpetual virgin within the marital relationship and to be unduly tempted by Satan *(I Corinthians 7:5)*.

Many verses from the word of God plainly prove that both of these teachings are blatantly false. One simple proof concerns the designation of our Lord and Saviour Jesus Christ as her *firstborn* son.

(KJB) Matthew 1:25 And knew her not till she had brought forth her firstborn son: and he called his name JESUS.

For the Lord to be the *firstborn* son of Mary, she had to give birth to other boys, too. The NIV conceals the truth by eliminating the word *firstborn*. This change eliminates one foolproof text that could easily dispel the Roman Catholic Church's false claims concerning Mary's supposed *perpetual virginity*.

(NIV) Matthew 1:25 But he had no union with her until she gave birth to a son. And he gave him the name Jesus.

Mary did have other children. Not only does the Old Testament foretell that the Lord would have brothers and sisters, but the New Testament confirms this truth as well. The Old Testament prophecy illustrates that the Lord would not be Mary's only child: *"I am become a stranger unto my brethren, and an alien unto **my mother's children"** (Psalm 69:8).* The context shows this verse in Psalms to be a reference to the Lord Jesus Christ. Now, read the next verse found in the same chapter: *"**For the zeal of thine house hath eaten me up...**" (Psalm 69:9).*

Comparing Psalm 69 with the book of John conclusively proves that Psalm 69 is referring to Jesus. *"And said unto them that sold doves, Take these things hence; make not my Father's house an house of merchandise. 17 And his disciples remembered that it was written, **The zeal of thine house hath eaten me up** (John 2:16-17).*

The Pharisees' question concerning Jesus' family members reveals that Mary undeniably had other children: *"Is not this the carpenter's son? is not his mother called Mary? and **his brethren**, James, and Joses, and Simon, and Judas? 56 And **his sisters**, are they not all with us? Whence then hath this man all these things? (Matthew 13:55-56).* The NIV makes it much more difficult to show the Catholic the errors taught by his church. The scripture plainly teaches that Mary was not a perpetual virgin, but had a normal healthy relationship with her husband *(Hebrews 13:4).*

V. Both Elevate Idol Worship

Under the Law, the Lord gave many rules concerning meats, drinks, and special days. These things drastically changed following the cross. The Apostle Paul writes that the handwriting of ordinances was nailed to the cross, and no man was to judge another pertaining to the Old Testament ordinances. Although strict warnings are given against those that command to abstain from meats *(I Timothy 4:1-3)*, one warning remains intact – the warning regarding idol worship.

*(KJB) I Corinthians 10:28 But if any man say unto you, This is offered in sacrifice **unto idols**, eat not for his sake that shewed it, and for conscience sake: for the earth is the Lord's, and the fulness thereof:*

No matter the period of time in which one lives, the command against idols remains constant. Why then does the Roman Catholic Church have idols everywhere, including its parishioners' yards, cars, and necks? The hierarchy of this church knows that the rebuke against idols must be eliminated. No problem. The NIV removes "idols" from the word of God, circumventing God's clear admonition against them.

(NIV) I Corinthians 10:28 But if anyone says to you, "This has been offered in sacrifice," then do not eat it, both for the sake of the man who told you and for conscience' sake-

The whole point of the passage in the word of God (KJB) was the warning against eating food offered **to idols.** The NIV conceals this truth by removing any reference to the idol in this passage. Second Samuel contains another passage that indicates the dangers involving idols or images and commands obedience to God's clear and explicit instructions concerning idols and images: *"The graven images of their gods shall ye burn with fire: thou shalt not desire the silver or gold that is on them, nor take it unto thee, lest thou be snared therein: for it is an abomination to the Lord thy God" (Deuteronomy 7:25)*. David and his men, knowing the command and the consequences of disobedience, obeyed implicitly.

*(KJB) II Samuel 5:21 And there they left their **images**, and David and **his men burned them**.*

To avoid any possibility of the images contaminating God's chosen people, God required that the idols be **burned**! David and his men (and the whole nation) would be in grave danger to do any less. Besides the editors of the NIV, who else would not want you to know how God feels about idol worship? Of course, Satan craves to steal the worship that rightfully belongs only to God *(Luke 4:5-8)*.

*(NIV) II Samuel 5:21 The Philistines abandoned their **idols** there, and David and **his men carried them off**.*

According to the NIV, what did David and his men do with the idols? In God's word, they obeyed by burning them. In contrast, the pro-Catholic NIV states that they "carried them off." No longer can the reader grasp the seriousness of the matter, nor can he read this account of their simple obedience. If Christians today would grasp this principle, we would have more book burnings, CD burnings, and probably some computer burnings due to the ungodly influence of the Internet and some people's idolization of it with their time and attention.

VI. Both Teach that it is Blessed to Remain Unmarried

A man is aroused by what he sees. Therefore, God commands *women* to dress modestly *(I Timothy 2:9)* and cautions against women that wear the attire of a harlot *(Proverbs 7:10)*. To help men avoid the pitfalls of lust, women are to dress modestly. Although men are more *visually* oriented, women generally are excited more by *touch*. Therefore, God instructs the man accordingly.

*(KJB) I Corinthians 7:1 Now concerning the things whereof ye wrote unto me: **It is good for a man not to touch a woman**.*

Take note that the Bible does *not* say that a man *cannot* ever touch a woman. God gives these instructions in order to help Christians understand how to avoid getting into trouble with the opposite sex. The NIV totally eliminates this necessary warning and adds credibility to the Roman Catholic Church's teaching of *celibacy*.

(NIV) I Corinthians 7:1 Now for the matters you wrote about: It is good for a man not to marry.

The consequences of the changes to this one verse are threefold. First, the text of the NIV teaches something not necessarily true. God ordained marriage and says that it is honorable *(Hebrews 13:4)*. Due to the weakness of our human flesh, it is not necessarily good for a man to remain unmarried; and, in many cases, to do so can be disastrous.

Secondly, this comparison should further dispel the myth that the newer versions simply modernize the English without changing the meaning of the text – the NIV does not mean the same thing as the word of God; therefore, they are not the same.

Thirdly, the NIV verse justifies the priestly celibacy alleged to be necessary by the Roman Catholic Church. This dogma is one of the most damnable of heresies due to the consequences suffered by the parishioners at the hands of these unmarried men. The normal God-given sexual desires become abnormal and perverted because of the devilish doctrines. *"Now the Spirit speaketh expressly, that in the latter times some shall depart from the faith, giving heed to seducing spirits, and **doctrines of devils;** 2 Speaking lies in hypocrisy; having their conscience seared with a hot iron; 3 **Forbidding to marry,** and commanding to abstain from meats, which God hath created to be received with thanksgiving of them which believe and know the truth" **(I Timothy 4:1-3).**

VII. Both Elevate Tradition

The Roman Catholic Church teaches that the traditions handed down from "the fathers" (those that set the policy for the Roman Catholic Church) are *equal* to scripture. The **Apostle Peter** warns against the elevation of any tradition by the new Christian believers, including the traditions established and promoted by their *Jewish* forefathers.

*(KJB) I Peter 1:18 Forasmuch as ye know that ye were not redeemed with corruptible things, as silver and gold, from your vain conversation received **by tradition** from your fathers;*

The NIV eliminates the Apostle Peter's rebuke against tradition. Failing to have any warning against tradition allows the Roman Catholic Church to elevate tradition to the same level as scripture (and in many cases, this church elevates tradition *over* God's word). Thus, the NIV eliminates a clear admonition against something that has created a considerable amount of heresy.

(NIV) I Peter 1:18 For you know that it was not with perishable things such as silver or gold that you were redeemed from the empty way of life handed down to you from your forefathers,

VIII. Both Fail to Teach their Followers *not* to Pray Repetitiously

*(KJB) Matthew 6:7 But when ye pray, **use not vain repetitions,** as the heathen do: for they think that they shall be heard for their much speaking.*

God wants to hear prayers that originate from our hearts. He promises that *"...the effectual fervent prayer of a righteous man availeth much" (James 5:16).* He does *not* want us to pray repetitiously, like the repetitive recitation of the Hail Mary. This is vain (empty, worthless). God wants to hear someone speak to Him as one would to someone he loves, rather than a canned prayer that has no heart and no thought. The Bible specifically rebukes *vain repetitions,* unlike the NIV which merely prohibits something as vague and imprecise as "babblings."

*(NIV) Matthew 6:7 And when you pray, **do not keep on babbling** like pagans, for they think they will be heard because of their many words.*

God wants us to pray from the heart, not just from the head. He wants to hear the sinner and saint alike pour out their lives and souls before Him. The vain, repetitious prayers of the heathen and Catholic alike make Him sick *(Revelation 3:16).* The **rosary** prayed by the submissive Catholic consists of:

15 - *"Our Fathers"*
15 - *"Glory be's"*
150 - *"Hail Mary's"* (*Hail Mary, full of grace . . . pray for us sinners.*)

Mary cannot pray for anybody...and she surely can't hear anyone pray to her. Notice that there are ten times as many prayers to Mary as to the Father. This is Mariolatry – the worship of Mary. The pope has given his full blessing to this type of behavior. Furthermore, the pope has never once preached the Gospel of the Grace of God. He has never once told anyone how to get to heaven and does not even know if he is going there himself!

A recent Catholic convert to Christ said he went to a Catholic Church with his wife and heard the priest say that he *hoped* he was going to heaven. What business does this man (the priest) have trying to teach others when he has experienced no spiritual rebirth in his own life *(John 3:3, I Corinthians 15:8)* and has no assurance of salvation? The Lord plainly gave warning concerning the result of the blind leading the blind *(Matthew 15:14)*. They both fall into the ditch.

Bible believers need to pray for their Catholic friends, neighbors, and family members. God wants everyone to understand the truth and be saved. *"For this is good and acceptable in the sight of God our Saviour; 4 Who will have all men to be saved, and to come unto the knowledge of the truth." (I Timothy 2:3-4)*. We must show them our love and true desire for their spiritual welfare. However, regardless of the depth of our love and concern for them, we must never turn a blind eye toward the error that Catholicism so freely propagates.

IX. Both Elevate Peter

The Roman Catholic Church incorrectly teaches that Peter is the rock of *Matthew 16:18.* Of course, every true student of the Bible knows that the rock mentioned in the passage refers to Peter's *confession* of Jesus as the Christ, the Son of the living God, rather than to Peter himself *("...that Rock was Christ" (I Corinthians 10:4)).* The Apostle John gives further proof that Peter is *not* the rock of Matthew chapter sixteen because the interpretation of his given name means "a stone" and **not a rock.**

(KJB) John 1:42 And he brought him to Jesus. And when Jesus beheld him, he said, Thou art Simon the son of Jona: thou shalt be called Cephas, which is by interpretation, A stone.

When the Lord says *upon this rock I will build my church*, He could not have been referring to Peter. Peter's name does *not* even mean rock, and you don't build a foundation upon a stone.[3] Peter is not the rock upon which the Lord promised to build His church. The NIV hides the true interpretation of Simon Peter's name, thus eliminating the possibility of using this passage to refute the claims made concerning Peter's elevated position by the Roman Catholic Church.

(NIV) John 1:42 And he brought him to Jesus. Jesus looked at him and said, "You are Simon son of John. You will be called Cephas" (which, when translated, is Peter).

From reading the NIV, people do not learn that Cephas means *stone*. Once again, the NIV eliminates another text that could be used to help Catholics see the false teachings of their hierarchy. Without the teaching of Peter as the first pope, apostolic succession becomes merely another fabricated concept. Dr. Bill Grady, in his book *Final Authority*, aptly points out the dilemma with claiming that Peter is the first pope.

For Catholics 'in the know,' however, 'Pope' Peter presents quite a paradox: he was so pontifical that he refused to have his toe kissed (Acts 10:26), was so infallible that Jesus called him Satan (Matthew 16:23), was so autocratic that Paul rebuked him to his face (Galatians 2:11), and was so celibate that he had a mother-in-law (Matthew 8:14). [4]

X. Both Condone the Selling of Masses

The selling of masses is probably one of the most disgusting, despicable practices of the Roman Catholic Church because it is used to prey upon the weak and the elderly. It is usually pressed upon those that are the most vulnerable – for instance, a widow during her time of grief.

(KJB) Matthew 23:14 Woe unto you, scribes and Pharisees, hypocrites! for ye devour widows' houses, and for a pretence make long prayer: therefore ye shall receive the greater damnation.

It is a historical fact that most wives outlive their husbands. When a Catholic man dies, the priest requires payment from his widow in order to say masses to shorten her husband's stay in "purgatory." Especially during the Dark Ages, many of the widows did not have the money to pay for the masses; therefore, they were forced to sign over their houses to the Catholic Church in order for the priest to receive payment for his prayers. The scriptures plainly condemn this type of spiritual extortion.

The Bible says for a pretence (a false reason – like money), these religious leaders make long prayer (like a mass). The Roman Catholic Church has billions of dollars in assets. Eliminating the church's opportunity to prey upon those most susceptible would result in a great financial loss to its coffers. Once again, the NIV translators did the Devil's bidding by yanking the entire verse out of the Bible. No more condemnation of this damnable heresy in the NIV!

(NIV) Matthew 23:14 [Missing]

For those that may doubt the direct connection to the Roman Catholic Church, the context of the whole passage plainly singles them out. The Roman Catholic Church is specifically condemned for devouring widows' houses and making long prayer for false reasons. Five verses earlier, those specifically condemned are also the ones taking upon themselves the religious title of *father*. *"And call no man your father upon the earth: for one is your Father, which is in heaven" (Matthew 23:9)*. These men are calling themselves fathers and, for pretence, making long prayers in order to devour widow's houses. The finger of God could not point any more clearly to the culprits of these despicable acts – the Catholic priest and their devilish system!

XI. Both Elevate the Priesthood System

The Apostle Paul's unique ministry to the Gentiles was disclosed soon after his conversion and again in his first book, Romans. His ministry was primarily to reveal the Gospel of the Grace of God to the Gentiles.

(KJB) Romans 15:16 That I should be the minister of Jesus Christ to the Gentiles, ministering the gospel of God, that

the offering up of the Gentiles might be acceptable, being sanctified by the Holy Ghost.

The KJB does not mention anything about the "priestly duty" of the Apostle Paul. This is not surprising since the main purpose of the priest is to perform the sacrifices to God. Paul knew that the Lord Jesus Christ was the final sacrifice *(Hebrews 10:12)*. Not so in the NIV.

(NIV) Romans 15:16 to be a minister of Christ Jesus to the Gentiles with the priestly duty of proclaiming the gospel of God, so that the Gentiles might become an offering acceptable to God, sanctified by the Holy Spirit.

The Roman Catholic Church elevates its priesthood system, and the NIV translators have been duped into following right along. The Roman Catholic system will usher in the Antichrist and the modern translations will be used to support his false teachings. Everyone is clamoring for unity. On the contrary, unity at the expense of the truth is never condoned by the word of God. Every **preacher** should keep in mind this one thought: as soon as he gets to the point where he is trying to please everyone, he will make the Lord very unhappy *(Luke 6:26)*.

XII. Both Teach Self-flagellation

J. Frank Norris once said that *"First Corinthians 9:27 is the most feared verse in the Bible."* His reasoning was quite simple. He knew the most fearful thing for a preacher was to lose his effectiveness and opportunity to preach because sin had overtaken his life.

*(KJB) I Corinthians 9:27 But **I keep under my body, and bring it into subjection**: lest that by any means, when I have preached to others, I myself should be a castaway.*

J. Frank Norris knew that he had to keep his body in subjection, lest he suffer the ministry-ending consequences. He also knew that the passage did *not* advocate abusing one's own body. *Volume I* of the *One Book Stands Alone* series (chapter four in this book) exposes the modern versions' heretical teaching of salvation by works. Because the NIV and the Roman Catholic Church both teach salvation by works, their teachings of abusing one's body to merit favor with God also concur.

(NIV) I Corinthians 9:27 No, I beat my body and make it my slave so that after I have preached to others, I myself will not be disqualified for the prize.

Monasteries contain thousands of men and women convinced that their abusive antics will somehow gain them favor with God. However, monks and nuns are not the only deluded souls. For instance, many Easter reenactments of the crucifixion take place in predominant Catholic countries by those desiring to physically suffer "for the glory of God." They abuse their bodies, convinced that this somehow pleases God. It does no such thing!

Here is another verse to demonstrate the perversion of these modern versions. Paul wished that those that were troubling the believers were cut off. This could simply refer to their opportunity to influence or speak to the believers. Simply their speech could have been "cut off."

*(KJB) Galatians 5:12 I would they were even **cut off** which trouble you.*

Now read the NIV and see if you arrive at this same conclusion. Was Paul desiring that these troublesome people mutilate themselves?

*(NIV) Galatians 5:12 As for those agitators, I wish they would go the whole way and **emasculate themselves!***

Emasculate means to castrate oneself. Where do you suppose the modern versions get this stuff? It originated in the Roman Catholic teachings and with men like Origen who castrated himself. Origen is the father of all the modern versions, and his influence can be seen when comparing these versions to the truth.

XIII. Both Attack those that Disagree with their Teachings

As we have seen, the modern versions clearly align themselves with the teachings of the Roman Catholic Church. One more comparison should further identify the propensity of these modern versions to conceal the actions of the Roman Catholic Church. The church's intolerance toward those that reject their dogma is historically apparent.

However, if someone rejects the true gospel, should Christians have a personal hatred toward them? The Bible says that the preaching of the cross will not be acceptable to the majority. Nevertheless, the world's rejection does not justify our hating or destroying those that disagree. The disciples wanted to destroy their critics, but the Lord instructs them otherwise.

> *(KJB) Luke 9:54 And when his disciples James and John saw this, they said, Lord, wilt thou that we **command fire to come down from heaven**, and consume them, even as Elias did? 55 But he turned, and rebuked them, and said, Ye know not what manner of spirit ye are of. 56 **For the Son of man is not come to destroy men's lives, but to save them.** And they went to another village.*

The disciples wanted to destroy their critics . . . just as the Roman Catholic Church has done to its critics for a thousand years. The Dark Ages was so named because Rome was in control – torturing, burning, killing, and destroying all those that disagreed with her teachings. Notice how short the same passage becomes when you read it in the NIV.

> *(NIV) Luke 9:54 When the disciples James and John saw this, they asked, "Lord, do you want us to call fire down from heaven to destroy them?" 55 But Jesus turned and rebuked them, 56 and they went to another village.*

If a modern version is your bible of choice, you no longer know *why* the Lord rebuked His disciples. He could have rebuked them because they asked Him for permission to destroy their enemies in public. Maybe the Lord rebuked them because He wanted to keep His desires a secret and they were letting "the cat out of the bag." See how much truth is missing in these modern perversions? The KJB makes it clear why the Lord rebuked them. They were asking amiss. He had no intentions of burning His critics. He came to *save* the lost, not to destroy them.

The Lord Jesus Christ will *not* set up His kingdom until sometime following the rapture of the Church. No matter how hard the various groups claim to be bringing in the kingdom, it will not happen until after the Lord's return. The Bible tells of a falling away in the last days *(II Timothy 3:1-5, II Thessalonians 2:3)*, not a spiritual awakening that ushers in the kingdom at the height of Christianity. The misunderstanding of this truth has caused much confusion. Jesus said his servants were not fighting to bring in His kingdom. *"Jesus answered, My kingdom is not of this world: if my kingdom were of this world, then would my servants fight, that I should not be delivered to the Jews: but now is my kingdom not from hence" (John 18:36)*. Those fighting are not of God. Rather, they are the wicked, even if they claim to be fighting in the name of the Lord.

*(KJB) Matthew 11:12 And from the days of John the Baptist until now the kingdom of heaven **suffereth violence**, and the violent take it by force.*

The NIV changes the entire meaning of the passage with its amillennial renderings. According to the modern versions, and contrary to the truth, those doing the fighting are *forcefully advancing* Christ's kingdom.

*(NIV) Matthew 11:12 From the days of John the Baptist until now, the kingdom of heaven has been **forcefully advancing**, and forceful men lay hold of it.*

This same false doctrine was used by the Roman Catholic Church to justify the Crusades. They martyred millions *in the name of the Lord.* Revelation chapter 17 reveals much about the Roman Catholic Church. It describes a city that has ruled the world politically and religiously and martyred the true saints of God. The Bible describes the location of the spiritual whore: *"...The seven heads are **seven** mountains, on which the woman sitteth" (Revelation 17:9)*. It is very interesting to note that Rome is called *the city of **seven** hills*. It is said of this woman – "the holy mother Catholic Church" that she is responsible for martyring the true believers of Jesus.

*(KJB) Revelation 17:6 And I saw the woman drunken with the blood of the saints, and with the blood of the **martyrs** of Jesus: and when I saw her, I wondered with great admiration.*

Someone does not want the world to know that Revelation chapter 17 points directly to the Catholic Church and its murderous past (and wicked future). The NIV does *not* point out the martyrs of the Roman Catholic Church.

(NIV) Revelation 17:6 I saw that the woman was drunk with the blood of the saints, the blood of those who bore testimony to Jesus. When I saw her, I was greatly astonished.

The Catholic Church controlled the world system for over a thousand years. They burned, tortured, and destroyed 68 million lives during the Inquisition (A.D. 1100-1800). The reason the explicit details of the Catholic atrocities are not clearly defined in our history books is that the Catholic Church has predominantly controlled the historians! History is written with a Catholic slant because the true saints of God were forced to go underground, lest they too become martyrs.

Dr. Sam Gipp, in his book *An Understandable History of the Bible*, succinctly states the truth:

The Roman Catholic Church has long been antagonistic to the doctrine of salvation by grace. If salvation is by grace, who needs "mass?" If salvation is by grace, who needs to fear purgatory? If Jesus Christ is our mediator, who needs the Pope? If the Pope cannot intimidate people into obeying him, how can he force a nation to obey him? The true Bible is the arch-enemy of the Roman Catholic Church. Rome can only rule over ignorant, fear-filled people. The true Bible turns "unlearned and ignorant" men into gospel preachers and casts out "all fear." [5]

The New American Standard Version

As mentioned in chapter one, one can trace most of the changes discussed in this book back to the NIV's predecessors. Unfortunately, many times the things that were footnoted in the earlier bible versions can now be completely removed from the text as Christians become less acquainted with the flow of the King James Bible. The verses could not be removed when the NASV was first marketed in 1960 because those types of changes would have been too blatant.

We will compare the same thirteen heresies found in the NIV, this time using the NASV.

Are you to confess your sins or faults?

*(NASV) James 5:16 Therefore, **confess your sins** to one another, and pray for one another so that you may be healed. The effective prayer of a righteous man can accomplish much.*

Was Mary blessed *among* women?

(NASV) Luke 1:28 And coming in, he said to her, "Greetings, favored one! The Lord is with you."

Was it *her* purification or *their* purification?

*(NASV) Luke 2:22 And when the days for **their** purification according to the law of Moses were completed, they brought Him up to Jerusalem to present Him to the Lord*

Who are the three that bear record?

(NASV) I John 5:7 For there are three that testify:

Was Jesus Mary's firstborn?

(NASV) Matthew 1:25 but kept her a virgin until she gave birth to a Son; and he called His name Jesus.

Did David burn the idols?

*(NASV) II Samuel 5:21 They abandoned their **idols** there, so **David and his men carried them away.***

Finally, we have a verse in the NASV that agrees with the King James Bible.

*(NASV) I Corinthians 7:1 Now concerning the things about which you wrote, **it is good for a man not to touch a woman**.*

Didn't Peter rebuke tradition?

*(NASV) I Peter 1:18 knowing that you were not redeemed with perishable things like silver or gold from your futile way of life **inherited** from your forefathers,*

Again, closer than the corrupt NIV!

*(NASV) Matthew 6:7 "And when you are praying, do not use **meaningless repetition** as the Gentiles do, for they suppose that they will be heard for their many words.*

Did you know that Peter's name means stone – he is not the rock of the Roman Catholic Church?

*(NASV) John 1:42 He brought him to Jesus. Jesus looked at him and said, "You are Simon the son of John; you shall be called Cephas" (which is translated **Peter**).*

The verses bracketed by the NASV are completely removed in the more modern versions.

(NASV) Matthew 23:14 ["Woe to you, scribes and Pharisees, hypocrites, because you devour widows' houses, and for a pretense you make long prayers; therefore you will receive greater condemnation.]

The footnote in the New American Standard Version says: "This verse not found in the earliest mss (manuscripts)." They are referring to the two Roman Catholic manuscripts – Vaticanus and Sinaiticus. The first is still located in the Vatican, and the second was stolen by Tishendorf from a monastery at Mt. Sinai.

Satan's attack grows bolder as Christians become further removed from the true readings found in the KJB. The brackets initially place the verse in doubt. The ultimate goal is to remove the verse entirely.

WAS PAUL REALLY A PRIEST?

(NASV) Romans 15:16 to be a minister of Christ Jesus to the Gentiles, ministering as a priest the gospel of God, so that my offering of the Gentiles may become acceptable, sanctified by the Holy Spirit.

One would have to be blind to miss the importance of this change. If Paul was a priest and we are to be followers of him *(I Corinthians 11:1)*, then Baptists and Protestants are wrong and the Roman system is the only one that is right. Priests offer a sacrifice…(i.e. the mass).

Discipline in the NASV becomes *beat* in the NIV!

(NASV) I Corinthians 9:27 but I discipline my body and make it my slave, so that, after I have preached to others, I myself will not be disqualified.

The previous verse may not go as far as the NIV, but the next verse far surpasses it. Should we really encourage and condone self-mutilation? The Roman Catholic system does, as do the modern versions.

(NASV) Galatians 5:12 I wish that those who are troubling you would even mutilate themselves.

Bracketed NASV means *removed* in the NIV!

(NASV) Luke 9:54 When His disciples James and John saw this, they said, "Lord, do You want us to command fire to come down from heaven and consume them?" 55 But He turned and rebuked them, [and said, "You do not know what kind of spirit you are of; 56 for the Son of Man did not come to destroy men's lives, but to save them."] And they went on to another village.

Rome does not want you to know about the martyrs!

(NASV) Revelation 17:6 And I saw the woman drunk with the blood of the saints, and with the blood of the witnesses of Jesus. When I saw her, I wondered greatly.

The New American Standard Version is just another Roman Catholic bible dressed up in Protestant robes. These changes are not by chance. They are a systematic attack against the truth. Rome wants to hide her wicked ways and practices... and the modern versions assist her in doing so.

As already demonstrated, the changes to the modern versions are quite serious and impact critical doctrines. In some cases, the changes constitute heresy! How can so many Catholics and non-Catholics alike be so deceived into accepting such anti-biblical doctrines? Consider a quote from a letter written by "Mother" Teresa. *"I am told God lives in me – and yet the reality of darkness and coldness and emptiness is so great that nothing touches my soul."* [6] This was written by a woman that the pope is now considering for sainthood! She is not the only one that has impacted the world wearing sheep's clothing. The two men covered in the next chapter are the men most responsible for the changes being made in every modern version on the market today. The reader should seriously consider their testimony.

Chapter 13 Endnotes

[1] Alexander McClure, *Translators Revived*, Maranatha Bible Society, Litchfield, MI, 1858 ed.), p. 71-72.

[2] The book, *From the Mind of God to the Mind of Man,* tries to find fault with the King James Bible and its translators over and over again. On page 154, the book lists the holy days found in the 1611 edition of the King James Bible and mentions that some would be unrecognizable by the modern reader. Of course, the two that they would like the reader to especially notice refer to the "blessed Virgin." These days do seem odd to us today, especially because of the unscriptural handling of Mary (i.e. The Virgin Mary) by the Roman Catholic Church. It seems that this unscriptural church has caused most of us to miss the mark. Every generation should recognize the blessed

position of the lowly woman given the great blessing of having birthed the eternal Son of God. Mary recognizes the blessing bestowed upon her: *"For he hath regarded the low estate of his handmaiden: for, behold, from henceforth **all generations shall call me blessed"** (Luke 1:48).* Evidently, the churches of centuries earlier were more scriptural than many of us today! They recognized that Mary was blessed. The Bible critic needs to consider his position more carefully, rather than trying to attack the one book that has done more good than all the others combined.

[3] A stone is generally a piece of a rock; usually larger than a grain, but smaller than a boulder. Rock is an aggregate of particles composed of one or more minerals forming the major part of the earth's crust (igneous rock, metamorphic rock, sedimentary rock). Foundations are built upon a solid rock foundation; not a stone. The same holds true for a spiritual foundation *(Matthew 7:5)*.

[4] Grady, *Final Authority, op. cit.*, p. 54.

[5] Gipp, *An Understandable History of the Bible, op.cit.*, p. 80-81.

[6] Newsweek, *Perspectives*, September 17, 2001, p. 23.

14

The Men behind the Madness

Textual criticism cannot be divorced entirely from theology. No matter how great a Greek scholar a man may be, or no matter how great an authority on the textual evidence, his conclusions must always be open to suspicion if he does not accept the Bible as the very Word of God. [1]

David Otis Fuller

As the previous chapter entitled *"The Road to Rome"* demonstrated, instead of being a mighty barrier to the advancement of the Popery (the Roman Catholic Church), the modern versions actually strengthen and reinforce the dogma of the Roman Catholic Church.

How did it All Begin?

The King James Bible indisputably reigned supreme from the 1600's through the late 1800's without any real competition. "Coincidentally," this period contained the world's greatest period of spiritual revival. However, in May 1881, the English Revised Version was published in England, selling two million copies within four days! Although it failed to gain lasting popular appeal, it opened the floodgates to later versions that would use the same corrupt foundation – the Greek texts designed by the Catholic sympathizers Westcott and Hort.

Most historians recognize the brutal persecution enacted by the Roman Catholic Church against all those who have disagreed with them. The most infamous of these was the system of tribunals known as the Inquisition used to torture and kill many of those that challenged the Catholic dogma. The methods they have used are notorious and include torture, imprisonment, and murder.

Hundreds of books have been written about the brutality of the Inquisition. Amazingly, the inquisitors kept detailed records documenting their atrocious acts. Dr. Bill Grady, quoting from *Foxe's Christian Martyrs of the World*, gives the following statistics:

> *Torquemada was chief inquisitor until his death, and during the eighteen years he ruled the Holy Office,* **ten thousand two hundred and twenty persons** *were burned alive, and* **ninety-seven thousand three hundred and twenty-two** *punished with loss of property, or imprisonment – numbers so large as to seem incredible, but which are given by Llorente, the Spanish historian of the Inquisition, who was well qualified to judge of their accuracy.* [2]

No matter how effective or oppressive Satan's wiles, God always provides a way to stand against them *(Ephesians 6:11)*. The Lord chose one of their own, a converted former Catholic priest named Martin Luther, to enlighten the world. He led Germany and the rest of the world into the Protestant Reformation. The encyclopedia tells us that the name *Protestant* originated with a group of German princes who *protested* against the pope in 1529. The term has come to be applied to those denominations that arose out of the Reformation era, including the Anglican, Lutheran, Methodist, and Presbyterian Churches.[3] (See endnotes for the reason that Baptists are *not* included in this list of Protestant churches.) [4]

The Westcott and Hort/Roman Catholic Church Connection

Soon after the Reformation began, the Catholic Church began a *counter-reformation* movement. In 1534, Ignatius de Loyola founded the Jesuits in an attempt to recapture nations lost to the Protestant Reformation. He also used this Jesuit priest organization to attack, discredit, and remove the *Textus Receptus* Greek Text from use and to support pro-Catholic Greek texts in its place. Eventually, the Jesuits' greatest accomplishment would be to supplant the *Textus Receptus* (the text used to give us the King James Bible) with the Westcott and Hort Greek text.

Their crowning achievement of the 20th Century would be the production of a plethora of modern versions. The NIV publisher, John R. Kohlenberger may have said it best when he linked all modern versions back to the Westcott and Hort Greek text. He said, "All subsequent versions from the Revised Version (1881) to those of the present...have adopted their basic approach...and accepted the Westcott and Hort (Greek) text." Thus, the majority of seminaries have also adopted this corrupt Greek text, in lieu of the one used by the churches for 1,600 years.

The historical accounts of corruption emphasize the importance of knowing the men and women behind the modern versions. Those claiming to make the Bible more readable, yet denying the inspiration of the Bible, should have their writings carefully scrutinized to determine their underlying beliefs and motives. Unfortunately, many revisers of the words of God have not even believed in the fundamentals of the faith, let alone the inspiration of the Bible. Two of the men most responsible for the corruptions found in the modern versions are Fenton J.A. Hort and Brooke Foss Westcott.

Those influenced by modern textual critics and their criticisms ignore or downplay the heretical beliefs of Westcott and Hort. For example, here is the standard position expressed in a book published in 1999, entitled *From the Mind of God to the Mind of Man.*

*But those who really brought the Alexandrian texts to the public's attention were two Church of England clergymen, Brook Foss Westcott and Fenton John Anthony Hort. In 1881, after some twenty-eight years of **careful** textual criticism, they published a Greek New Testament that gave primary (though not exclusive) precedence to the older Alexandrian readings...Some have vilified these men's intentions. But what has been amazing to me, as a preacher of God's Word who must rely upon the findings of* *textual critics, is that Westcott and Hort themselves believed that there is actually very little difference between the two major families of manuscripts.* [5]

The misinformation concerning these two men is very disturbing and destructive. The changes discussed in this book have resulted from the differences between "the two major families of manuscripts." Are they significant?

Westcott and Hort knew the importance of keeping their personal beliefs from public view. Their personal correspondence reveals that they knew the importance of displaying a public persona that looked fundamentally sound. However, it also reveals what they truly believed. Because of their lasting influence, seminaries have become breeding grounds for spiritual infidelity concerning God's words. We need seminaries to preach and teach a dependence upon God and His word, rather than a dependence upon scholarship and man's wisdom.

Who were Westcott and Hort? What were their Beliefs?

The best way to discover the beliefs of the dead is to study their writings. Both Brooke Foss Westcott and Fenton John Anthony Hort wrote extensively. Here are some of their beliefs, as revealed by their own writings:

- **Did not believe in the miracles of the Bible**

Westcott in 1847: *"I never read an account of a miracle* (in the Bible?) *but I seem instinctively to feel its improbability and discover some want of evidence in the account of it."* [6]

- **Did not believe in the infallibility of the scriptures**

Westcott to Hort in 1860: *"I reject the word infallibility – of Holy Scripture overwhelming."* [7]

Hort to Lightfoot in 1860: *"If you make a decided conviction of the absolute infallibility of the N.T. practically a sine qua non for co-operation, I fear I could not join you, even if you were willing to forget your fears about the origin of the Gospels."* [8]

• **Did not believe in the supernatural creation**

Hort to Westcott in 1860: *"...Have you read Darwin? How I should like to talk with you about it! In spite of difficulties, I am inclined to think it unanswerable. In any case, it is a treat to read such a book."*[9]

Hort to Ellerton in 1860: *"But the book which has most engaged me is Darwin. Whatever may be thought of it, it is a book that one is proud to be contemporary with. I must work out and examine the argument more in detail, but at present my feeling is strong that the theory is unanswerable."* [10]

• **Did not believe in the efficacy of the atonement**

Hort: *"The fact is, I do not see how God's justice can be satisfied without every man's suffering in his own person the full penalty for his sins."* [11]

• **Westcott and Hort were clearly Anti-protestant (pro-Catholic sympathizers)**

Hort: *"I think I mentioned to you before Campbell's book on the Atonement, which is invaluable as far as it goes; but unluckily he knows nothing except Protestant theology."* [12]

• **Believed in the necessity of purgatory**

Hort to Ellerton: *"But the idea of purgation, of cleansing as by fire, seems to me inseparable from what the Bible teaches us of the Divine chastisements..."*[13]

• **Believed in the communist system**

Westcott: *"I suppose I am a communist by nature."* [14]

Hort: *"I...cannot say that I see much as yet to soften my deep hatred for democracy in all its forms."* [15]

Hort: *"I cannot at present see any objection to a limit being placed by the State upon the amount of property which any one person may possess . . . I would say that – the co-operative principle* (Communism) *is a better and a mightier than the competitive principle* (Free enterprise system)." [16]

- **Believed in prayers for the dead**

Westcott: *"We agreed unanimously that we are, as things are now, forbidden to pray for the dead apart from the whole church in our public services. No restriction is placed upon private devotions* (to pray for the dead)." [17]

The Roman Catholic system has greatly profited from the money paid for saying Mass for loved ones that have died.

- **Believed in the worship of Mary**

Hort: *"I am very far from pretending to understand completely the ever renewed vitality of mariolatry. ...I have been persuaded for many years that Mary-worship and 'Jesus-worship' have very much in common in their causes and their results."* [18]

(**Westcott** compelled his wife Sarah Louisa to take the name Mary in addition to her given name.) [19]

- **Believed in the sacraments (sacrifices)**

Hort: *"Still we dare not forsake the Sacraments, or God will forsake us."* [20]

- **Believed in baptismal regeneration**

Westcott: *"By birth he may, if he will, truly live here; by baptism he may if he will, truly live forever. ...I do think we have no right to exclaim against the idea of the commencement of a spiritual life, conditionally from Baptism, any more than we have to deny the commencement of a moral life from birth."* [21]

Hort: *"We maintain 'Baptismal Regeneration' as the most important of doctrines...the pure Romish view seems to me nearer, and more likely to lead to the truth than the Evangelical."* [22]

- **Acknowledged their heretical positions**

Hort to Ellerton: *"Possibly you have not heard that I have become Harold Browne's Examining Chaplain. I have only seen him two or three times in my life, not at all intimately, and was amazed when he made the proposal, in the kindest terms. I wrote to warn him that I was not safe or traditional in my theology, and that I could not give up association with heretics and such like."* [23]

Westcott to Lightfoot: *"It is strange, but all the questionable doctrines which I have ever maintained are in it* (a particular book lacking the fundamentals). *"* [24]

- **Other significant problems with Westcott and Hort**

▸ Did not believe in a literal heaven. [25]
▸ Did not believe in the literal second coming of the Lord Jesus Christ. [26]
▸ Did not believe in the Lord Jesus Christ's literal 1,000-year reign on earth. [27]
▸ Did not believe in the reality of angels. [28]
▸ Denied the Trinity's oneness. [29]
▸ Doubted the soul's existence apart from the body. [30]
▸ Did not believe in a literal Devil. [31]

It is hard to imagine, after reading what these two men believed, how any Christian that espouses the fundamentals of the faith could align himself with the likes of these two characters. However, every person choosing a modern version over the King James Bible does just that. He aligns himself with two men who despised the very things that most Christians hold sacred. Their influence can be seen *directly* in the revision of 1881 and *indirectly* in every modern version since that time. To ascertain the extent of their influence, read the writings of their contemporaries, including Dean Burgon, another member of the Revision committee.

This is what Dean Burgon said about the new Westcott and Hort Greek text. *"The history of the 'New' Greek Text is briefly this: a majority of the Revisors....are found to have put themselves into the hands of Westcott and Hort."*[32] Dean Burgon knew that the majority of the men involved in bringing about a "revision" of the Bible were improperly influenced by these two men.

The King James Bible New Testament comes from the **Majority Text** (that is, from those manuscripts that agree with each other and are most prevalent). Unlike the translators of 1611, Westcott and Hort rejected the Majority Text and relied heavily on the Alexandrian manuscripts which included the Vaticanus and Sinaiticus manuscripts. One of the members of the committee pointed out that the *"Vatican Codex...is regarded by Hort as a first rate authority; even when it stands alone, its evidence is regarded as of very high value. When it agrees with some other of certain selected good manuscripts, especially Tischendorf's Sinai Codex, their joint testimony is accepted as almost decisive."* Westcott and Hort regarded both the Vaticanus and Sinaiticus manuscripts as authoritative. Yet, these two manuscripts disagree with each other over 3,000 times in the Gospels alone.[33] These two manuscripts have greatly influenced every modern version on the market today and form the basis for 99% of them.

When the Majority Text (of the King James Bible) was overruled by majority vote, many of the original 99 Revision Committee members resigned from the work. Dr. Newth states that the dropout rate from Hort's overbearing presence was about 88%, with an average attendance of sixteen, and most of the attending members declining to vote.[34]

The final outcome was that Westcott and Hort changed the Greek text of the *Textus Receptus* in 5,337 instances. Hort writing to Westcott on April 12, 1861 clearly shows that they were well aware of the fact that their positions would be viewed as heretical. *"Also - but this may be cowardice - I have a sort of craving that our text should be cast*

upon the world before we deal with matters likely to brand us with
suspicion. I mean, a text, issued by men already known for what
will undoubtedly be treated as dangerous heresy, will have great
difficulties in finding its way to regions which it might otherwise
hope to reach, and whence it would not be easily banished by sub-
sequent alarms." [35]

Some may still not be convinced as to the heretical beliefs of these
two men. Westcott and Hort did *not* even believe in the inspiration of
the original autographs. Writing in their *Introduction to the New Testa-*
ment in Original Greek they stated: *"Little is gained by speculating as*
to the precise point at which such corruption came in. They may be
due to the original writings or to his amanuensis if he wrote from
dictation, or they may be due to one of the earliest transcribes." [36]

These two men are directly responsible for the spiritual backbone
lacking in most pulpits because of the changes brought about through
their corrupt text. Consequently, the modern versions have contributed
to the heresies of man. Many of these revisions attack the very fabric of
everything Christians hold sacred. Whether you choose the NIV, NKJV,
NASV, Living Bible, or any other modern version does not matter. The
foundation of each of these modern versions is corrupt. This includes
the NKJV when it departs from the *Textus Receptus*, choosing to align
itself with the false and heretical readings of the Westcott and Hort text.

The choice is simple. One must choose to hear the words of God as
recorded in the King James Bible and thereby be likened to the man that
built his house upon a firm foundation. *"Therefore whosoever heareth*
these sayings of mine, and doeth them, I will liken him unto a wise
*man, which **built his house upon a rock:" (Matthew 7:24).***

When the trials of life come (and they will) the only way to withstand
the onslaught is to have the right spiritual foundation. *"And the rain*
descended, and the floods came, and the winds blew, and beat upon
*that house; **and it fell not: for it was founded upon a rock" (Matthew***
7:25).

If one chooses to ignore the changes made by these modern perversions, he can be likened to a man that built his house upon sinking sand.

"And every one that heareth these sayings of mine, and doeth them not, shall be likened unto a foolish man, which built his house upon the sand: (Mathew 7:26).

When the trials of life come, without the right foundation, the destruction is foretold. *"And the rain descended, and the floods came, and the winds blew, and beat upon that house; and it fell: and great was the fall of it" (Matthew 7:27).*

Each of us should carefully consider the Psalmist's question: *"If the foundations be destroyed, what can the righteous do?" (Psalm 11:3).* In light of the evidence, only one choice remains. The King James Bible stands alone. All of the modern versions are built upon the same corrupt sinking-sand foundation. The Bible says, *"Blessed is he that readeth..."* *(Revelation 1:3).* One can be blessed by simply reading the Bible, but it does matter which "Bible" one chooses. The blessings do not come from picking up one's favorite version. They come from reading God's book, and God only wrote one book!

Chapter 14 Endnotes

1   David Otis Fuller, *Which Bible?,* Grand Rapids, MI (Grand Rapids International Publications, 5th ed., 1975), p. 157.

2   Grady, *Final Authority, op. cit.,* p. 192.

3   David Cloud, *Way of Life Encyclopedia,* WAY OF LIFE LITERATURE, Oak Harbor, WA.

4   J.M. Carroll, *The Trail of Blood,* (Ashland Avenue Baptist Church, Lexington, KY, 1931) p. 3.
     BAPTIST: Baptists do not trace their heritage to the Protestant Reformation, but back to Jesus Christ and the apostolic churches. Baptists are not a by-product of the Reformation as Curtis Whaley so aptly explained:

     Though many Baptist groups sprang up during the Protestant Reformation, according to Collier's Encyclopedia, the Baptists have descended from some of the evangelical sects of the preceding age during which the Roman and Orthodox Churches dominated all of Europe and suppressed all dissent. A Catholic, Cardinal Hosius, President of the Council of Trent (1545-1563), wrote during the early years of the Reformation period, "Were it not that the Baptists have been grievously tormented and cut off with the knife during the past twelve hundred years, they would swarm in greater numbers than all the reformers."

Baptist is name for various groups of Christians who hold certain distinctives such as:
1. *Salvation by grace through faith (Ephesians 2:8-9);*
3. *Eternal security of the believer (Romans 8:35-39);*
2. *Baptism by immersion of believers only (Acts 8:36-38);*
4. *The Bible as the sole authority for the church – tradition and other writings are rejected as authoritative (Isaiah 8:20, John 8:47, II Timothy 3:16), including a rejection of infant baptism;*
5. *Priesthood of the believer – a separate priesthood within the church is rejected (I Peter 2:5-9, Revelation 1:5-6);*
6. *Regenerate church membership – professing Christians, giving evidence of salvation are the only ones qualifying to join the local church (Romans 10:13, Titus 3:5);*
7. *Autonomy of the local church – all hierarchical structures are rejected (Acts 13:1, Colossians 1:2);*

[5] Williams, *From the Mind of God to the Mind of Man, op. cit.,* p. 83-84.

[6] Arthur Westcott, *Life and Letters of Brooke Foss Westcott,* volume I (London: Macmillan and Co., 1903), 52.

[7] *Ibid.,* volume I:207.

[8] Arthur Fenton Hort, *Life and Letters of Fenton John Anthony Hort,* volume I (London: Macmillan and Co., 1896), 420.

[9] *Ibid.,* volume I:414.

[10] *Ibid.,* volume I:416.

[11] *Ibid.,* volume I: 120.

[12] *Ibid.,* volume I:322

[13] *Ibid.,* volume II:336.

[14] Arthur Westcott, *Life and Letters of Brooke Foss Westcott,* volume I (London: Macmillan and Co., 1903), 309.

[15] Arthur Fenton Hort, *Life and Letters of Fenton John Anthony Hort,* volume II (London: Macmillan and Co., 1896), 34.

[16] *Ibid.,* volume I:140-141.

[17] Arthur Westcott, *Life and Letters of Brooke Foss Westcott,* volume II (London: Macmillan and Co., 1903), 349.

[18] Arthur Fenton Hort, *Life and Letters of Fenton John Anthony Hort,*

volume II (London: Macmillan and Co., 1896), 49-50.

[19] Arthur Westcott, *Life and Letters of Brooke Foss Westcott*, volume I (London: Macmillan and Co., 1903), 8.

[20] Arthur Fenton Hort, *Life and Letters of Fenton John Anthony Hort*, volume I (London: Macmillan and Co., 1896), 77.

[21] Arthur Westcott, *Life and Letters of Brooke Foss Westcott*, volume II (London: Macmillan and Co., 1903), 160.

[22] Arthur Fenton Hort, *Life and Letters of Fenton John Anthony Hort*, volume I (London: Macmillan and Co., 1896), 76.

[23] *Ibid.*, Volume II, 165.

[24] Arthur Westcott, *Life and Letters of Brooke Foss Westcott*, volume I (London: Macmillan and Co., 1903), 290.

[25] *Ibid.*, Volume II, 49.

[26] Benjamin Wilkerson, *Our Authorized Bible Vindicated*, (Takoma Park, 1930), 197-198.

[27] Arthur Westcott, *Life and Letters of Brooke Foss Westcott*, volume II (London: Macmillan and Co., 1903), 268.

[28] Arthur Fenton Hort, *Life and Letters of Fenton John Anthony Hort*, volume I (London: Macmillan and Co., 1896), 219.

[29] *Ibid.*, 136.

[30] *Ibid.*, Volume II, 64.

[31] *Ibid.*, Volume I, 121.

[32] Burgon, *Revision Revised, op. cit.*, p. 40.

[33] Bill Grady, *Final Authority, op. cit.*, 98.

[34] *Ibid.*, p. 256.

[35] Arthur Fenton Hort, *Life and Letters of Fenton John Anthony Hort*, volume I (London: Macmillan and Co., 1896), 445.

[36] Westcott and Hort, *Introduction to the New Testament in the Original Greek*, (NY: Harper & Bros., 1982) p. 280.

15

What Happened to the Originals?

*All **critics** of the King James Bible will agree on two points of interpretation. First: the word scripture is always used in reference to the missing originals; and second: inspiration describes the **singular act** whereby God mysteriously breathed out the very words which comprise these autographs. Combining these two concepts implies that the breath of God is in some way limited to the venerable originals and, of necessity, reduces all subsequent copies and translations to an inferior status.* [1] [Emphasis mine]

Dr. Bill Grady

D r. Grady's above analysis is insightful. It is surprising that those who hate our beloved King James Bible are guilty of so blatantly disregarding God's omnipotence. Dr. Grady confirms this thought when he states that, *"Without infallible preservation, we are forced to conclude that God's breath evaporated with the deterioration of His originals."* [2]

The Bible contains 53 instances in which the words *scripture* or *scriptures* are used. In every single instance, the word *scripture(s)* refers to a *copy* and not to the *original autographs*. Not even the critics claim that Timothy *(II Timothy 3:15)*, Paul *(Romans 15:4)*, Apollos *(Acts 18:24-28)*, the Bereans *(Acts 17:10)*, or even Christ *(Luke 4:17-21)* had the *original* autographs. Yet, the copies that each of these men read are referred to as scripture. Not even one of these individuals ever claimed the need to correct his respective copy.

These simple yet profound truths do not bother the critic. He will point out that that which is applicable to a copy in the same language cannot be applied to a translation. These critics further claim that the translation must be a verbal (word for word) and plenary (completely and totally) identical copy for it to be inerrant, infallible scripture. This is a dishonest ploy on the part of any person trained in language studies and familiar with the work of translation. Such an educated person knows that one cannot translate from one language into another without introducing some variation, since certain words must be added in order to complete the sense of the new language. Thankfully, the King James translators indicated these added words by placing them in italics.

Take note that many of the *italicized* words in the KJB are included in the modern versions without any indication of their absence from the Hebrew or Greek. For instance, *Psalm 23:1* includes an italicized verb in the King James Bible in order to complete the sense of the verse: "The LORD *is* my shepherd; I shall not want." The NIV reads, "The LORD is my shepherd, I shall not be in want." The NIV gives no indication of the added word. [3]

In an attempt to degrade the King James Bible, the critic takes his two-pronged attack seriously. He magnifies the originals, while despising the italicized words. As is frequently the case, that which man magnifies, God generally abhors *(Luke 16:15)*. The critic places the originals on a pedestal. What does God think about the *originals*? One of the clearest examples of God's complete lack of reverence for the *originals* would be His "protection" of the *original* Ten Commandments destroyed shortly after God produced them.

There is more to the story than man generally recognizes. Many people think that these Ten Commandments written on stone were destroyed before the Nation of Israel had a chance to learn their contents. However, God gave the *original* Ten Commandments to the Nation of Israel *verbally* before any of the Ten Commandments were ever written in stone.

Therefore, the people of Israel actually heard God give these commandments directly to them. This is easy to prove. Follow Moses' travels up and down the mountain and note that Moses is present at the *bottom* of the mountain when the Ten Commandments are originally given (as recorded in Exodus chapter 20).

Moses goes up:

*Exodus 19:3 And **Moses went up** unto God, and the LORD called unto him out of the mountain, saying, Thus shalt thou say to the house of Jacob, and tell the children of Israel;*

Moses goes down:

*Exodus 19:14 And **Moses went down** from the mount unto the people, and sanctified the people; and they washed their clothes.*

Moses goes up:

*Exodus 19:20 And the LORD came down upon mount Sinai, on the top of the mount: and **the LORD called Moses up** to the top of the mount; and Moses went up.*

Moses goes down, as recorded in the **final verse** of chapter nineteen:

*Exodus 19:25 So **Moses went down** unto the people, and spake unto them.*

Moses is down off the mountain among the people when God speaks. The next verses (beginning in the first verse of chapter 20) give the Ten Commandments. Many people would declare that the chapter break caused them to miss this important truth. I think God purposely put His Bible together in this fashion so that only a person that is interested in taking the time to **study** the truth will see it *(II Timothy 2:15)*. Moses goes down to the people and God speaks to them (the people) and conveys His Ten Commandments.

Exodus 20:1 And God spake all these words, saying, 2 I am the LORD thy God, which have brought thee out of the land of

Egypt, out of the house of bondage. 3 Thou shalt have no other gods before me . . .

Thus begins the Ten Commandments in verse three. The Lord speaks the tenth and final commandment in verse 17. We pick up the sequence of events following the tenth commandment.

Exodus 20:18 *And all the people saw the thunderings, and the lightnings, and the noise of the trumpet, and the mountain smoking: and when the people saw it, they removed, and stood afar off. 19 And they said unto Moses, Speak thou with us, and we will hear:* **but let not God speak with us,** *lest we die. 20 And Moses said unto the people, Fear not: for God is come to prove you, and that his fear may be before your faces, that ye sin not. 21 And the people stood afar off, and Moses drew near unto the thick darkness where God was. 22 And the LORD said unto Moses,* **Thus thou shalt say unto the children of Israel, Ye have seen that I have talked with you from heaven.**

Why were the people afraid of God's speaking directly to them? Because they had just heard Him speak to them, and they did not enjoy the experience! As soon as God finished speaking *the originals* (verses 1 through 17), the people turned to Moses (verse 19) and spoke to him. The people told Moses that they did not want God to speak directly to them anymore!

The pronouns in verse 22 of *the King James Bible* will shed additional light on this passage. As you may recall, *thou* is a **singular** second person pronoun; whereas *ye* and *you* are two forms of the **plural** second-person pronouns. Therefore, the LORD is speaking only to Moses when He says, "Thus *thou* shalt say..." He is instructing Moses to speak to the children of Israel. He tells Moses to say the following to the children of Israel: "*Ye* (Israel) have seen that I (God) have talked with *you* (Israel) from heaven." By understanding God's use of the pronouns in the King James Bible, one can understand exactly what has just transpired in this verse. God spoke to the Nation of Israel directly. In addition, God gives us further proof.

In case a person continues to doubt the manner in which these events occurred, two other passages clearly prove that God spoke His *original* Ten Commandments directly to the people. In Deuteronomy, we find the record of Moses speaking to the Nation of Israel.

*Deuteronomy 4:10 Specially the day that thou stoodest before the LORD thy God in Horeb, when the LORD said unto me, Gather me the people together, and **I will make them** (the people) **hear my words,** that they may learn to fear me all the days that they shall live upon the earth, and that they may teach their children. 11 And ye came near and stood under the mountain; and the mountain burned with fire unto the midst of heaven, with darkness, clouds, and thick darkness. 12 **And the LORD spake unto you** (the people) **out of the midst of the fire: ye heard the voice of the words,** but saw no similitude; only ye heard a voice. 13 **And he declared unto you** his covenant, which he commanded you to perform, **even ten commandments;** and he wrote them upon two tables of stone.*

Deuteronomy chapter four says that God told Moses to gather the people together to make them hear His words. Verse thirteen says these words were the Ten Commandments. Still doubting? God knew some would have a hard time accepting the truth since the truth of the scripture contradicts the sequence of events as portrayed by Hollywood and Charlton Heston. Here is another proof from the dialog of Moses, speaking to the children of Israel.

*Deuteronomy 9:10 And the LORD delivered unto me **two tables of stone** written with the finger of God; and on them was written according to all the words, **which the LORD spake with you** (the people) in the mount out of the midst of the fire in the day of the assembly.* (As recorded in Exodus chapter 20)

The people had received the original Ten Commandments *verbally* from God prior to their being broken while Moses was receiving the *written* word on the mountain. Notice that the verse says that the Lord spoke with the people and then delivered the two tables of stone to Moses – written with the finger of God. Exodus chapter 31 tells us about these two tables of stone. These are the *written* originals (unless someone wrote them down when God first spoke them to the people!).

> ***Exodus 31:18** And he gave unto Moses, when he had made an end of communing with him upon mount Sinai, two tables of testimony, tables of stone, **written with the finger of God.***

Moses receives these two tables of stone written with the finger of God. Meanwhile, the people at the bottom of the mountain have gathered together to persuade Aaron to make a molten calf to be their god. They break the verbal commandments given to them by God *(Exodus 32:8)*. Moses then comes down the mountain with these written "originals." Remember that these tables technically are not even the *originals* since the original words were given verbally to the people.

> ***Exodus 32:15** And Moses turned, and went down from the mount, and the two tables of the testimony were in his hand: the tables were written on both their sides; on the one side and on the other were they written. 16 **And the tables were the work of God, and the writing was the writing of God, graven upon the tables.***

One might assume that God would think very highly of these prized *originals*, possibly even instructing Moses to take special care of them. But instead, we read that Moses breaks all Ten Commandments at one time.

> ***Exodus 32:19** And it came to pass, as soon as he came nigh unto the camp, that he saw the calf, and the dancing: and Moses' anger waxed hot, and **he cast the tables out of his hands, and brake them beneath the mount.***

There go the *originals*! What is God going to do? God thought so highly of them that they did not even make it off the mountain. Because Moses breaks the *originals*, God has to inspire some more copies. In chapter 34, Moses is told to make two more tables and God will again write the Ten Commandments upon them.

*Exodus 34:1 And the LORD said unto Moses, Hew thee two tables of stone like unto the first: **and I will write upon these tables** the words that were in the first tables, which thou brakest.*

Moses is told to hew out two new tables and **the Lord** will write upon them. We find later in the chapter that the Lord chose to write upon them with the hand of Moses! These *copies* are inspired. In verse four, Moses hews out the two tables of stone and goes back up the mountain.

*Exodus 34:4 And **he hewed two tables of stone** like unto the first; and Moses rose up early in the morning, and went up unto mount Sinai, as the LORD had commanded him, and took in his hand the two tables of stone.*

*Exodus 34:27 **And the LORD said unto Moses, Write thou these words:** for after the tenor of these words I have made a covenant with thee and with Israel. 28 And he was there with the LORD forty days and forty nights; he did neither eat bread, nor drink water. **And he wrote upon the tables the words of the covenant, the ten commandments.***

Moses is the one that writes the words, even though God said He would write them Himself (verse one). So, who wrote the words? God or man? God led Moses to write a perfect *copy* of the *originals*. This should give some indication of what God thinks about the originals and how He can inspire the copies as well. We should place no greater emphasis upon the originals than does Almighty God.

We should believe in the power and omnipotence of God. I do not have any problem believing the King James Bible to be the word of God to the English-speaking people. If the Lord wanted man to live by every word of God can He not guide the translators *by giving them the understanding* in *how* to translate His word? The Lord used natural means to write inspired scripture, thus proving His magnificence. **The fact that God could use men to do anything perfect should amaze us all. If He could lead them to write perfectly in the originals, what limits God from insuring a work of perfection in its translation?**

*II Peter 1:19 We have also **a more sure word of prophecy;** whereunto ye do well that ye take heed, as unto a light that shineth in a dark place, until the day dawn, and the day star arise in your hearts: 20 Knowing this first, that no prophecy of the scripture is of any private interpretation. 21 For the prophecy came not in old time by the will of man: but **holy men of God spake as they were moved by the Holy Ghost.***

This is what I believe about my Bible. Holy men of God spake as they were moved by the Holy Ghost. In the verses preceding this passage, Peter refers to being an eyewitness to Jesus' majesty. Then he concludes that we have **a more sure word of prophecy with the written word of God.** We have the written word of God. Holy men of God spake as they were moved by the Holy Ghost, and we have the results. Look at the next example for further insight into the mind of God concerning the *originals.*

*Jeremiah 36:1 And it came to pass in the fourth year of Jehoiakim the son of Josiah king of Judah, that this word came unto Jeremiah from the LORD, saying, 2 Take thee a roll of a book, and **write therein all the words that I have spoken** unto thee **against** Israel, and **against** Judah, and **against** all the nations, from the day I spake unto thee, from the days of Josiah, even unto this day.*

The insight you should first get from this verse is that the word of God is basically negative and *against* you. Here is the *original* being spoken to Jeremiah. Notice that the word of God has many negatives. It is against your thoughts, your actions, your sin, and you... if you are lost, backslidden, or reprobate.

*Jeremiah 36:4 Then Jeremiah called Baruch the son of Neriah: and **Baruch wrote from the mouth of Jeremiah all the words of the LORD,** which he had spoken unto him, upon a roll of a book. 5 And Jeremiah commanded Baruch, saying, I am shut up; I cannot go into the house of the LORD: 6 Therefore go thou, and read in the roll, **which thou hast written from my*** *mouth, the words of the LORD in the ears of the people in the LORD'S house upon the fasting day: and also thou shalt read them in the ears of all Judah that come out of their cities.*

Baruch wrote the words (the words of the LORD) spoken from the mouth of Jeremiah. The prophet tells him to read them in the LORD's house.

Jeremiah 36:10 Then read Baruch in the book the words of Jeremiah in the house of the LORD, in the chamber of Gemariah the son of Shaphan the scribe, in the higher court, at the entry of the new gate of the LORD'S house, in the ears of all the people.

Baruch obeys and reads all of *the words of Jeremiah*. But I thought they were *the words of God?* Do you see how this works? Jeremiah's words *are* God's words. Michaiah (verse eleven) then went to the king's house and told the scribes what he had heard.

*Jeremiah 36:14 Therefore all the princes sent Jehudi the son of Nethaniah, the son of Shelemiah, the son of Cushi, unto Baruch, saying, Take in thine hand the roll wherein thou hast read in the ears of the people, and come. So Baruch the son of Neriah took the roll in his hand, and came unto them. 15 And they said unto him, Sit down now, and read it in our ears. So Baruch read it in their ears. 16 Now it came to pass, **when they had heard all the words, they were afraid** both one and other, and said unto Baruch, We will surely tell the king of all these words. 17 And they asked Baruch, saying, Tell us now, How didst thou write all these words at his mouth? 18 Then Baruch answered them, **He pronounced all these words unto me with his mouth, and I wrote them with ink in the book.*** (II Peter 1:21: Holy men of God **spake** as they were moved by the Holy Ghost.)

One of the greatest indicators of the true word of God is its convicting properties on the tenderhearted, and thus we see the *fear* produced when it is read. After experiencing its conviction, the people want to know how this book came to exist. Baruch's simple answer seems almost to mock those who question him – *Jeremiah pronounced all the words with his mouth and I wrote them with ink in the book.*

The princes warn Baruch and Jeremiah to hide themselves and the book while the scribes go and tell the king. They know that the word and the messenger will be attacked. After the king hears the words, he tells Jehudi to get the roll out of Elishama's chamber.

> ***Jeremiah 36:21*** *So the king sent Jehudi to fetch the roll: and he took it out of Elishama the scribe's chamber. And Jehudi read it in the ears of the king, and in the ears of all the princes which stood beside the king. 22 Now the king sat in the winterhouse in the ninth month: and there was a fire on the hearth burning before him. 23 And it came to pass, that when Jehudi had read three or four leaves,* **he cut it with the penknife, and cast it into the fire that was on the hearth, until all the roll was consumed in the fire that was on the hearth.** *24* ***Yet they were not afraid,*** *nor rent their garments, neither the king, nor any of his servants that heard all these words.*

Notice that the king's bold attempt to destroy the word of God caused onlookers to lose the initial *fear* and conviction we read about in verse sixteen. This is much like the situation today. Critics attack the very words of God, causing people to lose their fear of God. The Lord does not find this attack upon His word an insurmountable problem. He simply creates another *original* (or is it a *copy of the original*?). Furthermore, take note that this copy contains many additional words not found in the *first original.*

> ***Jeremiah 36:27*** *Then the word of the LORD came to Jeremiah, after that the king had burned the roll, and the words which Baruch wrote at the mouth of Jeremiah, saying, 28* ***Take thee again another roll, and write in it all the former words that were in the first roll,*** *which Jehoiakim the king of Judah hath burned. 29 And thou shalt say to Jehoiakim king of Judah, Thus saith the LORD; Thou hast burned this roll, saying, Why hast thou written therein, saying, The king of Babylon shall*

certainly come and destroy this land, and shall cause to cease from thence man and beast?

Because Jehoiakim tries to destroy the word of God, the Lord pronounces additional judgments against him. These are also to be written in the new copy/original.

Jeremiah 36:30 *Therefore thus saith the LORD of Jehoiakim king of Judah; He shall have none to sit upon the throne of David: and his dead body shall be cast out in the day to the heat, and in the night to the frost. 31 And I will punish him and his seed and his servants for their iniquity; and I will bring upon them, and upon the inhabitants of Jerusalem, and upon the men of Judah, all the evil that I have pronounced against them; but they hearkened not. 32 Then took Jeremiah **another roll**, and gave it to Baruch the scribe, the son of Neriah; who wrote therein from the mouth of Jeremiah all the words of the book which Jehoiakim king of Judah had burned in the fire: **and there were added besides unto them many like words.***

Do you see what this *copy* contains? It contains all of the words of the first *original* plus many other words. Sort of makes one wonder about the italicized words found in the King James Bible. The additional words were added by Jeremiah . . . or Baruch . . . or God? All three! Who added the italicized words found in the King James Bible?

Chapters 45 through 51 record the text of the *copy*. Look what happens to the text of the judgment against Babylon. Jeremiah tells Seraiah to bind a stone to it and throw it into the Euphrates River. What does this do to one's opinion concerning God's method of supernatural preservation of the original autographs? God does not care what we think.

Jeremiah 51:60 *So Jeremiah wrote in a book all the evil that should come upon Babylon, even all these words that are written against Babylon. 61 And Jeremiah said to Seraiah, When thou comest to Babylon, and shalt see, and shalt read all these words; 62 Then shalt thou say, O LORD, thou hast spoken against this place, to cut it off, that none shall remain in it,*

neither man nor beast, but that it shall be desolate for ever.
*63 And it shall be, **when thou hast made an end of reading***
this book, that thou shalt bind a stone to it, and cast it into
the midst of Euphrates:

In other words, nobody is going to *burn* His "book" twice. What does God think of the beloved *originals* to which all of the Ph.D.'s are referring? He is the One that insured that they would not remain in existence. God will not allow us to worship the paper upon which the *originals* are written. This may also explain why God used predominantly Hebrew and Greek, two languages that He knew would be frozen in time, to pen His word.

God has forsaken and abandoned the originals. He has no use for them, and anyone who tries to dig them up or idolize them is not being led of God. Hezekiah had to destroy the brazen serpent because people were making it an idol, much the same way people would treat the originals if they still existed today. *"He removed the high places, and brake the images, and cut down the groves, and **brake in pieces the brasen serpent that Moses had made***: *for unto those days the children of Israel did **burn incense to it***: *and he called it Nehushtan" (**II Kings 18:4**).*

What does all of this *original* stuff mean to us today? Remember that the second original (copy) of Jeremiah chapter 36 had additional words added to it by God. The italicized words in the King James Bible are a good manifestation of this concept. There are many understood words when the Hebrew and Greek are translated into English or some other language. This is why the King James Bible translators were led of God to italicize these words. One such example is found in ***Deuteronomy 8:3***. Man is to live by every WORD that proceedeth out of the mouth of the Lord. "Word" is not found in the original and is therefore italicized in your King James Bible. Check it out!

Deuteronomy 8:3 *And he humbled thee, and suffered thee to hunger, and fed thee with manna, which thou knewest not, neither did thy fathers know; that he might make thee know that man doth not live by bread only, but by every **word** that proceedeth out of the mouth of the LORD doth man live.*

The word *word* is italicized in the King James Bible because it was not included in the *original* Hebrew. This is similar to the *second original (copy)* of Jeremiah chapter 36. It is a word which is added. However, when the Lord quotes *Deuteronomy 8:3*, as recorded in the book of Matthew, the word *word* is not in italics in the KJB. This fact is significant since this one example alone should nullify the critics' claim that understood words (the italicized words) should not be included in the English translation.

> *Matthew 4:4 But he answered and said, It is written, Man shall not live by bread alone, but by every **word** that proceedeth out of the mouth of God.*

Word is not italicized in Matthew chapter four when the Lord quotes Deuteronomy chapter eight. This is very important because it means that a word provided in the translation from Hebrew to English is included in the Greek original! This conclusively proves that the italicized words are not just words added by man, but are in fact part of the inspired scripture. Another good example of this concept is Peter's quotation of *Psalm 16:8 in Acts 2:25*. After all of the evidence given against them, you might be wondering why God would allow men to produce these modern versions. The answer is found in Deuteronomy chapter thirteen. Whenever these false prophets (or false bibles) come on the scene, God uses them to prove our love for Him *(I Corinthians 11:19)*. A false bible is very similar to a false prophet. Each purports to speak His word but is, in fact, false.

> *Deuteronomy 13:1 If there arise among you a prophet, or a dreamer of dreams, and giveth thee a sign or a wonder, 2 And the sign or the wonder come to pass, whereof he spake unto thee, saying, Let us go after other gods, which thou hast not known, and let us serve them; 3 Thou shalt not hearken unto the words of that prophet, or that dreamer of dreams: **for the LORD your God proveth you, to know whether ye love the LORD your God with all your heart and with all your soul.** 4 Ye shall walk after the LORD your God, and fear him, and keep his commandments, and obey his voice, and ye shall serve him, and cleave unto him.*

When we apply Deuteronomy chapter thirteen to the modern version phenomenon, we see why they exist. God wants to prove our love for Him and His word. These false bibles preach, teach, and prophesy something apart from the truth. We must remain true to God no matter the opposition. We must be strong no matter the magnitude of the attack by Satan and his scribes.

Who Killed Goliath?

One more example illustrates how the modern version supporter can get himself into some deep water. Who killed Goliath? David, right? According to the NIV, Elhanan killed Goliath.

*(NIV) II Samuel 21:19 In another battle with the Philistines at Gob, **Elhanan** son of Jaare-Oregim the Bethlehemite **killed Goliath the Gittite,** who had a spear with a shaft like a weaver's rod.*

The NIV claims that Elhanan killed Goliath the Gittite. Why does the NIV make this false claim? The phrase *"the brother of"* happens to be italicized in the King James Bible and therefore is not found in the Hebrew. However, it was "understood" by the translators and therefore added in the English language. Good excuse for the revisers to remove it, right? Not if you want truth. According to the true word of God, Elhanan did not kill Goliath. He killed Goliath's brother.

*(KJB) II Samuel 21:19 And there was again a battle in Gob with the Philistines, where Elhanan the son of Jaare-oregim, a Bethlehemite, **slew the brother of Goliath the Gittite**, the staff of whose spear was like a weaver's beam.*

If the authors of the NIV are so careless as to allow this error to remain unchanged in millions of copies, how much can you trust them with the remainder of the Bible? One would think that this glaring error would be easy for everyone to see and realize that the problems do not stop here. However, some will still reject the truth because they have painted themselves into a corner and cannot figure out how to get out. Their pride has overpowered any commitment to finding the truth and the word of God.

In order for a translation to be authoritative, strict adherence to the words of the Holy Spirit must be used. Therefore, a strict adherence to a word-for-word translation must be followed. The Hebrew and Greek must be carefully translated into the new language. The means employed by the translators of the KJB clearly displays their honesty and integrity. In order to achieve this exactness and authority, they placed in italics the words used in their translation that were not actually found in the original text. Jakob van Bruggen, commenting on this aspect of the King James Bible, asserts that:

> *To a large extent, the KJV owes its authority to the rule that inserted words were printed in italics. The Bible reader was thus able to see how carefully the translators treated God's Word. They were afraid to add even one word, but if they were not able to translate without adding a word for the sake of clarity, they indicated that it had been added.* [4]

Versions today do not adhere to the same principles followed by the translators of the King James Bible. Rather than a word-for-word translation, they have opted for a different set of manuscripts, utilizing the dynamic equivalency method. Therefore, not only are their methods different, but their foundation is also fundamentally flawed. Dynamic equivalency seeks to translate the *meaning* from one language to another. This allows the translators to determine the word used because they decide what God meant to say. When a different set of manuscripts establishes their foundation, one can easily see the potential for problems. This potential is borne out in every modern version on the market, as well as in those that have already fallen by the wayside and yet to be produced.

Study the italicized words found in the King James Bible. The producers of the modern versions have been the greatest critics of the italicized words of the KJB. That is why they frequently omit entire clauses from their respective versions. Imagine the confusion when the italicized words are excluded from the text. Satan thrives in an environment of confusion. The modern versions help to create just such an environment.

Now, compare the passages containing italicized words in the KJB with the same passages in a modern version. Wouldn't it be the height of hypocrisy to find many of these so-called added words in the modern versions? These problems emanate from the neo-orthodox view that the concepts or ideas are inspired, rather than the actual words themselves. This type of philosophy concerning the Bible allows the translator to change words, add words, and delete words, as long as he purports to convey the original concept. As we have seen, translators frequently fail to achieve their desired goals, and therefore fail to convey the truth. One book stands alone above all the hypocrisy, all the change, and certainly above all the Hollywood hype.

Chapter 15 Endnotes

[1] Grady, Final Authority, op.cit., p. 16,17.

[2] Ibid., p. 17.

[3] Ibid., p. 163.

[4] Jakob van Bruggen, The Future of the Bible (Nashville, 1978), p. 136-137.

16

Examining the "Errors"

*The preacher must learn to test the error by **the truth** and not the truth by the **error**. To fill one's mind with error, with a view to an appreciation of the truth, is not only most unprofitable but positively dangerous.* [1]

Alfred P. Gibbs

L ike many other new Christians, I was taken to the local Christian bookstore soon after becoming saved in order to buy a Bible. Of course, like most new converts, I was unaware that there were more versions of the bible to choose from than there are keys on a piano. I depended on others to guide me *(Acts 8:31)* in the selection process. My new Christian friends told me that they heard that the New American Standard was best; so, I paid about $50.00 for one of the best leather NASV's in stock.

Within a few months of my conversion, questions about "which bible" began to surface in my discussions with others. Thus, the inerrancy of the word of God was an issue of importance very early in my Christian walk. After the issue was plainly presented to me, I bought a King James Bible. I made this decision primarily on the basis of God's promise to supernaturally preserve His words for every generation *(Psalm 12:6-7)*. I knew the word of God (the KJB) told me about the Lord Jesus Christ and convicted and convinced me of my need for a Saviour. I knew that without the word of God, I had little or no chance of growing as a Christian. However, immediately upon becoming acquainted with the Bible issue, I was bombarded by those who did not think that a person should be limited to one Bible only. Did God really want me to pick and choose the verse in the version I liked best? Why was there so much confusion?

One of the individuals who questioned my early allegiance to the KJB was my supervisor in the Air Force. He was a Mormon. He and I frequently spent time discussing the Bible. He usually got the best of me in our early discussions since I was still a babe in Christ. Once he became aware of my introduction to a position of belief in the KJB alone, he brought me a book published by the Mormons which highlighted the "errors in the King James Bible." Since then their approach has somewhat changed. The Mormons advertise free books of Mormon or King James Bibles (freely printed and distributed) in order to snare unsuspecting people.

These events occurred in my life at precisely the same time that I left the Methodist church and began attending an independent Baptist church in Niceville, Florida. The eighteen-year-old young man that led me to the Lord was a Methodist, so I had begun attending his church. My new pastor and the men of the church clearly taught that the KJB was the infallible and inerrant word of God.

The book that my Mormon supervisor showed me was published by the Mormon "church." Its expressed purpose was to provide Mormon followers with the necessary ammunition to combat the claims of Christians asserting the King James Bible to be the infallible and final biblical authority. It is important to understand why the Mormon church would do this. There can only be one ultimate authority. The Mormon church claims to be this authority! One of the first things this cult (or any cult) must do in order to convert someone to its false teachings is to destroy anything or anyone else competing for authority in that person's life. The ultimate objective of such organizations is to become the sole authority in the life of the targeted individual.

My supervisor showed me the first "error" listed in his book. He said this one error was enough to convince him that the King James Bible could not be infallible and inerrant. I must admit, it floored me and created doubts as to what I was being taught at my new church. I could not respond and felt betrayed by those that had "misled" me about the King James Bible's perfection.

However, God's Bible principles always sustain the earnest child of God who is looking for the truth *(John 8:32)*. The Christian's outlook should match that of Joseph. His brethren tried to destroy him and, after many years of suffering with many doubts about God's prophecies, he saw God's plan and purpose for his life fulfilled. This is what he told his brethren: *"But as for you, ye thought evil against me; but **God meant it unto good..."** (Genesis 50:20)*. Praise God, He still miraculously delivers!

The Lord used the answer to this Mormon "error" to show me that I must believe in the infallibility of scripture *by faith* no matter the doubts created by Satan and his cohorts. The "error" contained in this book, to which I refer, concerned the differing accounts of Saul's trip to Damascus at the time of his conversion. There are three accounts of Saul's salvation experience given in the Bible. These three are found in Acts chapters 9, 22 and 26. We also read in Acts chapter 13, verse 9 that Saul's name was changed to Paul.

Each of the three accounts of Paul's conversion experience records that a light from heaven blinded him as the Lord appeared and spoke to him. Pay close attention to *Acts 9:7,* as compared to *Acts 22:9*. Acts chapter 9 indicates that the men with Paul *heard a voice*, while Acts chapter 22 records that they did *not* hear the voice of the Lord. The KJB "error," as asserted by this Mormon, concerns whether the men with Saul *did* or did *not* hear the voice of the Lord. My problem was figuring out how to reconcile these two seemingly contradictory accounts.

Even the self-proclaimed scholars have allowed these two "contradictory" accounts to convince them that the King James Bible contains errors. They have allowed these incorrect perceptions to convince themselves and others that the KJB contains errors just as the modern versions do. Such scholars are no better than the Mormon who attempts to undermine the authority of the word of God. What effect do these verses have on you? Read the next two passages, paying close attention to the two verses mentioned previously (verses 9:7 and 22:9).

Acts 9:3 And as he journeyed, he came near Damascus: and suddenly there shined round about him a light from heaven: 4 And he fell to the earth, and heard a voice saying unto him, Saul, Saul, why persecutest thou me? 5 And he said, Who art thou, Lord? And the Lord said, I am Jesus whom thou persecutest: it is hard for thee to kick against the pricks. 6 And he trembling and astonished said, Lord, what wilt thou have me to do? And the Lord said unto him, Arise, and go into the *city, and it shall be told thee what thou must do. 7 **And the men which journeyed with him stood speechless, hearing a voice**, but seeing no man*

Chapter 9, verse 7 plainly says that the men **heard a voice**. The issue presented to me was whether they did or did not hear the voice of the Lord. When this passage is compared with chapter 22, the supposed contradiction becomes evident. Chapter 22, verse 9 plainly says that the men that were with Saul **did *not* hear the voice**. Which is right? Or, are they both right? Do these two accounts in fact contradict each other and thereby prove that there are errors in the King James Bible? Satan wants you to think so. But what does God think? Pay close attention to verse 9.

*Acts 22:6 And it came to pass, that, as I made my journey, and was come nigh unto Damascus about noon, suddenly there shone from heaven a great light round about me. 7 And I fell unto the ground, and heard a voice saying unto me, Saul, Saul, why persecutest thou me? 8 And I answered, Who art thou, Lord? And he said unto me, I am Jesus of Nazareth, whom thou persecutest. 9 **And they that were with me** saw indeed the light, and were afraid; but they **heard not the voice** of him that spake to me.*

Read the two accounts together, closely comparing *Acts 9:7* with *Acts 22:9*.

*Acts 9:7 And the men which journeyed with him stood speechless, **hearing a voice**, but seeing no man.*

*Acts 22:9 And they that were with me saw indeed the light, and were afraid; but they **heard not the voice** of him that spake to me.*

Did they hear the voice or not hear a voice? Has the Devil put confusion and doubt into your mind already? Has your faith, like mine, been shaken by simply reading these two accounts? I say the Devil is responsible, because these doubts certainly do not originate from God. *"For God is not the author of **confusion**, but of **peace**, as in all churches of the saints." (I Corinthians 14:33).* Satan uses everything at his disposal to create confusion. However, God will give peace using the same tools that Satan uses to create confusion in the mind of the believer. For most people, one *supposed* contradiction would be enough to convince them that the KJB has errors. What about you? Have you failed to realize the necessary element of faith concerning God's supernatural book?

It is unmistakably clear that both accounts refer to the same event. What is the answer? Did these men with Saul hear the voice, or didn't they? Before we study the answer, each of us must realize that faith is necessary to believe that God has preserved His perfect word as promised. You must go to His word with a receptive heart and mind toward the truth. If you don't see the truth, it is not God's fault. It is yours *(II Timothy 2:15)*!

When I was presented with this problem, I could not answer it immediately. Someone had to show me the answer. But the questions initially shook my faith. I had to be willing to seek for an answer and to listen to the person that eventually provided the answer. Thank God that *"faith cometh by hearing, and hearing by the word of God"* **(Romans 10:17)**.

Many years later, I learned that the Devil was the one that caused me to doubt the accuracy of God's word. It was not God that had caused me to doubt! As a matter of fact, I now call this one of *"God's little rat traps."* Why would He allow such peculiar wording in His Bible to be used by cults to create doubts in the minds of believers? Didn't God know that people would take these two passages and try to prove that the King James Bible contains errors in these passages? Sure He did! Consider that He also knew that Satan would twist His words in Genesis chapter 3 with Eve in the Garden and *Acts 2:38* and the Church of Christ's position on baptismal regeneration. We have a responsibility to believe God, no matter how convincing the arguments, regardless of how our faith is initially shaken.

I came to realize that if a man decides to reject the truth, God will let him – actually providing the resources for him to do so. Consider a simple case in point: all those that reject the truth of the gospel and go into the Tribulation period will receive a lie *"from God."* The Bible says God is going to send them a strong delusion (a lie). This lie will be as damning as rejecting God's word is today. *"And for this cause **God shall send them strong delusion**, that they should believe **a lie"** (II Thessalonians 2:11)*. Satan will be the tool used by God to execute this lie *(II Thessalonians 2:3-4)*. He will allow Satan to sit in the temple of

God as though he is God; therefore, it is God that will send the strong delusion. This is a situation similar to the circumstances seen in the story of Job. Satan attacked Job, but God says He was the One that was moved against Job *(Job 2:3)*.

However, one must fully comprehend that it is not God's will for anyone to be ignorant of the truth and believe a lie. His will is clearly expressed: *"**Who will have all men** to be saved, and to **come unto the knowledge of the truth"** (I Timothy 2:4)*. God provides the truth, but He also points out that in the last days, men will be: *"Ever learning, and never able to come to the knowledge of the truth" (II Timothy 3:7)*. No matter the scriptural evidence against such positions, some men still claim that scholarship has reached new and higher levels than those that existed hundreds of years ago. The Bible teaches otherwise…and it is not good to call God a liar *(Romans 3:4)*.

The answer to this "contradiction" in the book of Acts can be easily understood with a little Bible study on our part. The same passages that convinced my Mormon supervisor (and the Mormon church) are also the ones that have stumped many a "scholar" who was ever learning, but never able to find the truth.

This "problem" in the book of Acts can actually be answered in a few different ways, but what if you could not find any answer? Should you believe God's promise of supernatural preservation any less? No! *Faith* in God's promises is the only sure thing that will help us avoid being children tossed to and fro. Paul tells us *"That we **henceforth be no more children, tossed to and fro, and carried about with every wind of doctrine**, by the sleight of men, and cunning craftiness, whereby they lie in wait to deceive" (**Ephesians 4:14**)*.

Some of the Possible Solutions

In chapter 9, the men with Saul were **standing** when it says **they heard a voice**. Therefore they heard **a** voice before they had fallen to the ground.

*Acts 9:7 And the men which journeyed with him **stood** speech-less, **hearing a voice**, but **seeing no man**.*

Once they had fallen to the ground, the Lord speaks so that *only* Saul can hear Him *(John 8:43)*. The men that were with him did *not* hear **the voice** of the Lord as He spoke directly to Saul. They also did not recognize that it was **the voice** of God because it says they **saw no man.** They were looking around for a man, not looking up.

Now, closely read the account in chapter 22. Saul falls to the ground and hears **a** voice speaking to him only. Notice that it is just **a** voice because, at this point, Saul did not yet recognize Who was speaking. It is only **a** voice until one recognizes the speaker. Then it becomes **the** voice of the person speaking.

*Acts 22:7 And **I fell unto the ground**, and **heard a voice** saying unto me, Saul, Saul, why persecutest thou me?*

Since Saul does not realize Who is speaking to him, he poses the following question.

*Acts 22:8 And I answered, **Who art thou, Lord?** And he said unto me, I am Jesus of Nazareth, whom thou persecutest.*

Later, Saul (Paul) relates his detailed account of these same events to the people. The other men with Saul saw the light, but did not hear **the** voice that spoke to him. Notice that he says it is *the* voice that they did not hear, not **a** voice. The Bible plainly says they heard **a** voice.

*Acts 22:9 And they that were with me saw indeed the light, and were afraid; but they heard not **the** voice of him that spake to me.*

As the story progresses, we are told that Ananias came to Saul and that Saul regained his sight. The message conveyed by Ananias is also directly from the Lord. Ananias says that the Lord appeared to Saul and he heard the voice from out of His mouth. Notice the **singular**, second person pronouns of *thee* and *thou* used to show that only Saul heard the Lord's voice. Ananias speaking:

*Acts 22:14 And he said, The God of our fathers hath chosen **thee**, that **thou** shouldest know his will, and see that Just One, and **shouldest hear the voice of his mouth**.*

Every word of God is pure. The Bible says that Saul – **thou** – *shouldest hear **the** voice of his mouth.* This excluded the other men because Ananias did not use the plural second person pronouns *you* or *ye*. Therefore, the other men heard **a** voice before they had fallen to the ground as recorded in Acts chapter 9, but they did *not* hear **the** voice or message of God which was revealed only to Saul.

Another way to understanding the difference between hearing **a** voice and hearing **the** voice can be explained as follows. A person will say he hears **a** voice (verse 4) if he cannot distinguish the origin of that voice. However, once it becomes apparent who is doing the speaking (that is, whose voice it is), he will say he hears **the** voice of a particular person. Perhaps the following example will clarify this point.

Suppose your pastor was talking to a group of people in another room, but you could not distinguish who was speaking. If someone asked you if you heard **the** voice of your pastor, you would answer "no" since you could not clearly distinguish that it was his voice that you were hearing. But if you were asked if you heard **a** voice, you could answer "yes" to this question – even if you could not discern the identity of the speaker.

With this in mind, realize that in chapter 9 the men heard **a** voice before they fell to the ground. But when God spoke to Saul, they did not hear **the** voice of the One that spoke to Saul only.

Acts chapter 26 sheds additional light on the matter. The timeframe of this chapter shows that they all had fallen to the ground by the time that Saul heard **a** voice (that he did not recognize). Notice that the Lord was speaking to Saul only.

*Acts 26:13 At midday, O king, I saw in the way a light from heaven, above the brightness of the sun, shining round about me and them which journeyed with me. 14 **And when we were all fallen to the earth, I heard a voice speaking unto me**, and saying in the Hebrew tongue, Saul, Saul, why persecutest thou me? it is hard for thee to kick against the pricks. 15 And I said, Who art thou, Lord? And he said, I am Jesus whom thou persecutest. 16 But rise, and stand upon thy feet: for **I have appeared unto thee** for this purpose, to make thee a minister and a witness both of these things which **thou hast seen**, and of those things in the which I will appear unto thee; 17 Delivering thee from the people, and from the Gentiles, unto whom now I send thee,*

According to Acts chapter 9, all of the men heard **a** voice, but only Saul heard **the** voice speaking directly to him. Saul says that when he first fell to the ground (verse 14) he heard **a** voice, but he did not realize Who was speaking. He then inquired concerning the identity of the speaker and learned that he was hearing **the** voice of the Lord. If you could ask the men who accompanied Saul what they heard, they would reply that they heard **a** voice, but they could not say that they heard **the** voice of the Lord. The Lord spoke only to Saul, and he was the only one that could account for its source.

But there is more. This is another place in which the "old, archaic" King James Bible provides revelation superior to that in all of the modern versions put together – and does so without changing one word. Note the use of the words "**thee**" and "**thou**" again in chapter 26. The modern translations, treating the Christian like an ignorant child, say that you cannot understand a verse with these pronouns in it; therefore, they change both singular and plural second person pronouns to the generic *you*. This thinking is extremely flawed and promotes a satanic lie used by the cults and critics alike!

By changing the words, the truth is hidden. With these singular second person pronouns (*thee, thou,* and *thy*) retained in the passage, the scripture is far superior. These specific pronouns refer to a **singular** subject. Conversely, *you, ye,* and *your* are used to make **plural** references. Note that the *singular* pronouns all begin with a "t" while the *plural* second person pronouns all begin with a "y." The device of these distinct pronouns is yet another way whereby to distinguish that Saul alone (consequently: *thee, thou, thy, thine*) heard the voice of the Lord. No such distinction is made in the modern versions.

When I showed this answer to my Mormon supervisor, he was in shock. From then on, he was much more careful in his attempts to shake my faith in the authority of God's book. I never did have the opportunity to lead this man to Christ. However, as a baby Christian, I was able to present a clear testimony concerning the promises of God relative to His supernatural preservation of His word *(Psalm 12:6-7)*. Not until many years later did I realize that the lines have been drawn and that Satan has launched his most vehement attack against God's preserved and perfect word.

My defense of the book today is rarely challenged by the cults as much as it is by educated, "scholarly" Christians. Here is a case in point concerning a book written by Robert A. Joyner, D.B.S., Th.D., Ph.D. He vehemently attacks the King James Bible... all the while denying that he does so. For instance, Dr. Joyner devotes an entire chapter to listing twenty errors in the King James Bible. Examine his "error" number fifteen:

> *In Acts 9:7 when Paul was converted, it says in the KJV the men "stood speechless hearing a voice, but seeing no man." In Acts 22:9 it says, "They heard not the voice of him that spake with me." Of course these verses make the Bible contradict itself. ...The KJV makes the Bible contradict itself....* [2]

Of course, we have seen that Dr. Joyner has just been caught in the rat trap. His conclusion after showing all these "errors" is as follows:

> *The KJV is a good translation. It is accurate in most places, but if you know about the mistranslations and obsolete words, it will help you to understand what God actually said in the Hebrew and Greek. There is no valid reason to reject the other good English translations we have today. In many places they can be a great help.* [3]

Here is a man that has an earned doctorate (Ph.D.) and does not understand how to explain these passages. Instead, his arguments align him with one of the worst, most deceptive cults in the world. He vehemently attacks the word of God with blasphemous remarks. At the same time, he condemns those that claim God has kept His promise of supernatural preservation.

Later in the same book, Dr. Joyner attacks again:

> *...throughout the KJV, in small things as well as big, the reader is being misled.* [4]

Dr. Joyner thinks man should trust in education rather than in the Holy Spirit. Shamefully, this is the common reaction against those that believe the book they hold in their hands to be the word of God. Read for yourself and see if this sounds like a spiritual answer.

Since God never promised a perfect translation, you may
have to occasionally check some detail in the original or
compare translations. . . .Let the textual scholars work these
few problems out. [5]

God does not expect the Christian to elevate the "textual scholars"
to the position of ultimate authority. His word holds that place. Now
read about the same issue from a Bible believing viewpoint. In his book,
Things That Are Different Are Not the Same, Dr. Mickey Carter expresses the necessity of having faith when considering God's promise of
preservation. God does not have to prove His promises true, but we
must believe them nevertheless. In the words of Dr. Carter:

We believe the King James Version is the preserved Word of
*God for the English-speaking people. If it is the **perfect** Word of*
*God, how can contradictions exist in it? There are **apparent***
contradictions in the Bible, while in reality there are none. We
need to approach these apparent contradictions with a strong,
steadfast, Bible-believing faith that there is an answer to them.
...But even if the answer cannot be found, why not trust God
with it? We can believe it is right because it is His Word. We
can trust Him that He will reveal the answer to us sometime
here on earth or, at the latest, when we get to Heaven. [6]

Amen! What saith the scripture? Does God expect faith to be a
necessary element in every aspect of a person's life and walk with Him?
*"For we walk by faith, not by sight" (**II Corinthians 5:7**). "...for*
*whatsoever is not of faith is sin" (**Romans 14:23**). "But without faith*
it is impossible to please him: for he that cometh to God must believe
*that he is, and that **he is a rewarder of them that diligently seek him"***
*(**Hebrews 11:6**).*

Now, we return to another critic of God's word – James White. He
refers to the subject passage and relates that, very early on, Mormon
missionaries showed him his first "alleged 'contradiction'" in the King
James Bible. Here is how he relates the story:

The first alleged "contradiction" that was ever shown to me
was based upon the KJV translation. Two young LDS mission-
aries, Elders Reed and Reese, were sitting in my sister-in-law's

*home, explaining to me that I could not really trust the Bible
because it had been "translated so many times." I was a young
person at the time (I was the same age as the missionaries),
and had not encountered too many real strong **challenges to my
faith**, so I asked them for examples of the "errors" they were
talking about. They took me to the KJV at Acts 9:7 and Acts
22:9.* [7]

Take note that Mr. White admits that someone attacking the King
James Bible was a **challenge to his faith**! However, he concludes his
comment concerning these passages with this statement: *"Such ambiguity is, unfortunately, a common problem in the KJV."* As we have seen,
this perceived problem completely evaporates with a little Bible study.
Instead of growing up in the Lord, Mr. White allowed these two cultists
to shake his faith and take him captive *(II Timothy 2:26)*. He has devoted much of his energies to accomplishing the same goal these Mormon missionaries had…destroying individuals' faith in God's supernatural promise of preservation.

God will reward the person that diligently seeks Him *(Hebrews 11:6)*.
This holds true concerning His word also. In many places throughout
the Bible, God personifies His word. That which is true concerning God
is also true concerning His word. The word of God is personified in
many verses *(Romans 9:17, Galatians 3:8, Hebrews 3:7)*. This application illustrates that anyone who diligently seeks for Him (or His word)
will find Him. The good news is that His word is not hard to find – just
go to the local bookstore and tell them you want a King James Bible.
(Be aware that most bookstore sales people will try to sell you anything
but a King James Bible, if they sense anything less than a total commitment toward its purchase.)

In closing, one should realize that a Christian does not have to explain every supposed error in the KJB. Instead, we must condition ourselves and others to embody a different mindset. Rather than encouraging an unbelieving heart that causes us to depart from God, we need to
encourage Christians and the lost to take God at His word. When we
doubt God, He says we have *"…an evil heart of unbelief, in departing
from the living God" (Hebrews 3:12)*. Paul commended the Bereans
because they readily received the word of God and then checked out the
truths in the scriptures *(Acts 17:11)*.

We limit God when we go to the Bible with an unbelieving heart. The Apostle Paul had the same problem with Christians in the first century. Many of them were not receiving the word of God, but were instead casting doubt upon its authenticity. Take careful note that Paul said the word of God only works effectually in those that **believe**.

> *I Thessalonians 2:13 For this cause also thank we God without ceasing, because, when ye received the word of God which ye heard of us, ye received it not as the word of men, but as it is in truth, the word of God, **which effectually worketh also in you that believe**.*

The Lord Jesus Christ made this same point to those to whom He ministered. The mighty works of God were limited because of their unbelief.

> *Matthew 13:58 And he did not many mighty works there **because of their unbelief**.*

If you have a difficulty concerning some aspect of God's word, the correct response is to believe and to ask God to help your unbelief.

> *Mark 9:24 And straightway the father of the child cried out, and said with tears, **Lord, I believe; help thou mine unbelief**.*

If one continues with an evil heart of unbelief, he opens himself up to the rebuke of the Lord.

> *Mark 16:14 Afterward he appeared unto the eleven as they sat at meat, and upbraided them with **their unbelief and hardness of heart**, because they believed not them which had seen him after he was risen.*

Let us not be guilty of unbelief and cause the mighty works of God to suffer. Those that witnessed the resurrected Christ proclaimed the truth to their fellow brethren. Shamefully, these disciples rejected the truth because they could not understand. The Lord rebukes them for not believing the truth from those who had witnessed His resurrection.

Shamefully, as we have seen, the cults are not the only ones that do not believe in God's promise of supernatural preservation. Christians have joined their ranks, have attacked God's infallible word, and have forsaken the truth. No longer do they believe God instructs *every* child of God to live by *every* word of God.

As evident from this simple example, one does not have to be in a cult to have a hardened heart of unbelief. There are many people that call themselves Christians and still do not believe the promises of God. One day we will all stand before the Lord Jesus Christ. It would be much better to stand before God having believed His promises "too much," than to be guilty of infidelity concerning His expectations and promises. For example:

> *Psalm 12:6 The words of the LORD are pure words: as silver tried in a furnace of earth, purified seven times. 7 Thou shalt keep them, O LORD, **thou shalt preserve them from this generation for ever**.*

God promises to preserve His word (in the King James Bible) and informs us that we are to live by *every* word of God. Is this possible using any other version of the Bible than the King James Bible?

> *Matthew 4:4 But he answered and said, It is written, Man shall not live by bread alone, **but by every word that proceedeth out of the mouth of God**.*

Are you busy proclaiming these truths, or are you a member of a cult that despises the truths of God? Are you busy defending the truth or are you a member of Satan's wrecking crew that destroys the faith of the unsuspecting? Don't straddle the fence *(Revelation 3:16)*. Choose you this day whom you will serve.

> *Joshua 24:15 And if it seem evil unto you to serve the LORD, **choose you this day whom ye will serve**; whether the gods which your fathers served that were on the other side of the flood, or the gods of the Amorites, in whose land ye dwell: but **as for me and my house, we will serve the LORD**.*

Chapter 16 Endnotes

1 Alfred P. Gibbs, *The Preacher and his Preaching*, (Kansas City, KS: Walterick Publishers, 1939), p. 319.

2 Robert A. Joyner, *King James Only?*, (Community Baptist Church, 1999), p. 18.

3 *Ibid.*, page 18-19.

4 *Ibid.*, p. 72

5 *Ibid.*, p. 44.

6 Mickey Carter, *Things That Are Different Are Not the Same*, (Landmark Baptist Press, Haines City, FL, 1993) p. 18-19.

7 White, *The King James Only Controversy, op. cit.*, p. 228-229.

17

Bible Roots

I build on no authority, ancient or modern, but the Scripture. I want to know one thing – the way to Heaven: how to land on that happy shore. God Himself hath condescended to teach the way. **He hath written it down in a book. O give me that book! At any price, give me that book of God.**
John Wesley

John Wesley understood the value of the scriptures. His quoted words were not spoken of either the original Greek or Hebrew texts. He knew that God had *also* given man His word within the pages of a book. Regretfully, man no longer seems willing to accept this simple truth. The same book used by John Wesley is the very book that helped establish and guide America's unprecedented achievement of individual liberty. It triggered the greatest revivals during the Church Age. But now, this same book has been "replaced" by hundreds of modernized versions which lack the power of their predecessor.

The influences of the modern Bible college and seminary must be examined to determine how they have helped spawn this move away from the book blessed by God more than any other. For the past several decades, many so-called conservative, fundamental Bible colleges and seminaries have weakened the faith of their students concerning the inerrancy of the scriptures.

Most of these schools require that the student, eager to learn the word of God, include Greek in his course of study. He is told that Greek is the language of the word of God, even though the Bible written in his own native tongue saved him and set his soul afire. He is placed under a teacher who may or may not believe in both the inspiration and the preservation of scripture. The purpose of these courses of study is *not* to strengthen the student's faith in God's infallible word, but to teach him to become its judge.

The young student's final authority is changed from the book he once loved and cherished to the Greek faculty and their lexicons. Soon, he is convinced that he doesn't have the word of God at his disposal and may even wonder if it exists at all. He is taught that better and more reliable manuscripts have been discovered that were not available to the translators of 1611. Gradually, he becomes convinced that the ignorant masses (uneducated in the original languages) have been led astray from the truth. He begins to believe that his education is the answer to the Church's woes *(II Timothy 3:1-2, 7)*. On the contrary, this philosophy of education has significantly contributed to the spiritual drought of these last days.

Eventually, the cycle continues when the Bible student graduates and moves on to serve in the pastorate. He unintentionally begins to convince his congregation that his knowledge of the *original languages* makes him spiritually superior to them. He becomes their final authority, and clergy/laity class divisions begin to emerge. One should recognize the similarities between this unfortunate scenario and that found in the Roman Catholic Church's exclusive use of the Latin language and institution of the priesthood system to blind the multitudes. Thus, many "Protestant popes" emerge, each seeking elevation on a man-made pedestal.

When Jesus spoke, *"...the common people heard him gladly" (Mark 12:37)*. In contrast, the majority of the scholars and religious leaders rejected and resisted Him. History repeats itself because *"there is no new thing under the sun" (Ecclesiastes 1:9)*. Bible colleges and seminaries need to teach the Bible as infallible and the original languages as a means to convince the gainsayers *(Titus 1:9)*, not as a tool to "correct" that which needs no correction. The moment a person runs to the Greek or Hebrew lexicon he is about to give you his private interpretation *(II*

Peter 1:20). This is true because the lexicon will have a choice of words that could be used, and he will have to decide which is right. [1]

The misdirection of one's final authority may not be readily apparent, but the confusion caused by the various versions of the bible is easily recognizable. Are all of the different versions necessary or inspired of God? Do multiple textbooks (bibles) make sense? Consider this: No teacher would ever teach a history, science, or math class and instruct everyone to bring his favorite textbook version to class. However, this identical situation is repeated in churches every Sunday. The preacher "preaches" out of one version and the people in the pews potentially have a dozen or more other versions from which they "follow along," creating confusion and chaos *(I Corinthians 14:33)!*

The King James Bible is *the* word of God for the English-speaking people. There is no other in use today. God provides, and Bible believers cite, many reasons for this truth. In any analysis, we should first consider the scriptural testimony. The Bible irrefutably tells us that God will *preserve* His word, and not allow it to pass away. Furthermore, scripture tells us that God *magnified* His word above all of His name. For these reasons and many others, Satan has reveled in creating doubt concerning the *authority* of the words of God.

As we study some of the facts concerning manuscript evidence, the first point to be understood is that there are over 5,200 ancient manuscripts in existence today. The vast majority of these manuscripts from all over the world (including Greece, Asia Minor, England, Ireland, Constantinople, Syria, Africa, Gaul, and Southern Italy) support the King James Bible. However, the two ancient manuscripts that are the major foundation for the modern versions come from one locale – **Alexandria, Egypt.** During the early Christian centuries, Egypt was a land in which heresies were rampant. Today, we find that the Muslims are the predominant group controlling this region. The same was true two thousand years ago – except under a different name.

One Bible stands alone, originating from a completely different source than all of the modern versions. The evidence supporting the rejection of the Alexandrian (Egyptian) texts and the acceptance of the manuscripts underlying the KJB is overwhelming. Keep in mind that many works have been dedicated to uncovering the scriptural truths and historical facts presented in summary form here. In any discussion, we must first consider the scripture supporting one's Bible position.

The Scriptural Evidence – Preservation

God promises to preserve His word for every generation. It is hard to believe how effectively Satan has used our Bible colleges and seminaries to convince many God-called men that God's promises have failed today.

> *Psalm 12:6 The **words** of the LORD are pure words: as silver tried in a furnace of earth, purified seven times. 7 Thou shalt keep them, O LORD, thou shalt **preserve** them from this generation for ever.*

Much like the promises of the Old Testament, the New Testament contains the same promise of supernatural preservation. God promises that His *words* will not pass away, contradicting the basic premise for the existence of the modern versions. The Bible does *not* say that preservation is limited to His *thoughts* not passing away.

> *Matthew 24:35 Heaven and earth shall pass away, but **my words shall not pass away.***

Just as Joseph Smith claimed to restore "true religion" by founding the Church of Latter Day Saints (the Mormon church), the modern day Bible critic claims to be restoring God's "lost" words by creating new bible versions. A common instigator works behind the scenes to create both false religions and false bibles. His satanic influence manifests itself in the production of rotten fruit. God magnifies His true word, whereas Satan magnifies the error.

The Scriptural Elevation – Magnification

Christians sing songs praising the precious name of Jesus Christ. According to God's word, we should be singing songs that not only praise His name, but also magnify His precious word. *To magnify* means to make greater in size or to appear greater or seem more important than a person or thing is in fact. Either of these definitions plainly reveals God's purpose and plan concerning His word. He wants His word magnified above even His precious name. This may seem foreign to Christians that love their Saviour, but it is scriptural and makes sense when considered in context.

> *Psalm 138:2* *I will worship toward thy holy temple, and praise thy name for thy lovingkindness and for thy truth:* **for thou hast magnified thy word above all thy name.**

While on a trip with the **Baptist History Preservation Society**, I traveled to Barren County, Kentucky. [2] There, I read the Articles of Faith of the Barren River Association adopted in 1830. There were twelve articles listed. The first and second are reproduced below. Pay particular attention to the order – the word of God comes first. These articles demonstrate these Christians' understanding of *Psalm 138:2*.

> *The Articles of Faith of the Barren River Association, adopted at her constitution at the Mount Pleasant Meeting House, Barren County, Ky., Sept. 15, 1830.*

> *1ˢᵗ We believe that the* **scriptures** *of the Old and New Testaments, as translated by the authority of* **King James**, *to be the words of God, and is the only true rule of faith and practice.*

> *2ⁿᵈ We believe in one only True and living God: Father, Word, and Holy Ghost.* [3]

Unlike so many contemporary churches, these men understood the importance divinely intended to be placed upon the word of God. In addition to their magnification of God's word, also take note that this church believed the King James Bible to be THE word of God over 170 years ago. Some may respond that these nineteenth century American Christians did not have all the bible version choices available to today's Christians. Amen *(I Corinthians 14:33)*!

Satan's Plan – A Subtle Attack

The fall of man began with this question from the subtle serpent: *"Yea, hath God said...?" (Genesis 3:1)*. This same question has been posed by *every* new bible version to hit the market. As a great preacher of old said: "The approved method of the present carnival of *unbelief* is not to reject the Bible altogether but to raise doubts as to portions of it..." Once one doubts the efficacy and inerrancy of the Bible, he falls prey to a never-ending search for truth. The Bible critic is *"Ever learning, and never able to come to the knowledge of the truth" (II Timothy 3:7)*.

The Lord Jesus Christ warned of Satan's mode of attack: *"Now the parable is this: The seed is the word of God... then cometh the devil, and taketh away the word..." (Luke 8:11-12)*. The easiest way to deceptively take something away is to replace it with something that seems similar. Replacing the genuine article with a counterfeit works effectively, whether the counterfeit be the *RV, Goodspeed, Riverside, American, Moffatt, ASV, Williams, RSV, Phillips, Berkley, NEV, NWT, Good News, NASV, New World, Amplified, Living, IV, NIV, NKJV, New Scofield, NCV, CEV, New Living, etc., etc., etc.*

Of necessity, the counterfeit must *look* like the real thing. Many times the modern versions do not remove every single instance of a particular doctrine. Thus, the changes incorporated into the new versions are limited, though they systematically attack key doctrines. The changes become progressively more pervasive as the public becomes accustomed to accepting change and grows further removed from the truth of the actual word of God. The true scriptures give us multiple witnesses, thus confirming God's system of judgment and justice. Consider *Matthew 18:16* (two or three witness requirement) and *Ecclesiastes 4:12* (a threefold cord is not quickly broken). God includes multiple witnesses to His truths for this purpose.

Satan has not altered his strategy much over the centuries. He still tries to deceive God's creation *(Revelation 12:9)*. If he attacked the word of God in the Garden of Eden, and used God's very words to tempt God Himself in the wilderness, he will use the same method with us today. The Bible describes his satanic *modus operandi*. *"But I fear, lest by any means, as the serpent beguiled Eve through his subtilty, so your minds should be corrupted from the simplicity that is in Christ" (II Corinthians 11:3)*. Satan still effectively deceives the unsuspecting. Too many Christians have neglected the spiritual battle and forgotten the identity of the one with whom they contend *(Ephesians 6:12)*.

Because of a rejection of the truth through sin and rebellion, the prophet Amos foretells of the day when men will hunger, not for food, but for the word of God. Although Amos' prophesy foretells God's judgment upon Israel, we have a similar situation occurring in churches today. Truly, history does repeat itself. *"Behold, the days come, saith the Lord God, that I will send a famine in the land, not a famine of bread, nor a thirst for water, but of hearing the words of the Lord: And they shall wander from sea to sea, and from the north even to the east, they shall run to and fro to seek the word of the Lord, and shall not find it" (Amos 8:11-12)*.

Since the 1880's, over 200 different English versions of the Bible have appeared. Has God authored each and every one of these? God could not have authored all of these *contradictory* versions, *"for God is not the author of confusion..." (I Corinthians 14:33)*. Can you guess who the author of this confusion might be? He is the same one who confused and beguiled Eve in the Garden; who used the scripture to tempt our Lord and Saviour in the wilderness; and who has blinded man and initiated his search for the ever-elusive "true word of God."

The Bible's Family Tree – Simplified

The "original autographs" refer to the actual manuscripts penned by the writers of each of the 66 books of the Bible. They were written in manuscript form by one of God's apostles or prophets. The *original autograph* was given to the nation of Israel (Old Testament) or a local New Testament church. Some New Testament epistles were sent to individuals such as Timothy, Titus, and Philemon. God, in His infinite wisdom and foreknowledge, primarily chose the Hebrew and Koine Greek languages to be used for the originals of the Old and New Testaments, respectively. Both of these tongues became "dead languages" within several hundred years after each respective canon was established. The words actually became "frozen in time." Thus, the words and their meanings could not change. They became, as Latin, dead languages with fixed properties of meaning.

In contrast, English is a living language. As such, new words are constantly being added to the English language, and old words remain in a state of flux. [4] For instance, the fourth edition of *The American Heritage Dictionary,* released in the year 2000, advertises its product with the following quote: *"This edition has nearly 10,000 new words and senses that **reflect the rapid pace of change in the English language today.**"* [5] Unlike the modern versions, the King James Bible was translated at a time when English was in its purest form. Since that time, the English language has progressively degenerated from what it was in 1611 to what it is today. Should God's word be forced to embody the degeneration of our language?

These original manuscripts (autographs) penned by the authors wore out from use. When certain other tribes, synagogues, churches, etc. desired a copy of a sacred writing, a copy was made for them. These copies are called "manuscripts" because they were written with pen and ink (prior to the advent of the printing press and typesetting).

Frequently, scribes were known to have destroyed old, worn manuscripts after the new copies had been made (a process analogous to our disposal of a weathered flag). These scribes were not concerned with holding onto the *originals* because they had faithfully copied the text. This faithful copying resulted in the faithful promulgation of God's word to subsequent generations. The only alternative explanation of the history of the Bible is that God's promise has failed and the words of God have indeed passed away *(Matthew 24:35).*

Other tribes, synagogues, churches, etc. made copies of these *manuscripts* until, eventually, copies of the sacred writings had been distributed all over the world. The *written* word of God spread in much the same way as the *verbal* word of God spread in the first century.

Acts 6:7 And the word of God increased...

Acts 12:24 But the word of God grew and multiplied.

Acts 13:49 And the word of the Lord was published throughout all the region.

Warning: Satan's henchmen were busy creating and copying some manuscripts at this time, too. Church history and the Bible warn about early corruption of the words of God. For instance, the Apostle Paul warns Christians in the first century of Satan's devices: *"For we are not as **many, which corrupt the word of God**: but as of sincerity, but as of God, in the sight of God speak we in Christ" **(II Corinthians 2:17).*** Nelson Floyd Jones' apt description of the early days of New Testament corruption contradicts the standard Bible critic's position.

*Hort said there were no signs of deliberate altering of the text for doctrinal purposes, but the Scriptures and the church 'Fathers' disagree with him. Again, II Corinthians 2:17 says that 'many' were corrupting the Scriptures during the time of Paul. From the letters and works of the Fathers, we know of Marcion the Gnostic who deliberately altered the text for doctrinal purposes as early as 140 A.D. Other corrupters of Scripture were named by the mid-second century by these church Fathers. For example, Dionysius (Bishop of Corinth from A.D. 168 to 176) said that the Scriptures had been deliberately altered in his day. Many modern scholars recognize that **most variations were made deliberately.**[6]*

God's Line of Manuscripts versus Satan's Line of Manuscripts

The copies that were proven to be good copies were "received" by the synagogues and local churches and became known as the "Received Text." Of the 5,262 Greek witnesses to the text of the New Testament, 80% are in full agreement with the true text; a full 90% of the witnesses agree 97% of the time![7] In addition, **ALL 2,143 Greek lectionaries** support the Received Text underlying the King James Bible. (Lectionaries are manuscripts containing scripture lessons read publicly in the churches. In other words, the churches that utilized the lectionaries **ALL** used the text that gave birth to the King James Bible!!!!!)

In 1382, John Wycliffe gave his people their first English translation of the Bible. He became known as the "Morning Star of the Reformation." Regretfully, because of his lack of knowledge in Greek and Hebrew, he based his work primarily on the Latin manuscripts, such as the Latin Vulgate. The Latin Vulgate was derived from Adamantius Origen's corrupted Greek Hexapla, commonly referred to as the Septuagint – LXX. Foxe confirms Wycliffe's use of the Latin in his comments about William Tyndale. Tyndale was the first individual to return to the original languages of Hebrew and Greek. All of the English versions before Tyndale were translations of a translation, all derived from the Vulgate or older Latin versions. [8]

Wycliffe was hated for his attempt to give the common people the words of God in the English language. In 1415, he was posthumously condemned for heresy by Pope Martin V at the Council of Constance. The Council ordered his bones exhumed and burned. The orders were carried out in 1428 when they unearthed them, burned them to ashes, and threw them into the river Swift.

In 1516, a scholar named Desiderius Erasmus (1466-1536) was led of God to produce the first *printed* edition of the Greek New Testament. Although he did not have a complete text, he used the manuscripts available to him to produce a Greek New Testament, which later became known as the *Textus Receptus*. Some claim that his work was inferior because he was supposedly ignorant of the competing text types. This is simply not true. Documentation exists to prove that he did in fact have knowledge of the Vaticanus manuscript and had regular correspondence with Professor Paulus Bombasius, the Papal librarian, concerning it. [9] Furthermore, a Catholic priest named Juan Sepulveda sent extracts of the Codex Vaticanus to Erasmus, in an attempt to convince him of its superiority. [10] After considering the material provided him, Erasmus rejected the Vaticanus as a variant text type. (Vaticanus is discussed further under Satan's line of manuscripts.) Thus, Erasmus knew of the text used by modern bible critics almost 100 years prior to the King James Bible, but considered Vaticanus, as well as the other Alexandrian texts to be variants.

Erasmus was the most unlikely candidate to be used of God. Yet, he was uniquely qualified. Who better to expose the fallacies of the Roman

Catholic Church than one completely familiar with its ways? Although
Erasmus had been raised and trained by Catholic monks, he was a true
man of character. He spent his life writing about and protesting the false
doctrines of the Roman Catholic system. His true friends were the Protestant scholars among whom he lived and died.

Cambridge historian Owen Chadwick said he was an *"ex-monk...a
Protestant pastor preached his funeral sermon and the money he left
was used to help Protestant refugees."* [11] He was buried at a Protestant
church in Basel. Erasmus shows up on Sebastian Frank's list of heretics
of the Roman Catholic Church. [12] The Council of Trent condemned
Erasmus' translation of the Bible because it did not match their corrupt
Vulgate translation, but rather the text of true Christianity. In 1559, the
pope placed Erasmus' writings on *The Index of Forbidden Books*, just
as the word of God had been placed on that list in 1229. [13] The Council
of Toulouse, which met in November of 1229 about the same time as
the crusade against the Albigensians, set up a special ecclesiastical tribu-
nal, or court, known as the Inquisition to search out and try heretics.
Twenty of the 45 articles decreed by the Council dealt with heresy. It
ruled in part:

> Canon 2 - The lords of the districts shall carefully seek out the
> heretics in dwellings, hovels, and forests, and even their under-
> ground retreats shall be entirely wiped out.

> Canon 14 - We prohibit the permission of the books of the Old
> and New Testament to laymen, except perhaps they might desire
> to have the Psalter, or some Breviary for the divine service, or
> the Hours of the blessed Virgin Mary, for devotion; expressly
> forbidding their having the other parts of the Bible translated into
> the vulgar tongue. [14]

No matter how much the Roman Catholic Church fought against
those that tried to spread the word of God throughout the world, truth
still prevailed. The *Textus Receptus* was eventually translated into other
languages, including **French, Dutch, Danish,** and **Czech**. Other well-
known Bibles were also produced from Erasmus' work. These included
the **Swedish** Uppsala Bible, the **Spanish** Reyna, the **Italian** Diodati
version, and Martin Luther's **German** Bible.

The English Bible – Purified Seven Times?

Many Bible believers teach that the book of Psalms prophesies of God's supernatural intervention and preservation of His word in the English language. *"The words of the LORD are pure words: as silver tried in a furnace of earth, **purified seven times.**" (Psalm 12:6).* There were six distinct editions leading up to our King James Bible, beginning in 1525 with Tyndale's Bible. The shortcomings of the earlier versions were commonly recognized, yet the Lord used each of these earlier works together for the greatest creation since Genesis one. If any of these earlier versions were the final English version, God would not have led in the creation of one final version, exiling the others to historical obscurity. The seventh was the King James Bible of 1611.

The fourteen rules of translation provided to the King James translators demonstrate the premise for this position. The fourteenth rule names the six translations considered by the KJB translation committee as true predecessors of the King James Bible. The translations to be used *"when they agree better with the text than the **Bishop's Bible** are the **Tyndale Bible, Matthew Bible, Coverdale Bible**, Whitchurch Bible* (which is also known as the Cranmer's or **Great Bible** printed by Whitchurch), *and the **Geneva Bible**."* These rules also show that justification exists for excluding the Catholic Douay Rheims Version and the Wycliffe Bible from the foundational versions since they were translated from the Latin. The seven stages of purification are detailed as follows:

1. Tyndale *(1525)* – William Tyndale was known as the "Father of the English Bible." He spoke seven different languages fluently (Hebrew, Greek, Latin, Italian, Spanish, English, and French) and was the sole translator of the first *printed* English New Testament. He had a price on his head and was hunted for eleven years by his king and the Roman Catholic Church. On October 6, 1536, he was tied to a stake, strangled, and *consumed with fire*. Before his strangling, he was given one last chance to recant, but refused to do so. He was allowed a moment to pray and cried out, *"Lord, open the King of England's eyes."* [15] God answered his prayer when King Henry officially sanctioned the publishing of two separate Bibles in the English language within a year of Tyndale's martyrdom. [16]

2. Coverdale *(1535)* – The Coverdale Bible was named after Tyndale's former proofreader at Antwerp – Miles Coverdale. He produced the first complete printed English Bible. His work consisted primarily of Tyndale's New Testament and Pentateuch, with the remaining Old Testament books rendered primarily from Luther's German translation. He omitted the marginal notes associated with the Tyndale Bible. King Henry officially sanctioned the 2nd edition printed in 1537. The Roman Catholic Church tried unsuccessfully to silence Coverdale. He escaped only days before they would have captured him.

3. Matthew *(1537)* – John Rogers (using the pseudonym of Thomas Matthews) continued Tyndale's work while Tyndale was imprisoned in a dungeon. After the death of Edward VI in 1553, Queen Mary came into power with the ambition of burning every Protestant who would not recant and submit to the church of Rome. John Rogers was burned first because he was the closest to William Tyndale. Over 300 leading Protestant scholars in England were burned at the stake during "Bloody Mary's" four-year reign. The others fled to **Geneva, Switzerland**.

4. Great *(1538)* – This translation was named the Great Bible because of its exceptional size – 16½ inches by 11 inches. This Bible was a revision of the Matthew Bible, not including Rogers' marginal notes. Henry VIII authorized by royal injunction the printing of 20,000 copies of this translation for distribution to every church in England. It has the distinction of being the first Bible officially authorized for public use in England's churches. Thus, Tyndale's dying prayer was quickly answered.

5. Geneva *(1560)* – Theodore Beza, John Knox, William Whittingham, and Miles Coverdale labored six years to produce the Geneva Bible. This translation included thousands of explanatory notes which promoted study and understanding of the text. The Geneva Bible was the first to feature numbered verses and italics, and the first English Bible translated entirely from the original languages. [17] It is quoted over 5,000 times in the plays of William Shakespeare. [18] The Geneva Bible came to America with John Smith in 1607, and later on board the *Mayflower* with the Pilgrims.

6. Bishops *(1568)* – The changes instituted in the Bishops Bible were mostly cosmetic, including many pictures, and thicker, more expensive paper. The Geneva Bible remained the people's Bible until the 1611 Authorized Version.

7. King James (1611) The King James Version of the Bible became the seventh purification of the English translation and is *as silver tried in a furnace of earth, purified seven times.* The "Puritans" vowed to remove the remnants of Roman Catholicism from the Church of England. Thus Dr. John Reynolds, president of Corpus Christi College at Oxford, suggested to King James that a translation be produced that the common people could understand, read, and love. This undertaking began when approximately one thousand ministers sent a petition to King James. [19] It was finally agreed that a new translation, absolutely true to the original Greek text, be made which would not include any marginal notes or comments. [20] No marginal notes were incorporated into this translation, except for explanations of Greek or Hebrew words and the provision of cross-references.

In 1604, a group of 54 of the best scholars in England were chosen to begin a new translation into English. In 1611, they completed the book that **later** became known as *the Authorized Version.*

The early editions of the Authorized Version included the Apocrypha. They included these books between the canonical Old and New Testament books to show that they were not inspired. All of the Apocryphal books were written in Greek, with the exception of one written in Latin. A 1613 edition of the KJB was printed excluding the Apocrypha. It is interesting to note that the Apocryphal books were distributed within the text of the Old Testament Vaticanus, Sinaiticus, and the other Egyptian manuscripts favored by the modern versions and the modern day textual critics. [21]

In the book, *From the Mind of God to the Mind of Man*, Paul Downey gives the distorted impression that the King James translators failed to distinguish between the non-canonical Apocrypha and the inspired scripture of the Old and New Testaments. He states that "the Authorized Version of 1611 had followed the Council of Trent..." [22] He fails to point out that the Apocryphal books were included in the KJB as they were in all other versions of the English Bible from the time of

Wycliffe (1384). Furthermore, the Council of Trent officially pronounced many of the Apocryphal books as inspired and canonical.

Satan's Line of Manuscripts

In 1475, a manuscript was logged into the Vatican library known as *Codex Vaticanus*. It was "rediscovered" almost four centuries later (in 1845) and has become instrumental in influencing modern scholarship. It dates to around A.D. 350.

In 1844, a second Alexandrian manuscript, called *Codex Sinaiticus*, was discovered in a monastery at the foot of Mt. Sinai. This manuscript also dates to about A.D. 350. Many scholars believe that these copies are two of the 50 copies that the Emperor Constantine instructed Eusebius to prepare for the new churches he planned to build in Constantinople. Thus, Origen (the Gnostic) influenced Eusebius (his favorite student); Eusebius influenced the Sinaiticus and Vaticanus manuscripts; and – in turn – every modern version taken from these two manuscripts was corrupted! Neither the Vaticanus nor the Sinaiticus was accepted as a "received" text. Thousands of changes have been noted within their pages by many different scribes throughout history.

In 1853, two men named Brooke Foss Westcott and Fenton John Anthony Hort set out to write a Greek text based on these two Alexandrian texts (*Codex Vaticanus*, and *Codex Sinaiticus*). Since these two texts by then disagreed with each other in some 3,036 places in the four Gospel books alone, the two men had to come up with a completely subjective text influenced by their heretical views. Consequently, they wrote an "eclectic" text, meaning they preferentially picked and chose certain portions of scripture from the Vaticanus manuscript and other portions from the Sinaiticus manuscript until they produced a rendering that satisfactorily conveyed their doctrines. (BUT *"...no prophecy of the scripture is of any private interpretation." II Peter 1:20.*).

Scrivener reported 15,000 alterations in the text of Sinaiticus *"brought in by at least ten different revisers, some of them systematically spread over every page, others occasional or limited to separate portions of the manuscript, many of them being contemporaneous with the first writer, far the greater part belonging to the sixth or seventh century, a few being as recent as the twelfth."* [23]

Therefore, it stands to reason that no matter how closely Vaticanus and Sinaiticus once agreed, with so many alterations these witnesses could no longer agree. Regarding the thousands of changes in the seventh century, Scrivener wrote: *"The one object of this corrector was to assimilate the Codex to manuscripts more in vogue in his time, and **approaching far nearer to our modern Textus Receptus."*** [24]

In 1898, a revision of Westcott and Hort's Greek Text was made and called *"Nestle's Greek Text."* The majority of Bible colleges today use Nestle's Greek text (the Aland-Nestle[26] or the UBS[3]) although it differs greatly from the *Textus Receptus*. Despite this fact, the new versions arise from these corrupted texts, while the King James Bible stands alone in its use of the *Textus Receptus* and its rejection of the readings from the corrupt texts. (Note: UBS[3] stands for the third edition of the United Bible Society.)

Westcott and Hort had an unusual rule of thumb for determining which Greek text to choose when there was a *variant* reading. They chose the "neutral" approach. Basically, this meant that the variant (the difference between the Greek texts) was approached from the perspective that the reading that should be chosen would be the one that reflects the *least doctrinal bias* (i.e. the one that is most neutral). For instance, they chose to use the word *who* or *he* in *I Timothy 3:16* rather than *God* (used in the *Textus Receptus*) because they *hypothesized* that some well-meaning scribe inserted *God* into the passage. According to their theory, the variants were caused by God's people, rather than those who had set out to corrupt the scripture *(II Corinthians 2:17)*. This is preposterous and anti-scriptural!

Typical of this philosophy, James White justifies the changes in the modern versions using various unproven hypotheses such as: "scribal expansion," [25] "parallel passage corruption," [26] "scribal harmonization," [27] "parallel corruption," [28] and "parallel influence."[29] Johann Jakob Griesbach concurs with this theory that the *corrupted* text is the one that *contains* a dogmatic position on doctrine. Read the illogical conclusions for yourself:

When there are many variant readings in one place, that reading which more than the others manifestly favors dogmas of the orthodox is deservedly regarded as suspicious.[30]

If the subject were not so serious, this absurd position would be humorous. Such a theory certainly has no basis in the spiritual realm. We are not talking about just any book. We are discussing a book that Satan hates! Ignorance of the truth has always been his greatest ally. To attribute the changes to "well-meaning godly men," rather than to satanic influence borders on lunacy. Dr. Samuel Gipp succinctly speaks from the Bible believing, spiritual perspective.

If Satan can eliminate the Bible, he can break our lifeline to Heaven. If he can only get us to doubt its accuracy, he can successfully foil God's every attempt to teach us. [31]

Westcott and Hort's theory of corruption has been proven false by unquestionable evidence. Dean Burgon dedicated 84 pages of evidence to support the KJB rendering of *I Timothy 3:16 "God was manifest in the flesh"* and to invalidate the modern version rendering of *"He who was manifest in the flesh."* Out of 254 manuscripts and translations in other languages personally examined by Dean John Burgon, 252 contained the reading supporting the KJB. [32] This equates to greater than 99% agreement with the King James reading and less than 1% siding with the readings found in the modern versions.

Compare the magnitude of evidence from the correct reading with the typical footnote found in most modern versions: *"Some manuscripts read God."* The modern version editors fail to tell you that the two manuscripts supporting the corrupt reading are the Vaticanus and Sinaiticus. According to the critic's theory, these two manuscripts should be given precedence because they do not contain as dogmatic a doctrinal stand. Here is the standard line of the liberals and neo-fundamentalists as excerpted from the book, *From the Mind of God to the Mind of Man.*

The discovery of some ancient Greek manuscripts late in the nineteenth century produced a revolution in the understanding of the Greek New Testament. These discoveries have

*changed the editing of Greek texts into a new quest to de-
fine the original text. These texts are based on new witnesses
not previously known and new approaches to interpreting
the variations. Beginning in the 1880s, printed Greek New
Testaments were developed with significant differences from
the traditional Textus Receptus Greek Text.[33]*

According to this modern philosophy, God's promise of providential
preservation of the scriptures failed until Tishendorf, Tragelles, and
Westcott and Hort "providentially" discovered it in the mid-nineteenth
century. Consider the dire implications – the text used by the church for
1,500 years and the same one that aided the cause of the Protestant
Reformation was really not the preserved text. Instead, infidels rediscovered it during a time of great unbelief – the time of evolution, liberal-
ism, Freud, and Marx. True biblical historians trace the great confusion
and discord among believers today back to this period of uncertainty
and unbelief.

Scriptural Support for Rejection of Alexandrian (Egyptian) Texts

From the scripture that follows, one can easily see that the LORD
dispels any notion that Egypt should be treated as any other country.
This is the very land from which the Vaticanus and Sinaiticus manuscripts originated. One can be certain that He did not send His Levitical
scribes to Egypt and bless them *there* with the task of preserving His
holy word. Instead, the LORD says He is going to consume (kill) them
all. He wants His people OUT of Egypt.

> *Jeremiah 44:26 Therefore hear ye the word of the LORD, all
> Judah that dwell in the land of Egypt; Behold, I have sworn
> by my great name, saith the LORD, that my name shall no
> more be named in the mouth of any man of Judah in all the
> land of Egypt, saying, The Lord GOD liveth.*

His name will not be named by those Israelites dwelling in the land
of Egypt. The Egyptians, of course, are Arabs. Most of the Arab countries are determined to eradicate the nation of Israel at any cost. Some
might point to Anwar Sadat of Egypt as a leader of an Arab nation
willing to consider peace with Israel. Consider this politician.

The first year he became premier of Egypt, he led Egypt into war with Israel! The encyclopedia calls him a pragmatist…(i.e. he could not wipe out Israel so he would try to negotiate). *"A pragmatist, Sadat indicated his willingness to consider a negotiated settlement with Israel and shared the 1978 Nobel Peace Prize with Menachim Begin as a result of the Camp David Accords. He was assassinated by Muslim extremists, who were opposed to his peace initiative with Israel."* [34]

Now consider the background: Sadat signed a peace treaty with Israel in 1979 and was assassinated two years later. He was assassinated because of the peace treaty, and the assassination occurred while he was reviewing a military parade that *marked the eighth anniversary of the crossing of the Suez Canal.* In other words, he won the Nobel Peace Prize, but continued to celebrate his country's attack on Israel! Is he a good example of Egypt's acceptance of Israel? He was a politician who did things that were politically expedient. Muslims hate Israel, America, and anything non-Muslim. [35] The scripture continues its condemnation of the Jews in Egypt.

*Jeremiah 44:27 Behold, I will watch over them for evil, and not for good: and all the men of Judah **that are in the land of Egypt** shall be **consumed** by the sword and by the famine, until there be an end of them.*

God allows us to find the truth through a search of the scriptures. The LORD wanted His people out of Egypt. He consumed any of them that remained there. The modern critic wants us to believe that God then used this same region to preserve His word through the Roman Catholic Vaticanus and Sinaiticus manuscripts. God emphatically differentiates between His words and those of the Jewish Egyptians!

*Jeremiah 44:28 Yet a small number that escape the sword shall return out of the land of Egypt into the land of Judah, and all the remnant of Judah, that are gone into the land of **Egypt** to sojourn there, **shall know whose words shall stand, mine, or theirs.***

It sounds as if God insured that the remnant of Judah would be able to differentiate between His words and theirs. It is unfortunate that man does not seem to possess the same capacity to discern truth from error today. Consider some of the other biblical passages which cast a definite negative light on Egypt.

Genesis 12:10-13 – Because of the Egyptians, Abraham is concerned for his life and the safety of his wife. Also note that this concerns the genealogical line of Christ *(Matthew 1:1-2)*.

Genesis 37:36 – Joseph is sold into Egypt as a slave. Did Egypt bring upon itself the curse of God pronounced against all those that curse Israel *(Genesis 12:3)*?

Genesis 50:25-26 – The first book of the Bible ends with Joseph's being placed into a coffin in Egypt.

Exodus 1:11 – Israel is persecuted in Egypt *(Genesis 12:3)*.

Exodus 12:12 – God passed through the land and killed all the firstborn of Egypt, judging all their gods.

Exodus 20:2 – Egypt is called the *"house of bondage."*

Deuteronomy 4:20 – Egypt is called the *"iron furnace."*

Deuteronomy 17:16 – The LORD ends the warning by stating, *"Ye shall henceforth return no more that way."*

Jeremiah 42:13-19 – God warns Judah pointedly, *"Go ye not into Egypt: know certainly that I have admonished you this day."*

Jeremiah 46:25 – God promises punishment on Egypt.

Ezekiel 20:7 – God commands Israel not to be associated with Egypt's idolatry.

Hosea 11:1 – God called His Son out of Egypt.

Revelation 11:8 – God compares Jerusalem in apostasy to Sodom and Egypt.

In spite of all of the scriptural evidence against the possibility of God's using Egypt to preserve His word, the Bible critics continue to hold to this unscriptural position. The following comments plainly reveal their position. According to an article written by Gary Hudson, Bob Ross theorizes the following concerning Egypt:

> *We should also remember the wonderful Providence of the Lord in regard to Moses, Joseph and the Israelites in Egypt, as well as how the infant Jesus was taken to Egypt as a means of escaping death in Israel during the time of Herod's campaign of infanticide. The Lord is Sovereign in Egypt as well as in Antioch, Jerusalem, and Rome! He works His wonders all over! In fact, if you had to have the "right place" in which the Lord could do His work, it would have to be a "wrong place," as the whole world is defiled by sin.* [36]

In other words, the right place would have to be the wrong place. This position ignores God's specific condemnation. Read Jeremiah chapter 44 again. This theory makes as much sense as attributing all the variations between the *Textus Receptus* and the modern versions to God's people. According to the critics, the modern versions are necessary because God chose Egypt (and the Catholic Church) to preserve His word which had been corrupted by well-meaning, over zealous scribes. Sounds like some of the logic displayed in the Garden of Eden!

God's promise of supernatural preservation has not failed during the last century. Man needs to believe the book God has provided, rather than trying to correct that which needs no correction. God used Antioch *(Acts 11:26)*, not Alexandria, Egypt *(Acts 27:6, 28:11)* to preserve His word. As we look at the cast of characters in the next chapter, consider which group was most likely entrusted by God to keep His beloved word!

Chapter 17 Endnotes

[1] Dennis Spackman, *The Certainty of the Words of Truth*, (New Zealand), p. 155.

[2] Baptist Historical Society, 504 Grace Avenue, Kannapolis, NC, 28083.

Jeff Faggart, founder (704)938-1335.

3 C.P. Carothorn & W. L. Warnell, *Pioneer Church Records of South Central Kentucky and the Upper Cumberland of Tennessee 1799-1899*, 1985), Reprinted by Church History Research & Archives, Dayton, OH., p. 23.

4 Jones, *op. cit.*, p. 10, 11.

5 The American Heritage® Dictionary of the English Language, Fourth Edition. Copyright © 2000 by Houghton Mifflin Company. Published by the Houghton Mifflin Company.

6 Jones, *op. cit.* p. 134.

7 Grady, *Final Authority, op. cit.*, p. 28.

8 John Foxe *et al., Foxe's Christian Martyrs of the World* (Westwood, NJ: Barbour & Company, 1985) p. 362.

9 Samuel Prideaux Tregelles, *An Account of the Printed Text of the Greek New Testament with Remarks on Its Revision upon Critical Principal Together with a Collation of Critical Texts*, (London: Samuel Bagster and Sons, 1854), p. 22.

10 Marvin R. Vincent, *A History of the Textual Criticism of the New Testament*, (New York: MacMillian, 1899), p. 53; F.H.A. Scrivener, *A Plain Introduction to the Criticism of the New Testament*, 4th ed., ed. Edward Miller, 2 Vols., (London: George Bell and Sons, 1894), Vol I, p. 109.

11 Owen Chadwick, *A History of Christianity,* (New York: St. Martin's Press, 1995), p. 198.

12 Roland Bainton, *Erasmus of Christendom* (New York: Scribner's, 1969), p. 257.

13 *Ibid.*, p. 277-278.

14 Pierre Allix, *Ecclesiastical History of Ancient Churches of the Albigenses*, published in Oxford at the Clarendon Press in 1821, reprinted in USA in 1989 by Church History Research & Archives, P.O. Box 38, Dayton Ohio, 45449, p. 213.

15 Fox, *Fox's Book of Martyrs*, Edited by William Byron Forbush, D.D. (Grand Rapids, Mich.: Zondervan Publishing House, 1967), p. 184.

16 Grady, *Final Authority, op. cit.*, p. 137-138.

17 *Ibid.*, p. 139-140.

18 *The Forbidden Book*, New Liberty Videos.

19 Alexander McClure, *The Translators Revived*, (Litchfield, MI: Maranatha Bible Society, 1858), p. 57.

20 *Ibid.*, p. 58-59.

21 Samuel C. Gipp, *An Understandable History of the Bible*, 2nd edition, (Northfield, OH: Daystar Publishing, 2000), p. 335.

22 *From the Mind of God to the Mind of Man*, James B. Williams, ed., op. cit., p. 45.

23 Prebendary Scrivener, *Full Collation of the Codex Sinaiticus with the Received Text of the New Testament*, Introduction, p. xix.

24 Cecil J. Carter, *The Anti King James Version Conspiracy*, Prince George, BC, Canada, 1997, p. 27.

25 White, *The King James Only Controversy, op. cit.*, p. 252.

26 *Ibid.*, p. 253.

27 *Ibid.*, p. 254.

28 *Ibid.*, p. 257.

29 *Ibid.*, p. 264.

30 J.J. Griesbach, *Novum Testamentum Graece* (Halle: 1796), p. 62.

31 Samuel C. Gipp, *An Understandable History of the Bible*, 1st edition, 1987, p. 26.

32 Burgon, *Revision Revised*, p. 492.

33 Williams, *From the Mind of God to the Mind of Man*, op.cit., p. 171.

34 Encyclopedia.com.

35 The followers of **Islam** are known as **Muslims** and number around 1 to 1.5 billion people worldwide. They teach that Islam is the only true religion for salvation and eternal happiness. The **Koran** is Islam's "bible" and Allah its god. The followers of Allah and His prophet **Muhammad** teach that Muslims everywhere must make **jihad** (holy war) against the evil forces that they believe are trying to destroy their religion.

"I (Muhammad) *have been commanded to fight against people, till they testify to the fact that there is no God but Allah, and believe in me* (Muhammad) *as the Messenger* (from the Lord)*...and when they do it, their blood and riches are guaranteed protection on my behalf except where it is justified by law."* (Muslim 1: 31)

"A martyr (in Jehad) *is dressed in radiant robes of faith: he is married to houries and is allowed by Allah to intercede for seventy men* (i.e. he is authorized by God to recommend seventy men for entry into paradise, and his intercession is sure to be granted.) (Ibn-E-Majah, Vol. 2, p. 174)

"Whatever one spends to facilitate Jehad, Allah shall give him a reward which will exceed his contribution 700 times." (Tirmzi, Vol.1, p.697)

"A man who was eating dates, said to the prophet 'Where shall I be if I am killed in Jehad?' He replied: 'In paradise.' The man threw away the dates and fought until he was killed." (Sahih Muslim: 4678)

"He who murders another, property of the murdered becomes property of the murderer." (Ibn-E-Majah, Vol. 2, p. 183)

Islam is the only approved religion of Allah (V. 5) and no other religion is acceptable to God (III: 75). Thus, all non-Muslims have been declared enemies of Allah. They are taught to give their enemy (infidels) *three choices:*

1. Invite them to embrace Islam (which actually means acknowledging the Lordship of Muhammad).

2. If they do not accept the proposal, then they must surrender and pay tribute, and

3 .If they reject both alternatives, then fight them mercilessly:

When the **Taliban**, the Islamic fundamentalists who had been one of the forces fighting the Soviet occupation of Afghanistan, was establishing its control of most of the country in mid-1996, Osama bin Laden left Sudan and relocated his base outside the eastern Afghan city of Jalalabad. Weeks after relocating to Afghanistan, Osama bin Laden issued a **fatwah** entitled **"Declaration of War Against the Americans Who Occupy the Lands of the Two Holy Mosques."**

The fatwah announced *"there is no more important duty than pushing the American occupier out"* and it praises Muslim youth who are willing to die to get rid of the enemy. *"Youths only want one thing,"* Osama bin Laden wrote, *"to kill you so they can go to Paradise."*

[36] Gary Hudson *"KING JAMES ONLYISM"* and the *"Egyptian Corruption"* Argument.

18

Noteworthy vs. Notorious

Every time we hire a scholar we need to have a revival. [1]
Dr. Bob Jones, Sr.

Many of the proponents of the modern versions (including James White) boldly claim that there is no grand conspiracy by those producing these new bibles. This may be true in some cases. However, Mr. White and the others fail to point out that the *underlying manuscripts* have had a satanic influence on their modern version counterparts; therefore, the translations produced from them contain the errors of Origen, Semler, Kittel, Westcott, Hort, and a cast of other infidels. Satan has used these men and others like them to cast doubt upon the very words of God.

For example, does your bible version completely omit some or all of the following verses, or cast doubt upon them in its footnotes – *Matthew 12:47, 17:21, 18:11, 21:44, 23:14, Mark 7:16, 9:44, 9:46, 11:26, 15:28, 16:9-20, Luke 17:36, 22:43-44, 23:17, John 5:4, 7:53-8:11, Acts 8:37, 15:34, 24:7, 28:29, Romans 16:24?* The following footnote from the NIV is representative of the typical attack upon the word of God: *"[The earliest and most reliable manuscripts and other witnesses do not have John 7:53-8:11.]"* [2] This footnote and others like it show that the NIV follows the two critical Greek manuscripts, Vaticanus and Sinaiticus!

Provided here is a simple Bible version checklist, followed by some important facts about the Bible issue debate. Answers to the checklist will help determine whether any particular version follows God's line of manuscripts or Satan's line. Once the problem identified, we need to distinguish whether an individual has had a noteworthy or notorious impact upon Bible history.

Bible Version Checklist:

a. Does your version make Jesus a sinner when he gets angry in *Mark 3:5* and *John 2:15*? It does if it takes out the phrase *"without a cause"* in *Matthew 5:22*!

b. Does your version change "Lucifer" to "morning star" in *Isaiah 14:12*, when *Revelation 22:16* clearly identifies Jesus Christ as the morning star?

c. Does your version change the word *"prophets"* to *"Isaiah"* in *Mark 1:2*, when the verse quoted actually comes from *Malachi 3:1*, thus necessitating the use of the word *prophets* as found in the KJB and not a single book (Isaiah).

d. Does your version say that Elhanan killed Goliath in *II Samuel 21:19*, when everybody knows David killed him?

e. Does your version omit the last fourteen words of the Lord's Prayer in *Matthew 6:13*?

f. Does your version admit that people *worshipped* the Lord Jesus Christ in *Matthew 18:26* and *Matthew 20:20*?

g. Does your version cast doubt on the deity of Christ by adding the words *"nor the son"* to *Matthew 24:36*?

h. Does your version omit the Lordship of Jesus Christ in any of these verses: *Mark 9:24, Luke 23:42 and Romans 1:3*?

i. Does your version make it hard for *everyone* to enter the kingdom of God in *Mark 10:24*?

j. Does your version cast doubt on the virgin birth of Christ by calling Joseph His father in *Luke 2:33*?

k. Does your version tell you *what* to live by in *Luke 4:4*?

l. Does your version cast doubt once again on the deity of Christ by calling Him a *"chosen one"* in *Luke 9:35*?

m. Is Jesus the *"only begotten"* Son of God in *John 1:14 & 18, John 3:16 & 18,* and *I John 4:9*?

n. Does your version forget to tell you in *whom* to believe in *John 6:47*?

o. Does your version admit that Jesus is in heaven in *John 3:13, John 16:16,* and *I John 5:7*?

p. Does your version reduce Jesus to God's *servant* rather than His *Son* in *Acts 3:13, 3:26, 4:27,* or *4:30*?

q. Does the Ethiopian eunuch get saved in *Acts 8:37* in your version?

r. Does anyone fast in the following verses: *Acts 10:30, I Corinthians 7:5, II Corinthians 6:5,* or *II Corinthians 11:27*?

s. Does Christ have a Judgment Seat in your version of *Romans 14:10*? The KJB says that we give an account of ourselves to *God* (vs. 12) at the Judgment Seat of Christ (vs. 10), proving the deity of Christ!

t. Does your version promote pride and boasting by changing *II Corinthians 1:12 & 14, 5:12, 7:4, Galatians 6:4,* and *James 1:9-10*.

u. Does your version place Jesus at the creation scene in *Ephesians 3:9* or *Hebrews 2:7*?

v. Is Jesus robbed of His deity again in *Philippians 2:6*?

w. Does your version exalt the deity of Christ by admitting that *God* laid down His life for us in *I John 3:16*?

x. Can you find the Trinity in *I John 5:8*?

y. Does your version contain footnotes such as, *"some manuscripts say..."* or *"the oldest and best say...?"* Does this not leave you to your own private interpretation of scripture, contrary to *II Peter 1:20*?

z. Does your version contain the command to study it and the revelation of how to do so in *II Timothy 2:15*?

This Bible Version Checklist gives a snapshot view of a few of the problems associated with the modern versions. The KJB was accepted as the final authority for over 300 years before the new versions became popular during the last few generations. Who caused all of the confusion with multiple versions? The basic premise of Westcott and Hort suggested that it was the Christians who had deliberately altered the scripture. They also insisted that men such as Adamantius Origen (a Gnostic who did not believe in the deity of Christ) were the ones responsible for causing the scripture to be restored after it was "lost" for some 1500 years!

According to these men, the text used by the Protestant reformers was the most *un*reliable because the true text was not restored until the late nineteenth century when the pope brought the Vaticanus manuscript out of his library and the truth was "rescued" by Tischendorf out of a monastery trash can! Where is the providence of God? Where is the spiritual discernment of God's people? Does it make sense that good, godly scribes corrupted the text and that infidels have rescued it? Pause for a moment and reflect on the absurdity of this position! Now, we turn our attention to some of the issues not completely covered thus far.

Copyrights on Derivative Works

All bible versions are *derivative* works because they are adapted from other works. In many ways, they are similar to a play written about a book by another author. To be copyrightable, a derivative work must be **different** enough from the **original** to be regarded as a **new work or must contain a substantial amount of new material.** Making minor changes or additions of little substance to a pre-existing work will not qualify the work as a new version for copyright purposes. In other words, the modern versions must by law read significantly different from their predecessor versions in order to qualify for a copyright.

In order to protect their financial investment and receive income from their work, bible publishers must copyright their work. Every modern version has a **financial** copyright, and thus an owner. According to the New Standard Encyclopedia, a copyright is *"the legal protection given to **authors** and artists to prevent reproduction of **their** work without **their** consent. The **owner** of a copyright has the exclusive right to print, reprint, publish, copy and sell the material covered by the copyright."* [3]

The text of the King James Bible is the only text of over 200 English translations that has *no financial copyright*! (Note: The copyright notices found in the King James *Study* Bibles do not cover the actual text of the Bible. They pertain only to the publisher's notes and comments.) The text of the King James Bible does not have a *financial* copyright. On the other hand, all of the modern versions have a copyright to protect their investment! The legal requirements of derivative works necessitate the use of assorted synonyms with greater and greater imprecision. Although the modern versions read more like our degenerating language today, their claims to be easier to understand are simply false and misleading. Understanding the truth of God's word and understanding the untruths conveyed by these modern bibles are two different things. Even their claims to be on a lower reading level are spurious.

Grade Level Indicator

The appeal of the new bible translations stems from their perceived ability to communicate, not from their fidelity to the actual words of God. However, their ability to communicate does not mean that the right message (the truth) is being communicated. The publishers that produce and print them are *not* as concerned with a faithful rendering of the true text as they are with corporate profits and the bottom line. Purchasing power, not the Holy Spirit of God, is the driving force (*I Timothy 6:10*).

Shamefully, the criteria for acceptance of a bible has become its perceived readability rather than its accuracy. When in fact it is the Spirit of God that gives a person the understanding of God's word *(I Corinthians 2:14)*. If it seems as though one can more easily read and understand the modern versions, this may have nothing to do with the Holy Spirit, the truth, or God's will. One may be understanding something conveyed to him by Satan rather than by God.

The claim of an easier reading bible is a major modern version sales pitch. Is the KJB really harder to understand than the modern versions? According to all the sales hype, this is true. Contrary to popular opinion, the Flesch-Kincaid research company's computerized Grade Level Indicator reveals that the King James Bible is the easiest of all the versions to read. In a selected analysis, the KJB reads on a 5.8 reading grade level, while the NIV reads on an 8.4 grade level, the NASV on a 6.1 grade level, Today's English Version on a 7.2, and the NKJV on a 6.9 grade level.

Flesch-Kincaid Grade Level Indicator
Selected Books I

	KJB Grade Level	NIV Grade Level	NASV Grade Level	TEV Grade Level	NKJV Grade Level
Gen. 1	4.4	5.1	4.7	5.1	5.2
Mal.1	4.6	4.8	5.1	5.4	4.6
Mat. 1	6.7	6.4	6.8	11.8	10.3
Rev. 1	7.5	7.1	7.7	6.4	7.7
Avg.	5.8	8.4	6.1	7.2	6.9

Chart 1

To insure a well-rounded inquiry, one each of the three book types (Gospel, Pauline epistle, and general epistle) were surveyed. The resulting data further confirms the readability of the King James Bible.

Flesch-Kincaid Grade Level Indicator
Selected Books II

	KJB Grade Level	NIV Grade Level	NASV Grade Level	TEV Grade Level	NKJV Grade Level
Joh. 1	3.6	3.6	4.2	5.9	3.9
Gal. 1	8.6	9.8	10.4	6.7	8.9
Jam. 1	5.7	6.5	7.0	6.0	6.4

Chart 2

Why is the King James Bible truly easier to read? The KJB uses one or two syllable words, while new versions choose to substitute these words with more complex multi-syllable words and phrases. As we have seen, their "heady, high-minded" vocabulary hides the hope of salvation from those seeking the truth. *"This know also, that in the last days perilous times shall come ...for men shall be lovers of their own selves, covetous, boasters, proud, blasphemous...**heady, highminded**, lovers of pleasures more than lovers of God; having a form of godliness, but denying the power thereof: from such turn away" (II Timothy 3:1-5).* The consequences are far reaching. Not only do they contain errors and heresies, but they also cause unscriptural division *(I Corinthians 1:10)*. Even the simple things taken for granted by previous generations are no longer possible today. No longer can these multi-version congregations read the Bible in unison or even agree upon what the Bible plainly states.

The problems are individual as well as congregational. There is less scripture memorization going on today because people do not know which version they should be memorizing. In His divine wisdom, God gave us the Bible that is easiest to memorize. Because the KJB is written with a definte meter and rhythm, it is the translation easiest to memorize. Satan knows and fears the consequences of a Christian that memorizes scripture. *"Thy word have I hid in mine heart, that I might not sin against thee" (Psalm 119:11).* The Bible-memorizing Christian that brings these truths to mind in the midst of temptation has some divine protection.

Instead of producing the fruit of the KJB (i.e. the great revivals, godly living, etc.), the new versions have only accompanied moral decline in our nation. Have the modern versions given the church revival and created a God-fearing nation? No! Instead, they have made it easier for Satan to corrupt this once great God-fearing nation. What is it going to take for America to wake up? What is it going to take for Christians to wake up?

Some people wonder how such drastic changes could be perpetrated upon the public. Samuel Hemphill explains the phenomenon as a classic case of wolves in sheep's clothing. He points out this truth clearly in his book which addresses the history of the Revised Version. *"Nor can it be too distinctly or too emphatically affirmed that the reluctance of the public could never have been overcome but for the studious moderation and apparently rigid conservatism which the advocates of revision were careful to adopt."* [4] Hemphill asserts that there never would have been a Revised Version were it not for the moderation and conservative position outwardly displayed by the revisers. One can easily see that neither Westcott nor Hort was conservative or moderate in his beliefs. The same assessment holds for Origen and an entire cast of other infidels. We can trace Satan's hand in every corrupt work. Interestingly, some of the men involved in the preparation of the modern versions have come to discover the truth and to regret their involvement. Being men of character, these individuals have attempted to disassociate themselves from it. One such man was Dr. S. Frank Logsdon.

In the 1950's, Dr. S. Frank Logsdon was invited by his businessman friend Franklin Dewey Lockman to prepare a feasibility study which led to the production of the New American Standard Version (NASV). He was involved at the very beginning and continued throughout the work. He helped interview some of the men who served as translators for this version and wrote the preface for the NASV. Many accounts of Dr. Logsdon's participation in the translation of the NASV exist. After receiving much feedback from the NASV's publication, Logsdon tried to disassociate himself from the work. There are tapes and personal letters explaining his concerns. The following is one such letter, written by Dr. Logsdon to Cecil J. Carter.

When questions began to reach me (pertaining to the NASV), *at first I was quite offended. However, in attempting to answer, I began to sense that something was not right about the N.A.S.V. Upon investigation, I wrote my very dear friend, Mr. Lockman, explaining that I was forced to renounce all attachment to the N.A.S.V. ...I can aver that the project* (NASV) *was produced by thoroughly sincere men who had the best of intentions. The product, however, is grievous to my heart and helps to complicate matters in these already troublous times.* [5]

Like some others that have innocently associated themselves with these modern versions, Dr. Logsdon was convinced that a better, easier reading, more literal translation could be produced. When the questions began to surface, he began to regret his relationship with this corrupt bible. His character and integrity prompted him to do the right thing by attempting to rectify his error. Many other men less principled than S. Frank Logsdon have refused to admit their errors and their susceptibility to satanic influence. Unfortunately, the man that discovered the Sinaiticus manuscript is such an individual.

Sinaiticus

In May 1844, Constantine von Tishendorf discovered *Codex Sinaiticus* in a wastebasket in St. Catherine's Monastery. The Greek text called Sinaiticus is believed to be one of the 50 manuscripts from those produced by Eusebius for the Emperor Constantine I. Tiscendorf's find seemed to destroy his judgment. Previous to this find, he had produced seven editions of his Greek New Testament. After the seventh, he declared that it was perfect and could not be improved. After he found the Sinaiticus manuscript, he produced his eighth Greek New Testament, which differed from his seventh in some 3572 places!!! Thus, a Greek text was born that differed significantly from the *Textus Receptus*. Tischendorf's own words describe his discovery.

It was at the foot of Mount Sinai, in the Convent of St. Catherine, that I discovered the pearl of all my researches... In visiting the library of the monastery, in the month of May, 1844, I perceived in the middle of the great hall a large and wide basket full of old parchments; and the librarian, who was a man of information, told me that two heaps of papers like these, molded by time, had been already committed to the flames. What was my surprise to find amid this heap of papers a considerable number of sheets of a copy of the Old Testament in Greek, which seemed to me to be one of the most ancient that I had ever seen. The authorities of the convent allowed me to possess myself of a third of these parchments, or about forty-three sheets, all the more readily as they were destined for the fire.[6]

Evidently, the antiquity of Sinaiticus convinced Tischendorf of the superiority of this manuscript. His Greek New Testament certainly reveals that he thought the St. Catherine's trash can held the most important find of all time. The monastery was constructed at the foot of Mount Sinai by order of the Emperor Justinian to house the bones of St. Catherine of Alexandria. However, the bones of many others are housed there as well. The skulls of monks from across the centuries are heaped in a large room in the Chapel of St. Triphone, also known as the Skull House. Reportedly, this heap of skulls is seven to eight feet high. The skeleton of one monk is left chained to the door adjacent to the mound of skulls as an ageless guard. Many visitors of this monastery have vividly described its satanic atmosphere. Did God really choose this wicked place to restore his "unfulfilled" promise of preservation?

The Sinaiticus manuscript had been kept by these monks for centuries, until it was discovered by Tischendorf, taken to Germany, and ultimately sold to Great Britain. It is now housed in the British Museum in London.

The Sinaiticus and Vaticanus are the two primary manuscripts that have been used to bring about the majority of the modern version changes. The justification used to convince the seminaries of the superiority of these texts is simply their age. The claim is made that the older a manuscript is, the closer it is to the original source and the less the chance that it embodies corruption. Westcott and Hort used these manuscripts to produce their own text. First, however, they had to convince the revision committee that the prevailing text type was ecclesiastically sanctioned and corrupted in Antioch prior to A.D. 400. These men were able to convince the revision committee to reject the majority readings based on their fabricated theory.

The Lucian Recension Theory

Westcott and Hort concocted an incredible fantasy to convince the committee members to reject the Majority Text and accept their text as authoritatively superior. They claimed that a council officially condemned and repressed the "true" readings (Alexandrian) while endorsing and propagating the "false" (Antiochian). [7] Thus, they concluded, the great majority of manuscripts in existence supporting the King James Bible were Satan's handiwork and not the providence of God.

This belief contradicts the historical record. For instance, Dean Burgon examined the writings of 76 church fathers. From fathers that died before A.D. 400, there were 2630 references to the Traditional Text and only 1753 to the Westcott-Hort type text. This fact conclusively proves that the Traditional Text was present before A.D. 400 and the Traditional Text outweighed the Westcott-Hort type text by three to two. Again, this fact conclusively disproves the Westcott and Hort theory that the Received Text **originated** during the fourth century.

Westcott and Hort had to invent this theory so they could claim that they were following the "oldest and best" manuscripts. The testimony of the church fathers proves that the Traditional Text existed long before the era that Westcott and Hort claim. Westcott and Hort deliberately set out to construct a theory that would destroy the Received Text and support their "neutral" text. Jack Moorman gives an outline of their attack. These nine points form the basis for rejection of the Received Text and the acceptance of all future modern versions. [8]

- **In textual criticism, the New Testament is to be treated like any other book.** (History reveals that Satan has always leveled his most vehement attack against the incarnate word and the written word. The Bible cannot be treated like any other book when Satan hates it so much.)

- **There are no signs of deliberate falsification of the text.** (Thus, no reason exists to reject any of the readings that contain a doctrinally inferior position.)

- **The numerical preponderance of the Received Text can be explained through genealogy.** (Basically, this means frequent copying of the same kind of "defective" manuscripts has given us the majority.)

- **Despite its numerical advantage, the Received Text is merely one of several competing text types.** (By considering the Majority Text together as a group, its numerical superiority has no bearing on one's decision concerning which text "type" to choose. Although 95-99% of the texts may agree with the text behind the King James Bible, when considering the manuscripts from a text type perspective only, this places the corrupt texts on equal footing numerically with the Majority Text.)

- **The Received Text is fuller because it is a *conflated* text that combined the shorter readings of the other competing text types. This conflation was hypothesized to have been produced with the official sanction of the Byzantine Church during the fourth century.** (Historical truth must be altered because Received Text readings existed prior to the time this alleged conspiracy took place.)

- **There are no distinctive Received Text readings in the writings of the church fathers before A.D. 350.** (Dean Burgon and others have conclusively proved this premise to be absolutely false. The Syrian Text dating back to the second century disproves this theory.)

- **The shorter reading is to be preferred** (on the assumption that a scribe would add material to the text). **Also, the harder reading is to be preferred** (on the assumption that a scribe would attempt to simplify the text).

- **The primary basis for a Greek text is to be found in Vaticanus and Sinaiticus.** (According to Herman Hoskier, these two "witnesses" disagree strongly with each other in 3036 locations in the Gospels alone.) *(Mark 14:55-56, Isaiah 8:20).* [9]

- **Harmonization. Parallel passages in the New Testament were made to say the same thing.** (There is no proof offered for this theory, and it eliminates the established two or three witnesses requirement.)

Many witnesses have disproved these false premises and theories, but they still form the basis of every modern version. Having learned the truth about Westcott and Hort and their fictitious suppositions, many modern version proponents try to distance themselves from these men. However, new version translators basically accept and use the theories of Westcott and Hort and their text, disregarding the inconsistencies. They claim to use all the manuscript evidence (an eclectic approach); however, they still hold to the Westcott-Hort theories. The Westcott-Hort text is given preeminence in all the new versions.

The Preservation of the Syriac Peshitta Version

Westcott and Hort knew that the existence of any Traditional Text readings prior to their self-proclaimed ecclesiastical corruption date would disprove their theory. The Syriac Peshitta, a text dating to about A.D. 150, was the historic Bible of the whole Syrian Church. It closely agrees with the Traditional Text of the King James Bible! It is the oldest Byzantine text and was attacked by Hort. J.J. Ray in his classic book, *God Wrote Only One Bible*, irrefutably disproved the fabricated claims of Westcott and Hort. An excerpt from this work reads as follows:

> *A number of good textual authorities state that the Bible of the Syrian Church, the Peshitta, was translated from the Greek Vulgate into Syrian about 150 A.D. . . . This Peshitta version is admired by Syriac scholars as a careful, faithful, simple, direct, literal version, clear and forceful in style. These characteristics have given it the title "The Queen of the Versions." Antioch was the capital of Syria where the early believers were first called Christians (Acts 11:26). In a few years the Syrian believers could be numbered by the thousands. Their Bible, the Peshitta, even today, generally follows the Received Text. This is another proof that the foundation for the King James Bible is older and more reliable than the Vatican manuscript, which was elevated to the chair of authority by Westcott and Hort.* [10]

Because it dates back to the second century and pre-dates both Vaticanus and Sinaiticus, the Peshitta's antiquity had to be denied by Westcott, Hort, and others of like mind. Such individuals also assert that all of the Byzantine texts were corrupted in unison (all over the world) in an attempt to explain why these texts read so similarly. Floyd Nolen Jones, quoting Burgon, Hills, and Pickering, conclusively proves that Hort's theory was false and that the Peshitta bears witness to the KJB readings 100 years prior to either Vaticanus B or Sinaiticus. [11] There are still approximately 350 copies of the Peshitta in existence today!

> It was at Antioch, capital of Syria, that the believers were first called Christians. And as time rolled on, the Syrian-speaking Christians could be numbered by the thousands. It is generally admitted that the Bible was translated from the original languages into Syrian about 150 AD. This version is known as the Peshitta (the correct or simple). This Bible even today generally follows the Received Text. One authority tells us this - The Peshitta in our days is found in use amongst the Nestorians, who have always kept it, by the Monophysites on the plains of Syria, the Christians of St.Thomas in Malabar, and by the Maronites on the mountain terraces of Lebanon. [12]

Westcott and Hort put forth a now-discredited theory in support of a later date for the Peshitta. Many liberal scholars recognize how wrong Westcott and Hort were, but our fundamental-evangelical "experts" still buy into their rewriting of history and accept their text as authoritative. This disappointing truth parallels the promulgation of evolutionary theory. No matter how many fundamental flaws are discovered, the evolutionary principles continue to be taught, disregarding the fact that the underlying premises supporting the position have been disproved. When the foundation is faulty, the building crumbles. Sadly, science and theology both sometimes play by an unfortunate set of rules which ignores logic and truth.

The Noteworthy and the Notorious

The cast of characters used by God to preserve the word of God have been greatly maligned. We will discuss only a few of these men from the last five centuries. These men are *noteworthy* in any study of church history or manuscript evidence for their faithful stand on the word of God and for the furtherance of the gospel. They truly were men of God.

Identifying Satan's henchmen is much more important because these *notorious* men have done much damage through their dastardly deeds, all the while masquerading as "good godly men." While many purport these men to be in the same vein as those that have stood for the Received Text, they are more aptly identified as *infidels*. The word of God that they worked to undermine actually warns us against them (*II Corinthians 2:17*)!

The Noteworthy

Erasmus, Desiderius (1469-1536): Dutch intellectual known as the "journalist of scholarship" credited with producing the world's first printed Greek New Testament. His decided preference for the readings of the *Textus Receptus* over those of *Codex Vaticanus* (as supplied to him by the Catholic Sepulveda) found its fruition in the adage, "Erasmus laid the egg and Luther hatched it."

King James Translators: The KJB translators faithfully translated the *Textus Receptus* into English. In 1604, a group of 54 scholars was chosen and divided into six teams, with each team assigned the task of translating a different portion of scripture. Each man on each team had to translate every word of his team's assigned portion. Then, these individual translations were collectively compared with those of the other team members. Discrepancies were voted on, bringing each team to agreement on its assigned portion of the scripture. Then, each team passed its work on to each of the other teams for their scrutiny and approval. Thus each scripture was examined at least **fourteen** times! The work took **seven** years and was completed in 1611. See Alexander McClure's *Translators Revived* (Maranatha Publications) or Gustavus S. Paine's book, *The Men Behind the King James Version* (Baker Book House, 1959) for further information.

Scrivener, Prebendary F.H.A. (1813-1891): Conservative Anglican scholar of Trinity College who contested with Hort for the *Textus Receptus* and readings throughout the decade of work done by the Revision Committee of 1871-1881.

Burgon, Dean John William (1813-1888): Outstanding conservative scholar of nineteenth century Anglicanism. Dean of Chichester, he repudiated Westcott and Hort and their text and principles with scholarly accord. He supported the Traditional Text since he believed that God preserved it through the church fathers as evidenced by their writings. Transmission of God's word, according to Burgon, was not naturalistic but through supernatural means. This position contradicted the position underlying Westcott and Hort's text.

The Notorious

Marcion the Heretic (d. 160): Ancient enemy of the Church, known for his repeated mutilation of the New Testament scriptures.

Origen, Adamantius (185-254): One-time headmaster of Alexandria's catechetical school of theology and philosophy in Egypt. Hailed as the Church's first textual critic. He denied the existence of hell and believed stars were living creatures in possession of souls for which Christ died. After his Alexandrian excommunication for castrating himself, Origen took his mutilated manuscripts and migrated to Caesarea where he set up another school. Expiring in 254, he bequeathed his library to his favorite pupil Pamphilus. Upon his own death in 309, Pamphilus passed the corrupted readings of Origen on to Eusebius, thus infecting all subsequent generations.

Eusebius of Caesarea (260-340): Ancient scholar known as the "Father of Church History," who was commissioned by Emperor Constantine to produce fifty new bibles. Many believe Vaticanus and Sinaiticus to be two of these 50 copies.

Jerome (342-420): Catholic scholar who produced the Latin Vulgate by "revising" the Itala version (or, *Old Latin*) according to the readings of *Codex Vaticanus*.

Semler, Johann Salomo (1725-1791): Professor of Theology at Halle. He looked at the Bible as a man-made book. He rejected the deity of

Jesus Christ and the supernatural infallibility of scripture. Semler was the father of German rationalism and author of the "accommodation theory," asserting that the Lord Jesus Christ and the Apostles accommodated themselves to the prejudices, errors, and superstitions of their time. [13] He set forth the principle that it is morally permissible to lie about one's beliefs when speaking publicly because the audience doesn't have the background to understand the full truth. Thus, it was taught that the preacher could assert from the pulpit that he believed the scriptures were verbally inspired, inerrant, etc. in order to "accommodate" his congregation who was unlearned in textual criticism. Semler "was the leader of the reaction in Germany against the traditional views of the canon of scripture." [14]

Griesbach, Johann (1745-1812): Published three Greek editions between 1774-1806, proposing several families of witnesses: Alexandrian, Western, and Byzantine. He listed fifteen canons for textual criticism and produced a text on these principles, departing from the *Textus Receptus*. He was a pupil of Semler.

Lachmann, Karl (1793-1851): A German rationalist. He was basically a classicist rather than a theologian. He desired to produce a text based on the fourth century manuscripts. He thought it impossible to produce the text of the originals, and rebuked his critics for following a "late, impure" text (the Received Text). [15] His text is based on two to four manuscripts (predominantly Vaticanus) and is considered to be the first critical text entirely casting aside the *Textus Receptus*. He treated the Bible like any other classical writing. However, his work was taken seriously by the textual critics because he furthered their objective of undermining the authority of the Received Text.

Tischendorf, L. F. Constantin (1815-1874): German textual critic who discovered *Codex Sinaiticus* in a trash can at St. Catherine's Monastery in 1844. He produced eight editions of his Greek New Testament. He had a distinct respect for the conclusions of Griesbach and Lachmann.

Tregelles, Samuel Prideaux (1813-1875): Published a critical text based on his own independent study. He was influential in the field of textual criticism in England. His theories of textual criticism paralleled those of Lachmann.

Schaff, Philip (1819-1893): Ecumenical church historian and professor at the apostate Union of Theological Seminary selected by the English Revision Committee to chair their American advisory board.

Westcott, Brooke Foss (1825-1901): Liberal Anglican professor at Cambridge who conspired with Dr. Fenton Hort from 1853-1871 to produce a radical Greek New Testament predominately predicated on *Codex Vaticanus*. Their corrupt text then became the catalyst for the English Revision Committee of 1871-1881 which resulted in the equally corrupt Revised Version New Testament of 1881. Their committee had not been charged with revising the Greek Text but with updating the English. When their work was published, they came under widespread condemnation for exceeding the authority of their appointment.

Hort, Fenton John Anthony (1828-1892): Cambridge professor who joined Brooke Westcott in producing a Greek New Testament predominantly built upon the *Codex Vaticanus* and German scholars such as Lachmann, Griesbach, and Tischendorf. During the ensuing Revision Committee of 1871-1881, Dr. Hort took the lead in cramming this corrupt text down the throats of his fellow committee members. The end result was the equally perverted Revised Version New Testament of 1881. Westcott and Hort said they venerated the name of Greisbach "above that of every other textual critic in the New Testament." [16]

Nestle, Eberhand (1851-1913): German scholar whose initial Greek New Testament of 1898 has undergone 26 editions to date. Used in the majority of Bible colleges and seminaries, the Nestle's text is basically identical to the text of Westcott and Hort.

Kittel, Gerhard (1888-1948): He edited the ten-volume standard reference work used in New Testament Greek word studies, the *Theological Dictionary of the New Testament*. In Gerhard Kittel, Satan found a man used to destroy both the seed of Israel and the "incorruptible seed" of the word of God. He was a dedicated Nazi who enthusiastically supported Adolph Hitler. His works were used to theologically justify exterminating the Jews. Kittel was put on trial for his key role in the extermination of two-thirds of Europe's Jewish population. [17] His father, Rudolph Kittel, was the author of *Biblica Hebraica* – used by the new versions to translate the Old Testament.

Notorious – Twenty-first Century Critics (A few examples)

The true Bible believer knows that his purpose in life includes being a defender of the faith. However, many men and women seem to have purposes contrary to this God-given objective. Instead of standing up for the pure, preserved word of God, they expend their energies undermining the truth. We have discussed a few of the individuals involved in this insidious attempt by Satan to destroy the truth of God. Here are the comments of a few more of the Bible critics.

Kutilek, Doug: *The Westcott and Hort text is much simpler to define. This is the Greek New Testament edited by B. F. Westcott and F. J. A. Hort and first published in 1881, with numerous reprints in the century since. It is probably the single most famous of the so-called critical texts, perhaps because of* **the scholarly eminence of its editors** (meaning the "esteemed" infidels of Westcott and Hort), *perhaps because it was issued the same year as the English Revised Version which followed a text rather like the Westcott-Hort text.*

It needs to be stated clearly that the text of Westcott and Hort was not the first printed Greek Testament that **deliberately and substantially departed from the textus receptus on the basis of manuscript evidence** (evidence from the corrupt Vaticanus and Sinaiticus!). *Westcott and Hort were preceded in the late 1700s by Griesbach, and in the 1800s by Lachmann, Alford, Tregelles, and Tischendorf (and others),* **all of whose texts made numerous revisions in the textus receptus on the basis of manuscript evidence** (Vaticanus and Sinaiticus, etc.)*; these texts, especially the last three named, are very frequently in agreement with Westcott and Hort, against the textus receptus* (peas in a pod!).

None of the major modern English Bible translations made **since World War II** *used the Westcott-Hort text as its* **base** (because Westcott and Hort's corrupt text has produced the corrupt Nestle's and United Bible Society texts). *This includes translations done by theological conservatives—the New American Standard Bible, the New International Version, the New*

> *King James, for examples—and translations done by theologi-*
> *cal liberals—the Revised Standard Version, the New English*
> *Bible, the Good News Bible, etc.* **The only English Bible trans-**
> **lation currently in print that the writer is aware of which is**
> **based on the Westcott-Hort text is the New World Translation**
> **of the Jehovah's Witnesses.**

Reader, do you recognize what Mr. Kutilek has just admitted? He
says the Christ-rejecting Jehovah Witnesses are the only ones that still
use the Westcott and Hort text! What does that reveal about this text and
the Vaticanus and Sinaiticus from which it came? What does it say about
all the modern versions' following the same ungodly line of corruption?.

> Mr. Kutilek continues: *On the other hand, the* **defects** *of the*
> *Westcott-Hort text are also generally recognized,* **particularly**
> **its excessive reliance on** *manuscript B* (**Vaticanus**), *and to a*
> *lesser extent, Aleph* (**Sinaiticus**). **Hort declared the combined**
> **testimony of these two manuscripts to be all but a guarantee**
> **that a reading was original.** (What a clear condemnation of
> their position). *All scholars today recognize this as being an*
> *extreme and unwarranted point of view. Manuscript B*
> *(Vaticanus) shows the same kinds of scribal errors found in all*
> *manuscripts, a fact to be recognized and such singular read-*
> *ings to be rejected, as in fact they sometimes were rejected by*
> *Westcott and Hort (e.g., at Matthew 6:33).* [18]

> **Ross**, Bob L.: *"The Inspired word of God came in the origi-*
> *nal Hebrew and Greek writings (2 Peter 1:21). A "transla-*
> *tion" into English or any other language is the "inspired"*
> *word of God to the extent it properly translates the languages*
> *in which the scriptures were first written. I have never read a*
> *commentary or respectable book which did not at one place or*
> *another clarify or correct what was regarded by the writers as*
> *a misleading or erroneous translation. One of the primary*
> *purposes of books and the study of them is to* **determine the**
> **true meaning of the Hebrew and Greek writings, as we do**
> **not always have it complete in any single translation."** [19]

Hudson, Gary R.: Here are two interesting statements which reveal this critic's knowledge of the variations and existence of the varying texts. *"The 'word-omission' and 'verse-comparison' charts distributed by KJOs* (King James Only's) *would not work to discredit the NKJV because the NKJV New Testament had retained all of those words and verses 'omitted in the new bibles' (Acts 8:37; I John 5:7; etc.)....All translations must be evaluated on the basis of their accuracy to their own underlying texts."* [20]

Using this evaluation standard would mean that any version that accurately translates the underlying text is acceptable whether or not that underlying text is accurate. This is shear lunacy! Hudson's infidelity again becomes evident in the next statement made by him: *The following is a brief list of readings from the KJV where ambiguity and/or mistranslation obscures the true meaning of the original."*[21]

Carson, D.A. In 1979, Carson released his book deceptively entitled, *The King James Version Debate:A Plea for Realism.* Here is one quote to give a clear sense of his Alexandrian position.

> *What shall we say too about the vast majority of evangelical scholars, including men in whom were found the* **utmost piety and fidelity to the Word**, *along with* **a scholarship second to none**? *These men hold that in the basic textual theory Westcott and Hort were right, and that the church stands greatly in their debt.* [22] [Emphasis mine]

Had the vast majority of these scholars read the *Life and Letters of B.F. Westcott,* by his son, and *Life and Letters of F.J.A. Hort,* by his son, they would realize that Westcott and Hort were not of the "utmost piety and fidelity," nor had they attained to a scholarship level "second to none." Instead, Westcott and Hort deliberately set out to deceive those they could influence through their outward appearance of orthodoxy.

Not only did Carson have an incorrect view of the two most insideous men to ever influence the Church, but his position also undermines the supernatural approach to scriptural preservation. He takes a naturalistic approach apart from God. The supernatural approach starts with God's promise of preservation and ends with His perfect word. Anything short of this method is humanistic, rather than spiritual. Carson also ignorantly stresses conflation and harmonization just as James White's book proclaims many years later.

A clear distinction and division between those that have stood for the truth and those that have been busy undermining it should now be readily apparent. When truth and error are examined side by side, the facts become clear. Continually highlighting these dividing lines remains the job of those familiar with the issue. Shamefully, our seminaries have frequently become the instigators behind this propagation of error, rather than the advocates of truth. Satan has used these institutions to convince young Protestant and Baptist Bible students that their Reformation Text is unreliable and their Authorized Version has grave inaccuracies. Furthermore, they have even taught that some of the modern versions are superior to the KJB.

Once these Greek and Hebrew professors have convinced their students that they no longer have God's word, these young men naturally attack their own English Bible and believe they are helping out God in the process. The extent of the problem will become evident to anyone that has listened to church advertisements condoning every conceivable, unscriptural method of gaining numbers. Check it out for yourself. Ask a pastor which version he and his church use to get a clear indication of the extent of the problem. There will be a clear distinction between those that stand for one book, and those failing to take a stand because they do not grasp the seriousness of the issue. The plethora of modern versions used from the pulpits bears witness to this phenomenon. If you pick and choose, you become the authority... and your own god!

Now that we have examined some simple facts about the Bible version debate, it is time to consider how these changes impact even the simplest of Bible truths. The next chapter is dedicated to a single topic sorely lacking in today's churches – prayer and fasting.

Chapter 18 Endnotes

1 Herbert Noe, *Messages to Magnify the Monarch*, (Livonia, MI: Galilean
   Baptist Church, 1987), p. 14.
2 NIV p. 796.
3 *The New Standard Encyclopedia, volume 3, page 565.*
4 Hemphill   *History of the Revised Version*, op. cit., page 25.
5 Letter to Cecil J. Carter on 6/9/77 from Dr. S. Franklin Logsdon, 1807
   Hemlock Ave., Prince George, British Columbia, Canada V2L1J3
   (maraanath@mag-net.com).
6 Tischendorf's report - *Codex Sinaiticus* Page 23 –24.
7 Grady, *Final Authority, op. cit.*, p. 32.
8 Jack Moorman, *Forever Settled (Part Five): A Survey of English Bible
   History* (NJ: Collingswood: Bible for Today), p. 197, 198.
9 Herman Hoskier, *Codex B. and its Allies,* Vol 1, *A Study and an
   Indictment,* (London: Bernard Quaritch).
10 Jasper James Ray, *God Wrote Only One Bible,* (Junction City, OR: The
   Eye Opener Publishers, 1955), p. 97-98.
11 Jones, *Which Version is the Bible?, op. cit.,* p. 164-167.
12 David Otis Fuller, *Which Bible?,* (Grand Rapids, MI: Grand Rapids
   International Publications, 1975), p. 197-198.
13 *If the Foundations Be Destroyed*, Trinitarian Bible Society Article,
   No. 14, p. 1.
14 Vincent, *A History of the Textual Criticism of the New Testament, op.
   cit.,* p. 92.
15 Metzger, *The Text of the New Testament, op. cit.,* p. 124.
16 Introduction, *The New Testament in the Original Greek*, p. 185.
17 Robert P. Ericksen, *Theologians Under Hitler: Gerhard Kittel, Paul
   Althaus, and Emmanuel Hirsch* (New Haven, Conn: Yale University
   Press, 1985).
18 Doug Kutilek, *Westcott & Hort vs. Textus Receptus: Which is Superior?, 1996.*
19 Bob L. Ross, *King James ONLY Hokey.*
20 Gary R. Hudson, *The Superior Accuracy of the NKJV to the KJV's
   Textus Receptus.*
21 Hudson, *Problems in the King James Version*
22 Carson, D.A. *The King James Version Debate: A Plea for Realism,*
   (Grand Rapids, MI: Baker Book House, 1979), p. 75.

19

Fasting Phased Out

And he said unto them, This kind can come forth by nothing, but
by prayer and fasting.

(Mark 9:29)

Prayer combined with fasting is a great spiritual weapon in the
Christian's arsenal against the world, the flesh, and the Devil.
That's why Satan takes such aggressive steps through the mod-
ern versions to destroy or neutralize this very important instrument.

The relative importance of any particular biblical subject can easily
be determined by studying the degree of vehemence with which it is
attacked in the modern versions. The modern versions' treatment of
fasting is an excellent case in point. Fasting is a sorely neglected Christian discipline, relegated by many to a practice only associated with the
Old Testament saint. For this reason, most Christians have never fasted
a single time in their lives.

The Purpose of Fasting

Fasting should be an important element of every Christian's life.
When God's intervention is desired in a particular matter, fasting is one
means to this end. Fasting is a practice which enables the *soul* and *spirit*
to overcome the desires of the *flesh*. The Apostle Paul states in the New

Testament that he had power with God because he kept his body in subjection. Paul did not allow his body and the desires of the flesh to control his life. As various aspects of fasting are discussed, keep the following verse in mind.

(KJB) I Corinthians 9:27 But I keep under my body and bring it into subjection...

Paul understood the importance of bringing his body into subjection to his soul and spirit, thus enabling him to do the will of God. When the body (or the flesh) controls a person's life, God no longer controls that life. Fasting enables an individual to overcome the flesh and helps to fulfill a person's desire to serve God. Fasting is a means for bringing the body into subjection, but it is *not* a means of abusing the body as the NIV insanely supposes.

*(NIV) I Corinthians 9:27 No, **I beat my body** and make it my slave . . .*

What is fasting all about? The most important aspect of fasting is that the practice requires a person to abstain from any physical pleasures during the period of the fast.

Forgoing Physical Pleasures

Three critical verses in the books of First and Second Corinthians reveal the importance of fasting as it applies to the Church today. The first of these verses reveals that a person must forgo participation in pleasures of the flesh, including physical intimacy, during the period of the fast in order to give himself to fasting and prayer.

*(KJB) I Corinthians 7:5 Defraud ye not one the other, except it be with consent for a time, **that ye may give yourselves to fasting and prayer**; and come together again, that Satan tempt you not for your incontinency.*

The critical truth of this verse from the KJB is that fasting does not simply entail abstinence from food, but from other physical pleasures as well. The NIV completely removes fasting from this verse, thereby destroying the true teaching and the intent of fasting. A person reading the NIV is not taught to forgo food AND other physical pleasures during a fast.

> *(NIV) I Corinthians 7:5 Do not deprive each other except by mutual consent and for a time, **so that you may devote yourselves to prayer**. Then come together again so that Satan will not tempt you because of your lack of self-control.*

The Apostle Paul's writings, as revealed in the KJB, instruct the Christian to abstain from physical relations with a spouse during fasting. The NIV makes very little sense when it omits fasting from the verse and leaves only prayer. Common sense lets us know that certain things are not to be done during prayer time!

Fasting occurs over an extended period, and is more continuous in nature than prayer. A person rarely prays without interruption for 24 hours; however, fasting must be uninterrupted in order to be a true fast. For any sane Christian, it is understood that one should refrain from physical relations during prayer. God does instruct the Christian to refrain from physical relations during a fast. This command to abstain can be applied to any other flesh-satisfying activities, including watching television, going bowling, or any of a variety of other actions. A person fasting should abstain from all activities naturally satisfying to the flesh in order to concentrate on prayer.

The NIV destroys most references to fasting. The New Century Version (copyright 1993) makes no mention of fasting in any of the passages known for their teaching on the subject in the KJB. The NCV is a member of the next generation of bible versions. Gradual deletions in the earlier versions including the NIV have culminated in the complete removal of all teaching concerning fasting from the NCV. Notice how the NCV matches the NIV in the following passage. As we will see in other passages, though, the NCV perverts the truth to a far greater degree than its predecessors do.

*(NCV) I Corinthians 7:5 Do not refuse to give your bodies to each other, unless you both agree to stay away from sexual relations for **a time so you can give your time to prayer**. Then come together again so Satan cannot tempt you because of a lack of self-control.*

Approving Ourselves as the Ministers of God

Paul testified to the fact that he fasted. He said that he approved himself as the minister of God "in much . . . fastings." Paul knew that fasting was one way to obediently do that which pleases God. He knew that God had instituted the fast in the Old Testament, and that fasting was an applicable practice for him (and for us) during this Church Age.

*(KJB) II Corinthians 6:4 But in all things **approving our-selves as the ministers of God**, in much patience, in afflic-tions, in necessities, in distresses, 5 In stripes, in imprison-ments, in tumults, in labours, in watchings, **in fastings**;*

The NIV destroys this record of the fact that Paul spent much time fasting. Simple hunger can arise for a host of reasons besides fasting.

*(NIV) II Corinthians 6:4 Rather, as servants of God we com-mend ourselves in every way: in great endurance; in troubles, hardships and distresses; 5 in beatings, imprisonments and ri-ots; in hard work, sleepless nights and **hunger**;*

Once again, the NIV destroys the truth, but the NCV does so to a greater degree. Following the lead of the NIV, the NCV states: "some-times we get no sleep or food." This passage from the NCV sounds less like a record of Christian fasting, and more like a testament of God's failure to provide for Paul's physical and material needs.

*(NCV) II Corinthians 6:4 But in every way we show we are servants of God: in accepting many hard things, in troubles, in difficulties, and in great problems. We are beaten and thrown into prison. We meet those who become upset with us and start riots. We work hard, and **sometimes we get no sleep or food**.*

Hunger versus Fasting

The following verse serves as another record of Paul's frequent fastings. God is faithful to catch the Devil and his cohorts in their diabolical actions. This verse from the KJB mentions not only fasting, but also hunger. Paul distinguishes between the two states. He was most likely involuntarily *in hunger*, but voluntarily *fasted* to promote submission of the body to spiritual matters.

> *(KJB) II Corinthians 11:27 In weariness and painfulness, in watchings often, in hunger and thirst, in fastings often, in cold and nakedness.*

Fasting is a very important aspect of the Christian's walk with God. If you have never fasted, note the following simple suggestions:

1. Don't eat anything (except maybe a breath mint).
2. Drink only water (or juice for a longer fast).
3. Pray about how long God would have you fast and stick to that time. Continue for a minimum of 24 hours, praying continually.
4. Abstain from anything that the flesh finds pleasurable.
5. Begin eating slowly and lightly after the fast.

Notice that the KJB says Paul was in hunger *and* fastings often. This verse denotes two distinctly separate actions or experiences. God knew that Satan would attempt to destroy the doctrine of fasting; therefore, He included mention of both fastings and hunger in the same verse. The NIV translators foolishly changed "fastings often" to "often gone without food".

> *(NIV) II Corinthians 11:27 I have labored and toiled and have often gone without sleep; **I have known hunger** and thirst and **have often gone without food**; I have been cold and naked.*

The NIV treats Christians as idiots. Can you imagine why Paul would say that he has known hunger and then, later in the very same verse, state that he has often gone without food? The Devil does not want you to know that our apostle fasted. Again, we see that the newest of the modern versions deletes this reference to fasting as well.

*(NCV) II Corinthians 11:27 I have done hard and tiring work, and many times I did not sleep. I have been **hungry** and thirsty, and many times **I have been without food**. I have been cold and without clothes.*

A person can't PREACH these new versions. They read much like the complaining of a whimpering baby. Can you imagine the Apostle Paul writing to the Corinthians in such a manner of self-pity?

Fasting is Not Optional

The Lord did not begin his discourse on fasting by qualifying His remarks with the word "if." Instead, He began: *"When ye fast..."*

*(KJB) Matthew 6:16 Moreover **when ye fast**, be not, as the hypocrites, of a sad countenance: for they disfigure their faces, **that they may appear unto men to fast**. Verily I say unto you, They have their reward. 17 But thou, **when thou fastest**, anoint thine head, and wash thy face; 18 That thou appear not unto men to **fast**, but unto thy Father which is in secret: and thy Father, which seeth in secret, shall reward thee openly.*

Notice that the Lord says "when" ye fast, rather than "if" ye fast. The Lord Jesus Christ never directly commanded Christians to fast. Instead, He took it for granted that they would fast, and went on to give instructions concerning regulation of the practice.

Many read Matthew chapter 6 and conclude that no one should ever know that you are fasting. Many Christians therefore wonder if it is permissible to tell others they are fasting. The Lord Jesus Christ pointed out the hypocrisy of people who were fasting with the wrong motive. One is not to *appear* to be fasting by the way he presents himself to others. **Any time you consciously attempt to appear spiritual before others, you do not possess true holiness before God**. Any person who fasts to be *seen* of men does not possess true holiness. Such hypocrisy is abominable to God.

Fasting is the best way to overcome an addiction and to allow a person to grow closer to God. Few things in life give the soul and spirit preeminence over the flesh as fasting does. Accordingly, God blesses the person who fasts scripturally.

The NIV removes every reference to the fasting of our apostle – Paul *(Romans 11:13, II Timothy 1:11)*. Satan waited until a later bible version to attack the passage in Matthew concerning fasting. All references to fasting retained in the NIV are removed from the NCV. The author was unable to find even a single reference to fasting in the text of the NCV. Remember that fasting does not constitute simple abstinence from food, but includes – among other things – abstaining from sexual intimacy with one's spouse.

> *(NCV) Matthew 6:16 "When you give up eating, don't put on a sad face like the hypocrites. They make their faces look sad to show people they are **giving up eating**. I tell you the truth, those hypocrites already have their full reward. 17 **So when you give up eating**, comb your hair and wash your face. 18 Then people will not know that you are **giving up eating**, but your Father, whom you cannot see, will see you. Your Father, sees what is done in secret, and he will reward you.*

"When you give up eating…" – Fasting means so much more than simply giving up eating. It involves a rejection of the things of the flesh. Eating is simply one of the more obvious and most prevalent flesh-satisfying activities in which we all engage daily. The NCV mentions the word *fasting* only in its footnotes, and defines the practice as giving up eating. As we have already seen, this is not a complete definition. No wonder the Bible foretells that Christianity will be shallow spiritually in these last days. A reader of the modern bible version cannot find out the truth unless he picks up God's true book.

Fasting should *never* become a religious ritual. Do not be like the religious Pharisee in Luke chapter 18. *"I fast twice in the week, I give tithes of all that I posses" (Luke 18:12)*. This Pharisee made a ritual of fasting . . . twice every week. Making a ritual of something leaves the heart out of the act. Instead, one should make it a rule to fast with the same frequency as the New Testament commands us to partake of the Lord's Supper: *"For as often as ye eat this bread . . . " (I Corinthians*

11:26). We are not told how often to partake of the Lord's Supper. This is a matter to be settled between the church (its pastor) and God, as the Spirit of God leads.

An individual should fast because his relationship and heart are right with God, and the Spirit of God has led him to fast about a specific matter or for a specific purpose. The act of fasting does not make a person spiritual. Fasting is a personal matter, as is the prayer within one's prayer closet. If God places it on your heart to fast, obey Him and He will bless. He will answer your prayer, and this disciplined practice will strengthen your soul and spirit over your flesh.

Biblical Examples of Fasting

The following three contexts for fasting are mentioned in the word of God: fasting for others, fasting in order to seek God's help, and fasting for God's guidance and direction. The importance of fasting cannot be adequately stressed. The purpose for fasting has now been completely erased in the newest modern versions. The NIV leaves the following verses somewhat intact, but the NCV completely destroys their treatment of the doctrine of fasting.

1. **Fasting for others**: When Haman plotted to kill all of the Jews, the only person in a position to intervene was Queen Esther. The only way to save the Jews was for Esther to approach the King *uninvited,* an action with the potential to earn her the death penalty. In preparation for the daunting moment, Queen Esther asks others to fast for her.

> *(KJB) Esther 4:15 Then Esther bade them return Mordecai this answer, 16 Go, gather together all the Jews that are present in Shushan, and fast ye for me, and neither eat nor drink three days, night or day: I also and my maidens will fast likewise; and so will I go in unto the king, which is not according to the law: and if I perish, I perish.*

> *(NCV) Esther 4:15 Then Esther sent this answer to Mordecai: 16 "Go and get all the Jewish people in Susa together. For my sake, give up eating; do not eat or drink for three days, night and day. I and my servant girls will also give up eating. Then*

I will go to the king, even though it is against the law, and if I die, I die."

Having dedicated thousands of hours to Bible study, the author sees no possible way to study the Bible using the NCV. The opportunity for cross-referencing is completely lost because Bible words are not retained in this and similar versions. After reading the story of Esther in the NCV, can one really conclude that she fasted?

What chance will the Christian of the future (without the KJB) have to know the truth when all references to many of these important truths have been completely destroyed? One can certainly imagine that some deluded soul will read of Esther in a future bible version and arrive at incongruous conclusions. For example, such a person might imagine that Esther has become fat eating the king's meat and knows that this displeases the king. Therefore, one might conclude, Esther gives up eating. Because she gives up eating (and consequently loses weight), she is able to courageously approach the king without suffering any negative consequences. This conclusion is just as reasonable as the action of replacing the word "fasting" with the limited definition of "abstaining from food."

2. **Fasting in order to seek the Lord and ask help of Him**: The children of Moab and Ammon came up to battle against Jehoshaphat.

(KJB) II Chronicles 20:3 And Jehoshaphat feared, and set himself to seek the LORD, and proclaimed a fast throughout all Judah. 4 And Judah gathered themselves together, to ask help of the LORD: even out of all the cities of Judah they came to seek the LORD.

Jehoshaphat proclaimed a fast for the people to seek the Lord. We too should fast if deeply troubled or burdened with some matter such as family problems, disobedient children, an addiction, etc. Fasting should be done to discern the will of God.

*(NCV) II Chronicles 20:3 Jehoshaphat was afraid, so he decided to ask the LORD what to do. He announced that **no one in Judah should eat** during this special time of prayer to God.*

The NCV simply says that no one should eat! The Devil knows the reader cannot draw the same conclusion using these different versions. He wants Christians to be ignorant of the truth! Satan most fears the dedicated, soul winning prayer warrior who understands the importance of prayer and fasting.

3. **Fasting to discern direction for the home**. A person should fast in order to determine direction for himself, his children, and his possessions.

> *(KJB) Ezra 8:21 Then I proclaimed a fast there, at the river of Ahava, that we might afflict ourselves before our God, to seek of him a right way for us, and for our little ones, and for all our substance.*

Fast to discern directions for:

- yourself
- your children and grandchildren
- your possessions, the things with which God has blessed you.

Prayer and fasting assist the Christian in learning God's will for every aspect of his life.

> *(NCV) Ezra 8:21 There by the Ahava Canal, I announced we would all give up eating and humble ourselves before our God. We would ask God for a safe trip for ourselves, our children, and all our possessions.*

Satan must take a sort of perverted comfort in re-writing the Bible, the history of the Bible, and the history of man. If we do not learn from the past, we are condemned to repeat the mistakes of our predecessors. We can easily become disillusioned by not knowing our rich heritage. The history of the United States includes many instances in which prayer and fasting have altered the course of events. As expected, however, these are not well-publicized instances since most people are generally very ignorant of the past as it relates to spiritual matters. Dr. Paul Tan relates the following story:

In the early spring of 1877, Minnesota farmers surveyed their lands, dreading the first hordes of locusts that had caused such widespread destruction the summer before. Another such plague threatened to destroy Minnesota's rich wheat lands spelling ruin for thousands of families.

Suddenly, Governor John S. Pillsbury proclaimed April 26ᵗʰ a day of fasting and prayer, urging that every man, woman and child ask divine help. A strange hush fell over the land as Minnesotans solemnly assembled to pray. The next morning the sun rose in cloudless skies. Temperatures soared to mid-summer heat. The people looked up at the skies in wonder, and to their horror, the warm earth began to stir the dreaded insects.

This was a strange answer! Three days passed. The unseasonable heat hatched out a vast army of locusts that threatened to engulf the entire Northwest! Then, on the fourth day the sun went down in a cold sky and that night frost gripped the earth. Most of the locusts were destroyed as surely as if fire had swept them away! When summer came the wheat waved tall and green. April 26 went down in history as the day on which a people's prayer had been answered.

Satan has spearheaded the rewriting of our rich Christian history. It is difficult to fathom what the future holds as upcoming generations are raised progressively further from the influence of God's word. Using bibles like the NCV, Satan will insure that future generations do not even understand the governor's proclamation concerning fasting. According to the modern versions, the governor should have instructed the people of Minnesota to observe a "day of not eating and prayer." What purpose is served by not eating unless a person understands the biblical principles of fasting destroyed in the modern versions? As we have seen, fasting means much more than simply giving up food.

Today, governors and mayors across this country are sued for so much as asking God's blessing on a high school graduating class or at the opening assemblies of a football game. This country has forgotten that it was founded based on freedom *of* religion, *not* freedom *from* religion. America needs a great awakening concerning its rich heritage. Some say our Christian heritage is a figment of our imagination. Read the Constitution or the Pledge of Allegiance to the flag. Our pledge says, "…one nation under God…" Our coins and paper money say "In God we trust." This is our heritage.

Consider America's heritage 20-50 years from now. Men like Minnesota governor Jesse Ventura will be remembered. In a November 1999 interview, during his comments concerning the legalization of prostitution, he made a statement that "*organized religion is a sham and a crutch for weak-minded people who need strength in numbers.*" He blames the "religious right" for the fact that prostitution is not legal in this country. Amen! Can there be any doubt as to why God's hand of protection on this country seems to be lifting from us? Our country desperately needs Christians to fast and pray down God's blessings and protection. Although our national need is great, we must not neglect our great personal need.

What are the Personal Effects of Fasting?

Fasting, like prayer, does not force God to do anything, but instead it helps resist supernatural strongholds and powers. Fasting has the greatest impact on the *soul*. The *only* way to know that fasting affects the soul is to search the King James Bible. No other version the author has researched allows one to realize this truth.

Most people understand from their Bible that they consist of three parts: spirit, soul, and body *(I Thessalonians 5:23)*. However, few people realize that their soul also consists of three parts . . . mind, will, and emotions. Fasting affects the soul (mind, will, and emotions) in three ways. Fasting *humbles* the soul, *chastens* the soul, and *afflicts* the soul. Nothing else in the Bible affects a person's soul in this manner. Therefore, fasting is a very important aspect of the Christian's walk with God.

The three parts of the soul are revealed in the scripture as follows:

• **Mind –** *Romans 7:25 "…with the mind I myself serve the law of God." II Corinthians 13:11 "…be of one mind…"*

- **Will** – *John 1:13* *"Which were born, not of blood, nor of the will of the flesh, nor of the will of man..."* *Ephesians 6:6* *"...doing the will of God from the heart..."*
- **Emotions** – *I Samuel 18:1* *"...the soul of Jonathan was knit with the soul of David..."*

Three passages in the King James Bible clearly communicate the effect of fasting on the soul. Although these examples are key points to understand concerning fasting, the NIV and the NCV completely destroy their effectiveness. The consequences are important to recognize. The Christian using a modern bible cannot determine why fasting should be an important part of his life. We live in a generation that is always asking "why?" The new versions fail to provide the believer with an answer.

Fasting Humbles the Soul

> *(KJB) Psalm 35:11 False witnesses did rise up; they laid to my charge things that I knew not. 12 They rewarded me evil for good to the spoiling of my soul. 13 But as for me, when they were sick, my clothing was sackcloth: I **humbled my soul with fasting**; and my prayer returned into mine own bosom.*

The KJB says that David *humbled* his soul with fasting. To humble one's soul means to abase, subdue, mortify, and crush it. This important aspect of fasting is destroyed in the NIV. Satan does not want the Christian to understand this aspect of the Christian walk; therefore, the NIV deletes any reference to the effects of fasting on the soul.

> *(NIV) Psalm 35:13 Yet when they were ill, I put on sackcloth and **humbled myself** with fasting. When my prayers returned to me unanswered,*

The NIV says that David's prayer returned to him unanswered; it also deletes any reference to the effect of fasting on the soul. The NCV takes a person even further from the truth and does not refer to being humbled or to fasting at all. Such a bible is worthless. How can one expect to see the truth if the possibility of cross-referencing is eliminated? Comparing spiritual things with spiritual things is one of the most basic Bible study tools.

*(NCV) Psalm 35:13 Yet when they were sick, I put on clothes of sadness and showed my sorrow **by going without food**. But my prayers were not answered.*

Again, the NCV changes fasting to "going without food." Fasting entails much more than simply going without food; it is a Bible word that denotes a *spiritual* act. A person *going without food* may simply not be hungry. God's word, the King James Bible, says that *fasting humbles the soul*. Try to imagine how important this truth is and who might want you to be ignorant of it. Every Christian wages an ongoing, daily battle with his flesh. Fasting is a powerful way to reject the flesh and to directly benefit the soul.

Consider this: when a person awakes in the morning, what is the first aspect of himself that he generally cares for? His flesh, of course! Brushing his teeth; taking a shower; drinking a cup of coffee; eating food. . . all of these activities serve the flesh. Would it not be refreshing to place top priority on something other than the flesh? Try fasting!

Until a person can begin awaking in the morning with the priority of communing with God or reading the Bible, his flesh will remain in first place. Let's give God the preeminence. Prayer and fasting are the best ways to positively affect the flesh and the soul.

Fasting Chastens the Soul

*(KJB) Psalm 69:10 When I wept, **and chastened my soul with fasting**, that was to my reproach.*

David again reveals another of the effects of fasting upon the soul. The soul is *chastened* through fasting. *Webster's 1828 Dictionary* defines chastening as correcting by punishment and the infliction of pain for the purpose of reclaiming. All of us need to reclaim our mind, will, and emotions for the Saviour. Fast and pray!

Once again, the NIV destroys the truth and the wisdom given to us by Almighty God. There is no way to find out what He truly wants us to know by reading the NIV or any of the other modern perversions.

(NIV) Psalm 69:10 When I weep and fast, I must endure scorn;

Unlike the KJB, the NIV does not reveal that fasting *chastens* the soul. People are naturally inquisitive. They want to know why they should do something and what makes it a beneficial practice. If preachers do not have the answers to these questions concerning fasting, they will not consider fasting to be a very important part of life. People seek wisdom and understanding, but find neither in the modern translations. The KJB, by giving knowledge, is used by God to encourage individuals to fast because of its positive impact on the soul.

Once again, the NCV perverts the truth even further than its modern predecessors. Both chastening and fasting are deleted from this verse.

(NCV) Psalm 69:10 When I cry and **go without food**, *they make fun of me.*

The New Century Version sounds so repulsive. It makes David sound like a wimp! Once again, fasting is eliminated and the second soul-impacting result of fasting is not conveyed. A Southern Baptist pastor recently stated to the author that the New Century Version is a good study bible. How deceived he is! Sadly, his congregation is no better off if it seeks for truth in such a modern perversion.

Fasting must be an important part of a Christian's life or Satan would not expend so much effort and energy to hide its importance.

Fasting Afflicts the Soul

(KJB) Isaiah 58:5 Is it such a **fast** *that I have chosen? a day for a man to* **afflict his soul?** *is it to bow down his head as a bulrush, and to spread sackcloth and ashes under him? wilt thou call this a fast, and an acceptable day to the LORD?*

Fasting afflicts the soul. To afflict means to trouble, to harass, and to distress. Fasting afflicts the soul – that is the will, the emotions, and the mind. Fasting helps to align these three with the will of God.

As we have seen, fasting humbles the soul, chastens the soul, and afflicts the soul. These truths are evident in the King James Bible. The NIV, consistent with its treatment of truth, omits any reference to the effects of fasting on the soul.

> *(NIV) Isaiah 58:5 Is this the kind of fast I have chosen, only a day for a man to **humble himself**? Is it only for bowing one's head like a reed and for lying on sackcloth and ashes? Is that what you call a fast a day acceptable to the Lord?*

The NIV guarantees that the Christian remains ignorant of the truth that God wants man to receive. One cannot find a single reference in the NIV to the tri-fold effect of fasting on a man's soul. Think about that. The fact that all the new versions eliminate these truths should serve as an indicator of how important they are to God. The soul-altering effects of fasting are not attributable to any other spiritual act.

The NCV does not include even half of the information contained in the pitiful NIV. Thus, the NCV guarantees complete and total ignorance of the necessity of fasting in a Christian's life and walk.

> *(NCV) Isaiah 58:5 This kind of special day is not what I want. This is not the way I want people to be sorry for what they have done. I don't want people just to bow their heads like a plant and wear rough cloth and lie in ashes to show their sadness. This is what you do on your **special days when you do not eat**, but do you think this is what the LORD wants?*

Special days when you do not eat?! The NCV follows the lead of the NIV and all previous perversions. In typical fashion, however, it goes a step further than its predecessors and purges all semblance of the truth. To whom do you attribute this gross perversion of truth? It is hard to miss the satanic influence behind these changes. His attack should convince us of the importance of fasting.

Principles of Fasting

In Isaiah chapter 58, the Lord rebukes a group of people who fasted for the wrong reasons. When God uses His word to correct the Israelites, Bible students should be careful to heed the correction, as well. Thus, much can be learned from studying this passage from the book of Isaiah. In this particular chapter, we read that Israel was fasting and yet finding pleasure in their daily routine. Any person who fasts should abstain from physical pleasures – such as watching television, playing sports, etc. – during the period of fasting and prayer.

> *(KJB) Isaiah 58:3 Wherefore have we fasted, say they, and thou seest not? wherefore have we afflicted our soul, and thou takest no knowledge? Behold, **in the day of your fast ye find pleasure**, and exact all your labours. 4 Behold, ye fast for strife and debate, and to smite with the fist of wickedness: ye shall not fast as ye do this day, **to make your voice to be heard on high**. 5 Is it such a fast that I have chosen? a day for a man to **afflict his soul?** is it to bow down his head as a bulrush, and to spread sackcloth and ashes under him ? wilt thou call this a fast, and an acceptable day to the LORD? 6 Is not this the fast that I have chosen? **to loose the bands of wickedness, to undo the heavy burdens, and to let the oppressed go free, and that ye break every yoke?***

Although this passage of scripture is a clear rebuke to the nation of Israel, one can find much truth here concerning principles of fasting. In verse 3, the Lord rebukes the Israelites for finding pleasure in the day of their fast. When a person fasts, he cannot simply continue with his normal activities. There are some things that are otherwise normal that must be avoided during this time. As we have seen, First Corinthians instructs the fasting Christian to abstain from physical intimacy with his spouse during the time of the fast. However, the application of this principle is much deeper when one considers the truth conveyed in this chapter from Isaiah.

During a period of fasting and prayer, one should not observe the habits of his daily routine as they involve feeding the flesh. How can a person's soul be affected when he is preoccupied with feeding his flesh? The NCV would have the Bible student believe that "going without eating" is the only requirement of a fast. (Really, one cannot even be certain from reading the NCV that going without eating constitutes a period of fasting.) These changes in the NCV are lies. A Christian fasts when he desires to get in touch with God. The actions and daily activities of the fasting Christian should be recognizably different from the individual's non-fasting routine.

Isaiah chapter 58, verse 4 says that a person fasts in order to make his "voice heard on high." This is an important part of fasting that people often neglect. True children of God want to be heard by God. Try fasting and prayer to produce a noticeable difference in your prayer life and spiritual well being. Second Samuel chapter 12 is an excellent example of the fruits of the biblical fast.

The Potential to Change God's Mind

The Bible contains many examples of individuals who understood the importance of fasting. David was just such a person. Nathan tells David in verse 14 of Second Samuel chapter 12 that his child will die. David fasts and prays in an attempt to change the outcome of this grave situation. *"David therefore besought God for the child; and David fasted, and went in, and lay all night upon the earth"* **(II Samuel 12:16).**

In spite of this well-intentioned fast, the child perished because of David's sin with Bathsheba. Your sin affects others, as well. David's fasting did not bring about the desired results in this particular instance; however, great truths about fasting are discerned from what David tells his servant later in the same chapter. *"And he said, While the child was yet alive,* ***I fasted and wept: for I said, Who can tell whether GOD will be gracious to me, that the child may live?*** *23 But now he is dead, wherefore should I fast? can I bring him back again? I shall go to him, but he shall not return to me"* **(II Samuel 12:22).**

God pronounced the judgment, and David fasted and prayed in an attempt to alter the outcome. David's fasting and prayer did not change the pronounced outcome concerning his child. However, as we shall see in the book of Jonah, fasting does hold the potential to change the mind of God concerning the affairs of men.

One should recognize the purpose of David's fast as clearly stated in his discussion with his servants. David was trying to change God's pronounced judgment. *He wanted his voice heard on high.* Once again, the NCV destroys this truth from God's word.

> *(NCV) II Samuel 12:16 David prayed to God for the baby.* **David refused to eat or drink.** *He went into his house and stayed there, lying on the ground all night.*

According to the NCV, David refused to eat or drink and lay on the ground all night. The NCV makes no mention of any spiritual purpose for David's actions. A reader of the NCV cannot discern why he refused to eat. Did David refuse to eat because he lost his appetite? Was he throwing a temper tantrum while lying on the ground all night? This passage from the NCV reads more like the story of a spoiled child, than of a contrite man trying to get in touch with God. Here is the rest of the story perverted by the NCV.

> *(NCV) II Samuel 12:22 David said, "While the baby was still alive,* **I refused to eat,** *and I cried. I thought, 'Who knows? Maybe the LORD will feel sorry for me and let the baby live.'* But now that the baby is dead, **Why should I go without food?"**

There is no comparison between the truth conveyed by the KJB and the nonsense of the NCV. The NCV says that David refused to eat and spent the night on the floor. These statements evoke connotations more juvenile than spiritual! The NCV says David "refused to eat, and cried," hoping that the Lord would *feel sorry* for him. In contrast, when the KJB uses the Bible word "fasting" in this passage, one automatically understands that there was an attempt on the part of David to accomplish some spiritual purpose.

The Ninevites Changed God's Mind

Does fasting and prayer change things? They certainly do! David fasted and prayed with the intent to bring God's grace and mercy upon him and his child. David believed that his actions (fasting and prayer) could change his situation for the better. David did not change God's mind. However, in the book of Jonah, the people of Nineveh *did* change God's mind and escaped His judgment through fasting and prayer. The people of Nineveh got their hearts right and changed their evil ways. Fasting and prayer can change you, too.

> *(KJB) Jonah 3:4 And Jonah began to enter into the city a day's journey, and he cried, and said, Yet forty days, and Nineveh shall be overthrown. 5 So the people of Nineveh believed God, and **proclaimed a fast**, and put on sackcloth, from the greatest of them even to the least of them.*

God heard the prayers of these people, saw the change in their hearts, and spared their city from destruction. God had pronounced His judgment, but prayer and fasting changed the outcome of the situation.

> *(KJB) Jonah 3:10 And God saw their works, that they turned from their evil way; and God repented of the evil, that he had said that he would do unto them; **and he did it not**.*

Once again, the modern perversions limit fasting to "not eating." Fasting involves so much more than the simple abstinence from food. The NCV gives no indication that the Ninevites did anything at all spiritual to spare their city.

> *(NCV) Jonah 3:5 The people of Nineveh believed God. They announced that they would **stop eating** for a while, and they put on rough cloth to show their sadness. All of the people in the city did this, from the most important to the least important.*

They stopped eating and put on rough cloth to show their sadness! According to the KJB, God honored the fast and its effects on the people. He will do the same for you, your family, your state, and your country. As the King James Bible has shown, fasting can change outcomes. Indeed, some areas of your life can be changed only through fasting and prayer.

The passage from Isaiah chapter 58 illustrates the true purpose and outcome of fasting. *"Is not this the fast that I have chosen? to loose the bands of wickedness, to undo the heavy burdens, and to let the oppressed go free, and that ye break every yoke?"(Isaiah 58:6).* God offers four results of fasting. No other practice yields these same results. A person should fast in order to:

(1) Loosen the bands of wickedness
(2) Undo the heavy burdens
(3) Let the oppressed go free
(4) Break every yoke

Smokers, drug addicts, alcoholics, those caught in the sin of pornography, etc. have little hope of ridding themselves of their respective vices and heavy burdens without salvation. What hope is there for the Christian who has strayed from God and become enslaved to these or other addictive behaviors? Fasting and prayer can make a difference in these lives. However, the application of fasting should not be limited to remedying someone else's sinful condition. A marriage that is on the rocks, children that are contrary to God, and individuals in any type of wickedness can all benefit from being submitted to the Lord through fasting and prayer.

Fasting: Overcoming Strongholds

In some cases, fasting and prayer are required to bring about needed results. For example, consider the man in the Gospels who begged Jesus to heal his son, possessed with a devil. This passage contains one of the most important truths conveyed in the Bible concerning fasting. When Satan has been allowed to gain a stronghold in a person's life, prayer and fasting may be the individual's only hope for deliverance.

Mark, in his Gospel book, tells the story of a man who came to the Lord concerning his son. The child had a dumb and deaf spirit – one that attempted to destroy him by casting him into the fire and water. The disciples had been unable to heal this young man. However, the Lord Jesus Christ rebuked the spirit and cured the boy. This passage best reveals the truths set forth in *Isaiah 58:6*. The disciples were unable to cast out this devil because fasting and prayer were necessary to *free the oppressed* and *break this yoke of bondage*. The disciples asked the Lord why they had lacked the power to help the man and his son.

> **(KJB) Mark 9:28** *And when he was come into the house, his disciples asked him privately, Why could not we cast him out?* *29 And he said unto them,* **This kind can come forth by nothing, but by prayer and fasting.**

The disciples tried to help this boy and his father, but could do nothing because they had not fasted and prayed over the matter. Prayer and fasting *release the bands of wickedness, undo the heavy burdens, and let the oppressed go free by breaking every yoke of bondage.* We know that Jesus fasted and prayed. This boy was not going to be freed until the Lord Jesus Christ loosed him. Is the same truth conveyed by the NIV?

> **(NIV) Mark 9:28** *After Jesus had gone indoors, his disciples asked him privately, "Why couldn't we drive it out?"* *29 He replied,* **"This kind can come out only by prayer."**

The NIV only mentions prayer! "What if" the King James Bible is right? The motive underlying these changes in the modern versions should be evident. One of the most powerful tools for affecting change in the life of the believer is not even available to one who reads something other than God's true word, the KJB. If a person reads the NIV, is he going to find out that fasting and prayer are the only ways to overcome some of the most damaging habits? NO!! Perhaps this is one of the reasons that many churches are so ineffective today. Maybe this is why churches have so many families falling apart with little hope in sight.

As we have seen, fasting is omitted when the story of the young man possessed by a devil is told in the Gospel of Mark. However, the Gospels generally retell the same stories; so, perhaps this truth can still be found in one of the other Gospel books. This story is repeated in Matthew chapter 17:

> **(KJB) Matthew 17:19** *Then came the disciples to Jesus apart, and said, Why could not we cast him out? 20 And Jesus said*

unto them, Because of your unbelief: for verily I say unto
you, If ye have faith as a grain of mustard seed, ye shall
say unto this mountain, Remove hence to yonder place;
and it shall remove; and nothing shall be impossible unto
*you. 21 Howbeit this kind goeth not out but by **prayer and***
fasting.

The King James Bible emphasizes the truth concerning prayer and fasting. Prayer *and fasting* are required to overcome the strongholds of Satan. The NIV does not simply change this verse in Matthew chapter 17. It omits the verse entirely. Why? Could fasting be that important for the child of God?

*(NIV) **Matthew 17:19** Then the disciples came to Jesus in*
private and asked, "Why couldn't we drive it out?" 20 He re-
plied, "Because you have so little faith. I tell you the truth, if
you have faith as small as a mustard seed, you can say to this
mountain, 'Move from here to there' and it will move. Nothing
*will be impossible for you." 21 **[omitted]***

As we have seen, both the King James Bible and the rich history of the United States attest to the power of prayer and fasting. However, most Christians today have no real understanding of the importance God has placed on fasting and prayer. Any Christian that is duped into believing that the modern versions will show them the truth should look for verse 21 in these versions. Try to find verse 21 in an NIV. This verse is ripped from the Bible because Satan does not want the average Christian to know the truth about fasting and prayer. He hates the fervent Christian on his knees and shudders at the thought of a prayer warrior who recognizes the significance of fasting and prayer.

The NCV also omits verse 21 of Matthew chapter 17, replacing it with a footnote. Why not just believe the Bible? It takes prayer *and fasting* to rid a person's life of certain infiltrations of the Devil and fleshly strongholds. If Satan has achieved victory in a particular area of your life – whether it is drugs, alcohol, tobacco, television, lust, lying, unforgiveness, pornography, etc. – why not implore God to intervene?

Barclay Newman, senior translator on the Contemporary English Version of the Bible, said: *"We have aimed at the ear more than the eye. You can read aloud without stumbling and hear without misunderstanding."* Newman, who holds a doctorate from a Southern Baptist theological seminary, claims that the CEV tries to remain loyal to "the meaning of the King James Version of the Bible" without being bound to its exact wording.

By comparing only a few of the scriptures, one can see how drastically the modern versions have affected major doctrines. Man cannot alter God's word and remain guiltless. God *will* hold him accountable. Americans are ignorant of their rich Christian heritage, just as they are ignorant of the impact of God's word upon our forefathers. Too many have failed to realize Satan's masterful work of deception. We had better wake up before it is too late. We need to pray and fast for ourselves, our families, our churches, and our nation. Humility is the key. America has somewhat of a unique responsibility. The world has viewed the United States as a **Christ**ian nation. Our designation comes from our association with His name – Jesus **Christ**.

> *II Chronicles 7:14 If my people, which are called by my name, shall humble themselves, and pray, and seek my face, and turn from their wicked ways; then will I hear from heaven, and will forgive their sin, and will heal their land.*

Our blessings came through our reverence to the Lord Jesus Christ. Only the Church's return to Him can restore our nation's true greatness; only the Christian's humble act of submission through prayer and fasting can effect the change this nation greatly desires and needs. Are you doing your part *(I Timothy 2:1-2)*?

Chapter 19 Endnotes

[1] Alfred P. Gibbs, *The Preacher and his Preaching, op. cit.,* p. 300.

20

1611 to 1769:
Blame it on the Press

The term "four major revisions" is a misnomer, and as such, is grossly misleading. There were no true revisions in the sense of updating the language or correcting translation errors. [1]
Floyd Nelson Jones

Men have been *"handling the word of God deceitfully" (II Corinthians 4:2)* since the Devil convinced the first woman to do so. From Cain to Balaam, from Jehudi to the scribes and Pharisees, from the Dark Age theologians to present-day scholars, man's corrupting hand has targeted the living words of the Almighty God. The attacks on the word of God are threefold: addition, subtraction, and substitution. From Adam's day to the computer age, the strategies have remained the same. Indeed, there is nothing new under the sun.

One attack which is receiving quite a bit of attention these days is a direct attack on the word of God as preserved in the English language: the King James Bible of 1611. The attack referred to is **the myth** [2] which claims that since the King James Bible of 1611 has already been "revised four times," there should be and can be no valid objection to other modern revisions. This myth was used by the English Revisers of 1881 and has been revived in recent years by fundamentalist "scholars" hoping to sell their newly produced version or to justify their support for their favorite translation.

Many examples can be provided to demonstrate this problem. For instance, read this statement from "The Committee on the Bible's Text and Translation" from Greenville, S.C., found in *From the Mind of God to the Mind of Man.*

> *In an effort to convey the inspired word in the language of the readers, more than one translation may be produced in one given language. In an effort to improve accuracy, these translations may go through numerous revisions. **(Even the revered King James Version has gone through at least four major and numerous minor revisions.)** These revisions are often necessary because living languages are constantly changing in their vocabularies and structures.* [3] [Emphasis mine]

Later in the same book we read: *"...there have been numerous **revisions** since 1611. During the next 33 years alone there were at least 182 **editions**, each differing in some way from the others."* [4] This statement on the surface is quite inflammatory (equating the printing of *editions* with the word *revisions*). It is complete spiritual infidelity for the contributor of the referenced book if he is implying that somehow these 182 editions from 1611 to 1644 can be equated to the textual changes "justified" by the modern version producers. However, if each edition did in fact differ from its predecessors even in minute ways, this further proves the inaccuracy of the early printing methods which is the premise of this chapter.

The intention of this chapter is to answer this argument. The purpose of the material herein is not to convince those who wish to deny preservation, but to strengthen the faith of those who already believe in a preserved English Bible. However, the present chapter provides believers in preservation with the tools necessary to convince the gainsayers *(Titus 1:9)*.

One major question repeatedly arises concerning efforts to counter attacks on the word of God. To what extent should an individual concern himself with satisfactorily answering the critics? If Bible believers were to devote themselves to answering every shallow objection raised to the infallibility of the English Bible, they could accomplish nothing else. Sanity must intervene and prevail. As always, the answer to this valid question lies in the pages of God's word.

*Proverbs 26:4 Answer **not** a fool according to his folly, **lest
thou also be like unto him**.*

*Proverbs 26:5 Answer a fool according to his folly, **lest he be
wise in his own conceit**.*

Obviously, there are times when a foolish query should be ignored,
but other situations in which such a question should be legitimately addressed. Consider the following rule of thumb: if answering the "question"
will cause you to appear as foolish as the attacker, the best answer is no
answer at all. For instance, if a Christian is told that the Bible cannot be
infallible because so-and-so believes that it is, and he is divorced, then it
is safe to assume that silence is the best answer. On the other hand,
serious questions and problems often arise which must be responsibly
and judiciously addressed.

To ignore issues of this latter sort would be to leave the Bible attacker wise in his own conceit. In the opinion of the author, the question
at hand concerning revisions to the King James Bible of 1611 belongs to
this second, legitimate class of inquiries. Had the King James Bible undergone four major revisions of its text, then to oppose further revisions
on the basis of an established English text would be unreasonable. Consequently, this attack should and must be addressed. Can this argument
be answered? Certainly!

I. The Printing Conditions of 1611

If God did preserve His word in the English language through the
Authorized Version of 1611 (and He did), then where is the authority for
the infallible wording? Is it in the notes of the translators? Or is it to be
found in the proof copy sent to the printers? If so, then our authority is
lost because these papers are lost. But, you may say, the authority lies in
the first printed page to come off the printing press. Alas, that copy has
also certainly perished. In fact, since the printing of the English Bible
followed the pattern of most printing jobs, the first pages printed were
probably discarded after careful scrutiny because of poor quality. That
leaves us with existing copies from the first printing. These are the copies often revered as the standard, against which all other King James

Bibles are to be compared. But are they? Did those early printers of the first edition not make printing errors? Does the preservation of God's infallible word rely precariously on perfect printing?

One principle must be established at the outset of this discussion. The authority for the preserved English text is *not* found in any human work. The authority for our preserved and infallible English text lies in God! Printers will fail at times and humans will continue to make plenty of errors, but God – in His power and mercy – will preserve His text despite the weaknesses of fallible man. Now, let us examine the pressures a printer faced in the year 1611.

Although the printing press was invented in Germany in 1450 by Johann Gutenburg (161 years before the 1611 printing), printing equipment changed only minimally during the intervening span of time. In the year 1611, printing remained an extremely slow, tedious, and laborious task. All type was set by hand, one piece at a time (through the duration of the entire Bible!), and errors were an unfortunate but expected element of any printed book. Because of this difficulty, and also because the 1611 printers had no earlier editions from which to profit, the very first edition of the King James Bible contained a number of printing errors.

As demonstrated later, however, these errors were *not* the sort of *textual alterations* freely made by the modern version publishers. Instead, they were simple, obvious printing errors of the sort that can still occasionally be found in recent editions in spite of the numerous advantages of modern printing technology. Such printing errors did not and do not render a Bible useless; however, they should be corrected in future editions.

The two original printings in 1611 of the Authorized Version demonstrate the difficulty of printing without making mistakes. Both editions were printed in Oxford. Both were printed in the same year: 1611. The same printers did both jobs. Most likely, both editions were printed on the same printing press equipment. Yet, in a strict comparison of the two editions, approximately 100 textual differences can be found. In the same vein, the King James critics can find only about 400 alleged textual alterations in the King James Bible after 375 years of printing and four so-called revisions! Something is rotten in *scholarsville*! The time has come to examine these alleged "revisions."Here is another example of this devious philosophy, as recorded in *From the Mind of God to the Mind of Man*.

> *"What is the significance of two separate 1611 KJV editions? How can I say I have an original 1611 KJV if there were two different editions with numerous discrepancies in the very first year of publication? A revision was done, probably 1613. 'Almost every edition from the very beginning, introduced corrections and **unauthorized** changes and additions, often adding new errors in the process' Though the changes in this edition were minor, they still numbered over three hundred."*
> [5] [Emphasis mine]

This statement says that these "changes and additions" were unauthorized! Could simple printing corrections be considered unauthorized? Where is the proof and documentation for these allegations?

II. The Four so-called Revisions of the 1611 KJB

Much of the information contained in this section is excerpted from a book by F.H.A. Scrivener entitled *The Authorized Edition of the English Bible* (1611), *Its Subsequent Reprints and Modern Representatives*. This book is as scholarly as its title conveys. An interesting point to note is that Scrivener, who published his book in 1884, was a member of the Revision Committee of 1881. However, he disagreed with the actions of the committee on numerous occasions.

In a section of Scrivener's book devoted to addressing the KJV "revisions," one initial detail is striking. The first two so-called major revisions of the King James Bible occurred within 27 years of its original printing. (According to the philosophy of modern version production, the English language must have been changing very rapidly in those days to warrant two revisions in 27 years!) The 1629 edition of the Bible printed in Cambridge is said to have been the first revision. A revision it was NOT. A careful correction of earlier printing errors it WAS. Not only was this edition completed just eighteen years after the 1611 translation was completed, but two of the men who participated in the 1629 printing, Dr. Samuel Ward and John Bois, had contributed to the original translation of the King James Bible.

Was anyone more eminently qualified to correct early printing errors than two of the men who had worked on the original edition? Only nine years later, and again in Cambridge, another edition of the King James Bible was published. This edition is purported to have been the second major KJB *revision*. Both Samuel Ward and John Bois were still alive, but it is not known if they participated in the printing of this edition.

Scrivener, who worked on the *English Revised Version of 1881*, agreed that the Cambridge printers had simply reinstated words and clauses overlooked by the 1611 printers and amended obvious errors. According to a study detailed later in the chapter, **72%** of the approximately 400 *textual corrections* in the KJB were completed by the time the 1638 Cambridge edition was printed – only 27 years after the original printing! **These *editions* were not instigated by a committee who decided that words had been translated incorrectly and needed to be updated! Instead, the later editions were necessary simply so that spelling could be corrected!**

The first two so-called revisions were actually two stages of one process: *the purification of early printing errors*. The last two so-called revisions were two stages in another process: *the standardization of spelling*. The two editions primarily dedicated to standardizing spelling were completed only seven years apart, in 1762 and 1769 respectively. The 1769 edition merely continued the process of spelling standardization begun in the 1762 edition. However, when the "scholars" are numbering revisions, two sounds better than one since it provides double the ammunition with which to justify infidelity to God's word. Very few textual corrections were necessary by this time, since the majority had been discovered and corrected in the first two editions. The *thousands* of alleged changes are in fact spelling changes that were made to match the established correct forms of word spelling. These spelling changes will be discussed later. **Suffice it to say at this time that the tale of**

four major revisions is truly a fraud and a myth. But, you may say, "changes are still changes – regardless of how many there are. What are you going to do with the changes that are still there?" Let us now examine the character of these changes.

III. The so-called Thousands of Changes

Suppose someone were to take you to a museum to see an original copy of the King James Bible. You approach the glass case where the Bible is on display and look down at the opened Bible through the glass. Although you are not allowed to flip through its pages, you can readily tell that some things about this Bible are very different from the characteristics of the one you possess. You can hardly read its words, and those you can make out are spelled in strange ways. Like others before you, you leave with the impression that the King James Bible has undergone a multitude of changes since its original printing in 1611. Not so! Beware, lest you be deceived by a very clever ploy. The differences you see are *not* what they appear to be. Let's examine the evidence. For proper examination, the changes made to the 1611 King James Bible can be divided into three categories: *printing changes*, *spelling changes*, and *textual changes*.

Printing Changes

Printing changes will be considered first. The type style used in 1611 by the King James translators was the Gothic type style. The type style you are reading right now and are familiar with is Roman type. Gothic type, sometimes called Germanic type since it originated in Germany, uses letters formed to resemble the hand-drawn manuscript lettering of the Middle Ages. Printing technology was invented in Germany, and Gothic was the only type style used for some time. Roman type style was invented fairly early in the history of printing, but many years passed before it became the predominate style in most European countries. In fact, Gothic style remained in use in Germany until recent years.

In England, the Roman type was already very popular and would soon supersede the Gothic style, but not until after 1611. The original printers of the King James Bible chose to use the Gothic style for its superior beauty and the embellishment it imparted to a manuscript. In 1612, the first King James Bible using Roman type was printed. Within a few years, all of the Bibles printed used the Roman type style.

Please realize that a change in *type style* alters the text of the Bible no more than does a change in format or type size. However, the modern reader, unfamiliar with Gothic, generally finds it very difficult to read and understand. In addition to some general change in form, several specific letter changes existed under the Gothic style format. For instance, the Gothic *s* looks like the Roman *s* when used as a capital letter or at the end of a word. However, when it is used as a lower case *s* at the beginning or in the middle of a word, the letter looks like our Roman *f*. Therefore, *also* becomes *alfo* and *set* becomes *fet*. Another variation is found in the German *v* and *u*. The Gothic *v* appears as a Roman *u,* while the Gothic *u* takes the form of a Roman *v*. (This explains why our *w* is called a *double-u* and not a *double-v*.) Sound confusing? It is until you get used to it.

Frequently, early American architectural design used the Gothic style lettering when lettering many of our government buildings. Inscriptions in many of our government buildings, especially in Washington, D.C., reflect this Gothic style. That is why the Covington County Court House reads "Couington Covnty Covrt Hovse." The format followed the Gothic style just as the early editions of the King James Bible did.

In the 1611 edition, *love* is *loue*, *us* is *vs*, and *ever* is *euer*. But remember, such examples are *not* even spelling changes. They are simply *type style changes*. In another instance, the Gothic *j* looks like our *i*. So *Jesus* becomes *Iefus* (notice the middle *s* looks like an *f*). *Joy* becomes *ioy*. Even the Gothic *d* is shaped quite differently from the Roman *d* with the stem leaning back over the circle in a shape resembling that of the Greek delta (δ). These changes account for a large percentage of the alleged "thousands" of changes made in the various editions of the King James Bible, and they do no harm whatsoever to the text. Such changes are nothing more than a smokescreen set up by the attackers of our English Bible, in a fashion typical of the Great Accuser *(Revelation 12:10)*.

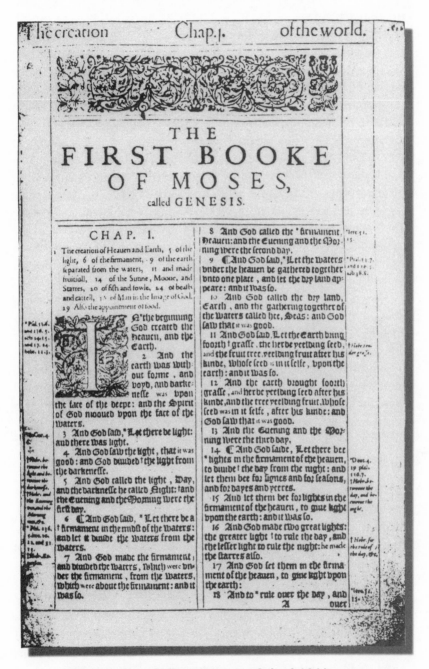

Photocopy of King James original 1611 page

Spelling Changes

Another kind of change made in early editions of the Authorized Version was changes of orthography, or spelling. Most histories date the beginning of Modern English around the year 1500. Therefore, by 1611, the grammatical structure and basic vocabulary of present-day English had long been established. However, English spelling was not yet stable and uniform at this time. In the 1600's, words were spelled according to whim. There was no such thing as *correct* spelling because no standards had been established. An author often spelled the same word several different ways in the same book, and sometimes on the same page. (And these were the educated people.) Some readers may believe the 1600's to have been a spelling paradise! Not until the 1700's did the spelling begin to stabilize. Therefore, in the last half of the eighteenth century, spelling in the King James Bible of 1611 was standardized.

What kind of spelling variations can you expect to find between your present edition and the printed edition of 1611? Although not every spelling difference can be categorized, several characteristic differences are very common. Additional *e's* were often found at the end of the words such as *feare, darke,* and *beare*. Also, double vowels were much more common than they are today. You would find *mee, bee,* and *mooued* instead of *me, be,* and *moved*. Double consonants were also much more common. What would *ranne, euill,* and *ftarres* be according to present-day spelling? See if you can figure them out. The present-day spellings would be *ran, evil,* and *stars*.

These typographical and spelling changes account for almost all of the alleged *thousands* of changes in the King James Bible editions. **None of these alter the text in any way**. Therefore, these changes simply cannot be *honestly* compared with the thousands of true textual changes blatantly forced on the unsuspecting reader by the modern versions.

Textual Changes

Our study has covered almost all of the alleged changes thus far. We now come to the question of actual textual differences between our present edition of the King James Bible and the KJB of 1611. There are

some differences between the two, but they are **not** the changes of a
revision or *mistranslation*. They are instead the *correction* of early
printing errors. By considering the facts, this truth becomes evident. We
will examine and consider:

1) The character of the changes
2) The frequency of the changes throughout the Bible
3) The time the changes were made

First, let us look at the character of the changes made since the time
of the first printing of the Authorized English Bible. The nature of textual changes made from the 1611 edition reveals them to be printing
error corrections. They are not textual changes made to alter the reading
of the scripture. In the first printing, words were sometimes inverted.
Sometimes the plural was written as singular or vice versa. At times, a
word was miswritten and mistakenly replaced with a similar one. In a
few instances, a word or even a phrase was omitted. The omissions
were obvious and did not have the doctrinal implications of those found
in modern translations. In fact, there is no comparison between the *corrections* made in the King James text and the *alterations* introduced by
the "scholars" of today.

F. H. A. Scrivener, in the appendix to his book, lists the variations
between the 1611 edition and later printings. A sampling of these
corrections follows. In order to be objective, the samples provided are
the first textual corrections on consecutive left-hand pages of Scrivener's
book. The 1611 reading is given first; then the present reading; and
finally, the date the correction was first made.

1611	**Present Reading**	**Year**
1. this thing	this thing also	1638
2. shalt have remained	ye shall have remained	1762
3. Achzib, nor Helbath, nor Aphik	of Achzib, nor of Helbah, nor Aphik	1762
4. requite good	requite me good	1629
5. this book of the Covenant	the book of this covenant	1629

6. chief rulers	chief ruler	1629
7. And Parbar	At Parbar	1638
8. For this cause	And for this cause	1638
9. For the king had appointed	for so the king had appointed	1629
10. **seek good**	**seek God**	1617
11. The cormorant	But the cormorant	1629
12. returned	turned	1769
13. a fiery furnace	a burning fiery furnace	1638
14. The crowned	Thy crowned	1629
15. thy right doeth	thy right hand doeth	1613
16. the wayes side	the way side	1743
17. which was a Jew	which was a Jewess	1629
18. the city	the city of the Damascenes	1629
19. now and ever	both now and ever	1638
20. which was of our father's	which was our fathers	1616

This sampling of 20 corrections reveals 5% of the *textual* changes made in the King James Bible in 375 years! Even if they were not simply corrections of previous printing errors, they pale in comparison to the modern version alterations. In fact, they are corrections of *printing errors*; thus no legitimate comparison exists. Examine the list for yourself. You will find only one variance which has potentially serious implications. In fact, in an examination of Scrivener's entire appendix, it is the only variation found by Dr. David Reagan that could be accused of having any doctrinal implications. The change referred to is found in *Psalm 69:32*, in which the 1611 edition stated "seek good." (See #10 above.)

Nevertheless, the facts reveal this discrepancy between the two editions to be nothing more than a printer's error. First, note the similarity between the spellings of the two words (*good* and *God*). How easily a weary typesetter could have misread the proof and inserted the wrong word into the text! Second, the error was so obvious that it was caught and corrected in the year 1617, only six years after the original printing and long before the mythical so-called first revision. The nature of the myth that there have been several major revisions to the 1611 KJB should be clearing up. But there is more.

Further research by Dr. Reagan reveals some interesting facts. In Middle English (up to the year 1500 or so), "good" was spelled in several ways. It could be spelled as *guod, gud, goed, goud, good* or *god*. The last spelling, *god*, was the most common spelling of good in Old English and corresponded to "gut" in German. The copyists may have thought they were only updating the spelling of *good* from the earlier spelling – *god*. No matter how the error crept in, it is obvious that neither this change, nor the others, support the claims of the modern version producers.

Not only does the *character* of these changes reveal them to be printing errors; so does their *frequency*. "Fundamentalist scholars" refer to the thousands of revisions made to the 1611 as if they were similar in magnitude to revisions found in the recent bible versions. They are not. The overwhelming majority of changes to the KJB 1611 are either type style or spelling alterations. The few remaining changes are clearly corrections of printing errors. The preceding list of changes from early editions of the King James Bible demonstrates the care taken by Scrivener to list all the variations. Yet, in spite of the tremendous effort he expended to this end, only about 400 variations are named between the 1611 edition and the modern King James copies. One can well imagine how difficult it must have been to typeset the entire Bible, one letter at a time. It was so difficult that 100 variations were found between the first two Oxford editions, both printed within the first year (1611) of publication.

Since there are almost 1200 chapters in the Bible, the average variation per chapter (after 375 years) is one correction for every three chapters. These are changes such as "chief rulers" to "chief ruler" and "And Parbar" to "At Parbar." Still, an additional piece of evidence proves that these variations were simply printing error corrections: consider the early date at which they were made.

The character and frequency of the textual changes plainly separates them from alterations in the modern versions. However, the **time** at which the changes were made settles the issue absolutely. The great majority of the 400 corrections were made within a few years of the original printing. Take, for example, our earlier sampling. Of the twenty corrections listed, one was made in 1613, one in 1616, one in 1617, eight in 1629, five in 1638, one in 1743, two in 1762, and one in 1769. Sixteen out of 20 corrections in the aforementioned sample, or 80%, were made within 27 years of the 1611 printing. In another study, made by examining every other page of Scrivener's appendix in detail, 72% of the textual corrections were made by 1638. This definitely does not indicate a long drawn-out series of revisions the "scholars" would have you believe. Thus, there is no "revision" issue. An imperfect method was used to print the Bibles, and the imperfections were simply found and corrected.

The *character* of the textual changes is that of obvious errors. The *frequency* of the textual changes is sparse, occurring on average only once in every three chapters. The *chronology* of the textual changes is early, with about three fourths of them occurring within 27 years of the first printing. All of these details establish the fact that there were no true revisions in the sense of updating the language or correcting any translation errors. There were only editions correcting early typographical errors. The source of authority for the exact wording of the 1611 Authorized Version is not in the existing copies of the **first printing**. Instead, the source of authority for the exact wording of our English Bible is in the preserving power of Almighty God. Just as God did not leave us the original autographs to fight and squabble over, neither did He see fit to leave us the proof copy of the translation. Our authority is in the hand of God, not the imperfections of man. Praise the Lord for that!

IV. Changes in the Book of Ecclesiastes

An in-depth study of the changes made in the book of Ecclesiastes should help to illustrate the principles previously stated. By comparing a 1611 reprint of the original edition published by *Thomas Nelson & Sons* with a recent printing of the King James Version, Dr. Dave Reese was able to locate four variations in the book of Ecclesiastes. The reference is given first, followed by the text of the Thomas Nelson 1611 reprint. The text is then followed by the reading of the present editions of the 1611 KJB. Finally, the date of the change is included.

Verse	Thomas Nelson	Present edition	Date
1:5	the place	his place	1638
2:16	shall be	shall all be	1629
8:17	out, yea further	out, yet he shall not find it; yea farther	1629
11:7	thing is it	thing it is	?

Several points should be noted concerning these changes. The last variation ("thing is it" to "thing it is") is not mentioned by Scrivener, who was very accurate and thorough in his analysis. Therefore, this change may be a misprint in the *Thomas Nelson* reprint. That would be interesting. The corrected omission in chapter eight is one of the longest corrections of the original printing, but notice that it was made in 1629. The frequency of printing errors is, on average, four errors for every twelve chapters. The most outstanding fact is that the entire book of Ecclesiastes read exactly like our present editions by the year 1638, since all printing errors in the book had been located and corrected by this time. That was over 350 years ago! By that time, the Bible was being printed in Roman type. Therefore, all – that's right... *all* – that has changed in 350 years in the book of Ecclesiastes is that the spelling has been standardized! As stated before, the main purpose of the 1629 and 1638 Cambridge editions was the correction of earlier printing errors. And the main purpose of the 1762 and 1769 editions was the standardization of spelling. So much for the attempts to discredit the King James Bible in order to justify scriptural infidelity and pass off the newest translation!

V. The Supposed Justification for Other Revisions

It should now be clear that the King James Bible of 1611 has not been revised, but only corrected due to the errors of an imperfect printing process. Why does this fact matter? Although there are several reasons why this issue is important, the most pressing one is that "fundamentalist scholars" are using this myth of past revisions to justify their contemporary tamperings with the text. For instance, the editors of the **New** King James Version have probably been the worst in recent years to use this propaganda ploy. In the preface of the New King James they state: *"For nearly four hundred years, and throughout several revisions of its English form, the King James Bible has been* *deeply revered among the English-speaking peoples of the world."* In the midst of their flowery rhetoric, they strongly imply that their edition is only a continuation of the revisions that have been going on for the past 375 years. This implication, which has been stated directly by others, could not be more false. To prove this point, we return to the book of Ecclesiastes.

An examination of the first chapter in the book of Ecclesiastes in the New King James Version reveals approximately 50 changes from our present edition of the King James Bible. In order to be fair, spelling changes (*cometh* to *comes; labour* to *labor*; etc.) were not included in this count. That means there are probably about 600 alterations in the book of Ecclesiastes and approximately 60,000 changes in the entire Bible between the KJB and the NKJV. This estimated count includes every recognizable change of the sort which were identified in analyzing the 1611 King James Bible. These criteria are only fair. Still, the number of changes is especially baffling for a version which claims to be updating the King James Bible in the same vein as the earlier "revisions." According to the fundamentalist scholar, the *New King James* is only the fifth in a series of revisions. How, then, did four "revisions" and 375 years produce a mere 400 changes, while the fifth revision brought about approximately 60,000 additional changes? If this is the case, the fifth revision made **150 times** more changes than the total number of changes made in the first four! That is simply preposterous!

Not only is the frequency of the changes in the New King James Version unbelievable, but the character of the alterations is serious. Although many of the alterations seem harmless at first glance, many are much more serious. The editors of the New King James Version were sly enough *not* to align themselves with the most serious blunders of the modern bibles. Yet, they were not afraid to change the reading in those places that are unfamiliar to the average fundamentalist. In these areas, the New King James Version is dangerous. Below are some of the more harmful alterations made in the book of Ecclesiastes in the NKJV. The reference is given first, followed by the reading from the King James Bible, and then the reading from the New King James Version.

Ref.	King James	New King James
1:13	sore travail	grievous task
1:14	vexation of spirit	grasping for the wind
1:16	my heart had great experience of wisdom	My heart has understood great wisdom
2:3	to give myself unto	to gratify my flesh with
2:3	acquainting	guiding
2:21	equity	skill
3:10	the travail, which God hath given	the God-given task
3:11	the world	eternity
3:18	that God might manifest them	God tests them
3:18	they themselves are beasts	they themselves are like beasts
3:22	portion	heritage
4:4	right work	skillful work
5:1	Keep thy foot	Walk prudently
5:6	the angel	the messenger of God
5:6	thy voice	your excuse
5:8	he that is higher than the highest	high official
5:20	God answereth him	God keeps him busy
6:3	untimely birth	stillborn child
7:29	inventions	schemes
8:1	boldness	sternness
8:10	the place of the holy	the place of holiness
10:1	Dead flies cause the ointment of the apothecary to send forth a stinking savour	Dead flies putrefy the perfumer's ointment
10:10	If the iron be blunt	If the ax is dull
10:10	wisdom is profitable to direct	wisdom brings success
12:9	gave good heed	pondered
12:11	the masters of assemblies	scholars

This is only a sampling of the changes in the book, but notice what has been done. *Equity*, which is a trait of godliness, becomes *skill* (2:21). The *world* becomes *eternity* (3:11). Man without God is no longer a *beast*, but just *like a beast* (3:18). The clear reference to deity in *Ecclesiastes 5:8* ("he that is higher than the highest") is effectively removed (and changed to "higher official"). But since *success* is what wisdom is supposed to bring us (10:10), this must be progress!? At least God is keeping the *scholars* busy (5:20). Probably the most revealing of the aforementioned changes is the last one listed, in which "the masters of assemblies" become "scholars." According to the New King James Version, "the words of **scholars** are like well-driven nails, given by one Shepherd." The *masters of assemblies* are replaced by the *scholars* who become the source of the Shepherd's words. That is what these scholars would like us to think, but it is not true.

In conclusion, the New King James Version is not a revision in the vein of former *editions* of the King James Bible. It is instead an entirely new translation, qualifying for its own copyright. As stated in the introduction, the purpose of this chapter is *not* to convince those who use the other versions. The purpose of this chapter is to expose a fallacious argument that has been circulating in fundamentalist circles. The proposition that the New King James Version (and others like it) is nothing more than a continuation of revisions made to the King James Bible since 1611 is simply an overblown myth. The most glaring error in this theory is that there have been no such revisions.

The King James Bible of 1611 has not undergone four (or any) major revisions. Therefore, the New King James Version is not a continuation of what has gone on before. The NKJV should, in fact, be called the *Thomas Nelson Version*. Thomas Nelson holds the copyright. The King James Bible we have today has *not* been revised, but purified. There is still no reason to doubt that the Bible we hold in our hands is the very word of God preserved for us in the English language. The authority for its veracity lies not in the first printing of 1611, nor in the character of King James I, nor in the scholarship of the 1611 translators, nor in the literary accomplishments of Elizabethan England, nor even in the Greek Received Text. Our authority for the infallible words of the English Bible lies in the power and promise of God to preserve His word! God has the power. We have His word on it.

Chapter 20 Endnotes

[1] Floyd Nelson Jones, *Which Version is The Bible?, op. cit.,* p. 71, 75.
[2] Adapted from *The King James Version of 1611 – The Myth of Early Revisions* by Dr. David F. Reagan (Knoxville, TN: Antioch Baptist Church, 5709 N. Broadway, Knoxville, TN 37918).
[3] Williams, *From the Mind of God to the Mind of Man, op. cit.,* p. 26 - 27.
[4] *Ibid.,* p. 147.
[5] *Ibid.,* p. 157.

21

Laying Down the Law

The man who does not know the nature of the Law cannot know the nature of sin.
John Bunyan

Too many churches today are busy trading converts rather than winning the lost for Jesus Christ. Trying to win souls takes a determined effort and sometimes has frustrating outcomes. Modern soul winning methods have further compounded the problem and stymied the labors of the potential soul winner. For example, an individual is said to have been *led to Christ* when he "bows his head and asks Jesus to come into his heart."

The simplicity of the gospel is a crucial truth. However, there is no scriptural justification for this unscriptural man-made method of "leading a soul to Christ." Not one verse can be produced showing that asking Jesus into one's heart has ever saved anyone. Witnessing has degenerated to proclaiming the *fruits* of salvation, rather than the scriptural mandate of repentance. This error confuses a person's real need.

This method of "soul winning" has led many to point their fingers at sincere well-meaning potential soul winners and accuse them of promoting a false gospel. Praise God that converts have been made in spite of these methods! The truly repentant sinner is saved when he realizes his spiritual need and desires God to forgive his sinful soul. Thankfully, asking Jesus to come into his heart may have been his way of admitting his lost and sinful condition, and trusting in his newfound Saviour for the remission of sins.

However, many non-repentant "Roman's Road conversion experiences" are no different from the Charismatic practice of "just-taking-Jesus-into-your-life." The *cure* is preached without convincing the lost man of his sinful *need*. Having already tried sex, drugs, and booze, he sees Jesus as just another fad attempt at fulfilling his desire to feel good. Martin Luther declared that *the first duty* of the gospel preacher is to declare God's law and show the nature of sin! [1]

Martin Luther was saved while studying the epistles of Romans and Galatians in order to teach these books at Wittenberg. His writing was powerful and reflected his understanding of the lost sinner's need. John Wesley, founder of Methodism, was converted to Christ upon hearing a reading of Luther's preface to Romans. Although Wesley reluctantly attended the Aldersgate meeting that preceded his conversion, God nevertheless opened his heart to the truth.

> *In the evening I went very unwillingly to a society in Aldersgate Street, where one was reading Luther's preface to the Epistle of Romans. About a quarter before nine, while he was describing the change which God works in the heart through faith in Christ, I felt my heart strangely warmed. I felt that I did trust in Christ, Christ alone for salvation; and an assurance was given me, that he had taken away my sins, even mine, and* **saved me from the law of sin and death.** [2] [Emphasis mine]

The founder of Methodism knew that his sins were "taken away." He knew he was **guilty of breaking God's law** and needed to be saved from *the law of sin and death*! Today, many Bible colleges basically teach that the ends justify the means. The law of God is ignored and replaced with a "lifestyle enhancement gospel" in an attempt to lead the lost to Christ. Potential converts are told to "just take Jesus, and you'll feel better." Preachers are actually teaching soul winning classes on how to trick a lost person into praying the "sinner's prayer." No wonder these "converts" are not experiencing the magnitude of change that true conversion brings because they remain unconverted.

Much insight is gained by considering the fourfold application of God's law (the Ten Commandments) to winning souls for the cause of Christ. The law of God:

I. Is an asset against sin
II. Gives an awareness of sin
III. Calls for an acknowledgment of sin
IV. Requires an adjudication of sin (or an accounting for sin)

If Christians understood the importance of using the law to lead sinners to Christ, they would be busy using it, rather than trying to convince the lost man that he simply needs Jesus. Yes, the Lord does enable a man to escape hell. However, the lost sinner needs first to understand that he is destined for hell and why that is so. People just don't see themselves as bad enough to need a Saviour. Even most convicts claim their innocence. This is true of lost sinners too! Most sinners have not seen their sin in the light of scriptural truth, and believe themselves to be undeserving of any punishment for their shortcomings. God's love has been overemphasized to the point that many a sinner cannot reconcile his image of a loving God with the biblical condemnation that arises from a just God.

I. The Law of God is an Asset against Sin

The law is one of God's greatest and most essential tools for dealing with mankind. God instituted the law as part of His plan to regenerate the fallen creature man and to reconcile humanity to Himself. God uses the law to accomplish His plan. Felix, a proud ruler, trembled when Paul witnessed to him concerning righteousness, temperance, and judgment to come *(Acts 24:25)*. Paul understood how to use the law in witnessing. He explains in the scriptures that the law is good if used lawfully *(I Timothy 1:8)*. However, it condemns the lost man if used **un**lawfully to convince the sinner that it is the means of reconciliation to God. Proverbs tells us that the law is light.

(KJB) Proverbs 6:23 For the commandment is a lamp; and the law is light; and reproofs of instruction are the way of life:

The King James Bible says that the law IS light. The law is not *a* light, like a flashlight, but it is light like God. *"...God is light, and in him is no darkness at all" (I John 1:5).* Every time an important point must be made, the modern versions pervert the truth. Our consideration of the law is no exception.

*(NIV) Proverbs 6:23 For these commands are a lamp, **this teaching is a light**, and the corrections of discipline are the way to life,*

These modern versions do not teach the truth and cannot be used to preach and teach the truth. Solomon refers specifically to the law and says that it *is* light; he does not communicate some nebulous "teaching" that it is "a light." Light shines through darkness, and *the law is light.* The law is perfect. Why, then, is the law not a central premise upon which the soul winner leads someone to Christ? The light of the law reveals the condition of the soul and its need for conversion. Thus, indirectly, the law converts the soul. The book of Psalms says:

*(KJB) Psalm 19:7 The law of the LORD is perfect, **converting** the soul...*

Does the NIV convey the same truth?

*(NIV) Psalm 19:7 The law of the LORD is perfect, **reviving** the soul...*

The law does not revive the soul. It condemns the soul and indirectly has its part in *converting* it. God's shining light (the law) plainly reveals all the dirt and sin concealed by spiritual darkness *(II Corinthians 4:4)*. Imagine God shining a bright light upon your sin – that is the essence of the law. The light of the law will reveal to the poor, lost sinner that he has transgressed against a holy, perfect, and righteous God. Conviction will cause that lost man to realize his hopeless state and his absolute inability ever to fulfill God's demand for perfect holiness. *"In the body of his flesh through death, to present you **holy** and **unblameable** and **unreproveable** in his sight" (Colossians 1:22).* God demands that we be holy, unblameable, and unreproveable in his sight! This cannot happen apart from the shed blood of the Lord Jesus Christ and the law reveals this truth to us.

The importance of using the law to reach the lost cannot be ignored. In order to avoid missing this important truth, no further comparisons with the modern versions will be given in this chapter. By now the reader should realize the significant differences and be willing to reject these modern perversions based upon the evidence. If you are in need of further evidence, more can be given...more will be given in the final two chapters. However, the emphasis of this chapter is directed toward those interested in a deeper understanding of the relationship of the law to winning souls.

II. The Law of God Gives an Awareness of Sin

Even in our hardhearted, sinful world, some people still readily accept that they are *sinners*. Unfortunately, this admission means very little to them since they recognize neither the extent nor the consequences of their crime *(Romans 3:23)*. The law serves as a schoolmaster to bring people to Christ, in that it clearly communicates the nature and severity of man's transgressions against a holy God. *Webster's 1828 Dictionary* defines a schoolmaster as *"he or that which disciplines, instructs or leads."* The purpose of the law today is to *lead* a lost person to Christ.

*Galatians 3:24 Wherefore **the law was our schoolmaster to bring us unto Christ**, that we might be justified by faith.*

The book of Galatians says we are justified by faith, and the law acts as our schoolmaster so that we may understand our need for God's grace. Historically, the Church knew these truths, but more recently, it has abandoned using God's law for a social type of gospel. One of the best known sermons of all time, Jonathan Edwards' *Sinners in the Hands of an Angry God,* strikes into the heart of even the casual reader the terrifying repercussions of having transgressed the law of Almighty God.

Similarly, hymn writers of centuries past understood the need to prepare the heart of the lost for the preaching of God's word. William R. Newell, in his song *At Calvary,* communicates great spiritual insight into the purpose and necessity of God's holy law in converting the soul. He knew that the word of God (the law) helped us grasp our sinful condition.

At Calvary

By God's Word at last my sin I learned;
Then I trembled at the law I'd spurned,
Till my guilty soul imploring turned to Calvary.
Mercy there was great, and grace was free;
Pardon there was multiplied to me;
There my burdened soul found liberty,
At Calvary.

Mr. Newell said his guilty soul turned to Calvary after he had trembled *at the law he had spurned.* The type of preaching and the scripture that brings about this reaction to one's sins is completely foreign to most churches. The lost man or woman has been brainwashed into thinking that *love* is the missing element in a "hell, fire, and damnation" sermon. However, the love for the lost sinner must be the impetus behind this type of preaching and usually is. These preachers know that the love of souls is more important than increasing membership by preaching popular, ear-tickling messages that never present the true convicting need of salvation to the lost person.

Another song written by John Newton reveals that **fear** leads us to Christ. Fear is a foreign element to the modern church that has already rejected the truth. Consider the second stanza of Newton's most famous song, *Amazing Grace. "'Twas grace that taught my heart to fear, and grace my fears relieved."* How does grace teach one's heart to fear? Of course, the sinner – when faced with the consequences of his sin – should fear and tremble at the law he has broken, the law of Almighty God. Once the sinner realizes that he is guilty of offending a holy and righteous God, he will yearn for the grace that brings true forgiveness of sin and peace with God.

The church has lost this focus today. The law is misunderstood and misapplied. Though the law does not provide redemption, it can and does bring conviction in a lost person's life. The law does not help you – it leaves you with a realization of your helpless state. The law does not justify you – it leaves you guilty before a holy, perfect Judge. The great preachers of a century ago understood the significance of the law.

E. M. Bounds wrote many significant books replete with spiritual insight. The *St. Louis Globe-Democrat* recorded the opening prayer of E.M. Bounds during revival meetings of D.L. Moody in that city. The opening sentence of his prayer reads as follows: *"Our Father, help us to come before Thee with humility and reverence, with some realization of our sinfulness, our guiltiness in Thy sight, some sense of Thy holiness and the demands of Thy law."* [3] (Emphasis mine) E.M. Bounds understood the absolute importance of the law! The sinner must recognize and understand that the law condemns the *unbeliever* in his sin and unbelief! No judge need pronounce the condemnation because the word of God proclaims it already.

> *John 3:18 He that believeth on him is not condemned: but **he that believeth not is condemned already**, because he hath not believed in the name of the only begotten Son of God.*

The best approach for reaching a lost man is determined by his unique spiritual condition. Is the lost person truly repentant or proud as a peacock? **True scriptural evangelism is always *law* to the proud and grace to the humble.** With the law we are to break the hardhearted, and with the gospel we can heal the brokenhearted. *"But he giveth more grace. Wherefore he saith, **God resisteth the proud, but giveth grace unto the humble"** (James 4:6).* Christians must be scriptural in their approach to reaching the lost. The proud need the law to bring to light their lost and sinful condition. The truly humble are ready to be told about the grace that can save their wretched soul from the punishment they admittedly deserve.

The proud sinner must see the law in a new light and realize his inability to fulfill its righteous demands. Without first recognizing that he is completely incapable of saving himself, a man can never truly believe on the One that fulfilled the law in all its points.

> *Galatians 3:13 Christ hath redeemed us from the curse of the law, being made a curse for us: for it is written, Cursed is every one that hangeth on a tree:*

The law condemns, but Christ took upon Himself every man's condemnation. The Lord Jesus Christ died on the cross of Calvary, taking upon Himself *our curse*. The sinner must see himself as guilty under the law before he can understand the awful price paid for his sins. *"...There is none righteous, no, not one" (Romans 3:10).* The law was made for him to reveal the ugly reality of his true identity apart from Christ.

> *I Timothy 1:8 But we know that the law is good, if a man use it lawfully; 9 Knowing this, that **the law is not made for a righteous man, but for the** lawless and disobedient, for the ungodly and for sinners, for unholy and profane, for murderers of fathers and murderers of mothers, for manslayers, 10 For whoremongers, for them that defile themselves with mankind, for menstealers, for liars, for perjured persons, and if there be any other thing that is contrary to sound doctrine;*

When we ignore the law, we produce damage rather than deliverance. This condemns the lost and offers false assurance of salvation. Christians need to proclaim God's law, the Judge, and the judgment and justice to come *(Jeremiah 23:5)*. The lost person must be shown why he is lost and condemned, and not merely convinced that accepting Jesus could enhance his quality of life. The sinner needs to be shown that the righteous Judge is awaiting execution day, and that God pardons only those who have accepted the payment made for them on Calvary by the Son of God. *Have you accepted this payment?*

Charles Finney said, *"The severity of the law should be unsparingly applied to the conscience until the sinner's self-righteousness is annihilated, and he stands speechless and condemned before the holy God."* What a difference between the expressions of Finney and the average preacher today! GUILTY sinners must be told that they have a Saviour Who has paid the debt they owe. *Has anyone told you about the debt, the payment, or the cure?* Preaching the pardon without first explaining the guilt makes no sense.

Modern evangelism has forsaken the law of God and its capacity to convert the soul. The law was given to drive sinners to Christ. Instead of preaching the law to the lost man, many try to convince him of his opportunity to improve his life. The lost sinner is told that he will never find true peace without Jesus Christ because of the *God-shaped vacuum* in his heart that only God can fill. There may truly be a God-shaped vacuum inherently existing within each of us, but Christians need to show the lost person why that vacuum exists. Instead, too often, the zealous soul winner instructs the potential convert to ask Jesus to come in and fill that vacuum when the person has little to no realization of Christ's suffering or of his own sin. Preachers must show the lost how and *why* they must trust in Christ to save them *(Ephesians 1:13)*.

Even if the sinner does come to Christ, modern methods of lifestyle enhancement witnessing leave the new convert disillusioned because he does not find the constant peace, continual joy, and lasting contentment he was promised. This unscriptural **motive** causes the convert to become disheartened when temptation, trials, and persecution enter his life *(II Timothy 3:12, Acts 13:50, Matthew 13:21)*. Need we wonder why the majority of true converts never become faithful members in a local Bible believing church? They quickly become backsliders because they were promised the easy life if only they would come to Christ.

The issue is *not* one of happiness, but one of righteousness. We should not preach and emphasize the *fruits* of salvation, but rather the absolute necessity of salvation. By offering the fruits of salvation, sinners will respond with impure motives, lacking the necessary repentance. Many of them will make a decision without any true conviction, and thus not truly be converted. Many churches that overemphasize church growth place a lost sinner on the assembly line and bring him out of the baptismal waters still on his way to hell. The church needs to wake up and quit using popular, unscriptural methods of "evangelism."

We need to preach the *Thou shalt not's* of the Bible. "Thou shalt not kill. Thou shalt not commit adultery. Thou shalt not steal. Thou shalt not bear false witness. Thou shalt not covet. Thou shalt not take the name of the LORD thy God in vain." Once the sinner recognizes that he has offended the true, holy, and just God, he anxiously wants to accept the payment made for his offenses. Many "good" people die and go to hell because they never realize they are not good enough!

Preachers must preach the law in order to show the lost sinner his sin. By failing to introduce the sinner to the law, we produce more "decisions for Christ" but fewer converts. Paul, a Jew converted to Christ, knew the law *(Philippians 3:6)*. He knew that without the law he would never have known what sin was. One hundred years ago, the lost man knew more Bible than most "faithful" church members today. Back then, even the public school elementary students knew about God's laws. The law must be preached in order to reveal the true nature of sin to the biblically illiterate generation in which we live.

> *Romans 7:7 What shall we say then? Is the law sin? God forbid. Nay,* **I had not known sin, but by the law:** *for I had not known lust, except the law had said, Thou shalt not covet.*

The early church understood the importance of the law, why then has modern preaching neglected it? The purpose of the law is to give man the knowledge of sin. Our repentance and understanding of sin must be more than a simple horizontal repentance for our sin against man. True repentance must be a vertical realization of having broken the commandments of a holy, righteous Judge.

> *Romans 3:20 Therefore by the deeds of the law there shall no flesh be justified in his sight:* **for by the law is the knowledge of sin.**

The law gives us the knowledge of sin. The knowledge of our sinful condition should make us speechless. It reveals our guilt before God. Man's tendency is to think of himself in a much brighter light until he recognizes that God judges him according to His perfect standard. God's law stops the mouth of the guilty by showing him his transgression and sinful state.

> *Romans 3:19 Now we know that what things soever the law saith, it saith to them who are under the law:* **that every mouth may be stopped, and all the world may become guilty before God.**

The lost man without conviction of his lost position thinks the statement "Jesus died for your sins" to be quite foolish *(I Corinthians 1:18)*. We must first show the lost man the law that he has broken. We must show him that he is guilty of breaking that law – the law of God. Until the sinner realizes his guilt, he will never come to the Saviour for the solution. The lost man must be convinced that he is a transgressor. Only God's law can convince him of such a thing.

> **James 2:9** *But if ye have respect to persons, ye commit sin, and are* **convinced of the law as transgressors.** *10 For whosoever shall keep the whole law, and yet offend in one point, he is guilty of all.*

The sinner must realize he is guilty (a law breaker) before he realizes his need for forgiveness. The gospel of Jesus Christ, and the redemption that it offers, makes little sense unless a person first realizes the transgression he has committed. An impenitent sinner *(Romans 2:5)* is not ready to receive Jesus Christ. The cross is foolishness to a man who has not realized his need for the Saviour.

> **I Corinthians 1:18** *For the preaching of the cross is to them that perish* **foolishness;** *but unto us which are saved it is the power of God.*

Convincing a man to bow his head and say the "sinner's prayer" only further hardens his heart. The sinner must first acknowledge his transgression before he realizes the payment that has been made for those transgressions.

III. The Law of God Calls for an Acknowledgement of Sin

Once a sinner is aware of sin, he must acknowledge his own personal participation in it. Unless he accepts and acknowledges his personal guilt in transgressing the law of God, he will simply ascribe the problem to others and miss the whole point in his own life.

The sinner under conviction must be like David. He had coveted another man's wife, committed adultery with Bathsheba, murdered her husband, and lied to cover his sins. Although David broke most of the Ten Commandments, he knew the horrific consequences of his actions. He knew he had sinned against a holy and righteous God Who could justifiably send him to hell. Only God's mercy spared this great king. When confronted with his sin, David pled his case the only way a sinner can – by placing himself in the hands of a merciful God.

> **Psalm 51:4 Against thee, thee only, have I sinned**, and done this evil in thy sight: that thou mightest be justified when thou speakest, and be clear when thou judgest.

Every sinner must have this same attitude concerning *his* sin. Each of us must recognize that we have offended God – the holy, righteous God of the universe. Too many times, we consider our sins offensive only to other men (horizontally) and not to God (vertically). All sin is against God, and He will ultimately judge the sinner accordingly!

Further insight may come by considering how our legal system handles a lawbreaker. Our system of government and our judicial system in particular were originally patterned after biblical precepts *(Isaiah 33:22)*. When man's law is broken, the courts have a system to handle the infraction. When someone steals from a store, the district attorney handles the case *for the state* against the perpetrator. The jury determines his guilt or innocence. The judge issues the sentence. The crime is considered one against society. The same holds true in the spiritual realm.

Your sin is against God. Following death, God will judge *you* and if *you* don't have Jesus, He will mete out pure justice and the sentence will have eternal consequences. God's *longsuffering* has been used by many people as a means of lasciviousness, rather than a time to consider the awful consequences of sin.

> **II Peter 3:9** The Lord is not slack concerning his promise, as some men count slackness; **but is longsuffering to us-ward, not willing that any should perish**, but that all should come to repentance.

Don't take God's longsuffering for granted. He is willing that all come to repentance, but there is a point in time when His longsuffering comes to an end. Joseph is another biblical example of someone that understood that sin is committed not only against man, but also against the heavenly Father. Potiphar's wicked, adulterous wife tried to seduce Joseph. Take special note of Joseph's response to her wicked proposal.

> *Genesis 39:9 There is none greater in this house than I; neither hath he kept back any thing from me but thee, because thou art his wife:* **how then can I do this great wickedness, and sin against God?**

Fornication seems to include only the individuals involved. But God sees things in another way. Fornication is a sin against God. Yes, it is also sinning against one's own body *(I Corinthians 6:18)*, but the greater sin is to offend a perfect, holy, righteous God. Your sin is against God! Your wickedness is against God! God will be your judge. **Have you ever thought about that? What will it be like in heaven for you to have your entire life flash before you and be judged accordingly?** If God does not see His Son, He will tell you to depart *(Matthew 25:41)*!

We must see our sin in the same light as the prodigal son viewed his sin. He returned to his father and confessed his sin to him, realizing that he had sinned *against God*.

> *Luke 15:21 And the son said unto him, Father,* **I have sinned against heaven***, and in thy sight, and am no more worthy to be called thy son.*

How do you feel about your sin? Do you consider it merely on a superficial level without considering its spiritual consequences? Do you think that a loving God will have to accept you because you are not that bad? Paul preached something we don't hear enough about today – repentance toward God.

> *Acts 20:21 Testifying both to the Jews, and also to the Greeks,* **repentance toward God***, and faith toward our Lord Jesus Christ.*

Repentance toward God! That is what we need in this sin-sick world. The law is our schoolmaster to bring us unto Christ. The role of the law in leading a person to Christ is to convince the lost man of his **sin** and its consequences. Sin is the transgression of God's law.

*I John 3:4 Whosoever committeth sin transgresseth also the law: for **sin is the transgression of the law**.*

Without the law, one does not have a realization of his sin and his sinful condition. The sinner will never be broken in contrition until he understands sin to be the transgression of God's law.

The lost man will be offended at the presentation of the gospel until he realizes what Jesus' sacrificial death means to *him*. He will be busy comparing himself with others whom he considers far worse than himself, though he be guilty of the same offenses. Romans chapter 2 describes this man's spiritual state. He is judging others and guilty of the same offense.

*Romans 2:3 And thinkest thou this, O man, that judgest them which do such things, **and doest the same**, that thou shalt escape the judgment of God? 4 Or despisest thou the riches of his goodness and forbearance and longsuffering; not knowing that the goodness of God leadeth thee to repentance? 5 But after thy hardness and **impenitent heart** treasurest up unto thyself wrath against the day of wrath and revelation of the righteous judgment of God;*

IV. The Law of God Requires an Adjudication of Sin

Adjudication means judgment of sin. The righteousness of God requires that He render judgment against sin. For a law to be effective and accomplish its purpose, it must be enforced. As **Romans 2:5** indicates, God will execute righteous judgment of sin. Only after a lost sinner acknowledges his own impending guilty verdict and forthcoming death sentence is he ready to appreciate and accept the one and only substitute – Jesus Christ.

God's goodness, forbearance, and longsuffering keep us alive long enough to make a decision – either for or against the truth of God. By refusing to repent of his sin, a man treasures up the wrath of God awaiting the day when His wrath will be revealed in righteous judgment. Our churches are filled with this type of "convert," sometimes easily recognizable. Such a person has little or no burden for his lost loved ones, friends, and neighbors. He is not concerned with living a holy, separated, Spirit-filled, God-honoring life. He is simply a worldly, nominal church member. On occasion, however, such a person is the most generous of givers *(I Timothy 6:10)* because giving soothes his guilty conscience. Sometimes he has the outward appearance of righteousness, but inside he knows that his life is a sham.

Charles Finney wrote: *"**Failure to use the Law** is almost certain to result in false hope, the introduction of a false standard of Christian experience, and to fill the church with **false converts**."* (Emphasis mine)

Once the law is preached to the sinner, he must come to understand the horrific consequences of breaking God's law. Following the death of the sinner, he will stand before God in judgment. Everyone will be judged...and without the righteousness of Christ, there is no hope *(II Corinthians 5:21)*.

*Hebrews 9:27 And as it is appointed unto men once to **die**, but after this the **judgment**:*

Are you ready for judgment day? God has appointed a day when He will judge the world. Now, compare this approach to the typical "soul winning" approach of today. When someone comes forward in a church service after hearing the plea to accept Christ, he is quickly told to bow his head before he changes his mind. Why the haste? Too many Christians are more concerned with a notch on their Bible, than with snatching lost souls from hell's flames. The sinner must realize that God commands all men to repent!

Acts 17:30 And the times of this ignorance God winked at; but now commandeth all men every where to repent:

True *conversion* to Christ produces within the new convert a yearning desire to keep the right type of relationship with his heavenly Father. True *maturity* in Christ reveals to a man that he is no longer under the law *(Romans 6:14-15)*. Unlike the scenario with a lost man, the law does not affect a Christian's relationship **with God**. The law does however apply to his relationship with *others*. (See chapter 14 in *One Book Rightly Divided,* by the author.) Nevertheless, a Christian will understand and be busy showing others that same law which can truly convert the soul by pointing the lost to Christ.

> ***Psalm 19:7*** *The law of the LORD is perfect, converting the soul...*

Historically, many of the great preachers knew the importance of the law in converting the soul. John Wesley suggested that evangelists should preach 90% law and 10% grace. Charles Spurgeon declared: *"They will never accept Grace until they tremble before a just and Holy Law."* Jonathan Edwards said, *"Almost every natural man that hears of hell, flatters himself that he shall escape it; he depends upon himself for his own security..."* [4] Are you willing to depend upon your own goodness to escape the coming judgment? Each of us must obediently follow Paul's scriptural injunction!

> ***II Corinthians 13:5 Examine yourselves,*** *whether ye be in the faith; prove your own selves. Know ye not your own selves, how that Jesus Christ is in you, except ye be reprobates?*

Are you redeemed from that curse?

> ***Galatians 3:13 Christ hath redeemed us from the curse of the law, being made a curse for us:*** *for it is written, Cursed is every one that hangeth on a tree:*

Christ paid the price *(I Corinthians 6:20)*. It was an awfully high price *(Mark 15:34)*. God forsook His Son when He took our sins upon Himself. God will pardon no one without application of the blood that washes away *(Revelation 1:5)* and purges *(Psalm 79:9)* sin.

A lost person will be judged unmercifully by the law of God at the judgment bar of God, also called the Great White Throne Judgment.

> ***Revelation 20:11*** *And I saw **a great white throne,** and him that sat on it, from whose face the earth and the heaven fled*

*away; and there was found no place for them. 12 And I saw the dead, small and great, stand before God; and **the books were opened**: and another book was opened, which is the book of life: **and the dead were judged out of those things which were written in the books, according to their works**.*

A saved person has his name written down in the Lamb's book of life *(Philippians 4:3)*. He will *not* be judged in the same fashion. Without Jesus, there is no hope. Without Him, the lake of fire awaits every man! *"And whosoever was not found written in the book of life was cast into the lake of fire" (**Revelation 20:15**).* Do you want to be judged on your own merits *(Romans 3:10)*, or on the merits of the Lord Jesus Christ? Wondering what to do – call for a light:

Acts 16:29 Then he called for a light, *and sprang in, and came **trembling**, and fell down before Paul and Silas, 30 And brought them out, and said, Sirs, **what must I do to be saved?** 31 And they said, Believe on the Lord Jesus Christ, and thou shalt be saved, and thy house.*

Romans 10:13 For whosoever *shall call upon the name of the Lord shall be saved.*

Yes, God's salvation is freely offered to *whosoever* will come. Are you willing to admit your sinful condition and need for a Saviour? Or are you convinced that a loving God could never reject you no matter what you have done with His Son? The truth reveals otherwise – *whosoever* calls upon the name of the Lord will not be in the *whosoever* of the next verse.

Revelation 20:15 And whosoever *was not found written in the book of life was cast into the lake of fire.*

Why not fall upon your face before a loving God that took upon Himself the form of a servant? *"For he hath made him to be sin for us, who knew no sin; that we might be made the righteousness of God in him" (**II Corinthians 5:21**).* He became sin so that we could become righteous!

Chapter 21 Endnotes

[1] Preface to the Letter of St. Paul to the Romans by Martin Luther, (Munich: Roger & Bernhard. 1972, vol. 2) p. 2254-2268.

[2] *The Journal of John Wesley*, ed. Percy Livingstone Parker (Moody Press, Chicago, IL), p.64.

[3] James Beller, *The Soul of St. Louis* (Prairie Fire Press, Arnold MO, 1998) p. 154.

[4] Jonathan Edwards, *Sinners in the Hands of an Angry God,* (Enfield, Connecticut, July 8, 1741).

22

The Fourth Witness

---

*...at the mouth of **two witnesses**, or at the mouth of **three witnesses**, shall the matter be established.*
(Deuteronomy 19:15)

Man's tampering with the word of God has negatively impacted the whole world. The most disheartening result within the church has been the creation of a very shallow type of Christianity. Nothing seems to please Satan more than producing superficial Christians. Regretfully, we have yet to fully witness the devastating outcomes caused by the modern version phenomenon. The consequences of their acceptance have been compounding at an alarming rate. Today, the majority of professing Christians have grown accustomed to complacently standing by while God's truths are ignored and perverted. Shamefully, those who profess to be making the Bible so easy to understand have caused the most serious damage.

These modern day Bible "correctors" with their *easy-to-read* versions have helped produce a type of Christianity that lacks authority and backbone. Too many church members want to be spoon-fed "the word" in small easily digestible portions contrary to God's method of spiritual growth. God wants newborn baby Christians to grow up and enjoy the spiritual meat of His word *(Hebrews 5:12-14)*. The Lord designed His word so that only those who obediently and faithfully study it can unlock its innermost secrets. Those who reject its infallibility are doomed to view it as a closed book – unworthy of the effort necessary to discover its truths.

God's true word is not difficult to recognize if one is willing to devote the time necessary to investigate this modern era issue. The false bibles are no better than a cheap counterfeit bill. All of us must learn to recognize the counterfeits. However, some are better trained at spotting counterfeit money than others. For instance, consider the difficulty encountered with passing counterfeit bills within a bank. Bank tellers are trained to identify the imposter by studying the genuine article. The same principle holds true with respect to the word of God.

The best method by which to discern whether the modern versions are corrupt is to compare them with the real thing – the King James Bible. Study the King James Bible, and you will be able to identify the counterfeit. We have diligently attempted to do just that.

True men of God have understood the principle that God magnifies His word above all His name. This is a remarkable fact considering how the "scholars" and the world in general treat His word. They look upon it contemptibly. Can you imagine what it will be like when they stand before the Lord accountable for their actions? Do you really want to be a part of the spiritual infidelity that has wrought havoc upon the Church and the world? What do *you* magnify – is it the same as what God magnifies?

> **Psalm 138:2** *I will worship toward thy holy temple, and praise thy name for thy lovingkindness and for thy truth:* **for thou hast magnified thy word** *above all thy name.*

Dr. Dennis Corle points out in his book, *Elements of a Godly Character (Volume II)*, an important truth that each of us must understand and recognize. *"One of the most outstanding things about the character of God is found in Psalm 138:2. He holds His Word above His name. Why?* **Because if a man's word is no good, his name is no good. If** *God's Word is no good, His name is no good."* [1] Now consider the motivation behind all of the modern versions ($) and the good names that have been tarnished due to their association with these works. A tarnished name is not worth all of the money in the world.

Proverbs 22:1 A good name is rather to be chosen than great riches, and loving favour rather than silver and gold.

Today, a man's word may no longer be his bond, but God's word is still His! Consider the facts conveyed in John chapter 5. The Lord tells us about the four witnesses that bore witness of Him. He begins with the lesser witness and moves on to the greater, until He reveals the greatest witness of all. The narrative given resembles a court proceeding, with witnesses giving testimony concerning the Lord, and with a court reporter taking down *the record* of the proceedings. The testimony (or witness) of a defendant during his own trial is received with suspicion; therefore, other witnesses must come forward on his behalf to substantiate the truth. Jesus said:

*John 5:31 If I bear witness of myself, my witness is not true.
32 There is another that beareth witness of me; and I know that the witness which he witnesseth of me is true.*

The First Witness: John the Baptist

John 5:33 Ye sent unto John, and he bare witness unto the truth. 34 But I receive not testimony from man: but these things I say, that ye might be saved. 35 He was a burning and a shining light: and ye were willing for a season to rejoice in his light.

The Second Witness – Greater than John: His Works

John 5:36 But I have greater witness than that of John: for the works which the Father hath given me to finish, the same works that I do, bear witness of me, that the Father hath sent me.

The Third Witness – Greater than John and the Works: the Father

John 5:37 And the Father himself, which hath sent me, hath borne witness of me. Ye have neither heard his voice at any time, nor seen his shape. 38 And ye have not his word abiding in you: for whom he hath sent, him ye believe not.

The Fourth Witness – Greatest of All: the Scriptures

John 5:39 Search *the scriptures; for in them ye think ye have eternal life: and* they are they which testify of me.

The listing moves from the lesser (John) to the greatest (the scriptures). God elevates His word (the fourth witness) above all other things. The importance and magnitude of these truths should not be taken lightly by anyone. That which God elevates and esteems, Satan hates and attacks vehemently. He is the god of this world *(II Corinthians 4:4)*. Therefore, one can understand why Satan and the world would attack the Saviour and His book. However, it is inexcusable for any believer to do so. God elevates His word to the supreme position. Satan wants to tarnish the character of God by attacking His word. If one cannot trust God's word, the very character of God can be called into question.

The Record of the Witnesses

As we have seen, John chapter 5 reveals the *testimony* of Christ's four witnesses. Three chapters later in the book of John, we read about the *record* of these witnesses. Our understanding of man's court system corresponds to the record referred to here. This record relates to the transcript (or record) of the witnesses' testimony produced by a court reporter.

John 8:13 The Pharisees therefore said unto him, Thou bearest *record* of thyself; thy record is not true. 14 Jesus answered and said unto them, *Though I bear record of myself, yet my record is true: for I know whence I came, and whither I go; but ye cannot tell whence I come, and whither I go.*

Why would Jesus say that the witness of Himself *(John 5:31)* would *not* be true, but his record (chapter 8) would be true? With a little understanding of legal proceedings, one can quickly ascertain this simple truth. Although *the testimony* of what the witness says may be disputed, *the record* of what that witness said is not disputable. Even if the witness falsely testifies, *the record* of his testimony (preserved by the court reporter) would be correct and indisputable because it is simply a record of the witness' testimony. *The record* of God's word far surpasses the testimony of man, the voice of God from heaven, and even the works of the Lord Jesus Christ during His earthly ministry. Here is one aspect of that record.

> **John 8:12** *Then spake Jesus again unto them, saying,* **I am the light of the world***: he that followeth me shall not walk in darkness, but shall have the light of life.*

The Lord Jesus Christ fulfilled all of the Father's will. Thus, the Father proudly proclaimed from heaven that He was well pleased with His Son. Peter, James, and John heard this proclamation from heaven *(Matthew 17:1-5)*. It must have been an incredible event to witness. However, the Apostle Peter says that the scripture **(or record)** is a *more sure word* than even the voice of God from heaven at the Transfiguration. Peter understood the principle – the record of scripture far surpasses one's own experience no matter how great or glorious. Here is the record:

> **II Peter 1:17** *For he received from God the Father honour and glory, when there came such a voice to him from the excellent glory, This is my beloved Son, in whom I am well pleased. 18 And* **this voice which came from heaven we heard***, when we were with him in the holy mount. 19* **We have also a more sure word of prophecy***; whereunto ye do well that ye take heed, as unto* **a light that shineth in a dark place***, until the day dawn, and the day star arise in your hearts: 20 Knowing this first, that no prophecy of* **the scripture** *is of any private interpretation. 21 For the prophecy came not in old time by the will of man: but holy men of God spake as they were moved by the Holy Ghost.*

The scripture is a *more sure word of prophecy*. It is even greater than any voice heard from heaven, even if that voice emanates from God Himself. Jesus proclaimed this truth; the Apostle Peter understood and expressed this truth. Why do the self-professed scholars and critics today miss the point all together? We desperately need light. Our only hope of light comes from the word of God. The word of God provides light by revealing to us the Son, the Saviour, and the supremacy of His word. Rejecting this truth perpetuates the darkness.

> *Psalm 119:130 The entrance of thy words giveth light; it giveth understanding unto the simple.*

God's true words give light – there is no contradiction in them. Selected verses throughout this book have been included as directed by the Holy Spirit of God in order to substantiate this truth. Thousands more could have been provided, but one more blatant corruption should suffice to reinforce the point. Take notice once again how these modern versions contradict themselves and the true word of God.

A single verse from John chapter 5 is compared to one in chapter 8. The New International Version first says that the Lord's testimony is *not* valid and then three chapters later claims that His testimony *is* valid. Can both be correct?

> *(NIV) John 5:31 "If I testify about myself, my testimony is not valid.*

> *(NIV) John 8:14 Jesus answered, "Even if I testify on my own behalf, my testimony is valid...*

Like its modern version counterpart, the New King James Version makes the same blunder, only using a different word. (Remember the copyright requirements!) The NKJV says His witness is *not* valid and then claims that it is valid.

> *(NKJV) John 5:31 "If I bear witness of Myself, My witness is not true.*

> *(NKJV) John 8:14 Jesus answered and said to them, "Even if I bear witness of Myself, My witness is true...*

The modern versions consistently fall into their own man-made traps. Their translators claim to translate a single Greek word identically every time it is used in the scriptures. That is why the NIV uses testimony in both cases and the NKJV uses witness both times. The same Greek word is found in both verses. The same Greek word can be translated either way. However, the King James translators were led by the Holy Spirit of God to translate the same Greek word two different ways because they had received understanding of the context. God blessed their efforts, and today we are blessed by their work and willingness to submit to the leading of the Spirit of God.

Since the King James translators used "witness" in chapter 5 and "record" in chapter 8, Christ does not contradict Himself in the KJB. When we study and consider the difference between the two words as we have done in this chapter we can see and understand the truth.

(KJB) John 5:31 If I bear witness of myself, **my witness is not true.**

(KJB) John 8:14 Jesus answered and said unto them, Though I bear record of myself, yet **my record is true***: for I know whence I came, and whither I go; but ye cannot tell whence I come, and whither I go.*

When we compare scripture with scripture in the King James Bible, we gain clarity and spiritual understanding. When we compare scripture with scripture in the modern versions, we see contradiction and confusion. God is not the author of confusion any more than He is the author of these modern perversions. Any diligent Bible student will arrive at this conclusion every time.

The book of Second Timothy both commands man to study the Bible, and explains the key that allows one to effectively do so. Interestingly, God uses a very descriptive noun in reference to the Bible student when He gives these instructions. God calls the student of His word a *workman*. This designation only applies to one who engages in difficult labor. In this case, the labor He is referring to is diligent study of His word.

II Timothy 2:15 Study to shew thyself approved unto God, a **workman** *that needeth not to be ashamed, rightly dividing the word of truth.*

Finding the truth takes work! Although the evidence points to the contrary, there are still those who would claim that the King James Bible is the more difficult translation to read. People say they can understand the modern versions better. Much of the perceived problem is self-inflicted because of man's unwillingness to put forth the necessary effort to study and understand the word of God. God has made unlocking of the truths in His word a laborious task. These issues are not just twentieth and twenty-first century problems – they were addressed over four centuries ago by William Whitaker. Consider his insight.

William Whitaker (1547-1595), a professor at Cambridge University, wrote *Disputations on Scripture* to refute the Roman Catholic dogmas.[2] Rome elevated the Latin Vulgate and the traditions of the Catholic Church as the rule of faith. Whitaker, like Bible believers today, held the scripture *alone* to be the rule of faith. Rome tried to discourage the common man from receiving the word by exaggerating the obscurities of the scriptures. Therefore, Whitaker answered these arguments and strategies by listing nine reasons why God insured that only the **workman** could unlock His precious truths. These obscurities in the scriptures are planned and purposeful. The following are Whitaker's nine reasons why God designed His word to be grasped and understood only by those who diligently study it.

1. God would have us be *constant in prayer*, and hath scattered many obscurities up and down through the scriptures, in order that we should *seek his help* in interpreting them and discovering their true meaning.

2. God wished thereby *to excite our diligence* in reading, meditating upon, searching, and comparing the scriptures: for, if every thing had been plain, we should have been entirely slothful and negligent.

3. God designed to *prevent our losing interest* in them; for we are ready to grow weary of easy things.

4. God willed to have that truth, so sublime, so heavenly, sought and found with so much labour, the *more esteemed* by us on

that account. For we generally despise and contemn (condemn) whatever is easily acquired, near at hand, and costs small or no labour...But those things which we find with *great toil and much exertion*, those, when once we have found them out, we esteem highly and consider their value proportionally greater.

5. God wished by this means to subdue our pride and arrogance, and to *expose to us our ignorance*. We are apt to think too honourably of ourselves, and to rate our genius and acuteness more highly than is fitting, and to promise ourselves too much from our science and knowledge.

6. *God willed that the sacred mysteries of his word should be opened freely to pure and holy minds, not exposed to dogs and swine.* Hence, those things which are easy to holy persons, appear so many parables to the profane. For the mysteries of scripture are like gems, which only he that knows them values; while the rest, like the cock in Aesop, despise them, and prefer the most worthless objects to what is most beautiful and excellent.

7. God designed to *call off our minds from the pursuit of external things* and our daily occupations, and transfer them to the study of the scriptures. Hence it is now necessary to give some time to their perusal and study; which we certainly should not bestow upon them, if we found every thing plain and open.

8. God desired thus to accustom us to a certain *internal purity and sanctity of thought* and feeling. For who bring with them profane minds to the reading of scripture, lose their trouble and toil: those only read with advantage, who bring with them pure and holy minds.

9. God willed that in his church some should be *teachers*, and some disciples; some more learned, to give instruction; others less skilful, to receive it; so as that the honour of the sacred scriptures and the *divinely instituted ministry* might, in this manner be maintained.

Whitaker conveys such profound truths applicable to every generation. His insights are absolutely correct, *even* in our twenty-first century context! A true student of God's word quickly realizes that the word of God is a book of inexhaustible truths, thus preventing his losing interest in the scriptures. He finds that his most exciting studies are those in which he expends the greatest effort. Those unwilling to be in a constant spirit of prayer, seeking the Lord's help, have frequently found their "spiritual nuggets" to be heretical pitfalls. Truly, only those in a spirit of prayerful humility are qualified to stand and teach the Bible. Furthermore, God's book will never be understood by the sluggard *(Proverbs 13:4)*, only by the workman! Praise God for His infinite wisdom and grace.

The real Bible issue revolves not around readability or understandability, but labor and **authority** *(Matthew 7:29)*. Compare the comments of Whitaker with those of Mr. James White. His book, *The King James Only Controversy*, as we have seen, virulently and unapologetically attacks God's book. Once again, he writes: *"...if the KJV has been your 'standard,' have you ever really looked into **why** you accept it as such?"* [3] His purpose is to attack the one book that can make a difference in a person's life. Without God's written word, we have no final authority! Hopefully, after reading *One Book Stands Alone,* and other works cited in the bibliography, you can affirmatively answer a resounding "yes" to Mr. White's inquiry. Having examined the evidence, the scriptural infidelity of the Bible critic is revealed to be an *inexcusable* sin (however, not an *unforgivable* one).

Since God has nothing to do with the production of their modern versions, they have no hope of writing a bible that is not self-contradictory. They are no better than blind leaders of the blind. They walk in darkness because only the entrance of God's word gives light. Since these versions choose to pervert the word, they produce darkness and cause others to stumble and fall. Our position is clear. We are to separate ourselves from those that cause division, and we are not to touch the products they produce.

*II Corinthians 6:17 Wherefore come out from among them, and be ye separate, saith the Lord, and touch **not the unclean thing**; and I will receive you,*

These modern versions are unclean. There is no need to read them, study them, or support them financially. This world needs a revival and a return to the things that make a country great, a family whole, and an individual pure. We hold the truth. *You* hold the truth. What are you doing with it? Times are coming when man will be searching for truth more than during any period in recent memory. Are you preparing yourself to obediently follow the scriptures? *"But sanctify the Lord God in your hearts: and **be ready always to give an answer** to every man that asketh you a reason of the hope that is in you with meekness and fear" (I Peter 3:15).*

Christian, are you preparing your heart, mind, soul, and body to be ready to give an answer to those in search of the truth?

Chapter 22 Endnotes

---

[1] Dennis Corle, *Elements of a Godly Character,* Volume II (Claysburg, PA: Revival Fires Publishers, 1996) p. 61, 73.

[2] Provided by Dr. Jerry Rockwell of THE SWORD OF THE LORD. *"Disputations on Scripture"* by William Whitaker. (PA: Soli de Gloria Publications).

[3] White, *The King James Only Controversy, op. cit.,* page 13.

23

Getting Off the Fence

I know thy works, that thou art neither cold nor hot: I would thou wert cold or hot. 16 So then because thou art lukewarm, and neither cold nor hot, I will spue thee out of my mouth.
(Revelation 3:15-16)

The goal of this book has *not* been to "heal the wounds" or to create any new ones, but rather to present the simple facts so that the reader may decide which side he is on. Bible believers are those that have prayerfully studied the issue without being swayed by personalities and alma maters. The Bible version controversy will only end when those that claim to be fundamental in the faith recognize that *one book stands alone* in presenting those fundamentals of the faith, and that all the other versions are simply pawns in the hands of the wicked one.

Each of us must decide what we believe about the issue of the word of God. There is no room for fence straddling, indecision, or lukewarmness. Jesus is coming back and He requires that we be found faithful *(I Corinthians 4:2)* concerning the truth. The underlying issue throughout *One Book Stands Alone* is one of authority – do you have a final, infallible authority under which you place yourself in submission? God's perfect, infallible word is the only thing that qualifies for this kind of submission. Where is it?

Jesus said, *"I am the way, the truth, and the life..." (John 14:6).* The reader really has only two simple choices – to follow the way of Jesus which is *the way of truth,* or to follow the way of the world. If one chooses to follow Jesus, he can avoid the very destructive course that so many others have stumbled along. David chose the way of truth. *"I have chosen the way of truth: thy judgments have I laid before me" (Psalm 119:30).*

Those mentioned in *II Peter 2:1* are false teachers among the believers. *"But there were false prophets also among the people, even as there shall be false teachers among you, who privily shall bring in damnable heresies, even denying the Lord that bought them, and bring upon themselves swift destruction. 2 And many shall follow their pernicious ways; by reason of whom the way of truth shall be evil spoken of" (II Peter 2:1-2).* Their destructive ways cause others to speak evil of the way of truth.

Every pastor, preacher, seminary professor, Sunday school teacher, and Christian must honestly decide where he or she stands on the issue of the Bible. Do we have God's word available today or did God fail to keep His promises? The wrong decision and position will cause others to speak evil of "the way" and put you in the same category as those individuals who openly and knowingly oppose Christ. It does not matter how spiritual one appears to be, or how many degrees he has earned.

Some people wonder how seemingly *great, godly, spiritual* men can be wrong concerning all of these modern versions. Ask yourself how so many intelligent people with earned doctorates are trying to find out how we evolved from apes and when the "big bang" took place. Without regeneration there is no illumination. Without a faithful belief in God's promise of supernatural preservation, there is no light. Spiritual and scriptural infidelity can happen to anyone, whether he is a pastor, preacher, or Bible teacher. Judas Iscariot, one of the twelve, fooled everyone around him, except the Lord. The Lord allowed him to continue in his position although he was a devil and eventually Satan incarnate *(John 13:27).* The Lord knew Judas Iscariot would eventually betray Him, but the others could not discern who the betrayer would be *(Matthew 26:22-23).*

John 6:64 But there are some of you that believe not. For
Jesus knew from the beginning who they were that believed
not, and who should betray him.

John 6:70 Jesus answered them, Have not I chosen you twelve,
and one of you is a devil?

Judas accepted the position knowing that he did *not* believe in the
work of the Lord. The Lord knew and Judas knew, but we have no
record that any of the other apostles even suspected him. Why? Because
Judas was a wolf in sheep's clothing. Although not all the Bible critics
are lost, many unbelieving men have infiltrated our seminaries. The Jesuits
were established for this specific purpose. They devoted the time and
effort to get the degrees (especially in the *original* languages) with the
sole purpose of destroying the Protestant movement and true Christianity.
They have infiltrated our seminaries and negatively influenced our schools
and pulpits around the world. Their diligent, determined attacks have
severely impacted the most influential position within the church – the
pastorate.

Young men enter the seminaries having obeyed the call of God on
their lives. They arrive on campus with zeal and a heart afire. But
something changes. For many of them, the book that saved them and
the one that set them afire is not reverenced by their teachers and is
actually ridiculed and questioned. By the time they graduate, they look
at that same book with disdain; some even apologize for reading from
such an archaic source. Why has God allowed this infiltration to occur?
The answer is quite simple. God has allowed these unbelievers and
spiritual infidels to infiltrate our schools in order to prove us, similar to
the way in which He proved Israel.

Judges 3:1 Now these are the nations which the LORD left, to
prove Israel by them, even as many of Israel as had not known
all the wars of Canaan; 2 Only that the generations of the
children of Israel might know, to teach them war, at the least
such as before knew nothing thereof;... 4 And they were to
prove Israel by them, to know whether they would hearken

unto the commandments of the LORD, which he commanded
their fathers by the hand of Moses.

God could have eliminated the heathen nations for Israel, but He
didn't. The four reasons why God allowed the wicked nations to remain
in the land are clear:

- To prove Israel *(verse 1)*
- To teach their succeeding generations *(verse 2)*
- To teach them how to fight *(verse 2)*
- To find out if they would obey the Lord *(verse 4)*

God wants to prove us, too. He does not want us to forget our rich
Christian heritage; He wants us to learn how to fight; and He wants to
know if we are willing to obey not only during times of blessing, but also
in times of trial as well. The churches are crumbling from within because
we have lost sight of the enemy. Shamefully, we have more fighting
amongst church members and between the deacons and pastor, than
against our real enemy. Israel failed miserably, too. Instead of learning
how to fight and how to submit obediently, they became as their enemies.
The infiltration by the enemy worked. Israel served their gods and forgot
the true God. Once the infiltration began, wicked alliances were forged
and Israel's demise was forthcoming.

Judges 3:6 And they took their daughters to be their wives,
*and gave their daughters to their sons, and **served their gods**.*
7 And the children of Israel did evil in the sight of the LORD,
*and **forgat the LORD their God**, and served Baalim and the*
groves.

We have been guilty of failing to learn the lessons of history *(I*
Corinthians 10:6, 11). The infiltration has occurred within our institutions
of higher learning – secular and religious. The Lord Jesus Christ warned
of men that would come in sheep's clothing. They would look like sheep,
act like sheep, talk like sheep, but their sole purpose would be clear – to
destroy the work of God. They are similar to the betrayer of the Lord.
Judas knew who he was and these individuals do as well.

Matthew 7:15 Beware of false prophets, which come to you in sheep's clothing, but inwardly they are ravening wolves. 16 Ye shall know them by their fruits. Do men gather grapes of thorns, or figs of thistles?

Their fruits will be the dead giveaway. What have all of these professors done to the way of truth and true biblical Christianity? What are their fruits? You can't look at the numbers, popularity, or money *(I Timothy 6:5)*. Big churches today are more easily built on falsehood and the lack of biblical truths, than on good hard scriptural preaching.

Counting the numbers does not reflect true fruit. They have produced a generation that knows not God. They have taken the cream of the crop in the seminaries and institutions of higher learning and systematically destroyed the faith of a generation. They continue to produce preachers with a *"form of godliness, but denying the power thereof."* When the student is taught to stand in judgment on the word of God, rather than allowing it to judge him, he loses his power *(Luke 4:32, Hebrews 1:3)*. Paul warned about these wolves entering in among the sheep.

Acts 20:29 For I know this, that after my departing shall grievous wolves enter in among you, not sparing the flock. 30 Also of your own selves shall men arise, speaking perverse things, to draw away disciples after them.

Once these wolves have entered in *(verse 29)*, their "converts" *(verse 30)* would rise **from within** to continue the cycle of degeneration and destruction. Times have not changed from Jesus' day. Religious hypocrisy ran rampant then just as it does today. Religionists were the Lord's staunchest critics and the very ones that nailed Him to the cross (using the Roman civil government). He issues the same warning for us today.

*Matthew 16:11 How is it that ye do not understand that I spake it not to you concerning bread, that ye should beware of the leaven of the Pharisees and of the Sadducees? 12 Then understood they how that he bade them not **beware of the** leaven of bread, but of the **doctrine of the Pharisees and of the Sadducees**.*

We do not have groups calling themselves Pharisees and Sadducees today among professing Christians. However, we have the same wicked philosophy and doctrine within many churches, Bible colleges, and seminaries. If the Lord were walking this earth today, He would be busy sounding the alarm against the apostate seminary professors that think themselves to be bible "correctors." Ezekiel gives a bleak survey of the spiritual condition in his day. The Church and world today clearly resemble Israel of old.

Israel's prophets devoured souls

> *Ezekiel 22:25 There is a conspiracy of her prophets in the midst thereof, like a roaring lion ravening the prey; they have devoured souls; they have taken the treasure and precious things; they have made her many widows in the midst thereof.*

Israel's priests refused to distinguish between the holy and profane

> *26 Her priests have violated my law, and have profaned mine holy things: they have put no difference between the holy and profane, neither have they shewed difference between the unclean and the clean, and have hid their eyes from my sabbaths, and I am profaned among them.*

Israel's princes were like wolves ravening their prey

> *27 Her princes in the midst thereof are like wolves ravening the prey, to shed blood, and to destroy souls, to get dishonest gain.*

Israel's prophets impersonated God's true spokesmen

> *28 And her prophets have daubed them with untempered morter, seeing vanity, and divining lies unto them, saying, Thus saith the Lord GOD, when the LORD hath not spoken.*

Israel's people oppressed the poor and needy

*29 The **people** of the land **have used oppression**, and exercised robbery, and have vexed the poor and needy: yea, they have oppressed the stranger wrongfully.*

Israel's God sought for a man

*30 **And I sought for a man among them, that should make up the hedge**, and stand in the gap before me for the land, that I should not destroy it: **but I found none.***

Passages like this give little hope of repair *from within* a corrupted nation, church, or "religious" organization or institution. The Bible tells us that God sought for a man AMONG THEM to stand in the gap. But he found none. Those that know the truth are going to have to get the job done, because there is little hope of these institutions ferreting out the wolves. We need men to stand up for the way of truth and be willing to fight to restore it. Will it happen from inside these organizations? Probably not, since God's pronouncement against Israel has direct spiritual application today. He found none among those that corrupted His way.

Having emphasized the battle so much, we must pause to consider how we are to be true servants of the Lord today. Israel went into a country or city and frequently annihilated it. How are we to handle things today. . . should we go in with guns blazing? No! Bible believers cannot allow the flesh to control their actions, but must spiritually handle the matter. We must scripturally instruct those that oppose themselves and those that oppose us. The Bible says that maybe God will *"give them repentance to the acknowledging of the truth."* What more can you ask for? What more can we pray for?

*II **Timothy** 2:24 And the servant of the Lord must not strive; but be gentle unto all men, apt to teach, patient, 25 **In meekness instructing those that oppose themselves**; if God peradventure will give them repentance to the acknowledging of the truth; 26 And that they may recover themselves out of the snare of the devil, who are taken captive by him at his will.*

True Bible believers must be instructors. We need to be instructing those that oppose the truth, that oppose the book, and that oppose those that stand for the truth and the book. Sadly, Christianity is ignorant of its great heritage. At the crux of the problem is the revisionist view of history so prevalent today. Even so-called Protestants are trying to forge new links with the Roman Catholic Church. They turn a blind eye toward, or simply fail to realize, the bloody history of that church and its loyalty to someone besides the Lord Jesus Christ. Protestants and Baptists have no business trying to find common ground with those that pervert the truth by mixing it with error. These groups elevate religion and try to destroy those that stand in the way of their building of an empire.

The professing church has always carried out the persecution of those that stood for the truth – consider Tyndale, Luther, Huss, etc. History reveals that those wearing the "clerical robes" are the main culprits causing spiritual darkness and apostasy. Paul warned that the majority of the corruption would come from within the "religious" community itself *(II Corinthians 2:17)*. These imposters will intentionally deceive the unsuspecting. They will use deceitful means to perpetuate their false doctrine.

> *II Corinthians 4:2 But have renounced the hidden things of dishonesty, not walking in craftiness, **nor handling the word of God deceitfully**; but by manifestation of the truth commending ourselves to every man's conscience in the sight of God.*

> *Ephesians 4:14 That we henceforth be no more children, tossed to and fro, and carried about with every wind of doctrine, by **the sleight of men, and cunning craftiness, whereby they lie in wait to deceive;***

The Apostle Paul says that there were many people corrupting the word of God by handling it deceitfully. Some of these men even had letters supposedly written by Paul *(II Thessalonians 2:2)*. Evidently, the Spirit-led Christians had the spiritual discernment to distinguish between the truth and the counterfeit. Finally, Paul directs the believers at Ephesus to grow up and quit being children swayed by every new thing they hear. We need greater spiritual discernment to ferret out these wolves, and only God's word can provide the necessary wisdom. Satan knows that he has to convince people to pick up a counterfeit bible before his master plan of deception can work. He has used many men and women quite effectively to attain his goals, but none as successfully as Westcott and Hort.

Westcott and Hort understood man's propensity to believe the outlandish. Their theory of textual history played upon man's sinful nature. Once Westcott and Hort were dead, the so-called scholars at some major conservative Bible colleges and seminaries accepted their theory of textual history because they feared the scholastic and intellectual ridicule that comes with standing for the truth. Try to imagine how anyone familiar with the magnitude of the evidence as presented here and elsewhere could allow himself to become entangled in this web of deceit. They feared loosing their position, their prestige, and their paycheck. *"The fear of man bringeth a snare: but whoso putteth his trust in the LORD shall be safe"(Proverbs 29:25).*

The real issue at stake is one of final authority. Having been presented with the evidence, you the reader must now decide your own course of action. However, your spiritual condition will affect your course and that of those you influence. It is time to quit straddling the fence. Choose your side. Choose your weapon. Will it be the sword of the Spirit – the word of God – or the modern version butter knife? Should you choose the sword, you will certainly be in good company:

I. The Lord Jesus Christ

No one could present the issue any more plainly or succinctly than the Lord. God in human flesh proclaimed that you are either for Him or against Him – no middle ground. He accepts no neutrality. You cannot serve two masters.

Matthew 12:30 He that is not with me is against me; and he that gathereth not with me scattereth abroad.

Matthew 6:24 No man can serve two masters: for either he will hate the one, and love the other; or else he will hold to the one, and despise the other. Ye cannot serve God and mammon.

God's man has always been given the responsibility of making people face the truth. A decision must be made. You must decide! Can you honestly hold your bible in your hand and say, *"Thus saith the Lord."*? Or are you going to hold your finger up to test the winds? If you are still licking your finger, you should get out of the pulpit, out of the classroom, and out of the way. You can only have one Master, and He demands that you choose which side you are on. God wants you either cold or hot *(Revelation 3:16)*.

II. Joshua

Joshua was a real man. He did not wait to see what everyone else was going to do. He did not wet his finger and stick it into the air to see which way the spiritual winds were blowing. When he gave his clear-cut position, he told his listeners to choose a side for themselves. Joshua let everyone know that his decision was not contingent upon the decisions of others. He plainly put the issue before the people as follows:

*Joshua 24:15 And if it seem evil unto you to serve the LORD, **choose you this day whom ye will serve;** whether the gods which your fathers served that were on the other side of the flood, or the gods of the Amorites, in whose land ye dwell: **but as for me and my house, we will serve the LORD**.*

What about you? Is your finger in the air concerning this issue before us? Or are you willing to be a Joshua and take the lead? The Lord made it clear that He does not want any fence straddling. God's man must be willing to stand and sometimes he must stand alone. The word of God demands that we choose.

III. Moses

Moses also points out that there is no middle ground, no middle of the road, and no fence straddling with God. Whose side are you on?

The neutral countries in a war sometimes suffer as many casualties as those that are actively involved in the battle. Innocent bystanders have the most to lose because they have nothing to gain. Are you trying to be neutral? Are you a bystander? Answer Moses' question:

> *Exodus 32:26 Then Moses stood in the gate of the camp, and said, **Who is on the LORD's side? let him come unto me.** And all the sons of Levi gathered themselves together unto him.*

Take a stand. Be willing to stand up and be counted. The time is now. The lines are drawn. Where do you stand? Is your God a god of your possessions, or the one and only true God and Creator of all things? God's word is pure! God's word is perfect! God's word has been preserved! Are you ready to proclaim this truth? Are you now convinced where to find it?

IV. David

Quite frequently our sinful condition interferes with our desire to do right. David asked the people to make a decision. He wanted to know if they were willing to consecrate (set apart) their life for service to the Lord? Are you willing to consecrate yourself to His service?

> *I Chronicles 29:5 ...And who then is willing to **consecrate his service** this day unto the LORD?*

Each of us must answer for himself. No one can make another person live a holy life. A familiar saying expresses this truth best: "The Bible will keep you from sin or sin will keep you from the Bible." Which will it be in your life? Sin and compromise... or holiness and steadfastness?

V. Elijah

Elijah put a choice before the people – the options were simple. Follow the LORD or follow Baal (false religion and a lie). The same holds true for any seminary professor that places his degrees, his alma mater, or his reputation above the word of God – the King James Bible. False religions like to claim that Jesus was a great prophet, but reject His deity. Seminary professors love to proclaim their love for God's word, but reject His promise of supernatural preservation. The truth is harmed more from within than from without. The unfaithful seminary professor is more destructive than all of the false religions put together.

> ***I Kings 18:21*** *And Elijah came unto all the people, and said,* ***How long halt ye between two opinions? if the LORD be God, follow him:*** *but if Baal, then follow him.* ***And the people answered him not a word.***

Elijah did his job. He made the people consider where they stood. Sadly, they behaved like many do today. They did not answer Elijah. Today, we are faced with the same situation. Either you are going to associate yourself with God's position, with Satan's position, or try straddling the fence. What will it be? Decide today while you still have an opportunity. Others are looking around for someone to take the bull by the horns. Maybe it is you. You could be the one that God is looking for to stand in the gap. Others will follow.

Lot

Shamefully, people would rather put the decision off – to delay facing up to their sin and sinful condition. Some people today are as guilty as Lot. He delayed making an important decision and it ended up costing him his city, his home, his position, his sons-in-law, his two daughters, his wife, his wealth, and his popularity. Indecision is not worth its high price.

> ***Genesis 19:16*** *And* ***while he lingered****, the men laid hold upon his hand, and upon the hand of his wife, and upon the hand of his two daughters;* ***the LORD being merciful unto him****: and they brought him forth, and set him without the city.*

God was merciful to Lot – his indecision did not cost him his life. However, any true man of God would rather die than live in disgrace like Lot. Your **in**decision will cost you dearly – maybe as much as it cost Lot. Maybe more! Furthermore, your hesitancy will make you very unstable. Unstable, indecisive people are some of the sorriest people with which to be associated. They adversely affect everyone around them and make godly Christians very uncomfortable.

James 1:8 *A double minded man is unstable in all his ways.*

God does not promise a reward to anyone who has wavering convictions. He wants every person to decide, and today is the day of decision. A person's unwillingness to make his position known causes others around him to fall. God despises the one that straddles the fence. He wants you to boldly let your position be known.

Revelation 3:15 *I know thy works, that thou art neither cold nor hot: I would thou wert cold or hot. 16 So then **because thou art lukewarm, and neither cold nor hot, I will spue thee out of my mouth.***

A wise person once said: *"When truth and error compromise, truth always loses, because error has nothing to lose."* Christians have much to lose once their Bibles are taken from them. We need some valiant men and women, unafraid of the potential for ridicule, to stand in the gap. This world has an abundance of wimps.

Jeremiah 9:3 *And they bend their tongues like their bow for lies: but **they are not valiant for the truth** upon the earth; for they proceed from evil to evil, **and they know not me**, saith the LORD.*

Has God shown you the issue? Are you willing to stand in the gap and show yourself valiant? If the Lord were walking this earth, I believe He would make each of us face this important decision. Whose word is most important to you?

Jeremiah 44:28 *Yet a small number that escape the sword shall return out of the land of Egypt into the land of Judah, and all the remnant of Judah, that are gone into the land of Egypt to sojourn there, shall **know whose words shall stand, mine, or theirs.***

Whose word will stand for *you*? God's or theirs? The King James Bible or the latest modern version? If we put ourselves under the authority of this one book, we may stray, but we won't stay away from Him for very long. If we stray, we will always know where to return. God wants us to worship Him in spirit and truth *(John 4:23-24)*. What is *your* decision? Where do *you* stand? There is no middle ground and no neutral position. You are either for God's word (the King James Bible) or you are against it. One book stands alone . . . will *you* stand with it? Or will *you* stand against it?

Glossary of Terms

absoluton – The false teaching of the Roman Catholic Church declaring the person innocent. They teach that the Catholic priest has authority to remit the sins of a person that confesses his sins to him, no matter how heinous the crime.

American Standard Version (ASV) – The English Revised Version printed in the United States in 1901. The great granddaddy of all the modern versions. (See the English Revised Version.)

a-millennial - The teaching that the 1,000 year period of Revelation chapter twenty is not a literal 1,000 years. According to a-millennialism, the events recorded about the millennium are to be interpreted symbolically. This means that the binding of Satan, the resurrection, and the 1,000 year earthly reign of Christ are simply symbols of the present Church Age and of the heavenly condition of saints, not literally future events yet to come.

Anno Domini – in the year of our Lord.

Baptist Historical Society – An organization created to restore Baptist Historical sites.

celibacy - The act of taking vows to become a priest or nun in the Catholic Church, pledging to remain unmarried.

Common Era (C.E.) – Used to denote *Anno Domini* – "in the year of our Lord," while refusing to recognize the birth and deity of the Son of God.

crusades – The wars fought against the Muslims to claim the Holy Land for the Roman Catholic Church. The church promised special privileges to the participants including the remission of sins, absolution for transgressions committed in the course of the Crusade, and cancellation of personal debt.

Cum Privilegio – Latin word meaning "with privilege." The King James Bibles printed in England must have this designation signifying that the Bible is being printed in the name of the Crown.

doceticism – A heresy which claims that Joseph was the father of Jesus. It attributes to the person of Christ only a manhood and not deity. This was especially prevalent during the early centuries A.D.

dogmatic – Unwaving. Asserting or disposed to assert with authority. Usually perceived in a negative way. However, every Christian should be dogmatic concerning Bible truths.

dynamic equivalency theory – A method of Bible translation that translates thoughts rather than words. During the last two decades, this new concept has been developed in the field of Bible translation which has affected the kind of bibles being produced. It is also known as "common language translation," "idiomatic translation," "impact translation," "indirect transfer translation," and "thought translation."

English Revised Version (ERV) – The project sanctioned by the Convocation of Cantebury in 1870 to revise the Authorized Version, which produced the Revised New Testament in 1881 and the Old Testament four years later. Drs. Westcott and Hort led in the 30,000 changes made to the text and completely ignored the Convocation's directive to *"introduce as few alterations into the text of the A.V. as possible..."*

Granville Sharp Rule – A rule of koine Greek developed by Granville Sharp in the late 1790s. This rule has been used by textual critics to justify the changing of many scriptures. It fails to recognize that the writers used a Hebraism called hendiady (en dia dis) which means "one by means of two."

Hebraism – (See Granville Sharp Rule).

hendiady – (See Granville Sharp Rule).

homophobia – Literally one who fears homosexuals. The name is misapplied by the pro-homosexual lobby attaching it to those that judge the sin.

immaculate conception – Decreed by pope Pius IX on December 8, 1854. The Roman Catholic teaching that Mary alone was born without sin. Along with this doctrine is the teaching that Mary did not commit sin at any time during her life. They ascribed to her the attribute of impeccability, which means she could not sin. Since, the wages of sin is death, a sinless Mary would never have died.

inquisition – Rome's answer to the Protestant Reformation was the inquisition under the leadership of the Jesuits, an order founded by Ignatius Loyola. He believed in absolute and unconditional obedience to the pope. Their supreme aim was the destruction of "heresy," which they defined as any thinking that differed from that of the pope. The primary methods of the Jesuits were schools, the confessional, and force. For example, they were responsible for St. Bartholomew's Massacre in France. They killed 70,000 separatist Christians in one night.

Lectionaries – Books containing selected passages of scripture employed by the early churches for congregational reading.

Living Bible – First copyrighted in 1972, a paraphrase written by Kenneth Taylor.

Morning star – Refers to the Lord Jesus Christ in *Revelation 22:16*. The modern versions change Lucifer to the morning star in *Isaiah 14:12*. Thus Lucifer is not revealed in the modern versions and is replaced by the Lord Jesus Christ.

neo-orthodox – The modernists restructured their agenda to present themselves as more orthodox in belief after realizing that they had moved too far to the left too quickly. Whereas the old modernism blatantly denied the Bible as the word of God, neo-orthodoxy professed to believe in inspiration, but gave the biblical term an unbiblical meaning; they taught that inspiration did not refer to the words themselves but the inspiration of the concept or ideas. The neo-orthodox theologian uses the fundamentalist's terminology, but the modernist's dictionary to define the words.

New American Standard Version – Copyrighted by the Lockman Foundation beginning in 1960. Updated again in 1995 changing some of the verses back to the King James Bible readings and many of the pronouns when referencing deity.

New World Translation (NWT) – First copyrighted in 1961 "C.E." The translation produced by the cult known as the Jehovah's Witnesses attacks key doctrines, especially the deity of the Lord Jesus Christ.

pedophiles – One that chooses children to satisfy their perverted sexual pleasures.

perpetual virginity – The false teaching by the Roman Catholic Church that Mary never consummated her marriage with Joseph and had no other children by him.

politically correct – Current political and moral climate causing many people to reject the truth in order to be more in tuned with the lax moral climate.

preservation – The doctrine of God's promise to keep His very words in every generation. The supernatural conveyance of the inspired text throughout all ages without loss or error. The same God that perfectly inspired the scriptures also promised to perfectly preserve the scriptures – not merely its teachings, but His very words.

progressive salvation – A heretical teaching that salvation occurs over a process of time and not instantaneously at the moment the person accepts Christ as Saviour.

protestant – Historically this term derived from the 16th century Protestant Reformation in Europe. The name originated with a group of German princes who protested against the pope in 1529, and has come to be applied to those denominations which arose from the Reformation era. Baptists are not protestant.

purgatory - According to Roman Catholic theology, a place or state where Christians go after death to suffer for sins not cleansed during their earthly existence. The doctrine of purgatory teaches that even when the guilt of sin has been taken away, punishment for it may remain to be cleansed after death. Without adequate penance for their sins, a cleansing must occur after death with punishment designed to purge away their debt. The Roman system teaches that the faithful on earth can help those in purgatory by offering for them the sacrifice of the Mass, prayers, almsgiving, and other religious deeds.

Revised Standard Version (RSV) – First copyrighted in 1952. The copyright page shows that it was a revision of the ERV and the ASV.

seminary – A school for training Christian workers, usually on a graduate level.

sexual orientation – The false teaching that those attracted to the same sex were born with this propensity. Therefore, they are not to be judged according to the condemnation against such actions found in the scriptures.

sexual preference – The true teaching about one's sexual propensities. It reflects that one's attraction to the same sex is a matter of choice.

Sinaiticus (or "Aleph") – The fourth-century manuscript rescued by Count Tishendorf from a trash can in St. Catherine's monastery. Although disagreeing with the Vaticanus in over 3,000 places in the gospels alone, it joins with Vaticanus to form the basis of the modern versions.

situational ethics – The thesis that what is right in a moral problem is more dependent on the immediate situation than on a general code. It is the opposite of moral absolutes as taught in the Bible.

variant – A difference in the spelling of a word or the wording of a text when comparing two or more manuscripts.

Vaticanus (or "B") – The fourth-century manuscript used with the Sinaiticus as the catalyst for the modern versions. It received its name after its Vatican guardianship – which is the headquarters of the Roman Catholic Church.

Bibliography

Allis, Oswald T. *The New English Bible, The New Testament of 1961, A Comparative Study.* (n.p., 1963).

Allix Pierre, *Ecclesiasitical History of the Ancient Churches of the Albigenses.* Oxford, 1821.

Alter, Robert. "Beyond King James," *Commentary*, September 1996, 61-62.

American Heritage Dictionary of the English Language, Fourth edition. Houghton Mifflin Company, 2000.

American Standard Version. Thomas Nelson and Sons, American Bible Society, NY, 1901, 1929.

Bainton, Roland. *Erasmus of Christendom.* New York: Scribner's, 1969.

Barker, Kenneth L. *The Accuracy of the NIV.* Baker Books, Grand Rapids, MI, 1996.

_____. *The NIV: The Making of a Contemporary Translation.* Grand Rapids, Michigan: Zondervan Publishing House, 1986.

Beller, James. *The Soul of St. Louis.* Arnold MO: Prairie Fire Press, 1998.

Bruggen, Jakob van. *The Future of the Bible.* Nashville, 1978.

Burgon, John William, B.D. *Revision Revised.* Paradise, PA: Conservative Classics, 1883.

Catholic Worker. Vol LXVIII, No. 3, May 2001. 36 East First Street, New York, NY.

Carothorn, C.P. & W. L. Warnell. *Pioneer Church Records of South Central Kentucky and the Upper Cumberland of Tennessee 1799-1899.* 1985, Reprinted by Church History Research & Archives, Dayton, OH.

Carroll, J.M. *The Trail of Blood.* Lexington, KY: Ashland Baptist Church, 1931.

Carter, Cecil J. *The Anti King James Version Conspiracy.* Prince George, BC, Canada, 1997.

Carter, Mickey. *Things That are Different are Not the Same.* Haines City, FL: Landmark Baptist Press, 1993.

Chadwick, Owen. *A History of Christianity.* New York: St. Martin's Press, 1995.

Cloud, David. *Way of Life Encyclopedia.* WAY OF LIFE LITERATURE, Oak Harbor, WA.

Corle, Dennis. *Elements of a Godly Character.* Claysburg, PA: Revival Fires Publishers, 1996.

Edwards, Jonathan. *Sinners in the Hands of an Angry God.* Enfield, Connecticut, July 8, 1741.

Encyclopedia.com.

Ericksen, Robert P. *Theologians Under Hitler: Gerhard Kittel, Paul Althaus, and Emmanuel Hirsch.* New Haven, Conn: Yale University Press, 1985.

Family Research Institute. *"Study Indicates Homosexual Acts Shorten Lifespan."* Colorado Springs, CO.

Fox. *Fox's Book of Martyrs.* Edited by William Byron Forbush, D.D., Grand Rapids, Mich.: Zondervan Publishing House, 1967.

Foxe, John. Foxe's Christian Martyrs of the World. Westwood, NJ: Barbour & Company, 1985.

Fuller, David Otis. *Which Bible?.* Grand Rapids, MI, Grand Rapids International Publications, 5th ed., 1975.

Gibbs, Alfred P. *The Preacher and his Preaching.* Kansas City, KS: Walterick Publishers, 1939.

Gipp, Samuel C., Th.D. *For His Pleasure.* Miamitown, OH: DayStar Publishing, 2005.

Gipp, Samuel C., Th.D. *An Understandable History of the Bible.* Macedonia, OH: Bible Believer's Baptist bookstore, 1987.

Grady, William P., Ph.D. *Final Authority.* Schererville, Ind.: Grady Publications, 1993.

Griesbach, J.J. *Novum Testamentum Graece.* Halle: 1796.

Hemphill. *History of the Revised Version.*

Hoskier, Herman C. *Codex B. and its Allies.* Vol 1, *A Study and an Indictment.* London: Bernard Quaritch, Publisher, 1914.

Hort, Arthur Fenton. *Life and Letters of Fenton John Anthony Hort.* volume I, London: Macmillan and Co., 1896.

_____. Arthur Fenton, *Life and Letters of Fenton John Anthony Hort.* Volume II, London: Macmillan and Co.

Hudson, Gary R. *"KING JAMES ONLYISM."* and the *"Egyptian Corruption"* Argument.

_____. *Problems in the King James Version.*

_____. *The Superior Accuracy of the NKJV to the KJV's Textus Receptus.*

Hymers, R.L. *The Ruckman Conspiracy.*

If the Foundations Be Destroyed. Trinitarian Bible Society Article, No. 14.

Jones, Floyd Nelson. *Which Version is The Bible?.* KingsWord Press, Woodlands, TX, 1999.

Journal of John Wesley, Percy Livingston Parker, ed. Chicago, IL: Moody Press.

Joyner, Robert A. *King James Only?.* Community Baptist Church, 1999.

Kutilek, Doug. *Westcott & Hort vs. Textus Receptus: Which is Superior?.* 5/24/96.

Lacy, Al. *Can I Trust my Bible?.* Littleton, CO: Al Lacy Publications, 1991.

Lerer, Seth, *The History of the English Language*, Lecture One, *The Great Courses on Tape*, 1998.

Lloyd-Jones, D. Martyn. *Preaching and Preachers.* Zondervan, Grand Rapids, MI, 1972.

Luther, Martin. *Preface to the Letter of St. Paul to the Romans.* Munich: Roger & Bernhard. 1972, vol. 2.

MacArthur Jr., John. *"Not His Bleeding But His Dying."* Letter to a member, 1976.

_____. *Hebrews, The MacArthur New Testament Commentary.* Moody Bible Institute, 1983.

Manhattan, Avro. *The Vatican Billions.* Chino, Calif.: Chick Publications, 1983.

McClure, Alexander. *Translators Revived.* Maranatha Bible Society, Litchfield, MI, 1858 ed.

Metzger. *The Text of the New Testament.*

Moody Monthly. June 1982.

Moody Magazine. 820 N. LaSalle Boulevard, Chicago, IL 60610, June 1982.

Moorman, Jack, ed. *Forever Settled.* Collingswood, NJ: Bible for Today, 1985.

New American Standard Version. Glendale: Gospel Light Publications, 1971.

News and Record, "Church Debates Homosexuality," Richard Osling, July 28, 2001.

Newsweek, "Perspectives," September 17, 2001.

Noe, Herbert. *Messages to Magnify the Monarch.* Galilean Baptist Church, Livonia, MI, 1987.

Paisley, Ian. *My Plea for the Old Sword.* Belfast Northern Ireland, 1997.

Parker, Percy Livingstone, ed. *The Journal of John Wesley.* Moody Press, Chicago, IL.

Phillips, J.B. *The Price of Success.* London: Hodder and Stoughton, 1984.

Ray, Jasper James, *God Only Wrote One Bible.* Junction City, OR: The Eye Opener Publishers, 1955.

Reagan, David F. *The King James Version of 1611 – The Myth of Early Revisions.* Knoxville, TN: Antioch Baptist Church.

Riplinger G.A. *New Age Bible Versions.* Ohio: Munroe Falls, 1993.

Robertson, A. T., "Language of the New Testament," in *The International Standard Bible Encyclopaedia,* 1956.

Sarna, Nahum M. "Biblical Literature," in *The New Encyclopaedia Britannica,* 15th ed., 1979.

Schaff, David S. *The Life of Phillip Schaff.* New York: Charles Scribner's Son's, 1897.

Scrivener, Prebendary. *Full Collation of the Codex Sinaiticus with the Received Text of the New Testament, Introduction.*

Spackman, Dennis. *In Pursuit of the Truth, A Personal Testimony.* 25 Ngaroma Road, Epsom, Auckland, NZ.

————. *The Certainty of the Words of Truth,* New Zealand.

Taylor, Kenneth. *The Children's Living Bible.* Tyndale House Publishers, Wheaton, IL, 1972.

The Citrus Chronicle, "King James Version 2000 Makes Language Plain," February 10, 2001.

The Evangelical Quarterly (Jan. 79). Reviews and Notices of *Preface Rev. Revised.*

The Forbidden Book. New Liberty Videos.

The Holy Bible, New King James Version. Nashville, Tenn.: Thomas Nelson, 1982.

The Montgomery Advertiser. "Homosexuality Not a Disorder, Experts Say." Chicago press release.

_____. *"Study Offers Challenge to 'Gay Gene'"* Washington press release.

_____. *Vermont House Approves Landmark Gay Rights Bill,* March 17, 2000.

The New Standard Encyclopedia, volume 3.

The New King James New Testament. Billy Graham Counselor's Edition. Nashville, Tenn.: Thomas Nelson, 1979.

The Oxford Companion to the English Language, 1992, s.v. "Biblical English."

_____. s.v. "Bible."

Tragelles, Samuel Prideaux. *An Account of the Printed Text of the Greek New Testament with Remarks on Its Revision upon the Critical Principal Together with a Collation of Critical Texts,* London: Samuel Bagster and Sons, 1854.

Tischendorf's report - *Codex Sinaiticus.*

Underwood, Mark A. *King James Bible Newsletter.* October 1998, Volume II, Issue 10.

USA Today. "Protestants Face Annual Sexual Divide." June 6, 2001.

Vincent, Marvin R. *A History of the Textual Criticism of the New Testament.* New York: MacMillian, 1899.

Waite, D.A. *Defects in the NKJV.* Collingswood, N.J.: Dean Burgon Society, 1988.

Westcott, Brooke Foss, and Fenton John Anthony Hort. *Introduction to the New Testament in the Original Greek.* NY: Harper & Bros., 1982.

Westcott, Arthur. *Life and Letters of Brooke Foss Westcott.* Volume I, London: Macmillan and Co., 1903.

_____. *Life and Letters of Brooke Foss Westcott.* Volume II, London: Macmillan and Co.

White, James R. *The King James Only Controversy.* Minneapolis, MN: Bethany House Publishers, 1995.

Wilkerson, Benjamin. *Our Authorized Bible Vindicated.* Takoma Park, 1930.

Williams, James B., ed., *From the Mind of God to the Mind of Man.* Greenville, SC: Ambassador-Emerald International, 1999.

Index

Scripture Index